The Romantic Movement

ALAN MENHENNET

CROOM HELM LONDON

BARNES & NOBLE BOOKS
TOTOWA, NEW JERSEY

© 1981 Alan Menhennet
Croom Helm Ltd, 2−10 St John's Road, London SW11

British Library Cataloguing in Publication Data

Menhennet, Alan
   The Romantic movement.
   1. Romanticism
   I. Title
   809'.91'4   PN751   80-41181
   ISBN 0-7099-0381-2

First published in the USA 1981 by
Barnes & Noble Books
81 Adams Drive,
Totowa, New Jersey, 07512
ISBN 0-389-20104-9

Typeset in Great Britain by
Pat and Anne Murphy Typesetters, Highcliffe, Dorset
Printed and bound in Great Britain by
Biddles Ltd, Guildford and King's Lynn

CONTENTS

ACKNOWLEDGEMENTS

It is a pleasure to be able to acknowledge my debt of gratitude to Albert Ward and Professor Philip Yarrow, both of whom read sections of the manuscript and made valuable comments and suggestions. Their readiness to give of their time to discuss and encourage was a crucial factor in the completion of this book. They are not, of course, in any way responsible for its defects.

A. Menhennet
Jesmond

ABBREVIATIONS

BG   Eichendorff, *Werke und Schriften*, ed. Baumann and Grosse (cf. Ch. 7, note 2)

DL   Deutsche Literatur. Sammlung literarischer Kunst- und Kulturdenkmäler, Leipzig, from 1928: Reihe Romantik, 24 vols.

DNL   Deutsche National-Literatur. Historisch-kritische Ausgabe, herausgegeben von Joseph Kürschner

EM   Hoffmann, *Die Elixiere des Teufels. Kater Murr* (cf. Ch. 14, note 2)

FN   Hoffmann, *Fantasiestücke. Nachtstücke* (cf. Ch. 14, note 2)

GW   Uhland, *Gesammelte Werke* (cf. Ch. 4, note 18)

K   Brentano, *Werke*, ed. Kemp (cf. Ch. 6, note 1)

KS   Novalis, *Schriften*, ed. Kluckhohn and Samuel (cf. Ch. 2, note 8)

M   Jean Paul, *Werke*, ed. Miller (cf. Ch. 11, note 8)

SB   Hoffmann, *Serapionsbrüder* (cf. Ch. 14, note 2)

SMN   Hoffmann, *Schriften zur Musik. Nachlese* (cf. Ch. 14, note 2)

SRE   Arnim, *Sämtliche Romane und Erzählungen*, ed. Migge (cf. Ch. 10, note 30)

1 INTRODUCTION

Some degree of vagueness attaches to all terminology in literary history, but nowhere is the problem more acute than in the case of Romanticism. The fact that the term has survived in spite of all the controversy which has raged around it[1] is proof enough that it is needed, but the confusion which exists as to its meaning makes it difficult to use. Some of that confusion is inherent in the phenomenon itself; some results from insufficient awareness of the variety of perspectives from which it can be, and is used.

This is our excuse for what might otherwise seem an unjustifiably long preamble. Our subject proper is the German literature of the last decade of the eighteenth, and the first three, approximately, of the nineteenth century, with some exceptions (notably Goethe, Schiller and Hölderlin). But to address ourselves to that material without first having placed it in its native, and indeed its European, historical context would be unwise. Goethe, for example, disapproved of the general trend of German romantic writing, but he admired Byron, who in turn admired and imitated him. Many non-German observers have seen him as a Romantic. Pushkin, for example, called him 'the giant of romantic poetry' (*Table -Talk*, XXV) and a more modern critic, Jacques Barzun, describes *Faust* as the 'Bible' of Romanticism.[2] It would be wrong to deny such people their right to see Goethe in this way but the specialist Germanist, from his perspective, is entirely justified in excluding him from that category. To place him in the same box as Novalis would be unfair to both parties.

The general romantic *tendency* was a European phenomenon, but it developed differently, and at different speeds, in different lands. Romantic *Movements* occur in individual lands when the tendency has reached the stage of its fullest valid development and the precise form which they take is conditioned by the national context. In Goethe, the romantic impulse is held in check by respect for reality and rationality, which in the German context makes him a non-Romantic, but which could well have made him more congenial to a French or English Romantic than Tieck or Brentano.

The romantic was one of two main tendencies which vied for pre-eminence in eighteenth-century European literature, the other being in essence rationalistic and classicistic in its thrust. Conditions in Germany

11

were such that the romantic tendency developed more quickly and in a
more radical form there than elsewhere, so much so that some critics
see it as being particularly congenial to the German temperament.[3]
From the late forties (with the 'Empfindsamkeit' of Klopstock and
others) to the early nineties of the century, we are dealing with what is
best seen, for our purposes, as a 'pre-romantic' phase, one in which the
tendency is clearly identifiable and active, but has not yet achieved full
intensity and dominance. This is not to imply that such writers (who
after all, include Goethe, Schiller and Herder!) failed to compose in
romantic vein because of some inadequacy of feeling or imagination.
No one who has read *Werther* or 'An den Mond' could think Goethe
incapable of envisaging and describing the romantic state of mind. He
was not a Romantic because he chose not to be.

A romantic tendency has been discerned even in Classical Antiquity,[4]
but this is possible only in the not very significant sense that all men
possess emotion and imagination. We can speak of a *significant*
tendency only when the romantic potential begins to be recognised and
consistently exploited as a path to reality and truth. The crucial process
is the emancipation of the 'Ich', the individual Self. As long as reality
and truth are 'given' to the Self, as long as the external world has
priority over the internal, the romantic potential cannot be fully
realised. Blake, in rejecting Joshua Reynolds' concept of a 'General
Nature' and asserting that 'all knowledge is particular,'[5] is stating a
fundamental romantic tenet. Religious writers, and above all mystics
and Pietists, were the most important precursors of the later Pre-
Romantics and Romantics. It is no accident that mystical thought
influenced Blake, or that Böhme was such a hero of the German
Romantic Movement.

A conscious decision in favour of freedom for the Self is the crucial
step. This does not mean a mindless wallowing in some indeterminate
'irrational' state, though a Romanticism which fails to grasp and
communicate, however indirectly, a *real* experience, to achieve what
we shall call 'substance' which may or may not be reducible to terms of
ideas, could subside into that condition. Such a Romanticism is that of
Karoline von Günderode (1780–1806), a sincere but sentimental
poetess who cannot articulate and control her relation to an uncongenial reality but takes refuge, as, for example, in 'Der Kuβ im Traum',
in a haze of unfocused and essentially escapist sentiment. Escapism is
the sign of an *inadequate* Romanticism. Nor is this movement
characterised by a flight from thought. Keats, for example, while he
endorsed the 'truth of the imagination',[6] wished to go beyond the

'pleasant wonders' of 'maiden-thought' to a more philosophical understanding of the world.[7] In Germany, Romanticism brought with it an
intensification of abstract speculation.

Similarly, while the romantic search for forms conducive to the
liberation of the Self often led to departure from the familiar forms
which appealed to the orderly and rationalistic mind, this did not
mean that organisation and control had vanished. Grove tells us that
the reviewer of the *Allgemeine Musikalische Zeitung*, writing in 1805,
found that Beethoven's 'Eroica' symphony 'seems often to lose itself
in utter confusion' and that Berlioz's mentor, Lesueur, on hearing the
Fifth Symphony, 'in trying to put on [his] hat . . . could hardly find
[his] head'.[8] But as Hoffmann points out, Beethoven's greater emotional
depth and complexity in no way rule out a firm 'inner structure' and a
high degree of mental control ('Besonnenheit') on the part of the
composer.[9]

The first stage of the rise of the romantic tendency in Germany is
the 'Empfindsamkeit' ('Sentimentalism') which came to the fore in the
late 1740s and corresponds to a cult of nature and feeling observable
in England and France at about the same time. Its major exponent was
Klopstock, whose influence remained strong into the seventies,
particularly among the writers of the 'Göttinger Hain', such as L. H.
Hölty and the brothers Fritz and Christian von Stolberg. J. H. Voss,
who was later to become the sworn enemy of romantic writers like
Brentano and Arnim, also had links with this group. A characteristic
situation for such writers is the contemplation of a landscape, leading
to a state of often melancholy reverie. The Self is not truly active; it
responds to an external stimulus with a vague feeling in which the
authority of rational logic is not so much denied as temporarily
suspended in what the Prince de Ligne, writing of an experience he had
one evening by the Black Sea, calls 'un de ces charmants anéantisse-
ments . . . lorsque l'esprit se repose tout à fait, lorsque l'on sait à peine
qu'on existe'.[10] The Prince feels tears come to his eyes, 'without
knowing why'. But there is no truly romantic mystery. Logic is waiting
in the wings, ready to reassert itself, as it soon does in a rather banal
reflection on the transitoriness of life. The journey into the inner Self
has been avoided. Similarly, John Dyer, a devotee of the 'musical',
'sweet' mood of melancholy,[11] indulges in the joys of contemplating
what he might perhaps have called a 'romantic landskip' in 'Grongar
Hill', but instead of carrying through the liberation of the inner, less
exclusively rational Self which the situation contains in potential, moves
smoothly into a conventional reflection on the age-old theme of the

superiority of 'rus' to 'aula': 'Be full, ye courts, be great who will . . .'
etc.

In these and countless other examples we might quote from Pre-
Romantics of all nations, logical thought remains in control of emotion
and nature is in essence a stimulant, not an entity with which one can
commune, thereby arousing the sense of a reality beyond the logical
and releasing the subconscious levels of the Self. Not until Romanticism
proper, with works like Lamartine's 'Le Vallon' or Wordsworth's
'Tintern Abbey' lines, does this become the general tendency in France
and England. But there is an important intermediate stage in German
literary history, beginning in the late 1760s, which requires separate
discussion and for which the traditional parochial formulae ('Sturm und
Drang', 'Klassik') are not wholly satisfactory in our present context.
This phase is still pre-romantic in our sense, but it contains writing of
the highest aesthetic importance, writing in which the romantic
tendency is expressed with a degree of intensity unparalleled elsewhere
in Europe. Goethe and Schiller, who dominate this period, were, in
fact, major influences on non-German Romantic Movements. The
process of spiritualisation of nature, for example, which we do not
really see in England until Wordsworth's generation, is carried so far by
Goethe in the lyrics of the 1770s and the following years that one feels
that the barrier between 'inner' and 'outer', 'Ich' and 'Welt', has
almost disappeared.

This never quite happens. The 'Stürmer und Dränger' recognised,
often with a deep sense of tragedy, that reality and logic constituted an
insuperable obstacle to the emotions and longings of the Self. This is the
case in Goethe's *Die Leiden des jungen Werthers* (1774), one of the
profoundest of all studies of the workings of the romantic tendency in
human psychology, written by a man who comprehends, but is not
comprehended by it. In the course of the 1780s, the 'Sturm und Drang'
generation developed in the direction which is normally designated by
Germanists as 'Classical'. The historical picture now becomes complex,
in that whereas the romantic generation comes to the fore from
approximately 1796 (e.g. with Wackenroder's *Herzensergießungen
eines kunstliebenden Klosterbruders* and Tieck's *Der blonde Eckbert*),
Classicism continues in full flower until at least 1805 (when Schiller
died), and Goethe's subsequent development till his death in 1832,
while highly personal, shows a considerable measure of continuity
with his 'Classical' period and never carries him unequivocally into the
romantic camp. A non-romantic literature of high calibre, then,
coexists with German Romanticism. In addition, there are outstanding

individuals who cannot be fitted into the pattern of any 'school'. These include Jean Paul (Richter) and Heinrich von Kleist who, on grounds of general affinity, are dealt with in this book and Friedrich Hölderlin, who is accommodated with the Classicists in a separate volume of this series.[12] A minor figure who deserves to be set apart from the common run of representatives of the residual 'Aufklärung' is Johann Peter Hebel, who also appears in this study, for reasons to be explained later.

In the context of these crowded years of the late eighteenth and early nineteenth centuries, the simple pre-romantic/romantic formula needs modification. Classicism respects the progress made by the 'Sturm und Drang' in understanding the complexities of individual psychology, and tries to build on it. It also continues the development of the romantic tendency by articulating and systematising the philosophical idealism which was implicit, but not always well expressed, in the earlier phase. Neither Goethe's *Torquato Tasso*, nor Schiller's *Über naive und sentimentalische Dichtung* (which provided considerable stimulus for Friedrich Schlegel), could have been written by an 'Aufklärer'. At the same time, Classicism distrusts subjectivism (Goethe's later attitude to his own *Werther* is a case in point) and is more willing than was the 'Sturm und Drang' to accept the limitations imposed by reality on the desires of the Self. It partakes of the romantic tendency and often analyses the same problems as engaged the attention of the Romantic Movement which was to a great extent contemporaneous with it, but it contains that tendency through checks and balances — expressed most clearly, perhaps, in its ideal of 'Greek' harmony and 'Humanität' — of a non-romantic character. This helps to explain the oscillation between enthusiasm and hostility which characterises relations between the Romantics and the older Goethe.

Finally, it should be recorded that romantic ideas and attitudes continued to exert a powerful influence in German literature and thought well into the nineteenth century, so much so that Ronald Taylor can legitimately include Schopenhauer and Wagner, for example, in the 'romantic tradition' and can even find evidence of romantic tendencies in Nietzsche.[13] One could, if one felt inclined, take the line even further. But none of the writers and thinkers involved are Romantics as we understand the term. One can also point in all cases — and Heine will later provide us with examples — to the rejection of basic romantic values. Our subject is the period in which the romantic tendency was fully developed as a coherent force. That it was also active outside these confines should not be allowed to confuse the issue.

Notes

1. Cf. R. Ullmann and H. Gotthard, *Geschichte des Begriffes 'Romantisch' in Deutschland* (Berlin, 1927), pp. 5 ff.; R. Immerwahr, 'The Word "Romantic" and its History' in S. S. Prawer (ed.), *The Romantic Period in Germany* (London, 1970), pp. 34–63 and H. Prang (ed.), *Begriffsbestimmung der Romantik* (Darmstadt, 1968).

2. J. Barzun, *Classic, Romantic and Modern* (London, 1962), p. 8.

3. Cf. E. L. Stahl and W. E. Yuill, *German Literature of the Eighteenth and Nineteenth Centuries* (London, 1970), p. 112: 'it may be considered the most typically German of intellectual attitudes.'

4. Cf. F. L. Lucas, *The Decline and Fall of the Romantic Ideal* (Cambridge, 1936), pp. 55 and ff. Lucas does not use the term 'tendency', but this is the only formula which can justify such an excursion into the distant past.

5. Blake, *Complete Writings*, G. Keynes (ed.) (Oxford, 1972), p. 459.

6. Letter to Benjamin Bailey, 22 November 1817.

7. Cf. his letter to J. H. Reynolds, 3 May 1818.

8. George Grove, *Beethoven and his Nine Symphonies*, reprint (New York, 1962), pp. 89 and 178.

9. Cf. Hoffmann's review of the work, SMN, 36–7. If it be objected that Beethoven retains elements of Classicism, we can still point to organised, if unclassical, form in Schubert (cf. H. Truscott's essay on him in R. Simpson (ed.), *The Symphony. Haydn to Dvorak* (Harmondsworth, 1966), pp. 190 and ff), and even in Schumann, who in a congenial form like the piano concerto, can show 'imagination . . . disciplined by a mind at the height of its powers' (Joan Chissell in R. Hill (ed.), *The Concerto* (Harmondsworth, 1952), p. 171).

10. Letter of 1787, quoted by R. Canat in *La Littérature française. Par les textes* (Paris, n.d.), p. 463.

11. Cf. *The Ruins of Rome; The Oxford Book of Eighteenth-Century Verse*, p. 276.

12. Cf. T. J. Reed, *The Classical Centre: Goethe and Weimar, 1775–1832* (London, 1980).

13. R. Taylor, *The Romantic Tradition in Germany* (London, 1970) (for Nietzsche, cf. p. 229).

2 THE ROMANTIC MENTALITY

One's first impression of German romantic literature — and it is not a false one — is of confusion. The logically rationalistic mentality sees categories and distinctions and achieves orderliness; the romantic, in which the liberated 'inner' spiritual faculties dominate, sees universal unity and therefore finds more truth in chaos than in divisive 'system'. 'Eros and Chaos', says Friedrich Schlegel, is the formula which constitutes 'the best explanation of the romantic'.[1] We are led to wonder how romantic art and thought are possible at all, how the Romantics can communicate in a coherent form.

Certainly, they did not find this an easy task. Many romantic works are either unfinished, or have perfunctory and inconclusive conclusions; much romantic thought takes a deliberately fragmentary form. On occasion, caprice runs riot, as in the 'scherzhafte Abhandlung' *Bogs der Uhrmacher* of Görres and Brentano and the result, while it may well be a valid expression of the romantic mentality, hardly deserves the name of thought. The question of genre, which the Classical Goethe and Schiller take very seriously and which even Jean Paul tries to approach systematically in his *Vorschule der Ästhetik*, is treated by the Romantics with cavalier freedom. A reason functioning on straight-forward logical lines, 'vernünftig denkende Vernunft', is for Friedrich Schlegel the enemy of poetry, whose first task is to suspend its operation and return us to 'die schöne Verwirrung der Phantasie . . . das ursprüngliche Chaos der menschlichen Natur'.[2]

This is not mere mindless iconoclasm. The Romantics talked in such terms as a necessary assertion of their revolutionary values; revolutionary above all in relation to the 'objective' rationalism of the Enlightenment, which Classicism and even 'Sturm und Drang' had not, to use a cliché of literary history, completely 'overcome'. This kind of rationalism cramps what are, for the Romantic, the supreme faculties, fancy and love, and its dominance in the mind and heart gives rise to what Brentano calls the 'Vernunftphilister'.[3] But rationality as such is not thrown out of the window. There is a romantic rationality which does not inhibit fancy and love and which, as Novalis says in the epigram 'Kennet euch selbst', constitutes the key to the truly 'rational man'. This is the basis of 'Besonnenheit', the inner balance and conscious control essential both in life and, as Novalis insists through Klingsohr in

Heinrich von Ofterdingen (Chapter 7), and as Hoffmann shows in the case of Beethoven,[4] in art. This is an essential protection against the danger of disorientation in the void of total subjectivity which the Romantics recognised, even though the 'inner', subjective reality was more important for them than the 'external', objective one. Most of them were indeed successfully engaged in practical occupations. Eichendorff, himself an efficient if not enthusiastic civil servant, saw such an occupation as preventive medicine against the sickness of 'Zerfahrenheit'.[5] Truly eccentric Bohemianism, such as that of Prince Pückler-Muskau, was not common among romantic writers. Even Hoffmann reserved this for his stories, contenting himself in reality with convivial evenings in the 'Weinlokal' with cronies like the temperamental actor Ludwig Devrient.

That the 'Zerfahrenheit' of which Eichendorff speaks really was a danger is illustrated by the case of Clemens Brentano. He had by no means given up the attempt to achieve control, but had difficulty in maintaining it. He indulged his fancy very heavily and, as he wrote to P. O. Runge (January 1803), had turned inwards into himself and 'consumed his own superfluity'. His self-awareness, he writes, is like a pastel-painting which, immersed in water, has floated to the surface, and which, by embracing, he has reduced to incoherence. Although, as his best work shows, he had not totally lost the capacity for internal control, the somewhat erratic course of his life and the almost capricious organisation of works like *Godwi* could give a negative impression. Heine, in his *Die romantische Schule*, finds more blame than praise for *Ponce de Leon*. He calls it 'zerrissen', a 'Maskenball von Worten und Gedanken' and sees no meaningful unity: 'nur der gemeine Wahnsinn bringt eine gewisse Einheit hervor.'[6] Allowance must be made here for the realist philosophy which — for all that he himself felt the effects of the romantic tendency — made Heine an acute, but not entirely fair, critic of the Romantic Movement. Even *Ponce* (which we shall be discussing later) is not as disorganised as Heine makes it sound. But even if this is more caricature than characterisation, he has put his finger on an important point, on a potential threat to all romantic writers.

The central romantic dilemma is that of the relation between spirit and reality. Pure spirit, infinite and eternal, is both everything and nothing. It is pure unified being, but if it is to achieve conscious *existence*, it must find an object, which means giving up some of its purity and admitting of a lower reality. In Fichtean terms, the subject, the intelligent 'I', is the first reality, the originating principle of all

'Freiheit des Denkens'. Intelligence is in itself merely 'ein Tun'; meaningful existence depends on interaction ('Wechselwirkung').[7] The 'I' *must* posit the 'Non-I'. A comprehensible reality entails the sacrifice of the absolute unity of the spirit and acceptance of a basic dualism in the world and the Romantics do accept this, even though they regard spirit as the only pure truth and the overcoming of the duality of existence, either inwardly as a foretaste of perfection or outwardly as a millennial restoration of harmony, as a consummation devoutly to be wished. To speak in terms of the individual personality (for Fichte's 'I' is an abstract epistemological principle), the true meaning and purpose of life lie in the finding and fulfilment of the *inner* Self, the dimension of it which transcends logical reason and forms the point of contact between the individual and the infinite spiritual reality. But while man is made to do this and can know no rest until he has, he is rooted, as man, in a material reality which stands in implacable hostility to that of the spirit, and which produces an inevitable, if tragic, adulteration of the spiritual life. He must feed, as far as possible, on the spiritual nutriment (above all, 'Poesie') which a benevolent Providence has distributed through the natural world and reduce his dependence on the material to a minimum. But to give in to the temptation to detach himself from the latter altogether would result not in Self-fulfilment, but in Self-loss. Truly, that way madness lies.

This does not mean that material reality, which is also the realm of objective logical rationalism, is accepted as intrinsically *valid*. The orientation of Romanticism is almost remorselessly subjective: 'Nach Innen', as Novalis says, 'geht der geheimnißvolle Weg.'[8] All romantic poetry, writes Eichendorff, seeks the Infinite.[9] Idealism, the philosophical attitude which Romanticism took to its highest pitch in Germany, is founded on the primacy of the truth of inner consciousness to that of 'external' objectivity, on the 'Freiheit und Selbständigkeit des Ichs', to quote Fichte again.[10] 'Wäre nichts im ganzen Dasein, was das Dasein wüßte,' writes Brentano in a letter of 1801, 'so wäre nichts da . . . Auf diese Weise ist der Mensch der Schöpfer der Welt.'[11] The 'magic idealism' of Novalis, in which fancy and love are not only perceptive, but also creative, is perhaps the most radical development of this tendency, but the primacy of Spirit, as Ego-principle (Fichte), World-Spirit (Schelling) or Idea (Hegel) is a fundamental principle of all romantic thought.

It is not hard to see from the foregoing that the romantic mentality favours religious feeling in the broad sense, though by no means always specific theological doctrine. Friedrich Schleiermacher, probably the

most important romantic theologian, himself shows this tendency when
he defines the essence of religion in the formula: 'Alles Beschränkte als
eine Darstellung des Unendlichen hinzunehmen.'[12] He sees this
approach in the thought of Spinoza, to whom he is correspondingly
kindly disposed, as are other Romantics such as Friedrich Schlegel, who
presents him as the philosopher of fancy and love in his *Gespräch über
die Poesie*, and Novalis, who calls him a 'gotttrunkene [r] Mensch'.[13]
It is Spinoza's supposed ability to see the infinite in nature which gives
rise to this enthusiasm and it is not the intellect, but the spiritual
faculties of the inner Self which, in the romantic view, give that
capacity. The most important quality of the student of nature, says the
Teacher in Novalis's *Die Lehrlinge zu Sais*, is a spiritual constitution
more often found in combination with simplicity of character than
with intellectual sophistication (KS I, 107–8). The understanding of
nature is not an intellectual insight but an emotional experience: 'Wem
regt sich nicht . . . das Herz in hüpfender Lust, wenn ihm das innerste
Leben der Natur . . . *in das Gemüt kommt!*' (p. 104, my emphasis).

The Romantics' concept of nature is one in which their belief in the
primacy of spirit over sense is expressed with special clarity. Goethe
stands closer to them in this field than anywhere else. He too felt that
the infinite could be experienced in nature and Schelling's formulation
(in the *Ideen zu einer Philosophie der Natur*), 'Die Natur ist der sicht-
bare Geist, der Geist ist die unsichtbare Natur,' attracted him. His own
studies of nature were congenial to romantic thinkers like C. G. Carus
and he was himself sympathetic to Carus's work.[14] He could have agreed
with Novalis that poets are the men best qualified to understand nature
(cf. KS I, 99). But he would not have endorsed Novalis's emphasis on
subjective imaginative faculties at the expense of objective observation.
For Novalis, 'creative contemplation' leads to 'Selbstempfängnis', in
which the dualism of subject and object gives way to an experience of
the one-ness of the Self with the universe (KS I, 101 f). Goethe's
'zarte Empirie' is rather a sensitive observation ('Anschauung') in which
the distinction between the observer and the thing observed is
maintained. The idea that truth can be perceived through 'Ahnung'
(perception without a concrete observation) would have seemed to him
to lead to an unacceptable nature-mysticism. And he was no mystic.

Romantic science, however, can accept a measure of mysticism. This
was the era of 'nature-philosophy', when physical nature was seen as a
series of variations on 'thoughts' of God, a vast unity formed and
informed by spiritual forces.[15] Lorenz Oken defines science as 'die
Wissenschaft von der ewigen Verwandlung Gottes in *die* Welt' (my

emphasis) and talks of God in terms reminiscent of both Fichte and
Böhme:

'Das Selbsterscheinen des Absoluten ist Selbstbewußtsein. Das
selbstbewußte Absolute ist Gott . . . Die Naturphilosophie muß die
Formen aufsuchen, in denen Gott denkt, und indem sie dieses tut,
stellt sie die Formen der Welt dar, die Naturphilosophie ist daher in
ihren höchsten Prinzipien Theosophie' (DL 13, 238–40).

Man is not God for the Romantics, and he is not a universe in himself.
He cannot know the infinite without some consciousness of a relation
to things outside himself. But it is in and through the inner world of the
Self, says Schleiermacher, that the universe and its laws are known:
'Darum ist es auch das Gemüt eigentlich, worauf die Religion hinsieht
und woher sie Anschauungen der Welt nimmt; im innern Leben bildet
sich das Universum ab, und nur durch das innere wird das äußere
verständlich' (DL 5, 95–6).

Imagination and emotion can be trusted in practical life too. 'Die
Leidenschaft', writes Bettina von Arnim, 'ist ja der einzige Schlüssel der
Welt' (DL 11, 120–1). Emotional involvement helps one to find the
truth: 'Aus sich selbst handeln . . . vermöge meines Charakters und
meiner Kraft handeln, und was ich überschaue auch bemeistern in
meinem Innern; das scheint mir der Herd des Lebens.'[16] Kant would
have frowned on such an accordance of priority to the individual over
the general. Freedom, for him, lies in a decision by the individual to
obey the indwelling, but super-personal 'Vernunftgesetz', which is often
in conflict with individual desire. The Romantics certainly have
morality, but could not accept one so restrictive of individual freedom.
Systematic 'Tugendlehre' is not adequate for Novalis, for example. The
conscience, the primary unifying force of the universe, represents God
on earth, as the essence of true human individuality ('der Menschen
eigenstes Wesen'). It provides the impulsion for the search for proper
moral culture ('Bildung') whose final stage is the state of 'mastery', the
one virtue which underlies all others and makes its possessor both
moral and individually free.[17]

While they reject a morality based on negative prescription, the
German Romantics do not share the interest of other Romantic
Movements in the activistic and anarchistic outlaw-hero, such as
Byron's Giaour or Espronceda's Pirate, whose 'god is liberty' and whose
law 'strength and the wind'. This kind of hero was left behind with the
'Sturm und Drang', after which he found a home in the popular

'Räuberroman' which trivialised the legacy of Schiller.[18] The German romantic hero is characterised by passivity and receptivity. Even in such a superficially 'active' character as Medardus, in Hoffmann's *Die Elixiere des Teufels*, the moral dimension seems to be not primarily a matter of will, but rather of subconscious impulses. Faith and an essentially pure heart are more important than reason and will. Grace is often required and where it does not abound, we often find a dark fatalism, even nihilism, as in Tieck's *William Lovell* or the conclusion of *Die Nachtwachen des Bonaventura*. A character can be drawn into an action in which his conscious will has no part, as when Wackenroder's Berglinger is drawn back by an 'irresistible force' to his destruction in the city.[19] Anton, the main hero of Arnim's *Die Kronenwächter*, comes to feel that men are 'Nachtwandler mitten am Tage'.[20] He is subject to unpredictable mental and moral vicissitudes, but does manage to preserve one area of freedom, the rather childlike spiritual purity of the inmost Self, a romantic counterpart to the 'Streben' of Goethe's Faust and Wilhelm Meister: 'mein Dasein wird ein ewiges Warten' (SRE I, 953).

In view of the dualism which we noted earlier between spirit and reality in the romantic experience, it is not surprising that dualism plays a significant role in romantic thinking. Certainly, harmony and reconciliation were longed for and sought, but it is usually only in myth or *Märchen* that the Romantic can find them. Contradictions, as Hegel states in writing of beauty, are endemic to actuality and beauty itself cannot remain in the vacuum of absolute spirit. Solger, a somewhat less rarefied thinker, still puts it in paradoxical and mysterious terms:

> In der Wirklichkeit ist daher die Schönheit nur da gegenwärtig, wo das Endliche in allen Gegensätzen sich ganz angefüllt zeigt von einem und demselben Wesen. Man sollte daher glauben, daß die Idee der Schönheit überhaupt alle Gegensätze aufhebt, und die Idee selbst in ihrer reinen Einheit hervortreten läßt. Darin aber liegt eben das Geheimnis, welches die Entwicklung der Idee der Schönheit schwer macht, daß zwar die Idee als eine und dieselbe wirklich werden, aber zugleich sich in die Gegensätze der Existenz entfalten muß, da sie sonst gar nicht zur Wirklichkeit kommen würde.[21]

Everywhere in romantic thought and art one finds recognition of the duality of life and the attempt to overcome, or at least contain, its destructive potential, from the systematic *Lehre vom Gegensatz* of Adam Müller to deliberate cultivation of chaos and 'irony', the

'Vorliebe für die Tollheit' shown by Klingemann in *Die Nachtwachen des Bonaventura*[22] or Hoffmann's recognition that 'die Erkenntnis der Duplizität'[23] is an essential prerequisite of self-realisation and -expression. No doubt the scorn felt by the Romantics for the philistines, the 'verständige und gefühlvolle Leute' as the night-watchman calls them, is genuine enough, but one doubts whether they were entirely happy at the thought that 'either normality was topsy-turvy, or they were.'[24]

The Romantics certainly disliked the reality which surrounded them, but whether this was a dislike of their specific environment, or of the limitations imposed by the deficiencies of material reality as such is not clear. Certainly, the discrepancy between poetry and 'alltägliche Beschränktheit', in A. W. Schlegel's formulation,[25] was acute enough in early-nineteenth-century Germany. There was little scope for the fulfilment of ideals in concrete form and apart from the passing excitement of the War of Liberation, little sustenance for the poetic spirit in public life. The mould of the *ancien régime* remained unbroken[26] and the period of reform of Stein and Hardenberg soon gave way to one of often xenophobic 'demagogy' — for example F. L. Jahn and Wolfgang Menzel — on the one hand and of sterile repression on the other. Germany, before and during the Metternich era, was a land where 'governments were strong and political life weak'.[27] The Romantics were not political radicals (at least after the early years), neither were they true reactionaries. They were conservative reformers, for whom the interest of political forms lay in their spiritual content and influence. Even the practical politician who stood ideologically closest to them, Gentz, was not really in sympathy with them and Metternich could find no role even for a thinker of the calibre of Friedrich Schlegel.[28]

The German Romantics disliked the spirit of the new age which was dawning and which they saw as spiritually crippled, 'arm in der Liebe',[29] ugly and anti-poetic in its industrialisation. The thrill, even if liberally admixed with horror, which at least some English observers felt at the sight of 'gigantic powers . . . compelled to serve the will of feeble-bodied Man' (Wordsworth, *The Excursion*, Book 8) is not felt in Germany. Justinus Kerner, the lover of 'Einsamer Nachtigallen Schlag In alter Wälder Nacht'[30] inveighs against the 'steam-mad age':

Die blaue Stille stört dort oben . . .
Kein Dämpfer und kein Segelschiff . . .
Nicht des Dampfwagens wilder Pfiff.

Laßt satt mich schauen in die Klarheit,
In diesen keuschen, sel'gen Raum,
Denn bald könnt' werden ja zur Wahrheit
Das Fliegen, der unsel'ge Traum.[31]

To preserve the ideal in such unpromising surroundings, they turned to
spiritual rather than political means, hoping to re-kindle in the Germans
their sense of identity, and the spirit of poetry in general, by persuading
them to concentrate their minds on sources and objects which breathed
a spirit at once Germanic and poetic, such as the Rhine, the 'Wartburg'
and the Middle Ages (including, for them, the sixteenth century) in
general. Even the drier historical and scholarly work of men like Jakob
Grimm and Savigny was largely directed to that end and Romanticism
and scholarship entered into a particularly fruitful partnership in the
literary field with the *Kinder- und Hausmärchen* of the Grimms, *Des
Knaben Wunderhorn* (the collection of folk-songs of Arnim and
Brentano), Görres's *Die teutschen Volksbücher* (1807) and the work of
editors and translators of the *Nibelengenlied* such as Karl Lachmann and
Karl Simrock. The last-named, for example, proclaims himself the
'disciple' of Fouqué in the Dedication (1826) of his translation, in
helping to communicate the epic's message of 'Lieb' und Heldenstreit',
which is 'unsres Volkes urerster Schirm und Hort'.

Their method was not, of course, 'realistic'.[32] But neither were they
necessarily obscurantists or escapists. It is easy to make fun of a
nostalgia for turreted castles, as it is to brush aside Brentano's attack
on the modern age in *Der Philister vor, in und nach der Geschichte*,[33]
as does a Marxist critic, as 'ein giftiges Pamphlet auf Humanität,
Aufklärung, Zivilisation und bürgerlich-fortschrittliche Entwicklung'.[34]
But when Friedrich Schlegel uses the poetic image of the 'Wartburg' to
point up the contrast with 'die gegenwärtige Armseligkeit', we realise
that romantic medievalism can have contemporary relevance and can
understand the hope which Schlegel voices that the 'sleeping lion' may
yet awake.[35] And while there are certainly dangerous, even unhealthy,
passages in Brentano's essay, there is also satire of the contemporary
world as trenchant and funny as any Heine-esque 'Zeitgedicht',
particularly in the portrait of the 'Musterphilister' (K 2, 987 ff). The
latter happens to be an 'Aufklärer', but that surely does not make him
immune against satire.

The Romantics had to eat and this meant that they, as poetic
people, had to find a footing in a prosaic society. They normally
managed to cope with the problem, but the familiar 'art-life' duality

affected them particularly strongly. Hoffmann, the musician who had to resign himself to earning his living as a legal official, was aware that his reputation as a writer would be anything but an advantage in his search for a situation. 'Unser Justiz-Großmogul', he wrote to Theodor Hippel, '[scheint] mich für ein exotisches Produkt zu halten, das in der Justiz sich nicht einbürgern kann.' Hippel himself, in trying to persuade the Prussian Minister of the Interior, Schuckmann, to employ Hoffmann, does what he can to dispel the artistic aura: 'von seinem früheren Fehler, zu großer Genialität, ist er völlig geheilt und aus dem Pegasus ist ein ganz tüchtiger ruhiger Ackergaul geworden.'[36] One can imagine the ironic 'Muskelspiel' this would have produced in the features of Hoffmann's Kreisler!

Social conditions, then, must have accentuated the Romantics' feeling of dualism between an 'inner' and 'outer' world. Their cultivation of the former made it inevitable that they should discover mysticism, which since the seventeenth century had had only an underground influence on German literature and thought. 'Der Sinn für Poesie', says Novalis, 'hat viel mit dem Sinn für Mystizismus gemein.'[37] Friedrich Schlegel sets out to combat false ideas of mysticism: 'Man scheue dieses Wort nicht; es bezeichnet die Verkündigung der Mysterien der Kunst und Wissenschaft, die ihren Namen ohne solche Mysterien nicht verdienen würden; vor allem aber die Verteidigung der symbolischen Formen und ihrer Notwendigkeit, gegen den profanen Sinn.'[38] Both poetic and mystical writing are relevations of an inner mystery.

Of the mystics who influenced the Romantics, the most frequently mentioned and praised is Jakob Böhme. Tieck, Novalis and Baader were among his admirers. Among the many echoes of his thinking in romantic literature, none is more striking than the dualism of inner and outer levels of experience, of which we have already had occasion to speak. This is essential to Böhme's concept of man's spiritual life in his fallen state. The 'animalischer Geist', as he puts it in *Aurora* (Chapter 19, paras. 18 ff) is still quickened by the divine source ('Qual', i.e. 'Quelle'), and can grasp infinite truth; the 'Thierischer Leib'

krieget nur einen Blick davon, gleich als wenn es wetterleuchtet: Denn also stellet sich die innerste Geburt der Seelen, wenn sie durch die äußerste Geburt in Erhebung des Heiligen Geistes, durch die Porten der Höllen reißet, aber die äußerste Geburt thut sich bald wieder zu . . .

Logical reason, which is caught up in the 'outer birth' (the fallen
spiritual state) of man, is no guide to divine truth. To know the latter,
Böhme maintains, we must be prepared to throw off the 'Vernunft-
Peltz'[39] and step into the circle of mystery, just as the Romantics
believe that we must shed the skin of reason if we are to enter into
what Tieck calls 'die süßen Geheimnisse des Gemüts'.[40] 'Es liegen sehr
viel tief verborgene Wunder in der Natur und im Menschen', writes
Justinus Kerner, 'die wir nicht kennen, weil unser Auge und Ohr sich
bloß mit den äußern Dingen beschäftigt.'[41] What prevents us from
seeing the higher spiritual truth is '[der] für die Welt berechnende
Verstand'.[42]

We have already seen indications of a clear hostility among the
Romantics to a certain kind of rationality. Georg Lukács, indeed, sees
Romanticism as guilty of deliberate 'irrationalism', the employment
of 'super-rational' faculties ('Ubervernünftigkeit') where rational
cognition is possible and desirable.[43] Others are inclined to minimise
the opposition between the two. H. Schanze, for example, justifiably
rejects the crude formulation of a romantic 'irrationalism' and points,
among other things, to the systematic study of philosophy undertaken
by Novalis and to his and Schlegel's use of the terms of mathematics,
as links with the Enlightenment.[44] In fact, neither of these views is
convincing. The Romantics were sophisticated intellectuals, whose aim
was not to destroy thought, but to extend its empire into realms
previously thought to be beyond its scope. One of the most mystically
inclined Romantics, Franz von Baader, rejects the view attributed to
Rousseau that 'man, when he begins to think, ceases to feel' as
'Poltronnerie gegen die Spekulation'.[45] The Romantics took a strong
and often highly professional interest in the development of the natural
sciences and much solid scholarship, as well as imagination, went into
the romantic re-creation of the Germanic past.

At the same time, all this and whatever else could be said in the same
vein is not enough to bridge the gap between Romanticism and
Enlightenment. The instincts of the men involved, who were often in
bitter opposition, did not lead them astray. The rationalism of the
Enlightenment was of the type which can accept mysteries only when
they can be shown to be not truly mysterious, capable of explanation,
that is, in a form which may be superficially and 'dialectically' complex,
but which in essence embodies the same laws as those which inform
practical common-sense logic. Mathematics, as we saw, are called in aid
by Schanze, but the Romantics were able to fit mathematics into *their*
view of the universe. Novalis certainly was not uniformly hostile to

rational thought-processes, but he did decide to abandon the 'Spitzberge der reinen Vernunft', as he wrote to Tieck (23 February 1800) in favour of poetry. Schanze suggests that with his call for 'Systemlosigkeit, in ein System gebracht' (KS II, 288–9) in the *Fichte-Studien*, Novalis is carrying the 'Systemdiskussion der Aufklärung' forward in a straight line.[46] But surely he is demanding that logic be transcended or, to continue the mathematical metaphor, that the circle be squared.

Rational speculation, in itself healthy, can be corrupted by a mentality which is, in Baader's term, 'irreligious'[47] and substitutes a 'self-made' reason for the God-given faculty. This self-made reason bolts the doors which could have led to the higher spiritual truth and is one of the main constituent features of the philistine. Arrogant rationalism 'destroys' the capacity for imaginative and emotional perception. However clever he may be, the rationalistic philistine lacks the capacity to employ the imagination in a creative way, as he lacks the organ for 'Ahnungen', the perceptions received when the *Gemüt* is opened to direct communication from the realm of spirit. Bettina gives a detailed and typically intricate description of this process:

> gestern abend fühlte ich vor dem Einschlafen, als ob mich mein Inneres in Liebe aufgenommen habe, und da schlief ich die Ruhe bis tief in meine Seele hinein und wachte von Zeit zu Zeit auf und hatte Gedanken . . . Der Geist ist Auge, je schärfer er sieht, je deutlicher wird die Ahnung, je reiner tritt das Spiegelbild der Wahrheit in der Empfindung auf.[48]

The directness and, as it were, innocence of feeling described in this passage make us think of the Romantics' admiration of the sure simplicity of feeling of the 'Volk' and of folk-song, but the convoluted sophistication of its prose reminds us that intellectual speculation is an inalienable part of their character, taken as a group. The flower, as a symbol of wholeness and innocence, is a favourite of Brentano's and is also used by Novalis in *Heinrich von Ofterdingen* in a similar way (KS I, 330). But the state of the plant, described by Novalis elsewhere as 'ein mangelhaftes Leben',[49] i.e. the stage before the powers and capacities which constitute proper life have developed, is not an option for man. He has to venture into life, risking the dithyrambic 'animal' state of 'übersättigtes Leben' and aiming to achieve 'ein freies Leben', as the same fragment puts it. This 'freedom' suggests what Novalis calls elsewhere the realisation of the 'transcendental Self', becoming 'the I of one's [own] I',[50] that is, presumably, infusing into the inner capacity for experiencing the infinite an element of conscious control. Brentano seems to be positing a similar ideal in his formulation: 'Ursprünglichkeit in vollem Bewußtsein'.[51]

There were more things in the romantic universe than had been dreamed of in the rationalistic philosophy of the eighteenth century, but for all their belief in a transcendent reality, the Romantics placed the greatest emphasis on man. There is no necessary contradiction here, for the mirror in which the infinite is reflected is the human *Gemüt*, that untranslatable word which renders the inner psychological life in its totality, and which is a favourite word of the romantic generation. It is in activating and articulating the deeper psychological processes that romantic literature is often at its most profound. Novalis, indeed, once defined poetry as 'Gemütserregungskunst' (DL 3, 218). It was this generation which accepted as valid subjects for scientific enquiry phenomena like dreams, somnambulism, 'animal magnetism' and the like. Men whose training and profession were unimpeachably scientific were willing, indeed eager, to take the 'Night-side' of nature, as the doctor and scientist G. H. von Schubert called it, entirely seriously. C. G. Carus, who was at once a qualified doctor and the author of a treatise *Über Lebensmagnetismus*, saw that the key to understanding our conscious psychological life lies 'nur in der Region des Unbewußtseins' (DL 18, 303). Even when external, 'fate'-ful forces or (to use Hoffmann's term) principles are invoked, the true Romantic will at least suggest a link between mysterious experiences and behaviour and individual psychology.

The *real* subject of romantic literature or art is often not the ostensible 'external' one, but the *Gemüt* itself and its both individual and infinite experience. The power and substance of a romantic 'Stimmung', such as that aroused by Eichendorff, lies in its psychological content and effect; it communicates the life of the author's *Gemüt* and stimulates that of the reader. Music, the art of 'the infinite in the finite',[53] is especially well fitted to such activity and has a corresponding attraction for the Romantics. In painting, C. D. Friedrich and P. O. Runge, particularly, often convey a symbolic and visionary quality, as if the real subject was the sensibility of the artist himself, and his apprehension of some transcendent reality. Runge himself remarks on the way in which, in landscape painting, our sense of the unity of all things calls forth in us words, thoughts and pictures and enables the painter to arrive at 'Symbole unserer Gedanken über große Kräfte der Welt' (DL 12, p. 170). C. G. Carus, writing on the same subject, describes how, by 'losing himself' through contemplation in the infinite, the painter finds that what previously only the spirit could apprehend becomes visible to the eye.[54]

It is above all the fact that it has psychological roots that enables the romantic imagination to retain the link with reality. Some critics do not accept that it achieves this. Ralph Tymms, for example, speaks of 'surrender to unbounded and unbridled imagination' and of the 'escapism' which 'lies at the heart of all Romanticism',[55] Tymms would not deny, of course, that man's imaginings, as psychological experience, are in at least one sense 'real'. But the implication of his remarks is that they are not 'true'. It is hard to see clear guidelines in this matter and psychologists themselves do not seem to agree on the extent to which dreams and fantasies contain truth. The Romantics themselves did not deny that there was such a thing as mental sickness. Loss of contact with reality, even in sympathetic figures like Hoffmann's hermit 'Serapion', is seen as pathological. But they did feel that departure from the everyday norm could well be a sign of enhanced spiritual awareness, as in the case of the eccentricity of the same author's Rat Krespel.

Certain trends in modern psychology seem to echo the romantic view. R. D. Laing, in *The Politics of Experience*,[56] accepts that there is a reality which our concept of normality obscures. Fantasy can be 'another mode of experience'. In an age characterised by a 'drive to control the external world and . . . an almost total forgetfulness of the inner world',[57] so-called 'psychotic' states can give transcendental experiences of real value.[58] It is interesting to note that the modern psychologist finds himself driven to speak of the same duality of inner and outer worlds which we noticed in romantic thought! He sees also a significant link between the artist and the psychologically abnormal. The artist, in venturing into fantasy, is setting out on a dangerous voyage. Some who essayed it were 'wrecked', others survived, thanks to their 'realistic appraisal of the risks'.[59]

The German Romantics were more willing than most to undertake this voyage and suffered shipwreck correspondingly more often. They knew the dangers of the poetic life and often wrote them out in 'wrecked' characters like Hoffmann's Kreisler or Wackenroder's Berglinger. Eichendorff formulates the problem of poetry in his late novel *Dichter und ihre Gesellen*, a work of romantic retrospect written by a survivor, in which a continued genuine faith in romantic values interacts with a sombre awareness of the dangers of the romantic mentality:

Es gibt nur wenige Dichter in der Welt, und von den wenigen kaum
einer steigt unversehrt in diese märchenhafte, prächtige Zaubernacht,
wo die wilden, feurigen Blumen stehen und die Liederquellen
verworren nach den Abgründen gehen, und der zauberische
Spielmann zwischen dem Waldesrauschen mit herzzerreißenden
Klängen nach dem Venusberg verlockt, in welchem alle Lust und
Pracht entzündet, und wo die Seele, wie im Traum, frei wird mit
ihren dunklen Gelüsten.[60]

It took a Romantic to write this. Rationalistic common sense can
neither grasp the phenomenon, nor provide an effective antidote to the
poisons which it undoubtedly contains for the unwary. Two main
possibilities offered themselves. One was to venture into the middle of
the stream, trusting in an inner moral and spiritual sense, almost
instinctive in its action and definable only in symbolic form. The
'stilles ernstes Wort' which Eichendorff finds in the forest and takes
with him as he goes out into the world ('Abschied') is one such
symbol. The second method was to set limits to the extent to which one
partook of the romantic tendency (as did Tieck) or to be possessed of a
temperament which has the same inhibiting effect (e.g. Chamisso and
Uhland).

There are works of a superficially romantic character in which the
imagination is used simply to provide a holiday from reality. But the
true romantic fancy constitutes a valid mode of perception, perhaps
even of thought. It calls for the scaling of heights which are no less
demanding and precipitous for the fact that they are less bare and
sharp than those of pure logic. Seen from the philosophical viewpoint,
as it is by Friedrich Schlegel in the *Gespräch über die Poesie*, this
tendency leads naturally to a form of thought in which allegory and
myth are the main media of truth. Schlegel calls for a modern
mythology as a universal framework which will enable the *Gemüt* to
set down its insights in a form which neither distorts nor emasculates
them, which is both concrete and spiritual ('sinnlich-geistig'). He cites
Spinoza (re-created in his own image) as a kindred spirit who, permeated
with 'transfiguring fancy and love', achieves the 'hieroglyphic
expression of surrounding nature'.[61] On a large or a small scale, we
often find romantic poets constructing myths and deliberately
cultivating the sense of legend which Brentano, in his essay on the
genesis of *Die Gründung Prags*, sees as the 'higher . . . eternal poetic
truth' (K 4, 528). Apart from this play, we can point in Brentano
especially to the *Romanzen vom Rosenkranz*, in Novalis to a generally

mythopoeic tendency, above all in *Heinrich von Ofterdingen*, in Arnim to *Die Kronenwächter*, in Hoffmann to the nature-myth of *Der goldene Topf* and the incipient redemption-myth of *Die Elixiere des Teufels.*

Schlegel more or less equates Spinoza's capacity for mythological vision with that apparent in the older religions. He concentrates, in the *Gespräch*, on the Greek, though the Indian is also mentioned, a point developed later in *Über die Sprache und Weisheit der Indier* (III, 1). As we have indicated before, we use the word 'religious' in the broad sense of an orientation towards the infinite when we introduce it in the context of the romantic mentality in general. Whether or not the individual has specific religious convictions, these are rarely in themselves the source of his romantic ideas. Fancy certainly finds religion more congenial than irreligion, but does not take kindly to having its free-ranging universalist tendency restricted by dogma.

In this broad sense, then, we can see fancy as a religious logic, which reveals order and harmony in an area where logical reasons can see only chaos. In its ability to find ways of 'combining' the apparently disparate, it is a truly 'productive imagination'.[62] It gives a thinker the power to 'experiment', to generate thought poetically through analogy and similar means. Novalis, who advocates such a poeticisation of thought in *Das allgemeine Brouillon*, considers that it is the lack of a capacity for 'experimenting' which makes both Kant and Fichte incomplete as philosophers.[63] For good or ill, he certainly possessed this capacity in full measure. Friedrich Schlegel wrote to him with justice: 'In deinem Geiste haben sich Poesie und Philosophie innig durchdrungen.'[64]

Just as we need to be able to attune our minds to the associative logic of the fancy in studying romantic thought, so we need a sensitivity to this kind of free combination if we are to overcome the initially alienating impression of 'formlessness' in romantic poetic literature, its apparently wilful delight in digression, repetition and variation of themes and flagrant disregard of architectonic principles. Here too, Romanticism goes further than 'Sturm und Drang'. It is true, for example, that A. W. Schlegel's proclamation of the principle of 'organic' form[65] recalls the aesthetic thinking of Goethe and Herder in the 1770s. But the way in which, in developing the theme, Schlegel dwells lovingly on the loose, even chaotic form, as he sees it, of English and Spanish drama, makes us inclined to feel that he stands closer to Novalis, who claims: 'In eigentlichen Poemen ist keine als die Einheit des Gemüts.'[66]

Fancy blended with intellect gives the romantic 'wit' which
Friedrich Schlegel prizes so highly and characterises in the 'Allegorie
von der Frechheit' in *Lucinde*. It is also closely connected with
romantic 'humour', a frame of mind in which the consciously free
spirit *enjoys* its sense of the discrepancy between itself and reality,
though not as intellectually as in the related and overlapping concept
of 'irony', which we associate particularly with Friedrich Schlegel.[67]
The great masters of humour in our period are Jean Paul (who, since
his status as a Romantic is questionable, is best left out of account
here), Arnim (in stories like *Die Ehenschmiede* and *Der Pfalzgraf, ein
Goldwäscher*) and Hoffmann. The portrait of the artist as clown in
Signor Formica is a fine representation of the humoristic character and
the juxtaposition of the story of the deeply spiritual musician Kreisler
with the self-revealing autobiography of a philistine feline in
Lebensansichten des Katers Murr produces a moving and profoundly
humorous total effect. Comic disorder is one of the primary effects of
romantic humour – indeed, there is often a tendency to the grotesque
which tempts us to speak of surrealism – and failure to respond
positively to it is a sure sign of philistinism.

Philistines can be 'worthy' people, like the sentimental, humani-
tarian, enlightened muskrat Piloris in Brentano's *Gockel, Hinkel und*
Gackeleia, described with delicious humour as 'fernher pilgernder
Menschenwohlbezwecker im schwarzen Frack und weißen
Unterkleidern' (K 2, 777). They can even fall in love though in their
love, as in their charity, their spiritual shallowness reveals itself. The
Romantics took this aspect of life very seriously, and rejected both
mere sensualism and the empty, sentimentalised shell, the platonic
'Seelenschwelgerei', as Friedrich Schlegel sees it, of F. H. Jacobi's
Woldemar.[68] Schlegel sought in love the height of sensual and
spiritual experience in a harmonious unity,[69] a synthesis of body and
spirit which, as Schleiermacher saw, probably better than the author
himself, is the true message of *Lucinde*, a book often interpreted as
merely a tract advocating free love. Love is not only what makes a true
marriage but also the central source of energy, in the inner *Gemüt* as in
the universe, of the life of the spirit. It fuels the religious impulse in
man: 'It is yearning for love which helps man to the enjoyment of
religion,' says Schleiermacher.[70] For Runge, it is the source of all art
and wisdom (DL 11, 137–8). It is ubiquitous as a force, just as poetry
is ubiquitous as a phenomenon.

Poetry means for the Romantic not only the work in which the poet
gives aesthetic form to his experience of the spirit, but also the

objective manifestations of the spirit in the world. Not only the artist, even the scientist can (indeed should) discern it. For J. W. Ritter, nature is 'ein vollkommenes Gedicht'[71] and the lectures of Henrik Steffens, according to Eichendorff, were poetic both in form and in content: 'sein freier Vortrag hatte durchaus etwas Hinreißendes durch die dichterische Improvisation, womit er in allen Erscheinungen des Lebens die verhüllte Poesie mehr divinierte als wirklich nachwies.'[72] There is no contradiction for the Romantic, indeed no real division between the activity of pure abstract spirit and experience of the outside world, with its 'immeasurable and inexhaustible' store of poetry, as described by Friedrich Schlegel in the opening section of the *Gespräch über die Poesie*. The true medium of romantic expression is neither realistic nor abstract, but one which shows a peculiarly intense interpenetration of the abstract and the sensuous. It is the absence of such an interpenetration which makes us reluctant, as it did Solger,[73] to describe Jean Paul's work as romantic.

The natural tendency of romantic poetry is thus towards the spiritualisation of reality, that is towards symbolism, though whether a *complete* symbolism is reached in all cases may be doubted. The outstanding formal characteristic of such poetic language is directness, even simplicity, as in much of Eichendorff's work. This does not necessarily make such writing easier to interpret: quite the contrary at times. The element of calculation and motivation is reduced more or less to vanishing-point. To understand what the poet says is one thing; to say what he means quite another. The symbol, as Friedrich Creutzer said in his *Symbolik und Mythologie der ältern Völker*, makes the infinite visible, not in the 'sukzessive Schlußfolge' which is the *modus operandi* of logical reason, but 'ganz und auf einmal' (DL 13, 91–2). It functions on the small scale in a way analogous to that of myth on the large.

The Romantics' predilection for the symbol, which arises out of their propensity for seeing the infinite in the finite, helps us also to understand their strong desire for musicality in the use of language. By this we mean not simply the cultivation of rich patterns and textures in sound, but a new and critical attitude to the assumed hegemony of logical 'meaning' in language. Direct expression, in which conscious logical reasoning is as little involved as possible, is the romantic ideal. 'Die Sprache hat sich prosaisiert,' writes Novalis in his *Monolog*, 'sie muß wieder Gesang werden.' With the example of music as a guide, it could, perhaps, recover what was seen as its true nature as a pure and direct medium of expression. 'Man verstehe die Sprache nicht,' runs the

message in *Die Lehrlinge zu Sais*, 'weil sich die Sprache selber nicht
verstehe, nicht verstehen wolle; die ächte Sanscrit spräche, um zu
sprechen, weil sprechen ihre Lust und ihr Wesen sei' (KS I, 79).
'Sprache ist Delphi.'[74] The Delphic and paradoxical utterance is likely
to be closer to the truth than the false clarity of the Enlightenment.

The romantic declaration of the independence of the Self inevitably
made the matter of social morality problematic. By and large, this
generation still accepted the traditional values, but now they had to be
seen to grow organically out of individual freedom. Just like the
Classicists, the Romantics talk of the achievement of humanity through
culture ('Bildung'), but they strive to reconcile this aim with the
principle of subjectivity. 'Harmonisch in schöner Sitte leben kann kein
anderer, als wer die toten Formeln hassend eigne Bildung sucht,' says
Schleiermacher (DL 4, 60). There is a paradox and a mystery at the
centre of this process: without any surrender of individuality, we are to
achieve the sureness and universality of pure morality. This would be a
state of god-like freedom; Novalis, indeed, never one to shrink from a
provocative paradox, declares: 'Gott will Götter',[75] and Friedrich
Schlegel, hardly less obscurely: 'Gott werden, Mensch sein, sich bilden,
sind Ausdrücke, die einerlei bedeuten' (DL 4, 20). Whether these sayings
provide much practical guidance may be doubted and to be fair, that
can hardly have been their purpose. Their purpose is to indicate the
nature of the ideal and to that extent it might be said that they indicate
a goal. The requisite strength to reach it, however, had to come from
faith, purity of heart, and in many cases, grace from an infinite source,
such as Eichendorff's Taugenichts seems always to have had, and as is
vouchsafed to others, often through love, as happens in the cases of
Arnim's Francœur and Hoffmann's Medardus.

Given the spiritualistic tendency of Romanticism and the fact that
society at large was dominated by other values, social integration was
bound to be a problematic matter for them. And, certainly, solitude has
its very strong attractions, above all as the state in which it is easiest to
come close to the infinite. Many romantic lyrics conjure up the
atmosphere of 'Einsamkeit', most notably 'Waldeinsamkeit', very
powerfully. And yet there is very often also a sense of danger, of
sinister forces symbolising a destructive isolation. Similarly, though
the figure of the hermit occurs not infrequently in the romantic novel
and is usually sympathetically portrayed, it never represents the final
wisdom for the author. Social integration as a 'Bürger', as happens in
the case of Wilhelm Meister, is hardly a romantic ideal: the small group
of like-minded friends, as portrayed by Hoffmann in the Serapion-

Brotherhood, is much more the thing. But the Romantics did have a sense of community, which is expressed in their attitude to the state.

As in the case of morality, the attempt is made here to achieve a relationship between the individual and general in which the former is not lost in the latter, but found again at a higher level. The state is anything but a system, an administrative machine, as the eighteenth century had conceived it, but in the words of Adam Müller, 'a great individual, encompassing a number of smaller individualities'.[76] In perhaps more scientific, certainly less elegant, language, K. S. Pinson speaks of the Romantics' 'organismic' concept of the state as a 'macroanthropos'.[77] The citizen should stand in a personal and emotional relationship to the state; Novalis phrased it, in the collection of his political fragments, as one of 'Glauben und Liebe'. When he experiences the idea of the state, says Schleiermacher, the individual should become aware of a higher, ideal form of human individuality in which he can feel himself merged and exalted (cf. DL 4, 55). This is perhaps not exactly nationalism, but it has much in common with it, above all the demand that political forms must satisfy the emotional as well as the physical needs of the citizen. That there are very real dangers in such idealism hardly needs to be emphasised, though we must remember that we speak with the wisdom of hindsight. It is hard to believe that the Romantics would have fallen victim to those who were later to peddle such a debased form of German 'Geist'.

It is difficult, even for a nation with a long history of unity and achievement, to feel itself *as a nation* without some special occasion. How much harder it must have been for the Germans at the beginning of the nineteenth century with no such unity and only so much history as their scholars and antiquarians could scrape together from memories of the distant past. A national consciousness of a kind had, of course, survived, but it needed the imaginative and emotional power of the romantic mentality to turn it into a political force. Scholars could help to re-create the sense of a German 'geistige Gemeinschaft' (Savigny[78]) through the study of language, legend and Germanic law, but it was above all the image of the Middle Ages, which it was able to conjure up, which confirmed the faith of the Romantic Movement, even in such a relatively 'realistic' thinker as E. M. Arndt,[79] in the real spiritual potential of the German people, at a time when the contemporary reality offered little but flaccidity and depression. The medieval period, as described by Görres in *Die teutschen Volksbücher*, was one of 'Andacht, Liebe, Heldensinn . . . der neue Garten der Poesie, das Eden der Romantik' (DL 10, 136). This has been followed

by a period of 'Todesstille und Verkehrtheit' (p. 146) from which the
Germans can escape only by rekindling the spirit of the Middle Ages.

But Germany could not be re-created on paper or on a stage, and
practical life showed up the dangerous weakness of the idealistic
romantic position. The purity and poetry of a vision are all too easily
lost in the attempt to translate it into reality. The practical tends to be
unpoetic and the poetic impracticable. It is hard to imagine a major
Romantic being fired by the politically not ineffective but aesthetically
unimpressive gymnastic movement of 'Vater' Jahn. A Wilhelm Hauff
could hymn the 'Schar im weißen Gewand' in his 'Turnerlust', but it is
impossible to conceive of a Novalis or an Eichendorff even contemplating such a step. Hoffmann, while he disapproved of the government's
persecution of him, found the man himself comic.[80] At the same time,
practically effective men are not always villains or philistines and poets
are not always saints, and the longing for realisation of a poetic vision
could lead a romantic idealist into dangerous paths. The enthusiasm for
a 'holy war' which some Romantics show, even though it is clear that
what attracts them is the realisation of a poetic spirit, not war as it is
fought but 'die Erscheinung überhaupt, in ihrer Reinheit gedacht',[81]
gives us pause.

In his study of Eichendorff, Paul Stöcklein quotes a passage from
Arnim's essay on the 'Volkslied' (in *Des Knaben Wunderhorn*):

> Ja, wer einmal im Tanz sich verloren und vergessen . . . der jemals
> vom jubelnden Taktschlage der Janitscharen hingerissen, einen Feind
> gegen sich, den mutigen Freund neben sich glaubte . . . der muß an
> eine höhere Kunst glauben, als die uns umgibt und begegnet, an
> einen Sonntag nach sieben Werktagen.

Stöcklein points with justice to the dangerous mixture of the idealistic
and the unworthy here and after quoting another passage in which
Eichendorff criticises self-indulgent emotionalism, adds that the
Silesian poet had none of Arnim's 'gefährliche[n] romantische[n]
Geistesart'.[82] To suggest that by showing an awareness of the dangers
of the romantic outlook one is demonstrating the un-romantic nature
of one's own mentality is to go too far. Eichendorff himself feels the
seductive pull of the irrational away from everyday reality and he knows
that there are positive as well as negative principles involved. As he
implies in 'Die zwei Gesellen', for example, a safe philistine life is not
self-preservation but a different, and more unworthy, form of disaster.

The Romantics knew, of course, that reality ultimately imposed

limits on self-fulfilment, for no man can live permanently in the realm
of the Self. German Romanticism, being so absolute in its desires, is all
the more susceptible to frustration and strain and so it is natural that
it should be specially characterised by the feeling of 'Sehnsucht':
longing for consummation and longing for release. The ultimate in
these experiences, both symbolically and in reality, is death, which we
shall have an opportunity to study in our discussion of Novalis.
Another variant is provided by music. Joseph Berglinger's hymn of
praise to music shows the author's consciousness that it contains both
bliss and temptation:

> Wohl dem, der (müde des Gewerbes, Gedanken feiner und feiner zu
> spalten, welches die Seele verkleinert) sich den sanften und
> mächtigen Zügen der Sehnsucht ergibt, welche den Geist ausdehnen
> und zu einem schönen Glauben erheben. Nur ein solcher ist der
> Weg der allgemeinen umfassenden Liebe, und nur durch Liebe
> gelangen wir in die Nähe göttlicher Seligkeit.[83]

To achieve romantic content at all, the writer must move whole-
heartedly towards the absolute. Half-measures bring disaster, as in the
case of Elis in Hoffmann's *Die Bergwerke zu Falun*. He must surrender
himself to it without losing himself in it, thus preserving the possibility
of a return to finite reality, however attractive the alternative. It is the
strength of the attraction and of the pain caused by the necessity of
compromise with everyday reality which enables us to distinguish most
clearly between the Pre-Romantic and the Romantic proper. The
great Romantics stand out by virtue of their ability to control the
process, in the full knowledge that they were thereby denying
themselves complete satisfaction. And the resultant 'Sehnsucht', a
positive spiritual impulse even if it contains a sense of deprivation, and
one which is not to be confused with sentimental self-indulgence, is one
of the most reliable signs of a genuine romantic mentality.

Notes

1. F. Schlegel, *Literary Notebooks*, H. Eichner (ed.) (London, 1957), no.
1760.

2. F. Schlegel, *Gespräch über die Poesie*, H. Eichner (ed.) (Stuttgart, 1968),
p. 319.

3. *Clemens Brentanos Frühlingskranz*; cf. Bettina von Arnim, *Werke und
Briefe*, G. Konrad (ed.) (Frechen, 1959), p. 63.

4. Cf. *Beethovens Instrumentalmusik* in FN, p. 44.

5. Letter to Leberecht Dreves, quoted in Eichendorff, *Werke*, W. Rasch (ed.) (Munich, 1966), p. 1567.

6. Heine, *Werke* (Bongs Goldene Klassiker-Bibliothek), Teil 9, H. Friedemann and R. Pissin (eds.) (Berlin, n.d.), p. 107.

7. Cf. DL, vol. 2, p. 102.

8. *Blütenstaub*, no. 17: Novalis, *Schriften*, P. Kluckhohn and R. Samuel (eds.) (Darmstadt, 1960–75) (cited as KS), vol. 2, p. 418.

9. Cf. the Introduction to his *Geschichte der poetischen Literatur Deutschlands.*

10. DL 2, p. 94.

11. C. Brentano, *Das unsterbliche Leben*, W. Schellberg and F. Fuchs (eds.) (reprint, Berne, 1970), p. 246.

12. Cf. DL 5, p. 84.

13. KS III, p. 651.

14. Their mutual sympathy is clear from Carus's book: *Goethe. Zu dessen näherem Verständnis*, E. Merian-Genast (ed.) (Zurich, 1948).

15. Hence the fascination of 'animal magnetism', the mysterious natural force seen as the basis of the hypnotic effects secured by Mesmer and his successors, and as confirming the existence of spiritual energies in nature (cf. G. H. Schubert, *Ansichten von der Nachtseite der Naturwissenschaften*, Ch. 13, and Hoffmann's treatment of the subject (below, Ch. 14)).

16. Cf. *Clemens Brentanos Frühlingskranz*, p. 92.

17. Cf. the conversation between the hero and Sylvester in Part Two of *Heinrich von Ofterdingen.*

18. For example, Ignaz Arnold, *Die Grafen von Moor* (1802). Arnold's *Der schwarze Jonas*, H.-F. Foltin (ed.) (Hildesheim, 1972), illustrates the coarsened image of the 'horrid' bandit in popular literature and makes specific reference to Schiller (pp. 21–3 and 256). Arnold is no Romantic nor (though they are less crude as workmen) are the principal practitioners of the genre, H. Zschokke (*Aballino*, 1794) and C. A. Vulpius (*Rinaldo Rinaldini*, 1798). The only major Romantic to show its influence in a mature work is Hoffmann, in *Ignaz Denner.*

19. Cf. Wackenroder, *Herzensergießungen eines kunstliebenden Klosterbruders*, A. Gillies (ed.) (Oxford, 1948), p. 97.

20. SRE 1, p. 573.

21. K. W. F. Solger, *Vorlesungen über Ästhetik*, reprint (Darmstadt, 1969), p. 77.

22. Ed. A. von Grolmann (Heidelberg, 1955), p. 55. For the authorship, cf. J. Schillemeit, *Bonaventura. Der Verfasser der Nachtwachen* (Munich, 1973).

23. Cf. *Die Serapionsbrüder*, W. Müller-Seidel (ed.) (Darmstadt, 1970), pp. 54 ff.

24. *Nachtwachen*, p. 66: 'Entweder stehen die Menschen verkehrt, oder ich.'

25. A. W. Schlegel, *Vorlesungen über dramatische Kunst und Literatur*, G. Amoretti (ed.) (Bonn–Leipzig, 1923), vol. 2, p. 279.

26. Cf. the satire of it in works like Arnim's *Die Majoratsherren* and Hoffmann's *Kater Murr.*

27. Agatha Ramm, *Germany 1789–1919. A Political History* (London, 1967), p. 40. For the nationalistic activities of Jahn and Menzel, see H. Kohn, *The Mind of Germany* (London, 1965), pp. 69–98.

28. J. Droz, *Le romantisme allemand et l'état* (Paris, 1966), pp. 171 ff and 251–2. For Gentz, and German attitudes to the Revolution, see G. P. Gooch, *Germany and the French Revolution* (London, 1920), pp. 91–103, 230–49 and 283–302.

29. Arnim, *Gräfin Dolores*, SRE 1, p. 88.

30. *Der Einsame*; Kerner, *Werke*, R. Pissin (ed.) (Hildesheim, 1974), Teil II, pp. 31 f.

31. *Im Grase*, ibid., p. 28.

32. Chamisso and Arndt are of a more practical turn of mind, but they are in very much of a minority.

33. A lecture delivered in 1811 to the Berlin 'Christlich-Teutsche Tischgesellschaft', whose name testifies to its conservatism.

34. Cf. J. Mittenzwei *et al.*, *Romantik* (E. Berlin, 1967), p. 267.

35. *Reise nach Frankreich* in F. Schlegel, *Europa*, reprint, E. Behler (ed.) (Darmstadt, 1963), p. 11.

36. Letters of 28 April and 3 May 1815; Hoffmann, *Briefwechsel*, F. Schnapp (ed.) (Munich, 1968), vol. 2, pp. 47 and 48.

37. Quoted by F. Hiebel in *Novalis*, 2nd edn (Berne–Munich, 1972), p. 351.

38. Cf. the essay *Literatur* in Schlegel, *Europa*, vol. 1, p. 51.

39. J. Böhme, *Sämtliche Schriften*, W.-E. Peuckert (ed.) (Stuttgart, 1957), vol. 5, p. 31.

40. In *Das alte Buch*; L. Tieck, *Novellen*, M. Thalmann (ed.) (Munich, 1965), p. 982.

41. In *Die Seherin von Prevorst*; Kerner, *Werke*, Teil IV, p. 30.

42. Ibid., p. 19.

43. Cf. *Die Zerstörung der Vernunft*; G. Lukács, *Werke*, vol. 9 (Neuwied, 1962), pp. 86 ff.

44. H. Schanze, *Romantik und Aufklärung* (Nuremberg, 1966), pp. 4–5.

45. F. von Baader, *Sätze aus der erotischen Philosophie*, G.-K. Kaltenbrunner (ed.) (Frankfurt, 1966), p. 55.

46. Schanze, *Romantik und Aufklärung*, pp. 2–3.

47. Baader, *Sätze*, pp. 54 ff.

48. Bettina, *Werke und Briefe*, vol. 2, pp. 362 and 363. Cf. Caspar David Friedrich: 'Heilig sollst du halten jede reine Bewegung deines Gemütes, heilig achten jede fromme Ahndung' (DL 12, p. 200).

49. *Blütenstaub*, no. 105; KS II, p. 462.

50. Ibid., p. 424.

51. *Clemens Brentanos Frühlingskranz*, p. 53.

52. Cf. his *Ansichten von der Nachtseite der Naturwissenschaften*. His chief work is probably the *Geschichte der Seele* of 1830. Goethe had serious reservations about this approach (cf. Carus, *Goethe*, p. 22).

53. Cf. Bettina von Arnim, *Goethes Briefwechsel mit einem Kinde* in *Werke und Briefe*, vol. 2 (1959), p. 96.

54. Quoted by M. Brion in *Art of the Romantic Era* (London, 1966), pp. 110–11.

55. R. Tymms, *German Romantic Literature* (London, 1955), p. 24.

56. (Harmondsworth, 1967), p. 23.

57. Ibid., p. 115.

58. Ibid., pp. 108 and 112.

59. Ibid., p. 116.

60. Eichendorff, *Werke*, ed. Rasch, p. 988.

61. Schlegel, *Gespräch über die Poesie*, p. 318.

62. Novalis's phrase, quoted by P. Kluckhohn in *Das Ideengut der deutschen Romantik*, 5th edn (Tübingen, 1966), p. 45.

63. Cf. E. Heftrich, *Novalis. Vom Logos der Poesie* (Frankfurt, 1969), p. 33.

64. Quoted by Heftrich, *Novalis*, p. 16.

65. *Vorlesungen über die dramatische Kunst*, vol. 2, pp. 111 ff.

66. Cf. E. Hederer, *Novalis* (Vienna, 1949), p. 329.

67. Novalis (*Blütenstaub*, no. 36) equates Schlegel's 'irony' with 'true humour'.

It may well be that a clear distinction between the two is not possible, but it is worth pointing out that 'humour' is wider in its psychological scope than 'irony', which always retains a certain theoretical element and is less poetically productive, giving rise at best to squibs like Tieck's comic 'Märchendramen'.

68. Cf. Schlegel's review of this novel.

69. Cf. P. Kluckhohn, *Die Auffassung der Liebe im achzehnten Jahrhundert und in der Romantik*, 3rd edn (Tübingen, 1966), pp. 345 ff.

70. Ibid., pp. 427–8. Cf. Novalis (KS I, p. 288): 'Was ist die Religion als ein unendliches Einverständnis, eine ewige Vereinigung liebender Herzen?'

71. Cf. Kluckhohn, *Ideengut*, p. 29.

72. In *Halle und Heidelberg*; BG 2, p. 1052. K. von Raumer compares Steffens to a magician (DL 1, p. 157).

73. Solger, *Vorlesungen*, p. 219.

74. Novalis, quoted by Hederer, *Novalis*, p. 108.

75. Cf. Hiebel, *Novalis*, p. 152.

76. Cf. Kohn, *The Mind of Germany*, p. 64.

77. K. S. Pinson, *Modern Germany*, 2nd edn (New York–London, 1966), pp. 43 and ff.

78. Cf. H. S. Reiss, *Politisches Denken in der deutschen Romantik* (Berne, 1966), p. 74.

79. Writing to G. A. Reimer (10 May 1812), he speaks of the 'herrliche Denkmäler des Mittelalters'.

80. At a menagerie, the 'wild' appearance of a 'berühmte[r] Hüpf-, Sprung- und Schwungmeister' calls forth the question: 'Wie heißt dieses wilde Tier?' (SMN, p. 642).

81. *Über das Mittelalter* in A. W. Schlegel, *Kritische Schriften und Briefe*, E. Löhner (ed.) (Stuttgart, 1965), vol. 4, p. 88.

82. P. Stöcklein, *Eichendorff* (Hamburg, 1963), p. 80.

83. Wackenroder, *Herzensergießungen*, p. 132.

3 THE ROMANTICS AND LITERARY THEORY

The primary function of this chapter is to serve as a transition to the consideration of literature proper, and it will be correspondingly brief. It is our intention to organise this discussion under the rubrics provided by the traditional distinction, still accepted by the Romantics and by no means redundant even today, of three fundamental *kinds* of poetic writing ('Dichtarten') namely lyric, dramatic and epic. The tendency of the romantic mind being to unite, indeed to merge rather than to divide, a few prefatory remarks on the typical attitudes of this generation to matters of literary theory in general, and of genre in particular, might well be in order.

This was the age which saw the death of poetics, the systematic discussion in comprehensive compendia of practical problems of the *craft* of literature, in favour of aesthetics on the one hand and imaginatively interpretative criticism on the other, a development which had begun with Herder and Winckelmann. Whereas Lessing, even in the *Hamburgische Dramaturgie* (1767–9), still uses Aristotle as a point of departure, has not given up the idea of a poetry which imitates 'nature' and has rules (e.g. Stück 19), and still discusses the practical, rather than the philosophical, issues of tragedy, we find Hegel concerning himself with the *spirit* of the genre in general, with such questions as the relation of 'Idee' to 'Wirklichkeit'. The 'Classical' Goethe and Schiller, albeit more subtly and sensitively than the 'Aufklärer', still try, as far as possible, to classify and define in a practical spirit[1] and the fact that Jean Paul, in his *Vorschule der Ästhetik* (1804), has still not truly emancipated himself from the tradition of the systematic manual on poetics, that he finds the distinction between epic and dramatic 'clear' ('hell': para. 63) and discusses such specific questions as the appropriate number of characters for each (para. 66), only underlines the fact that his relation to Romanticism is problematic. (He even finds himself saying that some of Shakespeare's plays have too many characters to be truly dramatic!)

Whether in systematic speculative aesthetics, or in the more intuitive (and often Delphic) utterances and *aperçus* of more poetic spirits, the burden of romantic pronouncements on literature is usually its general spirit rather than its precise form or technique. Their aim is a *romantic* poetry, one in which the infinite spirit finds expression,

41

whether it be seen philosophically as a 'Weltgeist' or more emotionally as '[der] beseelende Geist der ursprünglichen Liebe' (A. W. Schlegel's phrase), brooding anew over the waters of a productive 'chaos' which is still present under the ordered creation so beloved of the Classical taste, and which exerts its mysterious attraction on the romantic mind.[2] The free activity of the spirit is more important to the Romantic than the harmonious balance of objective Classical form, which, as Hegel observes in his distinction between Classical and romantic art, imposes an unwelcome restriction on that activity. It is not surprising, then, that the Romantics should tend to seek a form which is as *un*-finished, as fluid as possible, one which, as Friedrich Schlegel phrases it in his 116th *Athenäum*-fragment, 'ewig nur werden, nie vollendet sein kann' and that the tendency to 'mixtures' of forms and moods which A. W. Schlegel sees as characteristic of romantic poetry[3] should be regarded as a positive quality.

One of the chief aims of romantic poetry, as Friedrich Schlegel says in the fragment just quoted, is 'to reunite all the separated genres of poetry'. The traditional genres were indeed taken, and employed, but invariably with a romanticising intent, which brought them closer together. The lyric is less open to such manipulation, but this tendency is, as we shall see later, very pronounced in the romantic drama and novel. As a representative example of romantic practice in defining genre, we may quote here Novalis's fragment on the *Märchen*:

> Das Märchen ist gleichsam der Kanon der Poesie. In einem echten Märchen muß alles wunderbar-geheimnisvoll und unzusammenhängend sein . . . – die Zeit der allgemeinen Anarchie – der Gesetzlosigkeit – der Freiheit . . . Die Welt des Märchens ist die durchaus entgegengesetzte Welt der Welt der Wahrheit (DL 3, 230).

Novalis is not aiming here to distinguish the *Märchen* precisely from other literary genres, but rather to distil its essential spirit, which he uses as a symbolic representation of the character towards which all literary forms should strive. Whether he is in fact thinking here specifically of the fairy-tale as a form, or simply of the quality of 'das Märchenhafte', could be a matter for argument. We shall later see him claim that a novel can become 'märchenhaft', as indeed all poetry should, to the extent that this is possible within the particular form that the writer has chosen. This is the beginning, then, of the process of deliberate blurring of the distinctions between genres which, after a certain retardation in the nineteenth century, was resumed with the onset of modernity.

The romantic experience of the world was simultaneously one of infinite variety and of infinite unity and they sought forms which would convey that experience. The 'Verwischung der Grenzen' of which the young Friedrich Schlegel, still writing under the influence of Weimar Classicism, complains as a trait of the 'characterless' modern (i.e. romantic!) generation,[4] is not the result of lack of substance, but of the change from a clearly delimited to an infinite substance. The aim is to affect the reader in a way which makes him susceptible to wonder; as Hoffman says in *Der Dichter und der Komponist*: 'Nur im wahrhaft Romantischen mischt sich das Komische mit dem Tragischen so gefügig, daß beides zum Totaleffekt in eins verschmilzt und das Gemüt des Zuhörers auf eine eigne, wunderbare Weise ergreift' (SB 88). Examples of the mixture of lyric, dramatic and epic by Shakespeare, Cervantes and others were eagerly seized on and the tendency developed further, particularly in the novel. Hegel, for whom the essential character of romantic art lies in as complete a cultivation of the inner spiritual life as possible ('absolute Innerlichkeit'), sees its 'basic tone' as 'musical',[5] and as long as we remember to use this idea as an analogy, it can be useful. Certainly, the Romantic has a stronger sense of atmosphere than he has of architecture.

Just as there was a tendency in philosophy in general to see duality, and to seek to overcome it, in the world, so in aesthetic matters also. This gives rise to formulations – showing a broadly dialectical tendency – which are more impressive as abstract constructions than as applied literary criticism. A rising scale, from epic to dramatic, seems to be the general pattern, with the last named forming some kind of higher synthesis of the tendencies of the other two. The decisive factor is always the relation between Idea and Reality. For Solger, for example, there are two basic variants of this relation, the symbolic, in which the idea is merged in an object, and the allegorical, when it is present as the active agent which establishes the links between the various individual parts. The corresponding literary modes of expression are the epic and lyric. Such a pair inevitably, for a Romantic, calls forth the idea of a third, which unites the two. This, of course, is drama. For Hegel, the sequence is objective (epic)-subjective (lyric)-objective presentation of the subjective (dramatic).[6] For the Romantic, the drama, 'die höchste Erscheinung des An-Sich und des Wesens der Kunst' (Schelling: DL 3, 26) is, or should be, the supreme literary form, an ironic conclusion when one considers what the movement actually achieved in this field! In practice, the epic genres turned out to be much more congenial to the romantic taste, a fact which is reflected in the proportion of this book which is devoted to them. In theory, though, one can see that the drama must have looked inviting as a medium for the uniting of opposites, and the opera even more so. Novalis in fact refers to it as 'the highest stage of drama' (DL 3, 229), and Hoffmann, in *Der Dichter und der Komponist*, thinks along similar lines. One senses the shadowy and ungainly bulk of the 'Gesamtkunstwerk' lurking in the background.

There was, then, a strong tendency among the Romantics to minimise the differences between the three principal kinds of literary expression. At the same time, the temptation to abolish the distinction is resisted. Novalis does say that they are in fact all three present in all poetry, but adds in the same fragment that 'only that work is primarily an epic in which the epic attitude comes particularly to the fore' (DL 3, 228); in other words, he concedes that there are three distinct attitudes and that a work can be classified according to which of them predominates in it. If this is true for Novalis, the most daringly fanciful of romantic thinkers, and one in whom the monistic tendency is especially strong, it is *a fortiori* likely to be true for other Romantics. We feel fully justified, therefore, in using this threefold classification in the arrangement of the account of romantic literature which follows, though this must, of course, be done with a full awareness of the need for flexibility and for the occasional crossing and re-crossing of boundaries. Novalis's *Hymnen an die Nacht*, for example, will therefore be discussed under the rubric of 'lyric', the same author's *Heinrich von Ofterdingen* under 'epic' and Tieck's 'all-in-one',[7] *Kaiser Oktavianus*, under 'dramatic'.

Notes

1. A good example is the discussion *Über epische und dramatische Dichtung* in Goethe's *Über Kunst und Alterthum*, Band 6, Heft 1. Goethe finds the 'modern' tendency to blur distinctions between genres 'childish, barbaric and absurd', but recognises that he is swimming against the tide.

2. A. W. Schlegel, *Vorlesungen über dramatische Kunst und Literatur*, G. Amoretti (ed.) (Bonn–Leipzig, 1923), vol. 2. p. 114.

3. Ibid.

4. *Über das Studium der griechischen Poesie* in F. Schlegel, *Kritische Schriften*, W. Rasch (ed.) (Munich, n.d.), p. 117.

5. Hegel, *Sämtliche Werke*, H. Glockner (ed.) (Stuttgart–Bad Cannstadt, 1964), vol. 13, p. 134.

6. Cf. H. A. Korff, *Geist der Goethezeit*, 2nd edn (Leipzig, 1954), Teil IV, p. 730. For Solger, cf. *Vorlesungen über Ästhetik*, reprint (Darmstadt, 1969), pp. 260–73.

7. Cf. E. H. Zeydel, *Ludwig Tieck, the German Romanticist*, reprint (Hildesheim, 1971), p. 147.

4 THE ROMANTIC LYRIC (GENERAL)

A vast corpus of lyric poetry could be assembled from within the resources of German romantic literature. And yet, while the amount of high-quality work which it could contain is in absolute terms quite large, it does not form such a high proportion of the whole as might have been expected, given the radically 'inward' orientation of the Movement. The reason for this may be that it was *too easy* to write poetry of a certain romantic type. The forms most often used were simple and a wealth of suitable motifs and images lay to hand, particularly in the world of nature, which the romantic emancipation of the mind from strict logical control had thrown open to the poet as never before. Folk-poetry, legend and romance also offered ample opportunity. Deep philosophical thought was no longer required: feeling and melody, it would seem, were enough. But romantic simplicity is not, in fact, a simple matter. To achieve verse of *substance*, verse, that is, which has a significant romantic content, it is necessary to deploy more rather than less skill with words, as well as a stronger inner discipline in the use of the imagination, than other kinds of lyric would require. Cliché on the one hand and pretentious emptiness on the other are very real hazards. Some Romantics, indeed, were better able to achieve poetic effects in prose than in verse, competent as they were in the basic techniques.

Probably the most important of the lyricists who fall into this category are Arnim and Tieck, and *Tieck* is the more relatively successful of these. There are moments, in his work, of genuine lyrical effectiveness, as in 'Waldeinsamkeit' (from *Der blonde Eckbert*) and the following passage from the prologue to *Kaiser Oktavianus*:

> Mondbeglänzte Zaubernacht,
> Die den Sinn gefangen hält,
> Wundervolle Märchenwelt,
> Steig auf in der alten Pracht!

Here, a genuinely creative and disciplined fancy has been at work. 'Moon' and 'magic' could (and still can) be used as mere counters in the most shallow of would-be 'romantic' songs. But Tieck, whose aim here is to conjure up the spirit of ancient Romance, has succeeded, above all in the first line, in so arranging the words and sounds as to induce a powerful 'Stimmung', one of the most characteristic romantic effects. There is no way in which this could be interpreted in terms of precise 'meaning', but it is more than a pleasant playing of sense-impressions on the mind. The revelation of a spiritual reality, of beauty and wonder, which the world of the old romances clearly gave to Tieck and which caused him to re-tell so many of them in epic or dramatic form, is momentarily conveyed in an inspiration of some intensity, from which the rest of the work, unfortunately, falls rather sadly away.

Tieck, indeed, rarely manages to sustain lyric inspiration for more than a few lines at any one time. He finds it easier to conceive the ideal romantic poem than to realise it. He adumbrates many of the principles which more accomplished lyricists were to put into practice, as for example when he speaks of 'thinking in sounds',[1] a pronouncement echoed by Novalis in *Das allgemeine Brouillon* though in a more profound and practical form. Language, Novalis says, must free itself from the bondage of logicality, and be 'frei' and 'unbestimmt' in its action: '[die Sprache] ... muß wieder Gesang werden' (KS III, 283–4). Atmospheric quality and musicality are two of the most important characteristics of the romantic lyric in general and they are at least enunciated and prepared for by Tieck.[2] But in order to achieve these magical effects, a poet needs to be able to command the 'Zauberwort' which, as Eichendorff phrases it in 'Wünschelrute', can release the 'song which sleeps in all things'. This is in fact the result of a concentrated and disciplined sensitivity and Tieck's discipline as a practical poet wavers all too easily, his content can become superficial or even banal, his rhythms slack or monotonous. The true, as opposed to the merely superficially pretty, romantic potential of a theme needs to be articulated; Tieck tends to be satisfied with melodious vagueness, but one that leads nowhere. In section fourteen of *Die schöne Magelone* (1797), we are presented with a situation which is full of romantic possibilities. Lovers on a moonlit night, with an elopement in view: what could be more promising? Yet Sulima's song is disappointingly dull:

Es flüstern die Bäume
Im goldenen Schein,
Es schlüpfen mir Träume
Zum Fenster herein.

Ach! kennst du das Schmachten
Der klopfenden Brust?
Dies Sinnen und Trachten
Voll Qual und voll Lust? . . . etc.[3]

There is really no magic here, nor is there a sense of deep passion. Certainly the passage is romantic in intention and, at a relatively superficial level, in effect. It does create a sense, but only a mild one, of mystery and tension. Emil Staiger is justified in calling Tieck the inventor of romantic 'Stimmungskunst',[4] but he was hardly its most effective practitioner.

He was a competent, rather than an inspired writer of verse, but one still has the impression that he had it in him to be more effective than he in fact was. He often seems as much unwilling as unable to probe far into the deeper levels of consciousness. A truly effective and evocative beginning can tail off into something very ordinary. This characteristic, which we shall discuss again when we deal with Tieck at his best, as an epic writer, can usefully be illustrated here too, as this will help us appreciate better the greatness of other lyricists who came later. In *Franz Sternbald* there is a 'Waldhornmelodie' which begins with a really fine evocation of the forest atmosphere, another theme in which Tieck anticipates later poets of this era:

Hörst! wie spricht der Wald dir zu,
      Baumgesang,
      Wellenklang:
Komm und finde hier die Ruh . . . (Part I, Bk. II, Ch. 3)

Taken in isolation, these lines suggest a characteristically romantic psychological process; the journey into the subconscious. The idea of the forest as an active entity and the illogical, but to the associative imagination in no way disturbing, leap from 'Baumgesang' to 'Wellenklang', set us on that path. The continuation, however, sinks to the level of a rather banal love-poem, which even contains moments reminiscent of the conventional lyric of the earlier eighteenth century:

Ruhe aus in dem Gedanken
Daß sie dich ja wiederliebt,
Sieh, wie alle Zweige schwanken,
Echo Töne wiedergibt . . . etc.

'Nur am Geformten', says Friedrich Gundolf of Tieck, 'wird er produktiv.'[5] This is perhaps too harsh a judgement, but it does point to a historically important aspect of Tieck's activity, as a poet as well as a narrator. He performed a positive act of restoration in bringing material back from the popular to the literary level and in refurbishing the often stiff old-fashioned form in a romantic style. And in that process, he added a new and valuable dimension, namely an expression of his own, romantic response to the naïve charm of the original. A good example is his successful 'Kontrafaktur' of the hermit's song, 'Komm Trost der Nacht', from Grimmelshausen's *Simplicissimus* (Book I, Ch. 7):[6]

> Bald kommt des Morgens früher Strahl
> Und funkelt tief ins ferne Tal
> Und macht die Leutlein munter:
> Dann regt zur Arbeit alles sich
> Und preist den Schöpfer festiglich,
> Weicht Nacht und Schlaf hinunter,
>   Weil' nicht,
>   Süß Licht,
>   Morgenröte,
>   Magst die Öde
>   Hell entzünden,
> Gottes Lieb uns zu verkünden.[7]

The baroque poem, itself a distinguished work, is an expression of the deep and rather naïvely austere spirituality of the hermit which, as a remembered ideal, plays such an important part in the novel. There is little sense of a subjective response to nature as such. Tieck preserves the spirituality, but transposes it into a romantic key. He conveys a feeling, both of an infinite presence and of the sensuous reality of the natural world, and by creating an impression of brightness and animation and above all, of distance, manages to stir the inner levels of the *Gemüt*.

Tieck belongs, along with Novalis, Brentano, Eichendorff and Arnim, to the group of romantic writers whose lyrical work occurs largely in an epic (or, less frequently, a dramatic) context. This lyricism is on the whole of a higher quality, and more deeply and successfully romantic, than that of other writers who practise this genre independently and in an ostensibly 'pure' form. The mixture of genres improves the romantic product, it seems, or perhaps it is that the wider context helps the poet to concentrate his mind on the 'inner' and 'infinite' dimensions which provide the romantic lyric with its real substance but which cannot be introduced directly without the risk of an unacceptably high level of abstraction. However this may be, there is an inner, and an outer, circle of romantic lyricists and it is with the latter that we shall be dealing in the remainder of this chapter. There are several who produced poems of merit. The Schlegel brothers, for example, cultivated the sonnet with some success. Justinus Kerner, a member of the 'Swabian School'[8] and a prolific poet, sometimes achieved a pleasant, if not memorable, lyrical tone. We shall concentrate our attentions on the two most important poets of this 'outer circle', Chamisso and Uhland, with a complementary glance at Wilhelm Müller, and shall append a brief examination of the work of Johann Peter Hebel, one of Germany's foremost dialect-poets who, while not himself a Romantic, does not seem totally out of place in this company.

Adalbert von Chamisso is best remembered for a single short story,[9] but his literary production is dominated by poetry: songs, sonnets and ballads and a number of narrative works in *terza rima*. In his maturer work (from about 1819 onwards), he makes an impression which differs, at first sight, from the image of Romanticism which we might derive from a Novalis or Eichendorff. His nineteenth-century editor, Max Koch, is indeed convinced that he was not tainted with 'romantische Modetorheiten'[10] and Ermatinger calls him 'a realist at bottom'.[11] It is true that he writes with a certain clarity of style and a relative closeness to material reality which preclude a powerfully 'atmospheric' effect, true also that, while he does often use medieval material in his ballads, he does not yearn for a restoration of the romantic spirit of those days. Poems like 'Die Ruine' and 'Laß ruhn die Toten' show this. It is worth noting that he receives much more favourable mention in Heine's *Die romantische Schule* than is accorded to most other members of the generation.

There are factors in Chamisso's psychological and poetic constitution, then, which inhibit the romantic impulse in him and place him closer to the periphery than to the centre of the Movement. At the same time, that impulse remains the primary one in his writing. If we accept that his respect for material reality is high for a Romantic, a comparison with Heine, Stifter or even Mörike convinces us that his place is even less with them. While his poetry rarely reaches to the deepest levels of the inner consciousness, the life of the emotions, and to a greater extent still, the strange and mysterious, remain for him the source of poetry. There is no trace of the corrosive doubt which appears in the nineteenth-century writers. And while he may be politically out of sympathy with romantic medievalism, his 'Laβ ruhn die Toten' exhibits a *poetic* sympathy with the period, as well as a feeling that it can no longer help to solve modern problems. He is in his element in the world of the exotic, even horrific, and exploits his material with a genuine feeling for the romantic resonances, so that we can agree with Thomas Mann, who classifies Chamisso as a Romantic in spite of his 'Latin clarity and definition'.[12]

Love poetry forms a significant proportion of Chamisso's lyric output. His is certainly a serious, spiritualised love in the romantic manner and while his lovers are neither Heathcliff nor Heinrich von Ofterdingen, neither Juliet nor Jane Eyre, he can achieve some sense of exaltation at his more mundane level, an exaltation which has a genuine romantic content, as opposed to the sentimental stereotype which often passed (and still passes) for 'romantic love' in the popular imagination. The sadness of the girl left alone in the poem 'So still das Tal geworden' from *Lebens-Lieder und Bilder* (1831), for example, is much more than the pallid melancholy of Marie as she waits in the arbour in Hauff's *Lichtenstein* (Part I, Ch. 7):

> Marie saß traurig, in sich gekehrt; sie hatte den schönen Arm auf eine Lücke der Laube aufgestützt und das von Gram und Tränen müde Köpfchen in die Hand gelegt. Ihr dunkles, glänzendes Haar hob die Weiße ihres Teint um so mehr heraus, als stiller Kummer ihre Wangen gebleicht und schlaflose Nächte dem lieblichen blauen Auge seinen sonst so überraschenden Glanz geraubt und ihm einen matteren, vielleicht nur umso anziehenderen Schimmer von Melancholie gegeben hatten.

Here is an unhappy young lady the course of whose love-affair is not running smooth (though we feel that all will come right in the end), but who does not arouse the impression that the horizons of her love stretch wider than a happy domestic existence with the favoured male. Chamisso, on the other hand, while he does not rise to the vision of love as an infinite experience such as we shall see in Novalis, shows it as one in which the lover transcends everyday individual reality and which needs no validation but itself:

> Er hat, der Morgensonne gleich, dem Traume
> Dem nächtlichen, der Kindheit mich entrückt;
> Er schreite vor im lichterfüllten Raume,
> Es sinkt mein Blick geblendet und entzückt.

Ich werde nicht, einfältges Kind, begehren
Daß mir die Sonne nur gehören soll;
Mag flammend mich ihr mächtger Strahl verzehren,
Ich segne sie und sterbe freudenvoll.[13]

Chamisso writes in an expressive style, but not one which is enriched by the nuances and subtle undercurrents of the major romantic poets. An Eichendorff, describing Schloß Boncourt (Chamisso's birthplace), would have dissolved the object in 'Stimmung', using it as a key to unlock the inner doors of mind and heart. Chamisso's description is not quite solidly realistic and it does introduce the dream-motif, but in the context of clear observation of a specific scene:

Hoch ragt aus schattigen Gehegen
Ein schimmerndes Schloß hervor,
Ich kenne die Türme, die Zinnen,
Die steinerne Brücke, das Tor . . .

Dort liegt die Sphinx am Brunnen,
Dort grünt der Feigenbaum,
Dort, hinter diesen Fenstern
Verträumt' ich den ersten Traum. . . (*Werke*, 1, 49)

Chamisso's lyrical talent is not primarily for the simpler, more delicate short forms, though pieces like 'Rosen in dem Maien' (*Werke* 1, 71) and 'Seit ich ihn gesehen'[14] show at least quite high competence and in 'Die alte Waschfrau' (*Werke* 1, 212 f) he has created an image of the simple woman of the 'Volk' as effective as any in German romantic literature. It is in the ballad (also, of course, a form with strong folk-connections) and the narrative poem that this poet's greatest strength lies. Here too, he works with clarity and relative objectivity of tone. This is as well, for the subject-matter he chooses is often lurid, even gruesome, as in 'Das Krucifix', in which an artist crucifies his model in order to study the effects of the pain on the human body. Colour, excitement and exoticism abound in the material of Chamisso's ballads and this material is treated with the clear intention of making these potentially romantic factors tell in a romantic way, though without the psychological 'Verinnerlichung' characteristic of the German school. There is an almost rhetorical grandeur, for example, about 'Corsische Gastfreiheit', which tells how the Corsican law of hospitality triumphs even over a blood-feud. The wildness of the weather and of the natural

setting, recalling, perhaps, the Scott of *The Lady of the Lake*, enhance
the spectacular, if unsubtle, romantic effect and Chamisso's choice of
motifs and above all, of verbs and adjectives in these lines leave us in no
doubt that the effect is intended:

> Die Blitze erhellen die finstere Nacht,
> Der Regen strömt, der Donner kracht,
> Der mächtige Wind im Hochwald saust,
> Der wilde Gießbach schwillt und braust... (*Werke* 1, 144)

In similar fashion, Chamisso often deliberately and successfully sets
out to produce an impression of the uncanny, as, for example, in 'Das
Auge' or 'Die Sonne bringt es an den Tag', but without the psychological
depth which we shall see later in the stories of Tieck and Hoffmann.
His 'Nächtliche Fahrt' (1828) seems, particularly at the beginning, to
invite comparison with Brentano's ballad, 'Auf dem Rhein'. Each sets
out to tell, in a simple folk-metre, the story of a mysterious nocturnal
journey in a light skiff by a man and a woman. Each highlights, at the
beginning, the strange behaviour of the woman. But after the point has
been reached at which the woman has steered the boat to her desired
goal, Chamisso drops the mystery and indulges in a denouement which
is still romantic but, in contrast to Brentano, stays within the realm of
the concrete and comprehensible. The woman kills her faithless lover,
then herself, and the incoming tide washes up a wreck containing
'zwei Leichen/Gebadet in ihrem Blut' (*Werke* 1, 81).
    The best of Chamisso's narrative poems is *Salas y Gomez*, which
tells the story of an imaginary castaway on the sun-scorched rock in
the Pacific, near Easter Island, which gives the poem its name. He had
seen it during the expedition (of 1815—18) which he describes in his
Reise um die Welt and the rumour of a wreck there had stimulated his
fancy: 'Man schaudert, sich den möglichen Fall vorzustellen, daß ein
menschliches Wesen darauf verschlagen werden konnte' (*Werke* 2, 402).
The poem sets out to render this sense of horror at the idea of absolute
barrenness and isolation, with only moderate success in the parts which
deal with the thoughts and feelings of the castaway, but very
effectively in the description:

> Salas y Gomez raget aus den Fluten
> Des stillen Meers, ein Felsen kahl und bloß,
> Verbrannt von scheitelrechter Sonne Gluten,
> Ein Steingestell ohn alles Gras und Moos,

Das sich das Volk der Vögel auserkor
Zur Ruhstatt im bewegten Meeresschoß (*Werke* 1, 259).

Chamisso's is perhaps in the last analysis a romantic imagination
which needs an external prop, such as a dramatic story or setting. He is
not unreminiscent in this respect of Scott, who can bring together the
material for a great romantic novel, but lacks the 'passion', in the words
of E. M. Forster, required to instil real life into it.[15] The imagination of
such writers, judged by the most rigorous standards, is undeniably
coarse-grained. Not only Chamisso, but also Fouqué and perhaps even
Uhland, fall into this category. But we must not allow the best to
become the enemy of the good. All of those mentioned are capable of
distilling from their material a genuinely stirring romantic appeal. Nor
should their relative simplicity and accessibility be seen *merely* as
evidence of superficiality. This they certainly often are, but it is equally
true that the more profound romantic spirit, in its quest for the
Absolute, can lose itself in a fog of incomprehensibility and neglect
the real needs of the present, a point tellingly made by Arndt in
attacking the 'Apriorität' of Steffens.[16] To combine such accessibility
with genuine literary quality is not given to everyone and there are
times when one is grateful for a little firm ground under one's feet.

As in the case of Chamisso, so there are those who question the
romantic credentials of *Ludwig Uhland*. Friedrich Sengle, for example,
claims him for 'Biedermeier', as does Tymms.[17] This is hardly a dispute
which we can resolve here: the justification for our inclusion of this
writer must lie in the fruitfulness of our consideration of him under
the romantic rubric. Like Chamisso, he did his best work in the field of
the ballad. As with Chamisso, we find in his *oeuvre* a considerable
number of short pieces which are often pleasantly and melodiously
simple, but which only rarely, as in the case of the well known 'Die
Kapelle', reach a memorable level of achievement. Uhland differs from
Chamisso, however, in the degree of his theoretical insight into and
commitment to the romantic view of poetry. He accepts the need for
at least a measure of dreaminess, of the ability to make solid reality
become transparent, so that we can glimpse another reality through it.
In 'Der Mohn', he celebrates the poppy as the symbol of the poetic
mentality:

In meiner Tage Morgen,

Da lag ich auch einmal
Von Blumen ganz verborgen
In einem schönen Tal.
Sie dufteten so milde;
Da ward, ich fühlt' es kaum,
Das Leben mir zum Bilde,
Das Wirkliche zum Traum. . .[18]

'Die Welt wird Traum'! But this quotation (from Novalis's *Heinrich von Ofterdingen*) reminds us that Uhland's Romanticism, though genuine, is thin in texture. Even Tieck, by comparison, makes it appear sober-sided. The language in which Uhland conveys a radically romantic message lacks the romantic 'atmospheric' musicality and symbolic suggestiveness. We feel that the author's fancy functions best under the stimulus of an external object.

The Middle Ages provide Uhland with a fund of such objects. In the Introduction to the course of lectures which he delivered in 1830 on medieval German literature, he gives a genuinely romantic characterisation of that period. In medieval Christianity in general, in the Crusades, even in the old Germanic law (in discussing which he bases himself on Jakob Grimm's *Deutsche Rechtsaltertümer* (1828)), he sees the same spirit of 'Phantasie und Empfindung (or *Gemüt*)' which is also the basis of poetry (GW 4, 130–1). In his ballads, he is often able to bring this spirit to life for the modern reader, displaying the strengths and weaknesses which we might expect: a clear, strong plot-line, an eye for striking and evocative detail and a good sense of an effective ending, but at the same time a certain spareness in the general tone which inhibits the full development of the romantic effect present in potential in the material.

The ballad 'Harald' (1811) can serve as an example of what we mean. It tells a story which contains within it an archetypal romantic theme, that of the conflict between the conscious will and the forces of the irrational by which it is threatened as soon as it leaves the path of practical everyday decisions. Harald and his fellow knights ride home-ward in triumph after a successful campaign, but they do so 'in des Mondes Schein Durch einen wilden Wald'. The party is attacked by elves, who seduce all but Harald himself away to fairyland. The hero's superior ability to resist, his greater 'Besonnenheit', is effectively and economically symbolised by the description of his armour:

Nur er, der Beste, blieb zurück,

Der kühne Held Harald;
Er ist vom Wirbel bis zur Sohl'
In harten Stahl geschnallt (GW 1, 205).

But even his inner control is not sufficient, for he later removes his
helmet to drink at a spring, and falls into a sleep of centuries. The
ending skilfully combines a rounded conclusion with a romantic
'openness', a resonance which suggests a continuing battle between
spirit and sense and provokes a continuing activity in the reader's mind.
The figure acquires an almost legendary stature and with the
'Kyffhäuser' legend in mind, we do not find it too hard to see a potential
political interpretation coexisting with the psychological one:

Er schlummert auf demselben Stein
Schon manche hundert Jahr',
Das Haupt gesenket auf die Brust,
Mit grauem Bart und Haar.

Wann Blitze zucken, Donner rollt,
Wann Sturm erbraust im Wald,
Dann greift er träumend nach dem Schwert,
Der alte Held Harald (p. 206).

Broadly similar romantic effects are observable in others among
Uhland's best ballads, such as 'Der Fluch des Sängers', 'Das Glück von
Edenhall', 'Die Rache' and 'Die Jagd von Winchester'. In all of them, we
notice the poet's strengths and limitations. Psychological subtlety and
poetic 'Stimmung' are not his forte (the weakest part of 'Harald' is that
which deals with the elves); he often succeeds very well, on the other
hand, in conveying the sense of an old, naïve ethos in which heroism
and villainy march side by side in a world dominated by forces which
can neither be predicted, nor denied. 'Das Glück von Edenhall' (1834),
for example, shows the inevitable punishment of *hubris*, less brilliantly,
no doubt, than Heine's 'Belsatzar', but perhaps with a more authentic
naïveté. Uhland often displays considerable narrative skill and ability
to manipulate motifs, as for example in his use of the hunt-motif in
the description of the murder of the king in 'Die Jagd von Winchester'
(1810). First the King fails to shoot his quarry, then he becomes the
quarry of the murderer, who in his turn becomes the hunted:

Herr Titan fliehet durch den Wald,

Flieht über Land und Meer,
Er flieht wie ein gescheuchtes Wild,
Find't nirgends Ruhe mehr (GW 1, 204).

The motif is in fact carried through to the end of the poem. The hunt,
it seems, has a dynamic of its own which none of the participants can
control.

Dark, dramatic tales suit Uhland best, for there, the inherent power
of the material is well suited by his tendency to a laconic style. The
limitations of his unaided imagination show more clearly when he
attempts to present the sunnier, more idyllic side of the chivalric
world, as he does in poems like 'Das Singental' and 'Der Schenk von
Limburg'. He can really do little more than skim across the surface of
themes like nature and love and would never have been able to create
a *Taugenichts*. His best positive moments also occur in the heroic
context, most notably in 'Taillefer' (1812), a warlike but sunlit piece
dominated by the motifs of song and a 'hoher muot' reminiscent of the
Nibelungenlied. Taillefer, the servant who sings so beautifully as he
stokes the Norman Duke's fire, is made a free knight and brings the
same spirit to the battlefield of Hastings:

Und als das Rolandslied wie ein Sturm erscholl,
Da wallete manch Panier, manch Herze schwoll,
Da brannten Ritter und Mannen von hohem Mut;
Der Taillefer sang und schürte das Feuer gut...

Normannen sahen's, die harrten nicht allzulang,
Sie brachen herein mit Geschrei und Schilderklang.
Hei, sausende Pfeile, klirrender Schwerterschlag!
Bis Harald fiel und sein trotziges Heer erlag (GW 1, 237).

Many a young person to whom the complexities of the major
Romantics were impenetrable must have been inspired in the school-
room and perhaps even later by such poetry and the idealised
'Germanic' ethos which could be deduced from it. Writing in the period
which saw the outbreak of the First World War, W. Reinöhl counsels
German mothers to pack in their sons' knapsacks a copy of Uhland's
poems, 'wahrlich einen geweihten Frühling'.[19] Whether this was of
benefit to themselves or their country is a moot point. What we must
remember is that Uhland, like the other Romantics who brandished
poetic sabres, was writing in a weak and fragmented Germany, in which

the thought of a war of conquest would have been an absurdity and where the need for a national spiritual revival seemed imperative. Uhland does have a little of the 'helle Eisenfreude' of which Theodor Körner (1791–1813), one of the most bellicose of the nationalistic romantic poets,[20] speaks in his 'Schwertlied', but in context, it is much less sinister than might at first appear. In general, his is a genuine romantic striving and a genuine romantic achievement and it should not be scorned, either on account of later distortions, or because it does not represent Romanticism at its highest level.

Among the minor lyricists of the period, *Wilhelm Müller* deserves at least a passing mention, not only because he wrote the two cycles, *Die schöne Müllerin* (1820) and *Die Winterreise* (1824) which, as the world knows, were set by Schubert, but also because the verse of these cycles has genuine, if modest, merits. Its style is basically the romantic folk-style, with typical themes and motifs (love, nature, 'Wandern', mill-streams and mills). The poet has managed to feel his way into the emotions of his naïve main character and to render them with affecting sincerity. And there is some substance in A. P. Cottrell's claim that Müller sometimes manages to transcend the limitations of the restricted milieu and tone he has adopted and suggest a wider, more general context. When he writes of 'Wanderschaft', particularly in the poem which bears that title ('Das Wandern ist des Müllers Lust'. . . etc.), he does convey (albeit at a lower poetic level) something of the positive, fresh spiritual response to life which informs the great 'Wanderlieder' of Eichendorff. And the ending of 'Des Baches Wiegenlied' does indeed underpin the theme of death with a hint of the infinite:

> Der Vollmond steigt,
> Der Nebel weicht,
> Und der Himmel da oben, wie ist er so weit.

But to claim for these lines 'a mystical sense of infinity and eternity', as Cottrell does,[21] is to attempt to load too much weight of meaning on to a rather slight frame. Müller's nationalistic and political poetry, the early *Bundesblüten* and the *Lieder der Griechen,* 'blutrünstige Freiheitslieder' and 'versifizierte Leitartikel' as K. G. Just respectively describes them,[22] can safely be left in their decent obscurity.

It cannot be our brief to follow the further fortunes of the romantic tendency in the many nineteenth-century poets, like Rückert, Lenau and Mörike, in whom it was still, to some extent, at work.[23] But a niche must be found in any history of German literature for *Johann Peter Hebel*.

Hebel was born in 1760, which places him well after the generation of the major 'Aufklärer' and a decade before the first generation of the Romantic Movement. The nearest writers of significance to him in time are Schiller (1759) and K. P. Moritz (1757), neither of whom has close ties with the Romantic Movement. There is, however, some measure of connection, particularly in the case of Moritz, whose interest in psychology prefigures a major romantic preoccupation and whose novels show a definite pre-romantic sensibility and certainly influenced Jean Paul. Stahl and Yuill mention Hebel only in the context of Weimar Classicism and in his capacity as a prose-narrator.[24] As a High German poet, he shows affinities with the later-eighteenth-century Sentimentalists and their successors, such as Friedrich Mathisson (born 1761). There are certainly also traces of the rationalistic didacticism of the 'Aufklärung' in his 'Kalendergeschichten', collected in the *Schatzkästlein des Rheinländischen Hausfreundes* (1811), though his outstanding qualities in this field are rather a talent for anecdotal storytelling and a fine sensitivity, as a sympathetic sophisticated observer, to the spirit and tone of folk culture. It is in fact as a 'Volksdichter' that he is important and this gives him, arguably, a stronger affinity with Romanticism than with any other literary trend.

His outstanding literary work is to be found in the *Alemannische Gedichte* (1803), a collection of dialect-poems which demonstrates his near-perfect empathy with the people of South Baden, particularly of the 'Wiesenthal' area, with their ethos and their language. Their simplicity, humour and faith, and the stimulus of their legends and superstitions and of the stunning scenery of the southern part of the Black Forest, go to make up a medium in which Hebel's imaginative and emotional energies can express themselves more fully than in the conventional forms of High German poetry as they had come down to him. The *Alemannische Gedichte* are more, not less, technically complex than the other poems and more ambitious in their range. And they show an indisputable response to the non-rational and humorous. It is hard to imagine an 'Aufklärer', or even the Schiller who so solemnly and puritanically castigated G. A. Bürger, deriving great edification from a poem ('Sonntagsfrühe') in which Saturday, dog-tired, drags itself off to bed with the words 'I cha fast uf ke Bei me stoh', whereupon Sunday rubs the sleep out of its eyes and goes to knock up the sun:

Er pöpperlet am Lädemli,
Er rüeft der Sunne: 'd' Zeit isch do!'
Sie seit: 'I chumm enanderno.'[25]

Hebel does include an element of didacticism in some of his dialect-poems, but it occurs in such a genuinely popular tone that one thinks at most of the homely village schoolmaster; certainly not the 'enlightened' scholar in his study. It usually takes the form of a simple concluding moral, as in 'Der Mann im Mond':

Se hüt di vorem böse Ding,
's bringt numme Weh und Ach!
Am Sunntig rueih, und bet und sing,
Am Werchtig schaff di Sach (*Werke* 1, 44).

The rationalising effect of this is slight; it has more the tone of naïveté which the Romantics achieve in their best-observed folk-characters. Mere rationalism was in fact never enough for Hebel. This was in evidence already during his early years in Lörrach, when he participated with a group of friends in an enthusiastic 'Proteus Cult', also called 'Belchismus', from the fact that the group was in the habit of holding gatherings on the summit of the 'Belchen', one of the most 'romantic' heights of the Black Forest. Proteus was chosen as the patron spirit of this private society because he stood for the impermanence and constant flux of the physical universe. Hebel himself took the society name of Parmenides, thus identifying himself with a radically idealist philosophical position. It would no doubt be unwarranted if we were to attempt to read too much into these youthful activities, or to deny the feeling for reality which is present in Hebel's stories and poems, but it is certainly true that mere realism cannot satisfy him either. His dialect poetry in particular shows a strong sense of the transcendental and an awareness of the transitory nature of earthly things.

'Die Vergänglichkeit' is one of Hebel's finest achievements: a unique blend of the humorous and serious, the homely and apocalyptic. The fate of the ruined castle, the 'Röttler Schloß' which still overlooks the route from Southern Baden to Basel, is also that which awaits both the peasants who see it as they travel, and their own proud and solid house:

's Hus wird alt und wüest;
Der Rege wäscht der's wüester alli Nacht,
Und d' Sunne bleicht der's schwärzer alli Tag,
Und im Vertäfer popperet der Wurm. . .[26]

Even a simple song like 'Freude in Ehren', ostensibly a treatment of the pleasure-oriented 'carpe diem' theme, shows a strong consciousness of transience with pronounced eschatological overtones:

's währt alles churzi Zit,
Der Chilchof isch nit wit. . .

Wenn d'Glocke schalle,
Wer hilftis alle?
O gebis Gott e sanfte Tod!
E rüehig Gwisse gebis Gott,
Wenn d'Sunn am Himmel lacht,
Wenn alles blizt und chracht,
Und in der lezte Nacht! (*Werke* 1, 26)

Hebel is always looking for the opportunity to go beyond the narrow confines of everyday reality, much as he also enjoys the salt and savour of the latter. The personification of the river in 'Die Wiese' can certainly be related to the characteristic patterns of the folk-mentality, but Hebel does all he can to heighten the sense of movement, and of mystery when the spirit-world is mentioned:

Numme *stilli* Geister göhn *uf verborgne Pfade*
Us und i. . . (*Werke* 1, 17; my emphasis)

The terror of the story told in 'Der Carfunkel' outweighs, in its effect on the reader, the comforting tone of the homely framework within which it is placed. The theme (a pact with the Devil) is much less well contained here within the context of everyday life than is the case in Gotthelf's *Die schwarze Spinne*. And in the poetically impressive 'Der Nachtwächter um Mitternacht', there is an oscillation between homely ease and uneasy mystery which is typical of Hebel. In the churchyard episode, for example, death is related to the everyday at one point ('Du guten alte Franz se hen der di Bett scho gmacht im Grund'), whereas the sight of the peacefully sleeping village arouses thoughts of the Last Judgement. The final refrain does not resolve this tension between light and dark; it is endemic to Hebel's world, which derives its ultimate stability from a faith which almost recalls Eichendorff's:

Loset, was i euch will sage!
d'Glocke het zwölfi gschlage.

Und d'Liechtli brennen alli no:
d'Tag will iemerst no nit cho.
Doch Gott im Himmel lebt und wacht,
Er hört wohl, wenn es Vieri schlacht! (*Werke* 1, 85)

Notes

1. Cf. the poem 'Süße Liebe denkt in Tönen'.
2. Cf. also Ludoviko's remark in *Franz Sternbalds Wanderungen*: 'Warum soll eben Inhalt den Inhalt eines Gedichts ausmachen?'; *Werke*, M. Thalmann (ed.) (Munich, 1963), vol. 1, p. 928.
3. *Werke*, ed. Thalmann, vol. 2, p. 152.
4. Cf. 'Ludwig Tieck und der Ursprung der deutschen Romantik' in E. Staiger, *Stilwandel* (Zurich, 1963), p. 190.
5. Quoted with approval in Zeydel, *Ludwig Tieck*, p. 144.
6. Although Tieck's is a morning-hymn, the context makes it fairly certain that it is Grimmelshausen's version, rather than the original hymn by Philipp Nicolai ('Wie schön leuchtet der Morgenstern') that Tieck has in mind.
7. In Part II, Bk. 1, Ch. 6 of *Franz Sternbalds Wanderungen*.
8. The most important of the others were Ludwig Uhland and Gustav Schwab.
9. *Peter Schlemihls wundersame Geschichte*; cf. below, Ch. 12.
10. Chamisso, *Gesammelte Werke*, M. Koch (ed.) (Stuttgart, n.d.), vol. 1, p. 56.
11. E. Ermatinger, *Die deutsche Lyrik seit Herder* (Leipzig–Berlin, 1925), vol. 2, p. 20.
12. Thomas Mann, *Essays of Three Decades* (New York, 1947), p. 248.
13. Chamisso, *Werke*, H. Kurz (ed.) (Leipzig–Vienna, n.d.), vol. 1, p. 154. References will be to this edition.
14. *Werke*, vol. 1, p. 119. This is no. 1 of the cycle *Frauen-Liebe und Leben*, whose setting by Schumann has made it better known than much of Chamisso's poetry.
15. E. M. Forster, *Aspects of the Novel* (Harmondsworth, 1962), p. 38.
16. Letter to Schleiermacher, 23 November 1818.
17. F. Sengle, *Biedermeierzeit*, Part I (Stuttgart, 1971), p. 150; R. Tymms, *German Romantic Literature*, p. 345. The oscillation between 'romantic' and 'Biedermeier' in Uhland-scholarship is documented by H. Thomke, *Zeitbewußtsein und Geschichtsauffassung im Werke Uhlands* (Berne, 1962), pp. 14–17.
18. Uhland, *Gesammelte Werke*, H. Fischer (ed.) (Stuttgart, n.d.), vol. 1, pp. 62–3. References will be to this edition, cited as GW.
19. In the Introduction to his edition of Uhland's *Gesammelte Werke* (Leipzig, n.d. [1914?]), p. 10.
20. Among others who should be mentioned are E. M. Arndt (*Lieder für Deutsche*, 1813) and Max von Schenkendorf (1783–1813), author of 'Freiheit, die ich meine'.
21. Cf. A. P. Cottrell, *Wilhelm Müller's Lyrical Song-Cycles* (Chapel Hill, 1970), p. 31.
22. 'Wilhelm Müller und seine Liederzyklen' in K. G. Just, *Übergänge* (Berne–Munich, 1966), pp. 136 and 137.
23. For these, see G. W. Field, *The Nineteenth Century* (London–New York, 1975), pp. 62–75.

24. E. L. Stahl and W. E. Yuill, *German Literature in the Eighteenth and Nineteenth Centuries* (London, 1970), p. 107. We would certainly not wish to link him with the Romantics in this capacity.

25. J. P. Hebel, *Werke*, O. Behaghel (ed.) (DNL, 42), Teil 1, p. 78. 'Enanderno': 'right away'.

26. Cf. L. W. Forster (ed.), *The Penguin Book of German Verse* (Harmondsworth, 1957), pp. 281–2. The whole poem is printed here, with a translation. The passage quoted describes the effects of wind and rain, and the ticking of the death-watch beetle in the wainscoting.

5 NOVALIS

General Characterisation

Of the great German romantic poets, Novalis is the most problematic, not because he is less, but because he is *more* romantic than the others, because he approaches more closely to the ideal of Romanticism. He is not unique in this generation in saying that spirit is truth, but he is in the extent to which his is a direct, objective presentation of the naked truth, the absolute spirit. He can express a romantic vision with an almost Grecian directness. Again, he is in tune with other Romantics in seeing an opposition between spirit and material reality, but unique in the completeness of the victory which he accords to the spirit.

He was, by talent, temperament and circumstances, particularly well qualified to give poetic expression to the most daring flights of romantic thought. A strong spirituality was allied in him to impressive intellectual and imaginative capacities. Pietism, through his father, was part of his family background and the study of a number of thinkers, among whom Kant, Fichte, Hemsterhuis, Schleiermacher, Plotinus and Böhme stand out, and from whom he was able to assimilate what was relevant to his own needs, furthered and fed the idealistic and mystical bent of his mind. The 'Sophie-experience', to which we shall turn later, tipped the scale towards poetry, but a significant philosophical stratum remained and the mature poetic work shows, both in theme and in language, a unique blend of the sensuous and the abstract. If ever a style deserved the designation 'translucent', it is that of Novalis. The romantic tendency to seek the Absolute was present in him to a very high degree and the ethereal sensuousness which is characteristic of him is the product of his single-minded concentration on the task of reaching that goal through poetry, which, for him, was possible because poetry and truth were identical: 'Die Poesie ist das echt absolut Reelle,' he once said, 'Je poetischer, desto wahrer.'[1]

Novalis was not himself, of course, a disembodied spirit. He was in fact an able and energetic administrator, good company in society (Tieck speaks of his 'Virtuosität in der Kunst des Umgangs'[2]) and even capable of producing mildly amusing light verse. But he kept his inner spiritual life (his 'secret heart', as he puts it in the *Hymnen an die Nacht*) securely insulated from the influence of the outer, everyday level of existence. The capacity to do this so completely seems to

64

derive from the spiritual experiences connected with Sophie. A source
of power and insight welled up within him, the creative power which is
the heart of the spiritual life and which the Romantics called love.
Novalis is the romantic poet of love, in this ideal sense, *par excellence*.

That verse and poetry are not synonymous is true for all the
Romantics, but it is true for Novalis in a special way. He creates poetry
through a uniform process of 'poeticisation', a concentration of his
peculiar imaginative and emotional energy on his material. He is a
lyrical writer, but poetry, in his case, has less to do with actual verse
form than is the case with Brentano or Eichendorff. The language of
Novalis's verse is not necessarily more 'poetic' than that of the prose
which often surrounds it. For even when he is ostensibly describing a
material reality, the actual object is usually a psychological one, that of
the *Gemüt* itself.

The attempt to use language 'um der Dinge Willen', that is, as a
mere vessel, a subordinate instrument employed by the intellect for
the notation of a separate objective 'meaning' which the latter has
already grasped, rests, according to Novalis's *Monolog* of 1798, on a
superficial conception of its nature. In its true, 'inner nature', language
is a world apart, with its own, non-logical laws which reflect 'das
seltsame Verhältnisspiel der Dinge'. The true poet understands, and
attunes himself to this state of affairs, and therefore speaks as a
'prophet'. To quote once more *Das allgemeine Brouillon*, language
should affect the recipient in a musical, 'free and indefinite' manner:
'[die Sprache] hat sich prosaisiert. . . sie muß wieder Gesang werden'
(KS III, 283–4). The kind of re-poeticisation of language which
Novalis has in mind here is much more than the employment of
standard lyrical forms and techniques. The fact that Novalis's major
lyrical work, the *Hymnen an die Nacht*, is written largely in prose
should therefore not surprise us unduly. Nor should the fact that we
can make use of a prose passage to illustrate basic lyrical practice in
his work.

In the description of Schwaning's banquet in Chapter 6 of *Heinrich
von Ofterdingen*, the distinction between the functional narrative style
(plain reporting of facts) and the more ornamental is blurred by the
form in which the latter is introduced. Ornamental devices like simile
and metaphor are also used, but the most striking feature is that the
reporting style can, without any change in its *formal* nature, move
directly to the 'inner' poetic level. This chapter is constructed to lead,
in a pattern of escalation which is typical of Novalis's structural
technique, to the revelation of the nature of love. Its earlier stages,

from which we shall quote, deal with the allied phenomenon of
'Geselligkeit'. The pleasure enjoyed in a harmonious gathering of
morally and spiritually healthy people is itself a spiritual revelation, a
kind of social poetry:

> Alle unterhielten sich; Veronika lachte und scherzte mit ihren
> Bekannten. Mathilde erzählte ihm von Ungarn, wo ihr Vater sich
> oft aufhielt, und von dem Leben in Augsburg. Alle waren vergnügt.
> Die Musik verscheuchte die Zurückhaltung und reizte alle
> Neigungen zu einem muntern Spiel. Blumenkörbe dufteten in voller
> Pracht auf dem Tische, und der Wein schlich zwischen den
> Schüsseln und Blumen umher, schüttelte seine goldnen Flügel und
> stellte bunte Tapeten zwischen die Welt und die Gäste (KS I, 272).

From plain beginnings, the passage moves, smoothly and without a
break, to a radically poetic effect: the emancipation of the spirit from
the rigid laws of practical life and logic (here, 'die Welt'). At a later
stage, we even read that Heinrich 'understood the wine and the food'.[3]
Music plays an important part by inducing a free play of the emotions.
We are reminded of the remark in the *Monolog* concerning the 'strange
play of relationships between things,' strange, that is, to the logical
mind. This process is brought to full fruition in the description of the
wine, in which the language is emancipated from logical control. This
is no metaphor or allegory in the traditional sense. If that were the
case, we would be able to visualise the wine as a figure, coherent in
itself in its appearance and behaviour and related to an abstract
meaning through a series of logical correspondences. If it were to
function in this way, its location would need to be indeterminate. But
in Novalis, it is specifically located on the table, tripping lightly
between the knives and forks and placing gaily coloured tapestries
between the guests and everyday reality. The author is not departing
from that reality; without diverting our attention from it and its
relatively mundane detail, he is actively poeticising it before our eyes.

This, then, is a process of alienation. Beginning with a mundane
perspective, Novalis carries through a shift to the spiritual dimension,
often, as here, through the symbolic use of an image, and produces in
the reader the effect which, as it happens, he is also describing in the
narrative in this example. Alienation is the prerequisite of emancipation
and it is a process which is frequently renewed, by making the solid
transparent (as here), or by endowing the pure abstract with
sensuousness (as in the dream of the blue flower in Chapter 1, or in the

first section of the 'Astralislied' at the beginning of Part Two of
Ofterdingen). This is Novalis's typical poetic tone and it can occur as
easily in prose as in verse.

In a sense, Novalis's peculiarly intense concentration on the inner
processes makes all his writing lyrical to some extent. Even *Die
Christenheit oder Europa* is less a discourse on history in the conventional sense than a lyrical rhapsody on the past, present and anticipated
future fortunes of the spirit in this world, and in Novalis's eyes, not
necessarily the worse as history for that. It is, as the hermit in *Heinrich
von Ofterdingen* puts it (KS I, 259), the 'soul' of history which is
important, not the authenticity of the facts. All sciences, Novalis felt,
needed to be 'poeticised',[4] that is, carried on from a creative spiritual
perspective which enables us to see everything in terms of the eternal
and absolute One. There is only one science, he says;[5] this is the
spirit which informs the cult of 'Enzyklopädistik' in *Das allgemeine
Brouillon*, where the intellectual imagination plays on scientific fact
with an 'Analogiebesessenheit'[6] which may appear wilful to some, but
could also be seen as the logical application of the principle that the
spirit is king and that its foremost agents, fancy and love, should be
free to turn intellectual idealism into 'magic idealism', Novalis's special
creed. Even Fichte, as we saw, subjected the I (the free consciousness
of the Self) to limitation by the Non-I (consciousness of an objective
external reality). 'Magic idealism' lessens the restrictions on the subject
and enables it to 'experiment' in a 'freie(r) Generationsmethode der
Wahrheit'.[7] Whether or not this leads to 'sound' history, philosophy
or science, it guarantees the freedom of the spirit within the individual
Gemüt from interference by rationalistic or realistic impulses and lays
the foundation for a poetic symbolism which is very advanced for its
time.

The intensity of Novalis's vision of a spiritual resolution of the
duality of earthly life might mislead the casual reader into imagining
that he denied it altogether. Such a misunderstanding would rest on
the confusion of anticipation with actuality and of inner with outer
reality, a confusion which Novalis himself avoids, though the process
does involve him in paradox. His procedure is best illustrated through
his use of the concept of 'dream'. There are two modes of perception
for him, the earthly (logical) and heavenly (spiritual), and each has its
conception of reality and unreality, represented, frequently, by 'Welt'
and 'Traum' respectively. The two coexist, but if they are to do so in
harmony, the primacy of the spiritual must be accepted.

They are, in fact, more often in conflict and this means that their concepts of what is real are diametrically opposed. What is unreal 'Traum' for the one is often the highest reality for the other, When, therefore, a shift occurs from one perspective to the other, 'Welt' and 'Traum' can be said to change places:

Die Welt wird Traum, der Traum wird Welt (KS I, 319).

We must be careful, however, not to misinterpret what is a symbolic representation of a state of mind and at the same time a statement of a romantic millennium to be achieved one day in the future[8] as a declaration that the dualism inherent in present earthly life has been swept away. Novalis makes a clear distinction between the inner state of enlightenment, in which 'ein unnennbar süßer Himmel Mir ewig im Gemüte steht' (*Geistliche Lieder* 15) and which is preceded by a mystical, inner experience of death,[9] and the permanent removal of the barrier to full enjoyment of the ideal, which is achieved only through physical death itself. Till then, the final word for Novalis, as for other Romantics, is 'Sehnsucht'. As he said in another place, 'Das Leben ist kein Traum, aber es soll und wird vielleicht einer werden.'[10] His awareness of the essential unity of the world, of the fact that 'all the forces of nature are but one force' (cf. KS III, 659), is so particularly strong that while the exile from the realm of harmony (which is also the realm of love) continues, he can still find consolation and, simultaneously, a language in which he can articulate that sense of unity, in the fact that the world is full of correspondences, that all things stand in a 'symptomatic' relationship one to the other. This makes it possible for the poet, who is 'der Erfinder der Symptome *a priori*' (KS III, 35) to deal with highly abstract material in an essentially pictorial form.

It was his relationship with Sophie von Kühn and above all the experience which began with her death that deepened and developed romantic attitudes already present in Novalis and caused them to become rooted in his inmost personal consciousness in a way which amounted to a spiritual revelation. He made himself the prophet of such a renewal in fact, and it was no doubt this that prompted him to adopt as a *nom de plume* a name derived from a title once used by ancestors of his, 'von Rode' or 'de Novali' and which, as he wrote to A. W. Schlegel, seemed appropriate to his new outlook.[11]

The exact nature of the love which Novalis felt for Sophie, who was not yet thirteen when he first met her (in 1794), is something which not even Novalis felt able to define clearly. It was certainly deeply

serious and it wrought a thoroughgoing change in him. Whereas
previously, he seems to have lived lightheartedly, even flirtatiously,[12]
he now acquired stability and a firm spiritual orientation. Aware of
the possibility that fancy can be a deceiver, he examined his feelings
carefully, but remained convinced, as he states in the poem 'Anfang'
(KS I, 386–7), that this was 'kein Rausch'. Sophie was for him a
revelation of the spiritual perfection ('sittliche Grazie') which was (or
should be) the goal of all humanity. The extent to which this love was
also erotic in character can only be a matter for speculation, but of the
fact that the ideal of love which arose out of this experience did
contain a strong erotic element, intimately fused with an equally
strong spirituality, there can be no doubt.[13] Before that stage,
however, a new factor – and a crucial one – was added: the fact and
the experience of death. Sophie died in 1797. After the initial sharp
sense of desolation, this, by virtue of what one can only call a mystical
process, became a source of new strength as well as a powerful new
impulse to the natural romantic 'Sehnsucht'. By wrestling with the
thought of death, by sinking himself as deeply as he could into the
experience, Novalis managed to break through the barrier of negativity
imposed by the logical reason to a sure knowledge of the spiritual
reality of which Sophie had now become completely a part. The
experience of the 'breakthrough' itself, a common one in the field of
mysticism,[14] is described in the entry in Novalis's Journal dated 13
May 1797, on which the third of the *Hymnen an die Nacht*, the
'Urhymne' as Ritter rightly calls it,[15] is based.

Death now became for him, not only the gateway to Eternal Life,
but a spiritual revelation not identical with, but very closely related to,
love. Sophie, not as a symbol, but as a living source of faith and
strength, stood at the centre of this dimension of his inner life and
continued to do so, even after he had passed through the stage of
radical dissociation from material reality which was expressed in the
image of the 'Fremdling'[16] and reconciled himself to it to the extent
that he could become engaged to Julie von Charpentier. Julie's role in
his life seems to have been similar to that accorded to Cyane in
Heinrich von Ofterdingen who is sent by the dead (but still very much
alive) Mathilde to sustain the pilgrim on his way homewards ('immer
nach Hause': KS I, 325).

The conception of a 'home', a 'heavenly country' (*Hebrews*, 11, 16)
in which we shall be reunited with the divine source from which we
sprang, is of course a Christian one, and while Novalis's position may
well appear almost wilfully unorthodox and electic to many a believer,

he cannot be accused of using Christian concepts to evoke merely a passive, vaguely 'religious' mood. When he speaks of the urge to 'return home to our Father',[17] he is writing as a Christian. The Jesus who appears in his poems is the real crucified and risen Christ, who has 'raised the stone' (HN 5) and transformed death from a negating into a life-giving force. This reference to the raising of the stone brings to the fore the question of the relationship between Christ and Sophie in Novalis's mind. It is certainly one which stops short of identification, yet the Redeemer and the Belovéd are sometimes spoken of in similar terms. Jesus, for example, becomes the Beloved in the final section of HN 4 and in HN 6. The raising of the stone is used in the fourth of the *Geistliche Lieder* to render both the understanding of the Atonement and what is unmistakably the Sophie-experience. Novalis himself does not solve the problem for us. He indicates a link in the laconic remark in the Journal (16–29 June 1797), 'Xstus und *Sophie*' and in the final stanza of the fourth *Geistliches Lied*, but does not define it. All one can say with any confidence is that, without possessing equal status, both function as mediators between the 'heavenly' realm of absolute spiritual truth, and the 'earthly' one where man is at present domiciled.

Hymnen an die Nacht

The version of this work which we shall be discussing below is that printed in the *Athenäum* in 1800. Ritter feels that the changes which have been made from the manuscript version have increased the distance between the finished work and its original conception (which clearly lay in the Sophie-experience) to the detriment of its clarity and consistency.[18] We take what appears to be the majority view that without violating the integrity of the original inspiration, the *Athenäum* version presents a deeper and wider understanding of it. Its combination of individual and universal perspectives may well make for a more complex texture, but it is also one which is more truly representative of Novalis's mature outlook and method.

A hostile reviewer, writing in the *Neue allgemeine deutsche Bibliothek* in 1804, condemns the work for its 'lack of content': 'mit jeder Periode glaubt man etwas zu fassen und festzuhalten; und wird zuletzt stets überzeugt, daß man einem Dunstgebilde nachgejagt hat.'[19] Certainly, this is the kind of unfair criticism which results from a situation in which an un-romantic mind sits in judgement on an ultra-romantic work. Looking for what is not there, a clear 'theme' reducible to terms of logical thought, he misses what is, the romantic substance. Some critics more or less give up the idea of a statement of theme, seeing the *Hymnen* rather as an exploration of spiritual experience, culminating in something approaching a mystical union with the infinite reality.[20] This is true enough in itself, but it is so as a characterisation of the general tendency shared by all the major works of this author. There are also differences of emphasis between them.

In the *Hymnen an die Nacht*, Novalis sets out, not only to assert and demonstrate the primacy of the spiritual world over the material – an opposition from which essential elements of the cycle's structure are derived – but also to investigate one of the central mysteries of the spirit, namely love. It is love, both as an agent on the cosmic level and as it acts within the individual *Gemüt*, which is the driving force behind the work, love which is celebrated, and which triumphs in it. It opens man's eyes and frees him and it is his ultimate reward. The aim of preaching love transcendent and triumphant conditions all aspects of the cycle, which is anything but morbid or obscurantist. Pain and melancholy are but the necessary preconditions of freedom and illumination; as Astralis sings: 'Schmerzlich muß jenes Band zerreißen Das sich ums innre Auge zieht.' The final point reached is a strongly positive feeling, if still inevitably imbued with yearning, for man cannot entirely free himself from his earthly and finite state.

The 'inner eye' referred to is that of the inner, or 'transcendental' Self, of which Novalis speaks in *Blütenstaub* (No. 28). It is in taking possession of this inner Self that man achieves the true freedom which is the goal of all 'Bildung' and realises his capacity to be simultaneously terrestrial and transcendent. This Self is the chief protagonist of the *Hymnen*. It inhabits a cosmos which consists, in the terminology of the work itself, of two realms: those of light ('des Lichtes Reiche'; HN 6, stanza 1) and of love, where Jesus, the Virgin and Sophie, the three mediators, now dwell (cf. HN 5: 'das Reich der Liebe').[21] The first is subject to the laws of time, place and logic; the second is eternal and infinite and knows no restriction or separation of any kind. The Self is a native of the second realm, but exiled in the first and to some extent hampered by its restrictions. It feels a longing which is a sign of its infinite origin, but only with help from the infinite realm can it achieve inner illumination and freedom. Even after this breakthrough, it is not physically emancipated and still feels sadness and longing, but these now have a sense of direction and a productive quality which they lacked before, being imbued with love (cf. HN 4: 'sehnt sich und liebt').

Even in the romantic age, the cycle stands out for the radical nature of its departure from objectivity of presentation. If the Self is a mirror here, it is not a simple reflecting surface. Material may be presented to it, but it assimilates and re-fashions it and presents in its turn an image of its own. The laws which operate in the *Hymnen* are those of the *Gemüt*: we have no clear sense of place and while there are references to the past and future, both of the individual 'I' and of the collective 'We' of which it is a part, it is difficult to deduce a coherent progression in time from the sequence of the hymns. We are in the indeterminate 'Here' and 'Now' of the inner Self, where the laws of the 'realm of light' do not necessarily apply. The physical world appears as if broken in a prism and structures and progression are derived from the sequence of moods and the stages of illumination experienced by the Self.

Nor is there, in the strict sense of the word, any development of thought, Novalis simply unfolds what was present in potential in the first hymn. Essentially the same ground is traversed a number of times and echo and repetition are deliberately employed structural features, helping to create an impression of circular motion. The beginning of HN 6, for example, contains echoes of the first hymn:

Hinunter in der Erde Schoß,
Weg aus des Lichtes Reichen,
Der Schmerzen Wut und wilder Stoß
Ist froher Abfahrt Zeichen. . .

The first line recalls HN 1, para. 2: 'Abwärts wend' ich mich zu der. . . Nacht', the second, more remotely, para. 3: 'Wie arm und kindisch dünkt mir das Licht nun.' The third line has a parallel in HN 1, para. 2, in the reference there to 'tiefe Wehmut' and the 'frohe Abfahrt' of line four corresponds to the phrase in para. 3: 'wie erfreulich und gesegnet des Tages Abschied.' Similarly, the 'Abenddämmerung' of the concluding stanza of HN 6 recalls the 'Abendnebel' mentioned in No. 1.

The first two hymns establish the superiority of night to day and enunciate the main theme of the awakening of the Self to the reality of eternal and infinite love. The whole work is here in potential: even the theme of death is adumbrated in the conclusion of HN 1. This is in fact in itself an impressive emotional climax, but in the context of the whole, it represents an inferior level of insight. The perception is still fragmentary and vague. The Self is not yet aware of its own capacities and is still a passive recipient and a melancholy supplicant. There is longing, certainly, but it does not have the positive ring of faith and

the force of love which inform it in HN 6, after the Self has understood
the true nature of death and also of Jesus.

The third hymn describes the mystical experience at Sophie's
graveside, which predates the present time of the cycle itself ('Einst,
da ich. . .'), returning to the present in its final phrase. Its position in
the sequence is justified by the fact that it represents a step forward in
the progression of insight, though this is still at the level of unreflecting
emotion only. The Self is more active, both in the pain which precedes
the breakthrough and in the positive faith which follows it.

Hymn 4, in its prose section, expresses the new perspective on life –
and death – which comes from 'der Liebe Berührung'. The Self is now
freed, inwardly, from the dominance of the earthly mentality ('des
Lichtes Fessel', as it was called in HN 3), though it accepts that it is still
tied in its outer nature to Day and all its works. The inner, 'secret'
heart, however, is devoted to Night. The opposition of Day and Night,
first stated in HN 1, is set forth again, this time on a cosmic level. The
Self now knows it is a native of the 'Reich der Liebe', to which it
expects to return and as that would lead one to expect, is now able to
relate its individual experience to the heroic victory of Christ on the
cross. The ground was prepared by earlier Biblical references, to the
crystal stream of life (cf. Rev. 22, 1) and to Moses viewing Canaan in
para. 1 and (through the idea of the tabernacles) to the Transfiguration
in para. 2.

Jesus also figures, as the 'Geliebter', in the verse section, which
presents the experience of absolute love in terms of a personal union.
Formally, it is in large measure an anticipation of the coming of death,
as the prelude to the complete satisfaction of the infinite longing of the
Self. This anticipatory experience is possible because of the revelation
which the speaker has received, which has awakened the power of love
in him, but he still needs the aid of the Infinite Love which flows pure
and unrestricted in the transcendent realm ('O sauge, Geliebter
Gewaltig mich an'). He still awaits the state of complete 'slumber and
love'. The phrase which follows: 'Ich fühle des Todes Verjüngende
Flut' has what must be a deliberate temporal ambiguity. It can refer
both to the post-mortal state itself and – death being understood
symbolically as in the concluding lines – to the inner experience of love
available to the illuminated Self in the present. For however much
Novalis proclaims the triumphant emancipation of spirit from matter
(with the cross as 'Siegesfahne') there is no suggestion that the earth,
and Day, have been left totally behind:

Ich lebe bei Tage
Voll Glauben und Mut
Und sterbe die Nächte
In heiliger Glut.

Hymn five switches the attention abruptly from the personal to the
Christological perspective already prepared for in HN 4 and speaks for
the 'We' of the Christian congregation rather than the previously
dominant 'I'. There is a corresponding switch to the form and style of
the church hymn ('Geistliches Lied'), as opposed to that of the freer
'Hymne', in its concluding verse section. The theme is the problem of
death, which has defeated the Greeks but is overcome by Jesus Christ:
a radical and no doubt conscious reversal of the position which had
been taken by Schiller in 'Die Götter Griechenlands'. Though its tone
is quieter and relatively more 'objective' than that of the foregoing
hymns, it represents no real loss of intensity in the context of the
whole cycle, as it continues the escalation of insight into the supreme
reality of love to a new climax, expressed in what is probably the
noblest poetry of the work:

Die Lieb' ist frei gegeben,
Und keine Trennung mehr.
Es wogt das volle Leben
Wie ein unendlich Meer.
Nur *eine* Nacht der Wonne —
Ein ewiges Gedicht —
Und unser aller Sonne
Ist Gottes Angesicht.

The sixth hymn is a summation and a call to action, an 'Aufruf',
such as Novalis specifically provided for in the sketch-plan which occurs
early in the manuscript version of HN 5 (cf. KS I, 140). It gathers
together the threads of the cycle and gives it a more precise location
by its rejection of the modern age, which has lost the openness to love
of the early Christian 'Vorzeit'. It is a call, not to mass suicide, but to
an assimilation of the spiritual message of Christianity as conceived by
Novalis. He formulates it in a letter to Friedrich Schlegel (20 January
1799) in radical terms: 'Absolute Abstraction — Annihilation des
Jetzigen — Apotheose der Zukunft'. The Self (a collective one, though
the tone of the hymn is lyrical and subjective) is still 'bound' (stanza
10, line 5) to the realm of Day and 'Zeitlichkeit' (stanza 7, line 3), but

its longing has a positive and confident ring. What at the start was a
vague sense of an infinite spiritual reality and an uncertain hope for
union with it has become a certain knowledge and a secure faith. The
spring of spiritual truth flows unpolluted and strong within us. Perhaps
the most characteristic lines of the whole hymn are those which begin
stanza 9:

> Unendlich und geheimnisvoll
> Durchströmt uns süßer Schauer.

This blend of sensuous and abstract is typical of the poetic language
of the *Hymnen an die Nacht*. The imagery is taken as far towards
symbolism as one could reasonably expect to find in a pre-modern
work. In the verse, and in the rhythmically and often syntactically
complex prose, there is a general spirit of allusiveness, a symbolism of
outlook in which correspondences and connections can only be
discerned by a mind which is not restricted to merely logical thinking.
When, in one of the soberest passages of the work (the historical
narrative of HN 5), Novalis describes the end of the antique and poetic
period of Greek religion in terms of the withdrawal of the 'soul of the
world', 'ins tiefere Heiligtum, in des Gemüts höheren Raum' (KS I,
145), we are confronted with a confusion of spatial and psychological
categories which logic cannot unravel.

Literal meanings do have their part to play. They are those which
apply in the realm of Day, as for example in the opening paragraph of
HN 1, which seems almost to be there to point up by contrast with
what follows the difference between the two realms in this regard. As
the hymn progresses, the logic of the *Gemüt* supersedes that of the
intellect; with the very first phrase of the second paragraph, 'Abwärts
wend' ich mich zu der. . . Nacht', we have moved from a language
which describes, however 'poetically', to one which evokes. The
downward movement can only be understood in terms of a psychological process, a turning *inwards* into the *Gemüt*. Some degree of
interplay between literal and symbolic meaning continues in HN 1, but
by the beginning of the second hymn, the change from a metaphorical
approach (the light as a 'king' in HN 1, para. 1) to a symbolic one is
complete.

The two symbolic realms of Day and Night now generate two
chains of contrasting symbols which provide much of the texture and
even of the structural coherence of the work. This is still a *romantic*
confusion of logic — i.e. one which presupposes a unified and

meaningful universe which can be apprehended by the poetic mind – not a modern one. The 'verkehrtes Wesen'[22] of the daylight world conceals the real truth. One day, Novalis believes, it will be blown away; meanwhile, we must have recourse to a system of symbols, and one which reflects the dualism which, in the present fallen state of the world, must inevitably infect our apprehension of reality. The distorting effect of man's exile in the realm of light means that paradox is a constitutive factor in the symbolism of the *Hymnen*. The true light, which in the millenium will make our sun seem dark, must at present itself seem dark. Sophie, the emanation of Love, is 'die Sonne der Nacht'; the *truly* waking state (HN 1: 'jetzt wach' ich') is sleep in the terminology of the daylight reality and is sometimes described as such (e.g. in HN 2). Within this framework, Novalis has constructed a system of two contrasting sets of symbols, often corresponding in pairs, though not with too rigid an exactitude. Thus, rigidity and restriction are characteristic of Light and logic and fluidity and freedom of Night and love, but the images ('die dürre Zahl und das strenge Maβ ' and 'Es wogt das volle Leben wie ein unendlich Meer': HN 5) do not form an exact pair. These symbols are woven and interwoven, at times almost playfully, and produce a density of texture which could almost be seen as an equivalent of the Eichendorffian 'Stimmung'! This is a work in which uncompromising spirituality is married to a strong sensuous appeal. It demands that the reader shed some preconceptions and read with concentrated attention, but it offers as compensation for that effort a unique combination of beauty and profundity.

Geistliche Lieder

The full group of fifteen sacred songs published under this title (posthumously, in 1802) does not seem to constitute a planned and integrated cycle and it is probably idle to attempt to establish specific liturgical patterns and purposes within it. It is in fact in juxtaposition with the *Hymnen an die Nacht* that the *Lieder* (which will be cited as GL) reveal their character and unity. Both works belong to the last period, but retain an explicit link with the Sophie-experience. Each contains, formally, something of the other: the poem which concludes HN 5 is a 'geistliches Lied'; GL 7 is explicitly a 'Hymne'. There are correspondences and also important differences, which condition and are perhaps also conditioned by the choice of lyrical form.

Novalis was quite familiar with the tradition of the church hymn

and in particular, no doubt, with the emotionalistic songs of
Zinzendorf. In some notes which he wrote in 1799 in connection with
a projected series of writings of a more functionally religious character
than the *Hymnen*, he makes some comments apropos of the hymns of
J. K. Lavater which clarify his own attitude to the genre. Its function
should be to confirm and strengthen the 'heavenly' impulses in the
singer. Lavater has 'zu viel Irdisches'; presumably, he is too logical and
intellectually clever by half. The hymn should engage the heart and
elevate the singer and listener through 'sättigende, alles belebende
Begeisterung'. The *Geistliche Lieder* are less dynamically intense and
less abstractly complex than the *Hymnen*. No doubt they reflect the
relative reconciliation to the world which showed itself in the engage-
ment to Julie. But both works derive from the same set of experiences
and complement one another in their different emphases. The one
emphasises the process and the ecstasy of liberation, the other the
calm of liberation achieved. This may help to account for the fact that
the *Hymnen* have a unified structure (derived from the escalation of
insight), whereas the *Lieder* are a series of separate reflections.

GL 4 illustrates both the common source and the different
approaches of the two. It corresponds to HN 3 in that it describes the
moment of release from the anguish of deprivation. It too contains an
echo of the Journal in its reference to the wounds which remain open.[23]
It differs from the hymnic treatment in its serenity, which is not only
embodied in the simple and regular form, but expressly proclaimed,
and in striking terms:

> Wen ich sah, und wen an seiner
> Hand erblickte, frage keiner.
> Ewig werd' ich dies nur sehn;
> Und von allen Lebensstunden
> Wird nur die wie meine Wunden
> Ewig heiter, offen stehn.

The tendency of the *Lieder* is towards contemplation, as against the
analytical trend of the *Hymnen* and from that point of view, it is
fitting that the collection should end with a poem giving full expression
to the idea of 'seliges Schauen' mentioned by the hermit in his song in
Heinrich von Ofterdingen (Chapter 5):

> Ich sehe dich in tausend Bildern,
> Maria, lieblich ausgedrückt,

Doch keins von allen kann dich schildern,
Wie meine Seele dich erblickt.

Ich weiß nur, daß der Welt Getümmel
Seitdem mir wie ein Traum verweht,
Und ein unnennbar süßer Himmel
Mir ewig im Gemüte steht (GL 15).

Jesus, the Beloved of the soul in both works, is shown from different aspects. In the *Hymnen an die Nacht*, He tends to be a force which draws man out of the world while here, He is with us always, 'liebevoll gewärtig jeder Bitte' (GL 2). Nowhere is this more true, of course, than in the rite of Communion, which is the basis of GL 7. In this case, naturally enough, the tone is more individualistic and mystical than is usually the case in this collection, which helps us to understand why the hymnic free-verse form is chosen. At the same time, its place in the *Geistliche Lieder* is justified, for it deals with the experience of Christ in the here and now. The flesh and blood are solid and earthly.

Here too, man is seen as an exile from his true home. GL 12 has a reference to this life as 'das Elend', in the old Middle High German sense of exile. In GL 9, we are told that whosoever hears Christ's words 'kommt auch in Vaters Haus'. At the same time, the tendency to see more positive aspects to life in this world — through the presence in it of the Eternal — makes itself felt:

Jetzt scheint die Welt dem neuen Sinn
Erst wie ein Vaterland (GL 9, stanza 3).

This comes when we concentrate our minds on what we possess rather than on what we can have only in the future: 'Wo ich ihn nur habe Ist mein Vaterland,' Novalis declares in GL 5.

The experience of duality which is so strongly present in *Hymnen an die Nacht* plays but a minor role here and there is a concomitant reduction of the paradoxical element. Light and dark resume their traditional associations. Novalis has not lost his consciousness of the duality of earth and heaven, as the contrast between 'der Welt Getümmel' and the 'Himmel. . . im Gemüte' in GL 15 illustrates. But the outstanding characteristic of that poem is the poet's secure confidence in his ability to contain that duality. Nowhere is the 'Nazarene' quality discerned by Heftrich in Novalis[24] more in evidence than here.

Restriction of space precludes more than a passing reference to
Novalis's other verse. *Heinrich von Ofterdingen* contains a number of
fine pieces, both in the subtle and sensitive analytical style of the
Hymnen an die Nacht (for example, the 'carbuncle' stanza in the
'Atlantismärchen' and in the 'Astralislied' at the beginning of Part Two)
and in the more naïve and serene style of the *Geistliche Lieder* (e.g.
the hermit's song in Chapter 5 and the very impressive 'Lied der Toten'
among the sketches for Part Two). Perhaps we may allow ourselves one
quotation — Astralis' description, in iambic lines of great suppleness,
of the moment of her (spiritual) birth:

Ich duftete, die Blume schwankte still
In goldner Morgenluft. Ein innres Quellen
War ich, ein sanftes Ringen, alles floß
Durch mich und über mich und hob mich leise.
Da sank das erste Stäubchen in die Narbe. . .
Ich quoll in meine eigne Flut zurück —
Es war ein Blitz — nun konnte ich mich regen. . . (KS I, 317)

Astralis is a living testimony to the creative power of love, as it
fructifies sensitive and receptive spirituality. The blending of spirit and
sense, of intricate thought with imagery (which contains, incidentally,
clear reminiscences of Böhme)[25] provides a fine example of Novalis at
his lyrical best.

Notes

1. Quoted by J. Hegener in *Die Poetisierung der Wissenschaften bei Novalis*
(Bonn, 1975), p. 5.
2. Cf. the biographical sketch in Tieck's 1815 edition of Novalis's *Schriften*
(KS IV, p. 558).
3. KS I, p. 272; cf. *Geistliche Lieder*, 7, lines 19–22.
4. Letter to A. W. Schlegel of 24 February 1798. For a full study of this
concept, see Hegener, *Poetisierung.*
5. 'Alle Wissenschaft ist Eine.' Quoted by H.-J. Mähl, KS III, p. 238.
6. Cf. E. Heftrich, *Novalis. Vom Logos der Poesie* (Frankfurt, 1969), p. 29.
7. Ibid., pp. 35, and 32 ff and 52 ff.
8. Such a millennium was planned for the conclusion of *Heinrich von
Ofterdingen.* Having previously only dreamed of the Blue Flower, the hero was to
find it in reality and become the Messianic poet-king prefigured in the
'Atlantismärchen'. That this cannot be dismissed as *merely* symbol can be seen
from the concluding section of *Die Christenheit oder Europa.*
9. As Astralis sings, KS I, p. 319.
10. Quoted by E. Hederer, *Novalis* (Vienna, 1949), p. 144.

11. Cf. his letter to A. W. Schlegel of 24 February 1798. The title is derived from the name of an estate, Großenrode ('roden' is to clear woodland for cultivation, to break new ground).

12. Cf. *Am Sonnabend Abend*, KS I, p. 387.

13. Cf. for example *Hymnen an die Nacht*, No. 4, *Geistliche Lieder* 7, or the dream of the Blue Flower in *Heinrich von Ofterdingen*, Ch. 1.

14. Cf. for example Ch. 19 of Böhme's *Aurora*.

15. H. Ritter, *Novalis' Hymnen an die Nacht*, 2nd edn (Heidelberg, 1974), pp. 208–11.

16. Cf. the poem *Der Fremdling* and the later 'Der müde Fremdling ist verschwunden'.

17. 'Zum Vater wollen wir nach Haus': *Hymnen an die Nacht*, No. 6, stanza 2. This work will henceforth be cited as HN.

18. Cf. *Novalis' Hymnen*, p. 140. This book gives both versions and makes a meticulous study of the relationship between them.

19. Quoted in KS I, p. 126.

20. Cf. particularly F. Hiebel, *Novalis* (Berne–Munich, 1972), pp. 248 ff.

21. Cf. also Astralis: 'Der Liebe Reich ist aufgetan. . .' etc.

22. Cf. the fragment 'Wenn nicht mehr Zahlen und Figuren. . .' in the paralipomena to *Heinrich von Ofterdingen*.

23. Cf. *Journal*, 6 June 1797: 'Der Liebende muß die Lücke ewig fühlen, die Wunde stets offen erhalten' (KS IV, p. 44).

24. Heftrich, *Logos*, pp. 76–7. The 'Nazarene' school of German painters, whose chief representatives are Peter Cornelius and Franz Overbeck, aimed at a 'medieval' *naïveté*. To some extent, the Pre-Raphaelites form a parallel to them in English art, indeed direct influence has been discerned in the cases of Ford Madox Brown and William Dyce (cf. T. Hilton, *The Pre-Raphaelites* (London, 1976), pp. 19, 22, 25, and 126).

25. Cf. for example Böhme's use of 'quellen', of the return into the self and of the lightning-flash in his accounts of the creation process, e.g. in the *Mysterium Magnum*, paras. 12–26.

6 CLEMENS BRENTANO

Tauberauschte Blumen schließen
Ihrer Kelche süßen Kranz
Und die schlummertrunknen Wiesen
Wiegen sich in Traumes Glanz.[1]

This passage, from the lyrical description of night in Brentano's
Romanzen vom Rosenkranz (1802–11), is quoted here to establish at
the outset his romantic credentials. The work itself, by virtue of the
very fact that it is ostensibly epic in form – it is an attempt to create a
myth of a curse handed down, as with the Tantalids, from generation
to generation and eventually expiated – shows how essentially lyrical
Brentano's genius is. It remains in the memory for the keen sense of the
polarity of spirit and sense which it conveys, and above all for its
mastery of tone, colour and atmosphere. The extract quoted shows how
completely Brentano is in control of what amounts to a sub-genre
within romantic poetry, the night lyric. This provides the perfect
conditions for the *Gemüt* to slip its rational moorings and drift in
luxurious freedom, all tensions relaxed and full of a sense of the unity
of a world which, in common-sense daylight, is dominated by separation
and restriction. This is the time at which another dimension, a
'heimliche Welt'[2] is perceptible. Brentano lacks the philosophical
profundity and cosmic sweep of Novalis; instead, he offers extreme
sensitivity to sound and rhythm and an imaginative ability to penetrate
into the essential nature of a sense-impression (e.g. 'Traumes Glanz'
for moonlight) which act like a drug to liberate the mind from rational
control.

Nor does the fact that Brentano is aware that this is a dangerous, as
well as a sweet, release, that the mind could be seduced – as the figure
of the Siren indicates – into destructive illusion ('Wahn', p. 773), in any
way invalidate this 'Romanze' as an expression of the romantic outlook.
An awareness of the presence of demonic forces in the 'nocturnal'
dimension of the *Gemüt* is something with which we are familiar from
Eichendorff, Hoffmann and others.[3] There is, however, one word in
the description of the Siren's singing, namely the word 'giftig', which
does not seem to fit in with the general atmosphere. Its harshness of
sound and of associations disrupt the romantic tone which, however

strong the sense of duality may be at a given moment, never implies an endemic discord in the universe.

It is here, above all, that the Romantics part company with Kleist. For them, confusion is, or at least can be, an intermediate stage on the path to a deeper coherence. Kleist, on the other hand, lacks, as Eichendorff puts it, the capacity to see the 'dissonances of earthly existence' as 'rings in an invisible, eternal structure'.[4] Among the by-products of this, it can be argued, are his dislocated syntax and violence and harshness of subject-matter and tone. Brentano, for all his appreciation of Kleist's talent, speaks of the 'sharp' and painful impression which he makes,[5] yet he himself seems to have at least a tinge of this quality. Observers and critics have differed over the importance of this negative factor in his outlook. Eichendorff, for whom the religious sense is the power which protects both man and poet from such negativity, felt that Brentano, for all his external lack of order and system, possessed enough of this 'crystal stream' within him to keep him safe from such a radical disorientation. Korff, on the other hand, speaks of his 'Formlosigkeit', 'Zerrissenheit' and 'Haltlosigkeit'.[6]

There is certainly no lack of material in Brentano's work (and even more in his letters) to justify at least the raising of the question. The mere appearance of the one word 'giftig' in the context mentioned above does not, of course, of itself prove a great deal. But there are numerous other instances of a disruption of inner feeling: heavy and violent emotion, for example (as in 'Treulieb' or 'Palinodie'), imagery of a similar type (like that of the 'dagger in the bleeding mouth' in 'O Mutwill ausgesprochen') or the presence of dualism in a sharp and unconciliatory form, as in *Verzweiflung in der Liebe an der Liebe* or 'Wenn der lahme Weber träumt, er webe'.

There is also a certain tendency in Brentano to waywardness in the use of images, which appear in his poetry sometimes, not as symbols based on correspondences discerned by the free-ranging poetic fancy, but rather as counters, parts of a private code in which words are torn out of their normal contexts and whose effect, if powerful, is often disjointed. An example is the couplet which occurs on a number of occasions in Brentano's work and seems to have the force of a talisman for him. It forms the summation, for example, of the poem 'Eingang':

O Stern und Blume, Geist und Kleid,
Lieb, Leid und Zeit und Ewigkeit! (K 1, 619)

What we seem to find confronting us here is a romantic mentality
which has suffered serious disruption. The four word-pairs with which
we are presented all contain the dualism of 'heavenly' and 'earthly'
which we met in Novalis, but whereas the other poet feels sure ground
under his feet in that he has the inner capacity to resolve the duality,
and to control his life and art with the proper romantic 'Besonnenheit',
Brentano lacked that confidence. He had a positive romantic vision and
constantly sought, especially in his quest for love, to reach and lay
hold on 'Den Kristallgrund hell und reine', to use the symbolic image
of the 'Frühlingsschrei eines Knechtes aus der Tiefe'. He did not always
fail to do so, but neither was his grasp on it always secure. He could not
always conjure it up from within himself when he chose. And so the
'Eingang' couplet is not an assertion, but an incantation.

Brentano's letters are full of references to his need — for peace, for
childlike simplicity, above all for love — and motifs suggesting need,
such as that of poverty (e.g. the poor gleaner in 'Eingang'), or of the
pilgrim in the desert,[7] appear regularly in both his private and his
public writings. There is nothing exceptional, in romantic literature,
in such themes in themselves. The difference in Brentano's case is that
he feels not only the lack of certain qualities, but also the lack of the
capacity to attain them. He asks to be made whole, to be released from
the isolation, indeed exile,[8] of a world composed almost entirely of,
and by, himself. His love was certainly never without a strong element
of sensuality: this is as much in evidence in a late poem like 'Eine feine
reine Myrte', addressed to Emilie Linder, as it is in *Godwi*. But his most
serious love affairs, those with Sophie Mereau, Luise Hensel and
Emilie Linder, were all attempts to find wholeness and — paradoxical
as it may sound in his case — freedom. In childhood and early youth
he had been driven into, or had sought refuge in, the inner world of his
own fancy; as a result, one is forced to conclude, of the breakdown of
his relationship with his parents. With his father Peter Brentano, a man
of a hard, practical mentality, he could find no link at all and from his
mother, the intellectually and spiritually gifted Maximiliane Laroche,
whom he idolised and idealised, he was, by a combination of
circumstances, largely shut off. She died when he was fifteen. Thus a
pathological twist was given to a tendency which we recognise as
genuinely romantic, but which is normally held within safe bounds by a
compensating factor of objectivity, such as Brentano recognised, and
envied, in the 'Liebe, Ruhe und Wahrheit' of his brother-in-law,
Savigny.[9]

In the fragment *Der Sänger* (1800), one of his most subjectively autobiographical pieces, Brentano explicitly links this problem with the loss of his mother. When the Singer's mother dies, he seems to lose the power to relate to external reality: 'meine ganze äußre Welt sank mit ihr' (K 2, 505). He seeks a way of re-establishing the link:

> Wo lebt ein Wesen, das ich dicht umschlinge,
> Dem ich das Herz und den verwaisten Sinn
> Zur Pflege und zur Liebe wiederbringe? (K 2, 509)

It was to Sophie Mereau that he looked, at that time, to 'lead him into life', as he put it in a letter to her of 4 September 1803.[10] Love, which he presents as a Saviour in many works (e.g. *Godwi* and *Ponce de Leon*), was no simple matter for him. It represents 'integration', to use a fashionable word, at the highest level and locked inside his own consciousness, Brentano feels the lack of the ability to integrate, what he himself calls 'meine eigne Fähigkeit zur Welt und der Welt zu mir'.[11] The external world of actuality is not fully real to him: 'es war mir', says the Singer, 'als wären alle diese Dinge nicht mehr um mich, das wäre alles nur bloße Erinnerungen' (K 1, 506).

Brentano did, of course, exist and function in that world, but there were times when his link with it was not one of full human involvement, but one based on the faculty of 'Witz' which, as he expresses it in a letter to Luise Hensel (December 1816), grasps the 'flat' external world while a 'second soul' under the surface, as it were, sees the essential nullity of that activity:

> dann überlasse ich wieder die Worte ihrer innern lebendigen
> Selbsttätigkeit und die Rede wirtschaftet dann auf eigne Hand
> munter drauflos, während meine Seele in der Angst, Trauer und
> Sehnsucht liegt, und nur dann und wann, wie der Baß der
> Betrachtung, die reißende und hüpfende Melodie durchschneidend
> ordnet und einteilt.

This is a psychological state beyond romantic irony (where the inner Self is in control and enjoys its own freedom), and a highly complex one. It is hardly surprising, then, that Brentano should have great difficulty in devising a coherent language in which to communicate it and is sometimes reduced to oblique suggestion through images in a way more reminiscent of surrealist than of symbolist techniques:

> O Mutwill ausgesprochen

In Tränen ausgebrochen,
O Scherz von wenig Wochen
Indes das Herz gebrochen!
O Lächeln einer Wunde,
O Dolch im blutenden Munde (K 1, 1170–1).

This kind of 'Entstellung' (removal from context), to use Enzensberger's term,[12] is by no means always present in Brentano's style, but there are usually some signs of less-than-perfect control, such as an inability to form and finish a theme which goes beyond the normal romantic looseness of form,[13] and capriciousness in his poetic, as well as his personal, behaviour. This latter no doubt has its portion of romantic irony, but with an admixture of an alien element which almost always makes it sad as well as merry. 'Ich bin sehr arm', wrote to Emilie in 1837, 'sehr elend und muß immer gaukeln.'[14] Much of his playfulness, his manipulation of word-sounds and meanings (e.g. 'Wie wird mir? wer wollte wohl weinen. . .': K 1, 244 f), repetition and variation of whole phrases (as in 'Der Spinnerin Lied'), a mixture often laced with sharp paradox,[15] reflect not so much a serene detachment as a desire to overcome a sense of inner disunity and emptiness. His life and work certainly have an odd and mercurial quality and could give an impression of the merely frivolous indulgence of fancy, such as Ermatinger seems to imply with the formulation 'luftige Spiele einer überreichen Phantasie'.[16] But the very sadness which Brentano felt testifies to the presence in him of a more positive potential, in his writings, at any rate, that did not always remain unfulfilled.

Even in his earlier years as a writer, when his Catholicism was, to say the least, suspect, Brentano possessed an awareness of, and an ability to respond to, a reality beyond the merely personal. This, one feels, is the 'pure enthusiasm' of which he speaks in *Godwi* (K 2, 215). Whether in an overtly mystical context, as in 'Wenn der Sturm das Meer umschlinget',[17] or on the vaguer level of consciousness of 'fantasias' like 'Stille Blumen' and 'Guitarre und Lied', there is a concentration on the relationship between the individual and the absolute. The first-named poem clearly asserts the incompleteness of the isolated Self: 'In uns selbst sind wir verschlossen, Bange Fesseln uns beengen' (K 1, 46). For a moment, it could be thought that 'Stille Blumen' contradicts this view:

Und wer sich mit Liebe nicht selber umarmt,
Für den ist das Leben zum Bettler verarmt (K 1, 30).

But there is no contradiction. The Self and the infinite meet in both poems, for the love which is involved in our second example is both individual and universal and the inner experience is infinite as well as personal:

Doch blüht einem jeden das Ganze im Schoß
Und tief durch den Schleier, da weht es von ferne (K 1, 29).

This, and the companion fantasy mentioned earlier, have the melodious mistiness which is such a feature of Brentano's earlier poetry, but the cultivation of this atmosphere does not obliterate thought to the extent that Walther Killy seems to imply in his essay on Brentano's 'Gemütserregungskunst'.[18]

Nor does Brentano's 'Sehnsucht' entirely lack the positive content which, as we have seen from Novalis, romantic longing can and indeed should have: a positive awareness, that is, of a real object and even some degree of participation in it. In Margot's song of nightfall and moonrise in the unfinished *Märchen, Die Rose* (K 1, 57 ff; 2, 472 ff), whose function in the story is to reflect King Dringinwalde's need to achieve true humanity, we certainly have an image of Brentano's personal quest for wholeness. He was in fact constantly portraying himself, and even in works of a formally more than usually objective nature — ballads, for example — often falls into a kind of authorial intervention which is not irony (the narrator appearing *as narrator*), but, in a way, its opposite: the narrator suddenly becomes a participant, undermining rather than strengthening our sense of objectivity and detachment. 'Es ging verirrt im Walde', for example, tells in a straightforward third-person narrative the story of the princess carried up by her lover into his castle, but introduces a bewildering switch of perspective in its conclusion: 'Auf Felsen hoch *ich* wohne. . .'etc. (K 1, 135 (my emphasis)).[19] The process of making art out of personal experience demands the ability to 'externalise' the personal and Brentano had some difficulty in doing this. Yet even in *Godwi*, the most extreme case, he maintains sufficient control to produce a viable poetic work and sometimes, as in the episode from *Die Rose* from which we began here, the personal dimension is not perceptible at all. The song remains successfully on the general plane. The existence of a sphere of harmony and higher spiritual reality (symbolised by the stars) is convincingly posited and becomes the object of a positive romantic longing:

Das Leben erhebet,
Zum Himmel gewandt,
Den Busen und strebet
Sich wieder zu finden.
Die Sehnsucht erwacht
In schimmernder Nacht (K 1, 40).

Certainly, Brentano feels and expresses a deep sense of deprivation; the paradise of simplicity and wholeness has been lost. But he has not ceased to believe in its reality and he still possesses the ability to visualise it and to experience it inwardly. Childhood is one of the images in which he embodies it and the *Märchen*, *Gockel, Hinkel und Gackeleia*, for all its complexities, is in general imbued with that spirit. The creation, in collaboration with Achim von Arnim, of the outstanding folk-song collection *Des Knaben Wunderhorn* (1805–8) as a renewal of the 'frische Morgenluft altdeutschen Wandels', as he himself expressed it,[20] demonstrates his sympathy for the spirit of the people and original pieces like 'Der Star und die Badewanne' prove that he could kindle that spirit within himself.

He sought always an ideal of love which could give him both personal ecstasy and redemption from the unrest and pain of his individualistic isolation. A certain undefined religious feeling was associated with this even in the early period of the relationship with Sophie Mereau. This period contains the sweetest, but also the most diffuse, of his lyrics. In the unfulfilled love for Luise Hensel, he did seem to find his way to some degree of self-acceptance and began to rediscover his Catholicism. His poetry shed some of the luxuriant sweetness of the first period, but gained in strength, depth and mental discipline. He could never stifle all desire for happiness on earth, but he did manage to come to terms with the pain of life and to contain, at least, the tendency to self-pity and self-indulgence in general. His progress in this regard was undoubtedly furthered by contemplation of Christ and of His suffering. 'Mir hat das Kreuz geholfen,' he wrote later to Emilie Linder, 'und nicht die Bibel.'[21] This statement occurs, of course, in the special context of his attempt to convert her to Catholicism, but it still constitutes an accurate comment on the whole process.

The fine 'Frühlingsschrei eines Knechtes aus der Tiefe' (1816) illustrates the development to Brentano's more mature style. It is still intensely subjective and emotionally fluid and there can be no question of the childlike simplicity which, as we saw, Brentano set up as a psychological ideal. The language and imagery are in fact very complex. The poem deals with the parallel themes of the meaning of Easter and the individual's inner battle with sin and confusion, which are reflected in the imagery of the servant crying from the pit (cf. Ps. 88) and the Passion and Resurrection on the religious level, and the springtime renewal of nature and the mineshaft on the natural level. What has been gained is not a release from pain: rather, the sense of pain is sharper, as if the patient has emerged from a narcotic haze[22] to face and grapple with reality. Confusion has not been dispelled — for the reality is itself confused — but diffuseness has. Brentano's situation is still that of the exile, or the pilgrim in the desert, but after the meeting with Luise, the 'Engel in der Wüste',[23] the pilgrim is no longer 'without a star to turn to'. To speak of asceticism in Brentano's case would be absurd, but it is true that his existence now has a firmness in its loneliness which seems spiritually and morally healthier, and certainly is of benefit to his poetry. There is an ability to form experience and fix it in sharper phrases and images which more than makes up for the loss of the cloudier sweetness of the *Godwi*-period.

Even when the world reasserts its claims, in the Emilie-relationship, this firmness is maintained. Pieces like 'In tiefen Leiden' or 'Ich weiß wohl, was dich bannt in mir' seem to be formed from a metal forged in an intense heat:

> Die süße zauberhafte Zier,
> Der bangen tiefgeheimen Lust,
> Die aus mir strahlet, ruft zu dir,
> Schließ mich in einen Felsen ein,
> Ruft doch arm Lind durch Mark und Bein:
> Komm, lebe, liebe, stirb an mir. . . (K 1, 559)

This is a different kind of 'Lorelei', but still a romantic one. There is no magical 'Stimmung', but the poet's weapons and techniques are still the romantic ones of fancy and spiritual energy, or 'love'. The negative attitude which the older, more austere Brentano adopted towards his earlier poetic self[24] did not make him any less a poet. It is an extreme form of the insight into the relative vanity of earthly beauty and 'Ringen nach Verein', by comparison with the realisation of the meaning of the Cross, which he expressed (in poetry as fine as any he had previously written) in 'An Frau Marianne von Willemer' (K 1, 492 ff).

As a conclusion to this chapter, we intend to compare examples of the earlier and later styles. Our first example is a song which appeared in the play *Die lustigen Musikanten* (1802–3):

Fabiola. Hör', es klagt die Flöte wieder,
         Und die kühlen Brunnen rauschen.

Piast.   Golden wehn die Töne nieder,
         Stille, stille, laß uns lauschen!

Fabiola. Holdes Bitten, mild Verlangen,
         Wie es süß zum Herzen spricht!

Piast.   Durch die Nacht, die mich umfangen,
         Blickt zu mir der Töne Licht.

This is in fact a duet between the girl Fabiola and the blind singer Piast. The unseen flautist is Ramiro, a 'lost' Duke, eventually to be united with Fabiola, a similarly 'lost' princess, in a typically romantic ending of festive restoration. The song fits well enough into its context, but it can easily be detached and made to stand on its own. Not only does it have great beauty, it has a true, generally applicable romantic substance. In spite of his state of separation from the infinite spiritual reality, which is not accessible to him through ordinary means of perception, man can experience contact with and consolation from it through the inner powers of the *Gemüt*. Music makes a very appropriate image for this kind of direct apprehension of the infinite. 'The art of the infinite', in the words of Ricarda Huch;[25] it had a special importance, as we have seen, for the romantic generation as a whole.[26]

This is, then, not just a poem about the power of music (though Brentano was very susceptible to that power[27]), but a more general image of the inner experience of the *Gemüt*, which it aims to liberate and set in motion. Its aural richness does much to loosen the hold of logical reason, a process which Brentano takes to great lengths in his earlier poetry.[28] The synaesthesia (a device naturally much favoured by the Romantics) not only adds its own illogicality, but also a visual element to the sensuous world of the sound, which is further enriched by the reference to the coolness of the fountains. The function of the sense-impressions is not, however, to have a purely narcotic effect. The sound of the flute has from the outset a psychological force (it 'laments') and in the third couplet its melancholy is translated completely into the language of the *Gemüt*. 'Gold' has traditional associations of spiritual fulfilment and truth and coolness (recalling, no doubt, Biblical associations of physical and spiritual refreshment: e.g. Acts, 3, 19), and is a symbol used more than once by Brentano for a positive spiritual experience.[29]

This is one of those pieces in which Brentano has overcome his isolation to form an image of more than merely autobiographical significance. We can appreciate, of course, that the situation of the blind man imprisoned in night has a personal meaning for him, but we are not compelled to relate the poem to that situation. We know that images sometimes have a private meaning for Brentano but even in a case such as that of the 'Stern und Blume' couplet, which, as Elisabeth Stopp has persuasively argued, might even be said to be 'enciphered',[30] it is possible to speak of a measure of validity outside the private sphere. In our present poem, Brentano has escaped that net entirely. Its softness of texture and its successful assimilation of message into mood mark it as a product of the pre-conversion period, of the familiar, more obviously 'romantic' Brentano.

Our second example is the late poem 'O Traum der Wüste', which is too long, unfortunately, to be printed here in full. It was originally planned as part of a re-telling of the legend of St Marina, who attains sainthood through acceptance of an undeserved punishment. The place of her death becomes one of pilgrimage, and of grace and easement for all suffering hearts. Our poem was to have been the song of a later pilgrim (another self-portrait, of course!) who, on the journey from Babylon to Jerusalem,[31] reaches this spot. The 'Wüstentraum' is the place of release (cf. K 1, 625, lines 21–4, and 645, lines 525–9). This part of the 'Marina'-complex was not published during Brentano's lifetime, one assumes because of its much higher level of personal involvement. Christian Brentano, the editor of the *Gesammelte Schriften* of 1852–5, detaches it from its context and while one regrets that in some ways, it is certainly capable of standing on its own, without the legendary background, as an image of Brentano's own situation and beyond that, of the travail and hope of the soul torn between spirit and sense.

Structurally, as in other ways, this is a thoroughly romantic work. It eschews the logic of a narrative or argumentative sequence in favour of an emotional one which, as we saw in the case of Novalis's *Hymnen an die Nacht*, produces at least an initial impression of circularity. It remains throughout on the same ground: the present moment of pain and hope. The pain is that of Brentano torn between God and Emilie Linder, of the soul torn between sacred and profane love, longing for a harmonious release but suffering constant disappointment. The hope

is that given by the faith which makes the pilgrim into a pilgrim, namely
that through his suffering and through grace, he may find deliverance.
The emotional logic does in fact, as in Novalis's *Hymnen*, give rise to a
certain structural pattern, a progression of feeling which spirals its way
through constant repetition and variation of phrases and images, to a
final climax.

The opening (stanzas 1–3) states the situation; an 'endlos Sehnen
Blau überspannt vom Zelte', love in the desert, thirsting and constantly
frustrated. The intertwining of the spiritual and physical is thus
established at the outset in a romantic, but elliptical, symbolism which,
naturally enough, attracts the critic with modernist leanings.[32] The
erotic element is more prominent than the spiritual at this stage,
though there is a hint of the latter in the reference to Joseph's garment
(stanza 3; cf. Gen. 39, 12 ff) and the romantic motif of the dream,
enunciated in the first line and carried as a thread through the whole
work, indicates not only the discrepancy between the ideal and present
reality, but a hope, at least, of eventual fulfilment. The next section
(stanzas 4–9) provides a counterbalance by concentrating more on the
spiritual side of the equation. It makes direct use of religious images,
most of which are connected with the desert; the angel and palm-tree
(stanza 4), Hagar and Ishmael (stanza 5; cf. Gen. 21, 14–19), Christ
the Bridegroom (stanza 6), the burning bush (Exod. 3, 2) as a figure of
the Immaculate Conception (stanza 7), the voice crying in the wilderness (Luke 3, 4) and the honey in the lion's carcass (Judges 14, 8) in
stanza 8 and the cleft rock (Num. 20, 11) and the Bread of Heaven
(Exod. 16, 4), two more Old Testament figures of Christ, in stanza 9.
A third section (stanzas 10–15) switches attention to the things of
this world. The pilgrim is subject to temptation or in symbolic form,
he can fall among thieves.[33] The world offers many attractions, but
though they appear to offer love and refreshment, they turn out to be
barren, indeed destructive. All the images are held together by the
dominating and unifying central image of the wilderness. The final
stanza draws the threads together and states, in answer to the longing
and questioning which has gone before, a sombre but also a hopeful
conclusion. Suffering must be accepted, but at the moment of greatest
negativity, the grace of God will intervene:

O Liebe, Wüstentraum, du mußt verbluten,
Beraubt, verwundet, trifft der Sonne Stich,
Der Wüste Speer dich, und in Sandesgluten
Begräbt der Wind dich, und Gott findet dich! (K 1, 626)

This is a long poem: is it too long? Inordinate length and inability to
achieve 'concentration' of expression or 'inner form' are the chief sins
laid at Brentano's door by Korff.[34] It is certainly true that in many of
his poems, the inner energy source is an experience or a state of mind
which contains no possibility of development, or of movement in any
but a circular direction and which must, like a Catherine wheel, simply
burn itself out. That is not in itself a sufficient aesthetic justification.
Some of these poems simply die of weariness and cannot hold the
reader's attention. The poet's wit spins on and on, but the heart is
exhausted. In others, though, the energy is sufficient to maintain the
impetus of the work until a natural climax, or point of rest, has been
reached. Such is the case with what is Brentano's most systematically
repetitive and kaleidoscopic poem, 'Einsam will ich untergehen', and
indeed with our present example. There is no stanza in which the
intensity of feeling could be said to flag and whose removal would not
leave a patent gap.

While not neglecting the aural aspects entirely, Brentano's later
manner throws greater light and emphasis on the images. These do not
lose their romantic mystery, but stand out in sharper definition, are less
completely sensuous in character and have greater symbolic power than
those of the early lyrics. A stronger, sometimes astringent emotional
quality replaces the mistier sweetness of the early style. The image, for
example, of the 'Sehnsuchtspalme Die blütenlos Gezweig zum Himmel
streckt' (stanza 4), certainly speaks for and to the *Gemüt*, but it has a
hard edge and brings with it a keen sense of reality. In the same way,
the quality of the impression conveyed by the image of stones rattling
down a barren rock-face (representing the ache of unfulfilled longing)
conveys an impression of toughness and solidity, though there can
certainly be no talk of 'realism' in the description:

> Es saust das Haus der Schlangen und der Drachen
> Und prasselt nieder an der Felsenwand (stanza 12).

The primary images ('Wüste', 'Traum', 'Liebe') and their many
ancilliaries are shuffled and combined in phrases and sometimes in
compounds (such as 'Wüstentraumquell') in a pattern of infinite
variety and repetition which itself gives the sense of infinity. The
recurrence of the primary motifs in every stanza produces the effect of
an incantatory repetition, a device used by Brentano on a number of
occasions and with varying success. In our poem, the sense does not
falter, or become muffled in an atmosphere of playfulness for in each

separate formulation, at the beginning of the relevant stanza, an element is introduced which leads on to the new images and new facets of the theme which the stanza is to treat. Thus the revelation of God in the burning bush (stanza 7) is foreshadowed by the phrasing of the initial reference to the primary theme of love (i.e. here, 'das Wort der ew'gen Liebe'). In the following stanza, 'Durst der Liebe' (line 1) prepares for the image of the water gushing from the cleft rock.

Brentano is an uneven writer, whose immense talent is sometimes vitiated by the need to ventilate personal problems and whose inner fragility can lead to the dissipation of that talent in fragmentation and obscurity. But at his best he can control and counteract these tendencies and speak to the whole *Gemüt* in an authentic romantic tone, both sensuous and spiritual, individual and universal. Whether in the highly musical lyrical distillation of atmosphere and natural beauty and the individual re-creation of the spirit of the 'Volkslied' in the *Wunderhorn* and the Rhine-lyrics, or in the less immediately accessible and popular later poetry, he can find and hold fast to the 'crystal ground' of spiritual truth, control his experience and communicate it in a form appreciable by the world at large.

Notes

1. Clemens Brentano, *Werke*, F. Kemp (ed.) (Munich, 1968), vol. 1, p. 772.
2. Cf. the night-song which begins: 'Sprich aus der Ferne'.
3. Novalis would seem to form an exception to this rule.
4. Cf. Eichendorff's *Geschichte der poetischen Literatur Deutschlands*, BG 4, p. 365.
5. Cf. R. Steig, *Achim von Arnim und die ihm nahe standen*, reprint (Frankfurt–Berne, 1970), p. 302.
6. H. A. Korff, *Geist der Goethezeit*, 2nd edn (Leipzig, 1954), Teil IV, pp. 203, 205 and 448 respectively.
7. E.g. 'Einsam will ich untergehen', stanza 2; 'Ich bin durch die Wüste gezogen,' or 'O Traum der Wüste'.
8. Cf. 'Das Elend soll ich einsam bauen' (K 1, p. 440) and 'O schweig nur, Herz. . . baue dein Elend fromm' (ibid., p. 363).
9. Cf. his letter to Savigny (mid-July 1801) in *Das unsterbliche Leben*, pp. 214, and ibid., pp. 14 and 203.
10. 'Führe mich ins Leben hinein'; cf. W. Hoffmann, *Clemens Brentano. Leben und Werk* (Berne–Munich, 1966), p. 149. The poem quoted is echoed much later in that addressed to Emilie: 'Wo schlägt ein Herz, das bleibend fühlt?' (K 1, p. 531).
11. Letter to his sister Sophie, quoted by Hoffmann, *Brentano*, p. 87. Cf. also the letter to Bettina, ibid., p. 99.
12. H. M. Enzensberger, *Brentanos Poetik* (Munich, 1961). Enzensberger, himself a distinguished modern poet, is naturally interested in this aspect of Brentano's work and does perhaps overstress it (cf. Kemp, vol. 1, p. 1309).

13. Compare *Godwi*, a *truly* 'verwilderter Roman', with other romantic novels.

14. Brentano, *Briefe an Emilie Linder*, W. Frühwald (ed.) (Bad Homburg, 1969), p. 77.

15. E.g. line 31 of 'Eine feine reine Myrte': 'Mundes Wunde schmachtend lacht.'

16. E. Ermatinger, *Deutsche Dichter, 1700–1900* (Bonn, 1949), vol. 2, p. 243.

17. From *Godwi*; written in 1800. Critics have noted the closeness of this poem to Novalis's *Hymnen an die Nacht*.

18. 'Gemütserregungskunst: Clemens Brentano' in W. Killy, *Wandlungen des lyrischen Bildes* (Göttingen, 1956), pp. 53–72.

19. Cf. also the 'Lore Lay' ballad, *Auf dem Rhein* and 'Aus Köllen war ein Edelknecht'.

20. Quoted by R. Steig in *Achim von Arnim und die ihm nahe standen*, vol. 1, p. 177. Stein himself acknowledged the importance of the *Wunderhorn* in re-kindling the sense of German nationhood.

21. *Briefe*, ed. Frühwald, p. 37.

22. Contrast, for example, the atmosphere of this poem with that of *Guitarre und Lied*!

23. Cf. 'Ich bin durch die Wüste gezogen', K 1, p. 356.

24. Cf. his self-portrait as the 'Schreiber' in *Geschichte vom braven Kasperl und von dem schönen Annerl*.

25. Cf. R. Huch, *Die Romantik* (Leipzig, 1924), Teil 2, pp. 250–63.

26. Cf. above, pp. 28, 33.

27. As instanced in *Stille Blumen* or *Nachklänge Beethovenscher Musik*.

28. Some would say, too far; cf. S. S. Prawer's comments on *Der Spinnerin Lied* in *German Lyric Poetry* (London, 1952), pp. 121–6 and W. Killy, 'Gemütserregungskunst', especially p. 68.

29. E.g. 'Ich bin durch die Wüste gezogen', K 1, pp. 356–7.

30. E. Stopp, ' "O Stern und Blume": Its Poetic and Emblematic Context', *Modern Language Review*, vol. lxvii (1972), pp. 95–117.

31. The Babylon–Jerusalem dualism, symbolising the wrong and right paths in life, also occurs in 'Ich bin durch die Wüste gezogen', as does the motif of God 'finding' the pilgrim in the desert sand. From the Biblical perspective, of course, Babylon represents the World, in which the soul is exiled, and Jerusalem the Heavenly Home.

32. Enzensberger, *Brentanos Poetik* (pp. 55–70) devotes a long section to this poem.

33. The image of the man set upon by robbers is used in a letter to Emilie (*Briefe*, p. 53) as an allegory for life. Whether Brentano wishes to imply a reference to the Good Samaritan (and thus to Christ the Redeemer) is an issue which must be left open here, though one suspects that this is the case.

34. *Geist der Goethezeit*, IV, p. 203.

7 EICHENDORFF

It was Eichendorff who, writing of Brentano, coined the phrase '[die] wunderbare Süßigkeit der Romantik',[1] and he himself was able to feel and convey this phenomenon to his readers more acutely and consistently than any other poet of his generation. This is a dangerous quality in a poet, for simple feeling can all too easily degenerate into sentimentality and sweetness, divorced from spiritual savour, become a source of debilitating self-indulgence, as in the case of the sweet-toothed Brunies, who, in Grass's *Katz und Maus*, misuses Eichendorff in this way. And to those who read without due care and attention, a writer of this type could appear pretty but banal, perhaps even escapist. A supreme achievement like the story *Aus dem Leben eines Taugenichts* could be seen as no more than a pleasant relaxation from the stern business of reality. It seems at first glance so similar to other sugary confections of a type no doubt familiar to the reader. Relaxation, in fact, is a major problem for the reader of Eichendorff. We *must* relax while reading him, for he charms us into it whether we will or no, but to relax completely would be fatal. Eichendorff himself is well aware of this, for he knows that the magic of the romantic expedition into the interior of the *Gemüt* can lead, without proper control, to mental and moral disaster. He is constantly hinting to the reader to be on his guard, but the hints cannot be too broad if the charm is not to be destroyed, and so the active co-operation of the reader is needed. In 'Zwielicht', Eichendorff seems almost to be issuing a warning against the possible effects of his own magic: 'Hüte dich, bleib wach und munter.'[2]

Only in that way, indeed, will we recognise the *true* magic at all. The kind of banalicisation referred to above is the mark of the philistine whose tendency, as Eichendorff sees it, is to reduce what should be holy to the level of an existence divorced from all contact with the infinite spiritual dimension, to make it 'gemein'. He waged constant war against this species, notably in his 'dramatic fairy-tale' *Krieg den Philistern* and in satirical portraits, especially in his novels, of the most dangerous type, the 'cultured' philistine, who genuinely imagines himself to be a devotee of beauty, but who finds it in the debased form offered by authors like Lafontaine and Tiedge. In the sixth chapter of *Dichter und ihre Gesellen*, Eichendorff shows how true metal can be turned into base:

> Unterdes ging ein frisches Wehen durch die Wipfel, die letzte
> Wolkendecke zerriß, und die alte Stadtmauer und die Waldberge
> darüber standen plötzlich wunderbar beglänzt. Die Dame hatte sich
> erhoben und unter der Linde vor der Bank eine malerische,
> melancholisch-heroische Stellung genommen. Das Haupt in die
> rechte Hand an den Baum gestützt, sah sie eine Zeitlang, wie in
> Gedanken verloren, nach den Höhen — "Tiedge!" — sagte sie endlich
> bedeutungsvoll, und drückte Fortunat leise die Hand.[3]

The scene described at the beginning of this extract has an inherent
picture-postcard prettiness, but the romantic eye sees beyond this. In
describing the end of the storm, Eichendorff uses motifs which are in
themselves very common and simple and could easily degenerate into
mere pseudo-poetic clichés. But by a subtly indeterminate phrasing
([es] ging ein. . . Wehen durch die Wipfel'), by showing the sun breaking
through a barrier and 'suddenly' illuminating the scene and above all,
perhaps, by the judicious use of the words 'frisch' and (at the culminating moment) 'wunderbar', he endows the whole with a suggestion
of spiritual life.

The 'lady', on the other hand, is all sincere pose. Clearly not
unversed in German literature, she imagines herself playing Lotte to
Fortunat's Werther.[4] Reminded, perhaps, of some suitably 'elevated',
smoothly versified and decoratively phrased passage in Tiedge's
philosophical poem *Urania*, she thinks that she, like Lotte, has received
an intimation of a divine presence at the end of the storm. The irony is,
of course, that Eichendorff has clearly indicated such a dimension in
his initial description of the scene and as clearly indicated in his
description of the 'lady' that she is incapable of apprehending it. It was
probably because he realised that his particular kind of Romanticism,
which depends more than most on the evocation of atmosphere in a
formally simple style and with the use of a relatively restricted range
of easily accessible motifs, was especially vulnerable to distortion of
this kind, that he felt a hatred for the philistine which was strong even
for a Romantic.[5]

It is important that we should register formally the point that the
criticisms contained in the passage quoted above are not levelled
against Romanticism itself. They are to be distinguished from those in
which Eichendorff expresses his awareness that the romantic mentality
proper was also subject to real dangers. His many portraits of poets and

poetic characters show this clearly. And he did, in his later, retrospective essays on literary history, make some criticisms, not so much of
Romanticism as such, to which he remained faithful, as of individual
romantic writers. These had failed, as he saw it, to attain the romantic
goal, the totally admirable one of a regeneration of Germany, a
reorientation from earthly to heavenly values. Self-will, he feels, for
which Protestantism provided the opening, has perverted the basically
healthy romantic impulse towards freedom to produce non-holy and,
in Hoffmann's case, even unholy results. All this is of significance for
us, not as a commentary on Romanticism as a whole, which was not
necessarily obliged to produce a religious revival along the lines
desired by Eichendorff, but as an indication of the particular, perhaps
simpler and more contained, but still romantic variant of the movement
which we may expect to find in his case.

Eichendorff speaks, in his 'Wünschelrute', of a magic formula, a
'Zauberwort' which enables man to draw forth the 'song which sleeps
in all things'. No doubt he is thinking also of the spirit in which he
wishes to be read, but his primary concern here is the poet's art and, as
is usual in such cases, first and foremost his own. Leaving the technical
aspects on one side for the moment, we will concentrate here on the
element of magicality which is indeed central to Eichendorff's work and
in no way restricted to those areas which can be defined as broadly
'supernatural'. Even when sprites and similar beings are involved,
indeed, the real magic lies in the inner psychological effect, the
activation and heightening of psychological activity within the reader.
This is why Eichendorff so often succeeds in snatching poetry from the
jaws of cliché. As all critics agree, he is a poet of 'Stimmung', but his is
an atmosphere which has a real substance and energy. As opposed to
the inert, essentially empty prettiness of the sentimental writer, he
resembles Mozart, at least in the fact that his surface beauty and grace
conceal a spiritual depth and strength.

This occurs in secure situations as well as in those where the poet
introduces some element of overt mysterious unease. There may not be
fear, but there is at least a 'Schauer', that inner stirring which is
aroused by the recognition of a reality not contained in rational,
'normal' experience. It is precisely this which the popular sentimental
artist lacks or, if he senses the possibility, avoids. It is instructive in
this connection to see what the well known illustrator Ludwig Richter
made of Eichendorff's 'Waldeinsamkeit'. His woodcut, entitled
Waldeinsamkeit (reproduced by Stöcklein[6]), was designed as an
illustration to the following:

Waldeinsamkeit!
Du grünes Revier,
Wie liegt so weit
Die Welt von hier!
Schlaf nur, wie bald
Kommt der Abend schön,
Durch den stillen Wald
Die Quellen gehn,
Die Mutter Gottes wacht,
Mit ihrem Sternenkleid
Bedeckt sie dich sacht
In der Waldeinsamkeit,
Gute Nacht, gute Nacht! (BG 1, 294–5)

Richter (described by Brion as 'the unforgettable poet of an ideal
Germany'[7]) is certainly a 'poetic' artist who often uses romantic motifs
and can compose competent and often charming pictures. His charm,
however, is far removed from the Eichendorffian 'Zauber'; it has a
quality of cosiness, slightly tinged with sentimentality which is
epitomised by the centre foreground of the illustration under discussion,
which is occupied by a group of deer not mentioned in the original
poem. This latter first appeared in *Dichter und ihre Gesellen* as the song
heard by Otto just before he died. It was then taken to form the final
section of the cycle *Der Umkehrende*. There is comfort in Eichendorff,
as in Richter, but more mystery. In the precise contexts, we are dealing
with the final rest of a returned wanderer, but even without that
knowledge, it is surely possible to detect a suggestion in the special
solemnity of the description and the invitation to sleep that this is
more than merely an evocation of the peacefulness of a remote spot.
One does not, after all, go to such a place in order to sleep. Richter
gives no inkling of such a dimension and certainly does nothing to
induce the mood of solemnity. Similarly, he does not imbue his image
with the spiritual and psychological suggestiveness which is given by
Eichendorff's references to the Virgin Mary and her 'Sternenkleid' and
– most effective of all – to springs whose water moves, heard, one
assumes, but not seen,[8] through the 'quiet wood'. This indefinite
movement, introduced at the critical turning-point of the poem with
no clear logical link with what precedes or with what follows, cannot
but have the effect of creating a corresponding psychological movement,
of freeing the *Gemüt* from rational control.

The feeling induced by this process, one which occurs over and over again in Eichendorff's poetry, is certainly often a pleasant one of relaxation and freedom, but it is also a challenge. The liberation of the *Gemüt* is an awakening to spiritual freedom in the broadest sense and that brings with it dangers and responsibilities as well. We cannot simply indulge ourselves in the pleasurable sensation of the 'widening' of the heart in the presence of simple, unspoiled nature:

> Eh' es beginnt zu tagen:
> Der Strom geht still und breit,
> Die Nachtigallen schlagen,
> Mein Herz wird mir so weit! ('Wahl'; BG 1, 196)

The inner world of the *Gemüt* is anything but a safe and simple one for Eichendorff and he has no intention of by-passing this labyrinth. The only way to truth lies through it and he goes out of his way, in fact, to stimulate the subconscious into activity. Nature is for him not a vehicle for some vague pantheism, but a medium which, seen through the eye of the *Gemüt*, that is, with its visual solidity largely dissolved into sound, movement and indefinite sensations, can bring to the surface the subconscious thoughts which would otherwise remain hidden. In Gabriele's song in *Das Schloß Dürande* (BG 1, 235, as part of *Die Einsame*), the rustling of the wind in the treetops is part of the external world of nature, but the 'Klingen' which ensues is internal and psychological:

> Wenn die Wipfel über mir schwanken,
> Es klinget die ganze Nacht,
> Das sind im Herzen die Gedanken,
> Die singen, wenn niemand wacht.

The objective existence of the external world is never denied, but it exists, in Eichendorff's most characteristic lyrical work, primarily for, and is experienced in and through, the *Gemüt*. Oskar Seidlin over-dramatises somewhat when he claims that the opening line of 'Sehnsucht' ('Es schienen so golden die Sterne') 'verwandelt Lokal in Strahlung'.[9] We do not wish to lose completely the sense of the lonely observer looking out of the window at the starry sky: the aim should be, not to substitute abstract complexity for naïve simplicity, but to see a measure of the one in the other. Even so, Seidlin's point is valuable. The real life of the poem resides in the consciousness of poet and reader. It is the inner train of thought set off by the impressions received from the outside world that is of prime importance and Eichendorff's approach is almost always calculated to emphasise this, whether through simple parallelism (as in 'Der Glückliche': BG 1, 210), or through a less direct and rationally appreciable process. Sometimes, as in 'Die Nachtblume' (BG 1, 211), there is an almost complete fusion of the inner and outer worlds, which is also, inevitably, a confusion (cf. stanza 1, line 3). The night-world is described in terms of a natural phenomenon (a 'lindes Wellenschlagen'), but one which forms an image more appropriate to a train of thought than to the material outside world. Then, wishes, clouds, thoughts and winds seem to become, interchangeably, both internal and external at the same time:

> Wünsche wie die Wolken sind,
> Schiffen durch die stillen Räume,
> Wer erkennt im lauen Wind,
> Ob's Gedanken oder Träume?

Confusion is a necessary concomitant of the release of the 'eternal', 'unconscious' feelings which:

> Treten heimlich, groß und leise
> Aus der Wirrung fester Gleise,
> Aus der unbewachten Brust,
> In die stillen, weiten Kreise.[10]

That this has its dark side is well known to Eichendorff. Such a 'sweet enchantment' can constitute a 'net' in which 'the soul goes astray' (BG 1, 198: 'Das Frühlingsnetz'); 'die irren Lieder/Aus der alten schönen Zeit' form part of a dangerous 'Lockung' (BG 1, 98). The combination of a negative expression ('irr' and 'irren' almost always have this force for Eichendorff) with a positive motif here is a good illustration of the fact that the romantic sense of duality is present in Eichendorff too.

The motif of 'die alte schöne Zeit' is no doubt in part a reference to Eichendorff's own idyllic childhood days in Lubowitz. But it has a wider significance as well. Thoughts of the old days, the old garden, could certainly stimulate a nostalgic longing for a lost childhood (real or symbolic) which could only be regained by a denial of truth. 'Wir alle sind verirret,' Eichendorff says in 'Eldorado' (BG 1, 102). We cannot restore the situation by a simple unilateral declaration of independence[11] and there is no hope of a literal restoration of the

freedom and harmony of the 'old days'.[12] That is, as we hear in 'Der
Fremde', 'long since dead'. But in the *Gemüt*, it still lives a 'charmed'
life: *Soul, Mind, Heart, Feelings*

Kaiserkron' und Päonien rot,
Die müssen verzaubert sein,
Denn Vater und Mutter sind lange tot,
Was blühn sie hier so allein?

Der Springbrunn plaudert noch immerfort
Von der alten schönen Zeit,
Eine Frau sitzt eingeschlafen dort,
Ihre Locken bedecken ihr Kleid.

Sie hat eine Laute in der Hand,
Als ob sie im Schlafe spricht,
Mir ist, als hätt' ich sie sonst gekannt —
Still, geh' vorbei und weck sie nicht!

Und wenn es dunkelt das Tal entlang,
Streift sie die Saiten sacht,
Das gibt einen wunderbaren Klang
Durch den Garten die ganze Nacht (BG 1, 343).

In the story in which it first occurs (*Die Entführung*), this song
represents an awakening, and an attempt to regain lost innocence which
turns out to be abortive. Diana has immured herself in a life of wilful,
wild 'freedom' of a type which Eichendorff distrusts, as ballads like
'Die Räuberbrüder' and 'Die Brautfahrt' clearly show. She is inspired
by this song, which she hears as she looks at the neglected garden, to
attempt to return to natural simplicity ('ins Grüne', BG 2, 868–9), and
to invite her childhood friend Leontine, with whom she once played
there, to visit her. The impression made on her by Gaston has already
prepared the ground to some extent. But her attempt to respond to the
call and to return to a more natural path ends unhappily. Leontine, for
all her gentleness, is more free than she and has preserved the 'simplicity
in a pious heart' which gives the capacity *truly* to find 'the old garden'
(cf. 'An die Dichter', BG 1, 110).

Taken out of its context, this song is more ambivalent. The
activation, or re-activation of the spiritual world (or the level of
consciousness) symbolised by the charmed garden and the lady who

appears, at least, to be asleep, is seen to contain an element of risk (stanza 3). And yet it is the step into the romantic world, the world of beauty and wonder, and one has little doubt that Eichendorff feels that it must be taken. The subconscious level of the *Gemüt*, which can easily be seen as represented here by the flowing water of the fountain, is unpredictable in the state of freedom. But this is a call to a journey, just as much as are Eichendorff's many 'Wanderlieder', and in both cases it is a journey into the world of Romanticism which it is spiritual death to shun. Even a 'wild' freedom, like that of Diana, or Romana in *Ahnung und Gegenwart* who, in the song later known as 'Frische Fahrt', exclaims, 'ich mag mich nicht bewahren,' is a healthier reaction to the appeal to the subconscious – by Spring, in Romana's case – than is philistine caution. The risk has to be taken and the outcome can, in unhappy circumstances, be tragic, as it is in the case of Romana. But at least, she has not lived entirely without poetry, beauty and love.

The cause of failure in those who set out on the romantic journey – which is also a journey inwards, into the Self – is most often self-will, a failure to recognise that the Self cannot supersede God, but must be a vessel that He can fill. 'Ach Gott, führ uns liebreich zu dir!' Eichendorff exclaims at the end of 'Die zwei Gesellen',[13] aware that he too is unable to escape the confrontation with the 'waves of Spring' (BG 1, 64). Without an inner guide, the journey may well end in isolation and disorientation. Instead of the ideal we seek, we are likely to find nothing but – literally – ourselves, an unappetising double such as the one which confronts Romano in *Viel Lärmen um Nichts* (BG 2, 461). The solipsistic potential in the romantic outlook is a real threat and one to which Eichendorff, as a Romantic himself, is entitled to point, even if his judgements on some of his fellow Romantics are a little severe.

The journey can also, of course, end happily. The positive counterpart to Romano in *Viel Lärmen um Nichts* is Willibald, and the fact that he has a resoundingly Germanic name is no accident. Eichendorff's motifs often reflect this sense of a duality between a healthy Romanticism and one whose health is at least not secure. That of the 'Grund', for example, the hollow or valley-bottom, which usually suggests the inner recesses of mind and heart, can be positive or negative according to context. That of nationality normally resolves itself into a contrast between Italy and Germany. The former is colourful and exotic, but sultry and likely to present the unwary traveller with demonic temptations. Germany, with its forests, normally represents the spiritual health and simplicity which the Romantic

needs to have within him if he is to negotiate his perilous path
successfully. In Italy:

Da singt eine Fei auf blauem Meer,
Die Myrten trunken lauschen —
Mir aber gefällt doch nichts so sehr
Als das deutsche Waldesrauschen! (BG 1, 50: 'Rückkehr')

The positive figure in Eichendorff's work is, of course, the
'Taugenichts' of his best-known story; he too is a wanderer who enters
dangerous territory, but he carries, as it were, 'das deutsche Waldesrauschen' in his heart and thus is sure of a safe return. His 'Wanderlied',
the famous 'Wem Gott will rechte Gunst erweisen',[14] is a natural
complement to the more sombre 'Die zwei Gesellen'. It is more than a
simple hymn of praise to physical exercise or superficial 'enjoyment'
of the beauties of nature, worthy activities, but ones in which the
philistine can also indulge. Its relevance extends also to the housebound.
The real sin of those who 'stay at home' (stanza 2) is their moral and
spiritual inertia ('Trägheit'), their failure to respond to God's
revelation and to trust in Him. There is in Eichendorff's ideal of
romantic freedom an element of humility,[15] an acceptance of the
subordination of the individual to God, which not all Romantics have.
It is even possible to see this as a doctrine of the 'middle way':

Solange Recht regiert und schöne Sitte,
Du schlicht und gläubig gehst in sichrer Mitte. . .
Da trittst du siegreich zwischen Molch und Drachen. . .
                    (BG 1, 75: 'Memento')

We must not, however, confuse this kind of moderation with the
timidity of the 'Aufklärer' or the resignation of the 'Biedermeier'
writer. Simplicity and faith, indeed, are not characteristic features of
either of those generations. Eichendorff's ideal, the 'Einfalt gut in
frommen Herzen' of which he sings at the end of *Ahnung und
Gegenwart* (BG 1, 110: 'An die Dichter') is the sign of the spiritual
awareness of an age of faith and love and corresponds to the image of
the 'Vorzeit' in the sixth of Novalis's *Hymnen an die Nacht*. He knows,
as he says in the same poem, that the age of faith is past, 'the old glory
destroyed'. But that does not mean that these values have lost their
reality or relevance. What the poet presents, indeed, much more than
the most 'realistic' of practical thinkers, is 'des Lebens wahrhafte

Geschichte' (BG 1, 69: 'Nicht Träume sind's. . .').

The poem in which Eichendorff expresses his creed in its most satisfactory lyrical form is 'Abschied' (BG 1, 35–6). It is certainly a personal poem, in that it refers to the landscape of the poet's childhood, but its message is at the same time universal. The appeal of childhood and youth and of secluded and unspoiled nature in the early morning, important as these themes are in themselves, is here a stepping-stone to a higher theme which will remain after those other things have been left behind. It cannot be articulated – Eichendorff simply refers to 'ein stilles ernstes Wort' – and any attempt to do so must inevitably result in some lame generality. It is better to think in terms of a mental and spiritual state, the experience of a fundamental spiritual reality, which leaves behind a lasting conviction. This helps us to understand why this poem combines the serenity which is usual in Eichendorff with a more than ordinary solemnity. The consciousness of God which it contains is expressed without any of the 'mystische Überschwenglichkeit' which he criticised in some other Romantics.[16] It is the same consciousness as that which enabled him to write a sonnet-cycle on the death of his child (*Auf meines Kindes Tod*, BG 1, 256–61) whose tragic, yet assured simplicity amounts to grandeur. This is no formula for an escape into a world of pastoral prettiness, or the sham freedom of eternal studenthood. Like Willibald, Eichendorff has grasped and accepted the 'tragic seriousness' of life (cf. BG 2, 470). As various poems (such as 'Memento'), *Ahnung und Gegenwart* and *Der Adel und die Revolution*, as well as many letters show,[17] he was in fact anything but indifferent to the public issues and realities of his day. But there was no possibility that he could make common cause with the Young Germans, whom he saw as arrogant philistines, people who saw the lofty things in a materialistic, and therefore common ('gemein'), light and set themselves up, as a Golden Calf, as an object of worship.[18]

Technical mastery is the second pillar on which Eichendorff's magical simplicity rests. 'Was *wahr* in dir, wird sich gestalten,' he tells the poet in 'An die Dichter', but form is also important, indeed especially important in a poet like Eichendorff, whose aim is a direct simplicity, who eschews lexical, syntactical or philosophical complexity and sings 'aus frischer Brust' ('An die Dichter', BG 1, 111), and who operates with an arsenal of motifs which are not exotic or extraordinary and which recur frequently and almost predictably. Sensitivity and flexibility of rhythm and cunning orchestration of sound are very important for such a poet, and Eichendorff has these in full measure.

They all help in the all-important task of stimulating the activity of the deeper levels of the mind. The arrangement and treatment of the motifs often does even more. They are not striking in themselves, but are so interwoven with thoughts and emotions that they seem almost to arise out of the mind and to act as catalysts for its further activity. In 'An die Dichter', Eichendorff exhorts the poet to let his will be ruled by God and continues:

> Den Morgen seh' ich ferne scheinen,
> Die Ströme ziehn im grünen Grund,
> Mir ist so wohl! – Die's ehrlich meinen,
> Die grüß' ich all aus Herzensgrund! (BG 1, 112)

Even if we did not know from his general poetic practice that he associates the natural motifs mentioned here with positive, fresh spirituality, the context would force us to see them in that way. It is the interaction between reflection and a descriptive detail which deliberately avoids objective precision which we noticed earlier in this chapter in the case of 'Waldeinsamkeit'. It is a *quality* rather than a visual image that the motif of the rivers in the valley-bottom conveys, rather as happens in the opening lines of 'Das zerbrochene Ringlein':

> In einem kühlen Grunde,
> Da geht ein Mühlenrad. . . (BG 1, 346)

The dominant quality in both these cases is movement in stillness ('still' is an adjective often associated with 'Grund' in Eichendorff) and freshness: in the one poem a lateral movement leading away into the distance and suggesting the creative spirit at work in the soul, in the other a repeated circular one which sets the tone for the description of the disruption of the lover's inner peace.

Here, as in many other ways, Eichendorff shows what Stöcklein justifiably refers to as his 'musical instinct'.[19] It is not by profundity or originality of thought or boldness in imagery or linguistic usage that he impresses us, but by what does seem an instinctive feeling for the 'right' combination of simple elements; the one, that is, which will affect the *Gemüt* directly and draw from it an immediate response in which there is no trace of the conscious effort which, in their various ways, both Novalis and Brentano demand. If the instinct fails him, the result can be banal, even pawky, but when it functions efficiently, the experience which this poet affords us is, sad or joyful, one of fresh and spontaneous feeling. Eichendorff, rightly — that is, carefully and alertly — read, is a tonic, not a sedative.

Notes

1. Quoted in H. M. Enzensberger (ed.), *Clemens Brentano. Gedichte, Erzählungen, Briefe* (Frankfurt, 1958), p. 9.

2. Eichendorff, *Werke und Schriften*, G. Baumann and S. Grosse (eds.) (Stuttgart, 1957), vol. 1, p. 11. References are to this edition, cited as BG.

3. BG 2, p. 543. C. A. Tiedge (1752–1840), a popular poet of the period now languishing in deserved neglect, wrote mainly in elegiac and quasi-philosophical style and provided a diet much to the taste of the philistine: emotions and ideas reduced to a sweetened, mushy pap which could be taken by the unwary for a genuine poetic experience.

4. Cf. the passage in Goethe's *Die Leiden des jungen Werthers* (Bk. 1, letter dated 16 June) in which Lotte, watching the sun break through after a thunderstorm, is reminded of a passage in Klopstock's *Die Frühlingsfeier*, lays her hand on Werther's, and speaks the poet's name. Like Klopstock's before him, Goethe's sentiment released the sentimentality in others: 'Kaum war der Pistolenschuß verknallt', writes Eichendorff, 'womit sich Werther tötete, so überrieselte Lafontaine mit einer Tränenflut von Sentimentalität das ganze gerührte Deutschland' (*Novellen von Ernst Ritter*; BG 4, p. 897). August Lafontaine (1758–1831) was the 'master' of the popular sentimental novel and a *bête noire* of Eichendorff's.

5. Cf. P. Stöcklein, *Eichendorff* (Hamburg, 1963), pp. 130 ff.

6. Ibid., p. 91.

7. *Art of the Romantic Era* (London, 1966), p. 105. Richter's handling of romantic motifs is in general decorative rather than evocative, by contrast with that of Moritz von Schwind, who sometimes conveys a genuine sense of mystery.

8. The verb 'gehen', which Eichendorff not infrequently uses in contexts of this kind, gives an indeterminate quality to the movement involved. The plurality of the springs effects our sense of locality in the same way.

9. Oskar Seidlin, *Versuche über Eichendorff* (Göttingen, 1965), p. 55.

10. *Mittagsruh*, BG 1, p. 37; cf. *Der Abend*, ibid. The phenomenon of confusion is also explicitly treated in *Nachts* (BG 1, p. 12): 'O wunderbarer Nachtgesang. . . Wirrst die Gedanken mir. . .'

11. Cf. *Der irre Spielmann*: 'Seit ich da draußen so frei nun bin,/Find' ich nicht wieder nach Hause mich hin' (BG 1, p. 51).

12. W. Paulsen, in his study *Eichendorff und sein Taugenichts* (Berne–Munich, 1976), sees the poet as psychologically damaged, and his cultivation of childlike qualities as 'regressive' (pp. 35–40). As Paulsen admits, there is no documentary evidence on which we can base a precise judgement and the issue, in any case, is whether the message, rather than the man, is 'unhealthy'. Eichendorff seems to us to be quite sufficiently alert, as far as the obvious dangers of nostalgia are concerned.

13. Cf. also the endings of *In Danzig* and of *Die Nonne und der Ritter*.

14. In BG 1, p. 10, as *Der frohe Wandersmann*. Cf. also *Allgemeines Wandern, Der wandernde Student*, the cycle *Der wandernde Musikant*, etc.

15. Specifically expressed in the song of the 'Taugenichts'. Cf. also the second of Eichendorff's sonnets on the calling of the poet: 'O Herr, gib Demut denen, die da irren' (BG 1, p. 68).

16. Cf. *Geschichte der poetischen Literatur Deutschlands*, BG 4, p. 419.

17. A. Hillach insists, somewhat heavily but not entirely without justification, on the relevance to contemporary reality of all Eichendorff's works, the *Taugenichts* included (A. Hillach, *Eichendorff-Kommentar*) (Munich, 1971), vol. 1, 'Einführung'.

18. *Der deutsche Roman*, BG 4, p. 858.

19. Stöcklein, *Eichendorff*, p. 86.

8 ROMANTIC DRAMA (GENERAL)

Serious Drama

We saw in Chapter 3 that, however unsuited by talent and temperament the Romantics may have been to the dramatic form, they had a great interest in and respect for it. Coming to it partly from philosophical abstraction, partly under the inspiring influence of Shakespeare and Calderón — as *they* understood them — and partly impelled by a feeling for theatre as such (including its operatic aspects), they were able to conceive of a drama which would afford the opportunity for a realisation of the romantic vision more complete than the other genres could offer. Schelling and Hegel were able to see in the dramatic form, and particularly in tragedy, a complete embodiment of their abstract schemes. The interaction (or 'dialectic') of subjective and objective, ideal and real, and the resolution of this duality in a transcending unity are expressed in the dramatic conflict and its ending in eventual 'reconciliation'. More practically poetic minds (e.g. Tieck), influenced by the loosening of structure and mixture of forms and moods introduced by Shakespeare, conceived the possibility of realising the emotional and mystical romantic experience of the infinite variety and universal unity of the world. The little room of the stage could encompass infinite riches: vast tracts of time and space and the whole gamut of artistic expression, including music, song and spectacle.

It is still possible to distinguish comedy as a genre within romantic drama, but the designation 'tragedy' is more problematic in this context. The Romantics were not devoid of a sense of tragedy but (with the exception of Werner) they tended to express it better in epic than in dramatic form. The plays with which we shall be dealing in this section are sometimes — as in the case of Tieck's *Genoveva* — designated as tragedies by their authors, but the potentially tragic characters and situations too often take second place to other, serious, but non-tragic preoccupations. The real is too thoroughly dominated by the ideal. A case in point is the figure of Golo in Tieck's play which, had it been developed (as it was later to be by Hebbel), could have made the work tragic in a real sense.

The predecessors, contemporaries and successors of the Romantics all accepted that drama, as the presentation of a chain of events through dialogue and action, is more firmly tied than lyric or epic to the sphere of 'external' public and practical human behaviour. To romanticise it, that is to employ it as a vehicle for the idealist mentality, dominated by fancy and 'love', would have demanded a dramatic and theatrical genius of at least Shakespearian proportions. While some of his later plays, such as *The Tempest*, show a tendency in this direction, Shakespeare himself had not written plays of a purely romantic type and it is very doubtful whether he would have considered attempting the undertaking. Indeed, it could even be argued that the relative unsuitability of the dramatic form for the task of giving expression to the romantic spirit is implicit in Friedrich Schlegel's own definition, in the essay 'Literatur', of the purpose of poetry and its relation to the dramatic and epic genres. Having stated, not surprisingly, that idealism is a *sine qua non*, he goes on to distinguish between drama as 'exoteric' (i.e. presenting the ideal of beauty 'in dem Verhältnisse des menschlichen Lebens') and epic as 'esoteric' (the vehicle of that poetry which 'transcends the human sphere and strives to encompass nature').[1] This would lead one to expect that the epic mode would be the one most congenial to the romantic mentality. We shall see in due course that the Romantics are indeed more successful as epic than as dramatic writers and Schleiermacher does actually say: 'Wir sollten eigentlich gar keine Dramen machen, es werden doch alle romantisch,'[2] using the word 'romantisch' in this case in its older meaning of 'like a novel'.

Nevertheless, romantic dramas continued to be written and their most striking common factor is the attempt to achieve inwardness and transcendence in a form which still operates through the presentation of human beings in the external relationships of practical life. Whether the authors concerned would admit it or not, we are faced in the majority of cases with the use of dramatic form for undramatic purposes.

The romantic dramatist is usually on the look-out for ways of escaping from the tight net of the 'Verhältnis des menschlichen Lebens'. His tendency, therefore, is to give relatively little attention to specific characterisation, to the creation of tension in a close-knit action, or to a truly dramatic dialogue arising out of and furthering such an action. The common tendency of his most characteristic technical practices could be defined as that of loosening the framework imposed by the practical relationships between his characters, or making it transparent, so that a wider spiritual dimension is revealed. Such tendencies include deliberate mixture (e.g. of comic and tragic, of prose and a wide variety of verse forms), blurring of the sense of time and space and an epic rather than a dramatic attitude to the presentation of the plot.

Some romantic plays seem closer, structurally, to the medieval chronicle or to the picaresque novel[3] than to conventional drama.

Tieck, the Founding Father here as in several other spheres, is quite frank as to his intentions. In the Preface to Volume One of his *Schriften*,[4] he states that in his *Genoveva*, he has deliberately distanced himself from the traditional theatre and its forms:

> um größern Raum zu gewinnen, um einige Stellen ganz musikalisch, andere ganz malerisch behandeln zu können. . . und das Ganze durch Prolog und Epilog in einem poetischen Rahmen traumähnlich festgehalten und auch wieder verflüchtiget. . . auf keine andere Wahrheit, als die poetische, durch die Phantasie gerechtfertigte, Anspruch zu machen.

In a similar spirit, he praises Kleist for the way in which in *Das Käthchen von Heilbronn* — which Tieck, characteristically, sees as a 'Volkssage' — he employs a deliberately loose structural technique:

> Diese leichtere Art, welche Episoden zuläßt. . . Begebenheiten anreiht, die den Anschein des Zufälligen haben, verstattet dadurch einen Durchblick in die große, freie Natur.[5]

'Nature' represents here, as it often does for Tieck, the transcendental dimension, the 'All' or Infinite which is the constant ultimate goal of romantic poetry. It is because Shakespeare creates in him the state of mind in which he can experience 'nature', that which allows a man to transcend his individual self and find the 'spirit which speaks out of everything'[6] that Tieck valued him so highly and wrote about him at such length.

Serious romantic drama, then, has the tendency to focus on the infinite, to present the root of all being rather than the specific, finite human being. Its outcome is not the 'equilibrium' between the desires and interests of finite and infinite of which Schelling speaks,[7] but the assimilation of the one into the other. It is often overtly religious and if not that, shows a tendency in that direction. In view of this, the pre-eminent position accorded to Calderón by so many romantic writers on the theatre is hardly surprising. Schelling praises him for having reached the transcendental plane[8] and Friedrich Schlegel bases on him his conception of the ultimate romantic drama, the 'highest' type, which not only presents the mystery of existence, but provides a solution to it.[9] The triumph of spirit over matter (as redemption, the purification of human love, martyrdom, or in some other form) is the constant real theme of serious romantic drama and the true protagonists are the universal spiritual principles of good and evil. Arnim, indeed, even goes so far as to show, in one scene in *Halle und Jerusalem*, the crucified Christ and to quote some of the Words from the Cross (DL 21, p. 199). There *is* conflict of a kind, the same conflict as that waged in Medardus in Hoffmann's *Die Elixiere des Teufels*, but it is not easy to imagine how it could have been successfully portrayed on a stage.

Tieck does make some attempt at a portrayal of such a struggle in the most poetically successful of his serious dramas, the full title of which is *Leben und Tod der Heiligen Genoveva* (1799). St Boniface, who appears both as Prologue and as commentator-narrator, characterises it as 'Kunde aus der alten Zeit',[10] which is true, not only in the sense that it is set in the Middle Ages, but also in the symbolic sense in which we have already seen the motif of the 'old days' used by Eichendorff, representing a state of childlike faith and strong spirituality of outlook. The interplay of naïve subject-matter and complex modern sensibility which we saw in Eichendorff's 'Kaiserkron' song[11] is present here too. The essential story and its plain manner of narration and flat, two-dimensional characterisation recall the old chap-book on which this play is based. The author's manipulation and variation of poetic forms, on the other hand, together with his ability to evoke and analyse mood, add a modern romantic sophistication.

The story of the pure and pious woman who, when left by her husband in the care of his favourite Golo (who is not without attractiveness but cannot control his passions), resists both temptation and terror, is cast out and miraculously preserved to be vindicated before she dies, is told straightforwardly and with the clear intention of glorifying beauty, above all spiritual beauty. Tieck sees the world as a labyrinth full of delights and possible fulfilments for the human spirit, but also as a testing-ground in which each delight is also a danger. The danger consists essentially in the possibility of the entrapment of the individual in his own selfhood, with the consequent loss of his soul, his higher spiritual self. He has no great hope of emerging unscathed from the labyrinth unless his own inner vigilance is supplemented by divine grace. As Genoveva puts it:

Verworren wandern wir in bunten Reihen,
Und Tod und Unglück gehn durch uns dahin,

Wen du [i.e. God] mit deiner Milde willst erfreuen,
Der findet im Verderben den Gewinn (*Werke* 2, 389).

Tieck is not a great enough poet, nor is his religious feeling deep and
rich enough to enable him to realise this conception with complete
conviction. He comes nearest to success, from the dramatic point of
view, in the character of Golo, the tempter and tyrant, almost destined
from birth (like Hoffmann's Cardillac) to end in evil and driven to
destruction by an inner demon he can find no way to control, much
as he longs for the wisdom and strength to do so. Spurning the only
source of those qualities, the piety of Genoveva and Drago, he becomes
all the more inwardly torn, and therefore psychologically interesting.
Individual lines and passages show considerable sensitivity to the
complexities of the inner processes of the *Gemüt*, but, as in the lyrics,
Tieck's imaginative and poetic stamina is not sufficient to carry him
far without a lapse into rather banal images and metaphors:

O wie in mir Gedank' Gedanken drängen,
Wie's musiziert in mir mit tausend wechselnden Klängen!
Was kann ich, was soll ich beginnen?
Wohin, ihr rasenden Sinnen?
Wie von wilden Pferden fühl ich mich fortgerissen,
Die Erinnrung umgeschmissen,
Der taube Fuhrmann Vernunft im Hohlweg liegend (p. 440: Golo).

Tieck's most effective presentation of the romantic spirit in this
play occurs, not in his portrayals of Genoveva's spiritual beauty or of
the colourful and heroic world of chivalry,[12] but in the love episodes,
above all the scene in the moonlit garden. This has a sustained
sensitivity and poetic power such as one rarely finds otherwise in Tieck
outside the field of the novel and Novelle. There is a skilful mixture of
poetic forms, including a song which would not have disgraced
Eichendorff, and while the balcony scene probably owes its inspiration
to Shakespeare's *Romeo and Juliet*, its execution gives evidence of real
poetic power:

Genoveva   Wie still die Nacht des Tages Hitze kühlt,
(on the balcony). Wie sanft der Mondschein auf dem Grase spielt,
                 Wie süß das Herz sich nun beruhigt fühlt. . .

Golo   Sie schimmert wie ein neuer Sternenhimmel,
(below).   Ein neuer Mond ist sie emporgestiegen . . .
               Wie kann Natur so holde Schönheit zeugen,
               Sich selber durch die Schönheit zu beschämen,
               Sie muß sich vor dem eignen Werke neigen,
               Dies Wunder muß die innern Kräfte lähmen
                                      (p. 410).

This episode really does succeed in bringing to life the 'wundervolle Märchenwelt' which Tieck invokes in the Prologue to *Kaiser Oktavianus* (1804). In the latter play, the attempt to paint a romantic picture does not enjoy even the qualified success of *Genoveva*. Tieck's ambition, no less than a resuscitation of the whole world of medieval chivalry, outstrips his dramatic talent and the wide variety of national and social types and of animated and often exotic action, presented within an unmanageably wide spatial and temporal framework, ends in a bewildering, rather than inspiring, confusion. The basic plot, the story of Felicitas, Octavianus's wife, falsely accused and cast out, to be reunited with her husband twenty-one years later in an operatic reconciliation scene, is treated in a more outspokenly epic way than was the case in *Genoveva*. All this makes it more romantic in conception, but less effective as drama: its general effect is that of a megalomaniac *Märchen*. Tieck's other major drama, the two-part *Fortunat* (1815–16), is more urban and everyday in its settings and plot than the other two, but does not represent a radical departure from Romanticism. Its structure is still loose and episodic and the view of life which it conveys is still one in which human reason is unable to understand and control 'dieses bunte höchst verworrene Leben' (*Werke* 2, 773).

Of the other Romantics (excluding Werner) who tried their hand at this kind of drama, only *Achim von Arnim* enjoyed any measure of success. He, like Tieck, did his best things in the epic genres, but was better able than lyricists like Brentano and Eichendorff[13] to shape a romantic experience into at least a viable dramatic form. He composed a number of dramatic works of some merit, chief among them being *Der Auerhahn* and *Die Appelmänner* (1813) and the best-known, *Halle und Jerusalem* (1811) a two-part work consisting of a 'Studentenspiel' and a 'Pilgerabenteuer', the whole being designated in the idiosyncratic manner typical of Arnim as a 'Trauerspiel in zwei Lustspielen'. It grew

out of an adaptation of a drama by the seventeenth-century author
Andreas Gryphius, *Cardenio und Celinde*, which shows chaste and
carnal love in a conflict in which the former eventually triumphs, after
Cardenio has been brought to see the sinfulness of his ways and to
repent. Arnim keeps this basic structure, but makes it much looser. An
infinitely greater variety of characters, episodes and milieux is
introduced and the stately and statuesque baroque verse gives way to a
mixture of forms and a more psychologically expressive language.

The theme, too, is widened. Cardenio, the loss of whose beloved
Olympie 'has torn [his] existence out at the roots and cast it into the
river' (cf. DL 21, p. 113), has surrendered himself to the Devil (p. 88).
The Jew Ahasuerus,[14] who accompanies Cardenio through the action
like a benevolent shadow, knows that the enemy, the 'feurig wilde[r]
Drache der Eigenheit' (p. 115) can be overcome and redemption gained
in the purification of Cardenio's love, through a pilgrimage to the Holy
Sepulchre. The Jew is in fact Cardenio's father, who begat him in
sinful lust and therefore hopes to find his own redemption in this
process. The whole is a grandiose conception with an element of myth
which makes it all the more romantic and Arnim manages to endow it
with a sufficient amount of the energy which flows from romantic
fancy and 'love' to keep at least one reader's interest alive. His
imagination is, as ever, fertile and provides a succession of scenes with
an intrinsic romantic interest — student life in Halle, popular festivals,
a storm at sea, a siege, a pasha outwitted by his wives in his own harem,
a camel which puts its head through a hole in the wall and bites the
freethinker Bromley from behind — and ensures that that romantic
interest is brought out for the audience. This is not enough to save the
play as a stage drama, but it makes it at least a tolerable 'Lesedrama'.

Zacharias Werner is unique among the writers treated in this chapter in
that his imagination works in a truly dramatic way. Dialogue, for him,
really is a matter of communication and interaction between characters,
scenes follow one another in an effective sequence and many of them
are theatrically powerful. Poetically, Werner's verse remains behind
that of Tieck and his attempts at lyricism fall short of the standard
reached even by the merely competent Arnim. He is, on the other
hand, much more successful than they in the handling of blank verse
as a dramatic medium. *Das Kreuz an der Ostsee* (1806), for example,
contains many lines which would not look out of place in a 'Classical'
drama by Schiller, as for instance when Conrad von Landsberg remarks:

'Der Plätze gibt es viel, der Stunden wenig' (DL 20, p. 115), or
Agaphia: 'Der Zeiten Ernst erfordert ernste Tat' (p. 133). There is a
dramatic urgency and tension in lines like these.

The comparison with Schiller is not fortuitous. Werner had a high
opinion of Schiller's dramas and had to some extent modelled himself
on him, though he felt that the Schillerian form was on the whole too
restrictive for his vision. Even *Die Jungfrau von Orleans* was for him
only a *potentially* romantic play. His feeling demanded a more
positively religious orientation and a more active role for the supernatural. Had the Black Knight in the Schillerian tragedy been invested
with a really spectral aura, he would have constituted a disruptive
element in the play as it stands. The figure of the Minstrel in *Das
Kreuz an der Ostsee*, on the other hand, has to be seen as the
reincarnation of the martyred Christian missionary Adalbert, and
Werner does all he can to invest him with the appropriate qualities of
sanctity and mystery.

The battle between the forces of God and of Satan is a constant
theme in Werner's drama. With the exception of the martyr-drama
Die Mutter der Makkabäer (1816, published 1820), all his plays belong
to the period preceding his definitive conversion to Catholicism, a
period of strong and rather strained emotionalism in which a deep, but
theologically indeterminate, religious feeling played an important role.
The general tendency is anti-rationalistic and the dominant theme is
that of the opposition and interplay of the sensual and spiritual,
particularly in human love. In both his thinking and his writing, the
idea of 'purification', and of a love in which consummation consists in
the immolation of the body on the altar of spirit, is a central preoccupation. Deprivation and above all death become supreme
experiences for him and are presented in an atmosphere so thoroughly
compounded of pain and almost voluptuous ecstasy that one begins to
have doubts about the quality of his spirituality. It is true that he is not
the only Romantic to experience this mingling of the spiritual and
sensual — one thinks, for example, of Novalis and Brentano — and that
religious feeling is not necessarily invalidated in such circumstances.
But calm and control ('Besonnenheit' yet again!) are essential in this
situation if romantic exaltation is not to degenerate into a pathological
state and there are moments in Werner when we feel the control to be
wavering, at least.

Anything approaching a complete and detailed account of Werner's
oeuvre would require far more space than we can possibly allot him in
a book of this kind.[15] In addition to the plays already mentioned, it

includes *Die Söhne des Tals* (1803—4), which uses the story of the end
of the Order of the Templars to preach the gospel of 'purified
Catholicism' and culminates in the martyrdom of their leader, who is
eager to be united with the infinite through 'die herrliche Verwesung',
a phrase which contains an indication of the overheated nature of
Werner's spirituality. Then come *Martin Luther – oder die Weihe der
Kraft* (1806), *Attila, König der Hunnen* (1808), *Der 24. Februar*
(1809), *Wanda, Königin der Sarmaten* (1810) and *Cunegunde die
Heilige* (written 1808—9, published 1815). We shall be discussing two
examples of Werner's work in some detail below. Of the others, *Martin
Luther* created a considerable stir in its day and it certainly has the
colour and the theatrically effective scenes which one expects from
Werner but it suffers, as Kluckhohn says, from an inner disunity in that
the 'Weihe' of the love action is not satisfactorily integrated with the
theme of 'Kraft' (Luther's mission as the prophet of 'purified
Catholicism'). *Der 24. Februar* is a one-act play, a *tour de force* of
tight-knit construction which Werner produced in response to a
challenge from Goethe to write a truly 'concentrated' piece. It founded
a minor genre, the so-called 'fate-tragedy', whose standard pattern is
the working out of a curse, or prophecy of doom, in a more or less
melodramatic manner. Werner's play concerns the fulfilment of a
family curse when a father murders for gain a traveller who has taken
shelter under his roof on a date of fatal significance for the family. The
traveller turns out, not entirely surprisingly, to be his son, whom he
has not seen for fourteen years. In terms of dramatic technique, this is
a work of Spartan plainness; its romantic nature consists in the truly
powerful atmosphere which it possesses. A sense of Fate hangs over it
like a black cloud. It did not, however, found a tradition of any
distinction. Limitation of this kind was clearly uncongenial to Werner,
and his imitators, like Müllner and Houwald, lacked his talent.[16]

  Das Kreuz an der Ostsee is constructed round the conflict between
Christianity and paganism in which spirituality, represented by the
former, was eventually to emerge triumphant. Only the first part (*Die
Brautnacht*) of the two-part conception was in fact executed, but the
general outline is clear from this. The theme is treated both at the
general ideological level and in a personal relationship, the love between
the Christian girl Malgona and the formerly pagan Prussian Warmio.
The problem of integrating the general and the individual levels is more
successfully handled here than in *Martin Luther*, at least as far as the
dramatic effectiveness of the action is concerned. It is certainly a
romantic action, full of colour and incident, the central thread

consisting of an attack by the Prussians on the combined Christian forces of Poles and German knights. The pagans are driven off, but Warmio and Malgona are captured and taken away. In the Second Part, they would have suffered a sacrificial martyrdom which would have crowned not only their love (in which the spirit has already conquered the body in *Die Brautnacht*[17]) but also the victory of Christianity. There is an effective mixture of scenes of great animation and excitement with quieter ones of discussion and contemplation. Werner shows a commendable interest in and knowledge of folk history and folklore and an ability to put it to good dramatic use, particularly in the 'Dorotka' scene (Act III sc. 2) and his penchant for, and skill in, obtaining spectacular stage effects is demonstrated in a number of cases. Act III, sc. 1 is probably the best example. The Christians are under siege from the Prussians and a service of prayer for deliverance is being said in a chapel, visible through open double doors at the back of the stage. On the right, steps lead up to a watchtower, from which the battle is being observed. On the main stage, Malgona is first persuaded to leave the castle, whereupon her mother, Agaphia and other inmates of the fortress go through agonies of despair, shortly to be followed by transports of ecstatic relief.

The stage, then, is well and truly 'set'. Sound-effects also play their part, for the wild martial music which filled the interval between Acts II and III still resounds in snatches during this scene. To this are added a tolling bell, occasional blasts from the warriors' horns and muffled shouting from the attacking Prussians. Werner has equipped himself with an almost daunting range of theatrical resources and he makes full use of them:

Einige Polen. Der Feind ist auch am Wassertor!
Agaphia. Auch das!

(*Mit Ruhe*)
So sterben wir!
(*Sinkt langsam auf die Knie und betet in stiller Ergebung*)
Hereindringende Weiber
mit Kindern. Hülf — Rettung!
Die Priester (aufschreiend). Kyrie eleison!
Weiber. O unsre armen Kinder — weh! — die Teufel
Erwürgen sie!
Priester (aufschreiend). Kyrie eleison!
Wächters Stimme (von oben). Wehe!
Ein Feuerglanz! — die Burg brennt!

> *Die Priester (Mit stärkster Erhebung der Stimme*
> *Zugleich   schreiend)*. Ex profundis!
> *Das Volk (verzweiflungsvoll auf die Knie stürzend)*.
>   Mutter Gottes!
> *Einzelne Stimmen.*   O Heiland!
> *Priester (jammernd durcheinanderschreiend)*. Miserere, Kyrie!
>   (p. 177)

This is a theatrically powerful, if operatic and rather unsubtle, conception, but one feels some sympathy for the director and the actors who might be required to put it into effect.

Werner's treatment of his grandiose themes and high passions does in fact have a coarse-grained quality which, after the initial impact of his colourful and stagey plays has faded, leaves us with a feeling of dissatisfaction. The poetic garb is inadequate and the ideas too incompletely worked out to carry conviction. This applies particularly to Werner's all-important doctrine of love. It is in *Wanda* that he makes his most thoroughgoing attempt to build a tragedy around a love relationship. Wanda and Rüdiger, having fallen in love at the court of the prophetess-queen Libussa and been parted, meet again, but as the leaders of opposing armies. Only death can resolve the dichotomy of love for them and in a somewhat sultry scene at the end of Act IV, Wanda, having received guidance from the ghost of Libussa (appearing 'in einem stark erleuchteten Gewölke'), kills Rüdiger. She joins him in death in the following act in a spectacular self-immolation which must constitute the most blatantly operatic of all Werner's endings.

The intense dramatic conflict is typical of Werner, as are the link between love and death and the language in which the characters speak and in which he speaks of them, trembling as it does on the brink between passionate power and comic extravagance. Wanda's face is covered by 'ein[em] Strom ihr gewaltsam entquellender *süßer* Zähren' (my emphasis) and she describes herself in these terms: 'Ich Unglückseligste von allen Und doch allmächtig, schwelgend in Genuß' (p. 260). This is no doubt the 'Macht und Pracht der Qual' which Libussa, in sybilline verses, has said it is the lovers' destiny to make manifest to the world (p. 253). The fact that when Wanda has done the deed, the whole group on the stage is enveloped in a roseate haze emanating from the ghost of Libussa seems to symbolise the less than first-rate quality of thought and feeling which Werner brings to his themes. In the last analysis, competence in dramatic technique is not enough. He is an excellent showman and this helps to explain why he was highly esteemed at a time when Kleist was neglected. But the inadequacy of his powers of thought and of his poetic imagination to the task of realising the ambitious projects which he sets himself always makes itself felt sooner or later.

Comedy

The difficulty which plagued many an eighteenth-century writer of, or theorist on, comedy was the need to find a justification for the degree of relaxation which the genre brings with it: relaxation, that is, of the effort of concentrating on the serious aspects of life. This search for justification, which one meets primarily in the literary theory of the 'Aufklärung', even in Lessing,[18] is a reflection of the fact that the basic capacity for relaxation was defective, or inhibited. Even those two eighteenth-century writers who were most capable of the detached and (in a true sense) ironic frame of mind, Wieland and Goethe, cannot be said truly to have emancipated humour. The Romantics could, and did. In their theory and practice of comedy, those qualities which make for relaxation are the ones which receive most prominence. This does not mean, of course, that serious matters disappear from the scene entirely. Satire (directed in particular against the residual 'Aufklärung') still plays a part, and serious romantic ideals, above all that of love, can be brought to the reader's or spectator's attention. The difference lies in the atmosphere within which all this occurs. In romantic comedy, it is an atmosphere in which logical reason is no longer king; one more akin to the carnival spirit of fantasy and freedom. It is the atmosphere which Tieck tries to define (apropos of *Der gestiefelte Kater*) in the *Phantasus*-framework, in the phrase 'ganz Schaum und leichter Scherz'[19] and which was to be brilliantly realised in epic form by Hoffmann.[20]

The Romantics consistently aim, in comedy, to set the comic element free from restraint by didactic, or other considerations. Eichendorff considers that comedy should aim to produce a state of emancipation from the practical cares of the everyday world. The purpose of 'Lustspiel', he says, is 'eben nichts anderes, als die Lustigkeit'.[21] Shakespeare, naturally, was one model in this field but another, and more important, one was Aristophanes, in whom the Romantics found demonstrated all the qualities they valued most highly in this genre. Eichendorff describes him as soaring clear of all that is philistine by virtue of his 'fancy, wit and invention',[22] Friedrich Schlegel emphasises his 'schöne Fröhlichkeit' and 'erhabene Freiheit'[23]

and Tieck his capacity for 'true irony'.[24] The true sense of the comic,
which it is the task of the Romantics to restore, resides, for Brentano,
in the ability to detach oneself from, and 'play' with, reality.[25] Only
spiritual freedom can give this ability, and its restoration is therefore
also a step on the road to the restoration of spiritual freedom. Even in
those moments in eighteenth-century drama in which one feels that
humour is genuinely free — in some comic episodes in Lenz's *Der
Hofmeister*, for example, or in some of Goethe's 'Sturm und Drang'
squibs — it is still relatively earthbound. Romantic comedy on the
other hand aims at a genuinely fantastic effect and sets out to produce
a radical alienation of its events and characters from the plane of
everyday reality.[26] Even in a play like Eichendorff's *Die Freier* (1833),
where nothing impossible occurs, the complexities of the intrigue,
disguises and counter-disguises, the use of poetry and a general mood
of inconsequentiality produce an anti-realistic effect similar to that of
the *Taugenichts*. It is in the latter work, of course, that Eichendorff's
humorous vision achieves its truly representative expression: *Die Freier*
is not without charm, but by comparison, it is only a soap-bubble.

This leads us to our final introductory point: the relatively
unsuitable nature of dramatic form to the German romantic genius is
demonstrated by the example of comedy, just as it was in the case of
serious drama. The dramatist detaches himself from reality at his peril.
There may be some truth in Tieck's assertion that Shakespeare at times
shows an awareness of the 'odd' and 'artificial' nature of the process of
showing life proceeding on a stage,[27] in other words, that traces of
something analogous to romantic 'irony' can be detected in him.
Nowhere, however, does he strip material reality of all solidity,
probability and individual colour to the same extent as do the German
Romantics. The radical nature of the cult of the *Gemüt* in which the
latter indulge, and which enables them to excel in some fields, acts as
a barrier to achievement here. Humour does not flourish best in a
vacuum. Musset and Gogol (in *The Inspector-General*) prove that
romantic comedy of high quality is not an impossibility: the Germans
have nothing to compare with these.[28] Their comic sense, like the tragic,
finds a much more satisfactory expression in the epic than in the
dramatic genres; *Des Lebens Überfluß* is a much more successful comic
work than *Der gestiefelte Kater*, Arnim's *Das Loch* (1813) seems slight
beside the imaginative hilarity of *Die Ehenschmiede*, and even the most
satisfactory of all the German romantic comedies, Brentano's *Ponce de
Leon*, makes more demands on our tolerance than do his comic
Märchen.

Once again, we have to turn first to *Tieck*. He wrote three major pieces which are comic in tone and intention in the terms of our definition: *Der gestiefelte Kater* (1797), *Prinz Zerbino oder die Reise nach dem guten Geschmack* (1799) and *Die verkehrte Welt* (1799). In all of these, the same basic approach is adopted. Seriousness is stood on its head and irony reigns supreme. Plot and character matter very little; the important thing is that fancy should be free to assert itself at the expense of philistinism. As often happens when a formula is used more than once, the first occasion is the most successful. In the other two, we become aware from time to time of the exaggeration and heaviness of touch which usually accompany the attempt to repeat a former triumph.

Der gestiefelte Kater does tell the Puss-in-Boots story reasonably faithfully, but with the one major twist that the ogre who is eventually eaten, in the shape of a mouse, by the resourceful feline hero, becomes an allegory of the principle of Law. This represents a fitting integration of the play's deeper theme with its ostensible one. For the point of departure is the infringement of the law which, for all the relative flexibility which had been introduced by the pre-romantic phase, still stood in its essentials when the romantic generation appeared, namely the law which demanded that the dramatic illusion, even though we may be well aware that it is a convention,[29] should not be broken. A theatre which positively flaunts its consciousness of its own theatricality, as is the case in this play and in its successors, is a more iconoclastic departure than anything which the 'Stürmer und Dränger', with all their disrespect for enlightened rationalism, ever dreamed of.

Formally, this is a play about the *production* of a play called 'Puss-in-Boots'. The cast includes a prompter, stage-manager, actors (in both their mimic and their real capacities), the author and, most important of all, the public, which in the Prologue is seen discussing the play before the curtain rises and in the Epilogue pelts the author with rotten fruit. During the performance-within-a-performance, both during the Puss-in-Boots action and in the interludes (the *real* action), there are many comments and interjections from the public and exchanges between the various members of the central triangle formed by the public, actors and author.

There is certainly satire directed against specific figures of the current literary scene but the main target is the spirit of the Aufklärung' in general, conceived as an amalgam of common-sense rationalism and sentimentality. The play is a 'Publikumsbeschimpfung'

by the witty and for the witty. Its satirical *reductio ad absurdum* of
rationalism (one member of the 'public' even proposes that, since a
certain character is a foreigner, he should speak through an interpreter!)
is simultaneously an assertion of romantic freedom. There is a romantic
method in the play's 'madness', for only by losing one's (lower, merely
logical) reason can a man find the higher, romantic one. When the
philistine Fischer, in an interjection during the Puss-in-Boots action,
complains at the fact that the difference between fairy-tale and real
life should be pointed out by a talking cat, and adds: 'ich fürchte toll
zu werden' (DL 9, p. 31), we can appreciate a double irony.

This integration of satirical purpose with the broader romantic ethos
does much to ensure that the former shall not cloud the serene tone of
free humour which is the romantic ideal. There are in addition many
good ideas and inventions of a purely comic nature or, at least, moments
in which one is more conscious of comic than of serious satirical intent.
Thus at an inn just outside the border of the small state in which the
fairy-tale action occurs, a deserter holds the horses of the hussars who
have been pursuing him. 'Sprecht mir doch wieder zu, wenn ihr
wieder desertiert,' urges the landlord, when the deserter sets off to
re-enlist (p. 29). Certainly, we are expected to think of the peculiar
political constitution of the Holy Roman Empire, but it is enjoyment
of its crazy fragmentation rather than a serious satirical message that
Tieck conveys to us. This graceful, gay and inconsequential mood is
maintained throughout, but one becomes conscious eventually that it
has been bought at the price of loss of contact with life as a whole.
The texture is too thin and one begins to long for more substantial
fare. Man cannot live on *hors d'œuvres* alone.

Tieck's only serious rival in this field is *Brentano*, whose *Ponce de
Leon* (1801), while it is no masterpiece, is a work of merit. Heine, as we
saw,[30] did not have a high opinion of it. We can certainly concur in the
judgement that its construction leaves something to be desired. In
addition, it has to be said that it is slow-moving and over-long and that
Brentano's fondness for purely verbal humour, though it does
occasionally produce a kind of poetry of wit, can often be tiresome.
We can understand why it failed to find favour in Goethe's sight when it
was originally submitted as an entry for a prize competition announced
in the *Propyläen* in 1800. Nevertheless, the dismissive judgements on it
which were voiced throughout the nineteenth century and can still be
heard today are not entirely fair. With all its technical faults, it
succeeds in uniting the romantic freedom of the fantasy with an
equally romantic *substance*, which is provided by its treatment of the

theme of love. This is more than simply a motor to turn the wheels of
the plot. The Romantics, as we know, saw love as the primary
spiritual energy which gives direction and purpose to life and it is
this which Ponce finds, not merely a congenial partner with whom he
can leave the stage arm in arm at the close. Love is not shown here, of
course, in its most intense, mystical form, but as a creative, sunny and
reconciling spirit. Like the 'sunshine and happy wine' mentioned in the
Epilogue (line 53), it draws music from the 'hard rock of the heart'.[31]

Ponce, a young Spanish nobleman, is a character in search of a
character. He lives idly and capriciously, 'ein wunderlicher, wetter-
wendischer Kerl, der alle Leute unterhält und immer lange Weile hat',
as Valerio describes him (K 4, 149). Sarmiento, the *raisonneur* and
puppet-master (perhaps the Sarastro?) of the play, correctly diagnoses
Ponce's *ennui* as a sign of positive spiritual potential in him, to which
true love can give shape and direction. Ponce has engaged himself in an
affair with Valerio's daughter, Valeria, but cannot respond to her
devotion. He is taken with an ideal vision of Isidora, one of Sarmiento's
daughters, of whom her brother Felix has talked to him. Sarmiento
devises a means of resolving the amorous tangles in which his children
are involved by arranging that the whole group shall come together at
his country house. Felix 'elopes' with his beloved Lucilla (a scheme
devised by Sarmiento to test him) and Isidora and her sister Melanie
are provided for through Ponce and his friend Aquilar. Eventually,
though only after misunderstandings and heart-searchings, the couples
emerge in the correct configuration and Valeria, who has sublimated
her unrequited love in selflessness, is left free to accept the devotion of
Sarmiento's other son, Porporino.

This summary does not begin to do justice to the intricacy and
variety of the intrigue but it can at least serve to indicate that fancy
and not reason is the spirit which presides over this comedy. The spirit
of play is everywhere at work, in the inventive wit of the dialogue and
in comic inventions such as the scene (Act II sc. 22) in which Ponce
'dictates' a portrait to Porporino, who is masquerading at that point as
a painter. The masquerade motif is in fact a dominant one in the action,
from the *bal masqué* which is the central event of the first act to the
convoluted action of the last three, in Sarmiento's country residence.
Without translating us into a sphere of overt unreality, as does Tieck in
his 'Märchendramen', or Arnim in the 'Schattenspiel' *Das Loch*,
Brentano ensures that the atmosphere shall preserve its poetry
unpolluted by the practical spirit of everyday reality.

And it is in poetry, of a lyrical rather than a dramatic kind, that this play's greatest merit resides. The poetry is that of love, whose spirit seems to be diffused through the whole work and is given expression by Ponce, particularly in two episodes: the 'Sleep of Honour' speech in Act II, sc. 3 (K 4, 168) in which love is a dream-ideal and then later when it has become a reality, above all in Act IV. Aquilar may think Ponce long-winded, and it is unlikely that we are meant to take his making of his will in deadly earnest. But there can be no doubt that Brentano wishes us to see the love portrayed here as partaking of the infinite and absolute nature of the romantic ideal. The language in which Ponce speaks of his love may sometimes seem extravagant, but it is sincerely meant. This play is the nearest approach in the period to a comedy with a positive romantic content and, as such, it deserves its special place in this chapter.

Notes

1. F. Schlegel, *Europa*, reprint, E. Behler (ed.) (Darmstadt, 1963), pp. 48–55.
2. Quoted by P. Kluckhohn in DL 20, p. 11.
3. Tieck's *Fortunat*, for example, is a picaresque novel in dramatic form.
4. Berlin, 1828, pp. xxix–xxx.
5. Cf. H. Kasack and A. Mohrhenn (eds.), *Ludwig Tieck* (Berlin, 1943), vol. 1, p. 387.
6. Cf. *Briefe über Shakespeare*; Kasack and Mohrhenn, *Tieck*, vol. 2, pp. 17–18.
7. As quoted by H. A. Korff, *Geist der Goethezeit*, 2nd edn (4 vols., Leipzig, 1954), vol. IV, p. 734. A good, concise account of the thinking of the speculative romantic aestheticians on drama is to be found on pp. 730 ff of this work.
8. DL 20, p. 6.
9. Ibid., p. 7.
10. Tieck, *Werke*, ed. Thalmann (Munich, 1964), vol. 2, p. 362.
11. Cf. above, pp. 101–2.
12. Tieck certainly makes a serious attempt in both of these fields, notably in the description of Genoveva in the wilderness (pp. 507–13) and in the heroic portrayal of Karl Martell (pp. 393–4 and 407–8).
13. Brentano's *Die Gründung Prags* (1815) treats the founding of the Czech state in operatic style, in terms of the victory of light over darkness. Eichendorff handles the history of the chivalric 'German Order' in a not dissimilar way in *Der letzte Held von Marienburg* (1830). For a fuller treatment of all the playwrights discussed in this section, cf. P. Kluckhohn's introduction to DL 20.
14. This is of course the traditional name of the Wandering Jew, which enhances the suggestion of myth attaching to the character.
15. There are useful accounts in DL 20, pp. 14–31 and Korff, *Geist der Goethezeit*, vol. IV, pp. 404 ff.
16. See further Korff, vol. IV, pp. 427 ff.
17. They already regard one another as brother and sister: DL 20, p. 203.
18. Cf. *Hamburgische Dramaturgie*, nos. 28–9 and the discussion of laughter in *Minna von Barnhelm*, Act IV, sc. 6.

19. Quoted in DL 9 (*Satiren und Parodien*), p. 7. References to *Der gestiefelte Kater* will be to this edition.

20. Cf. Chapter 14 below, in particular the discussion of *Prinzessin Brambilla*.

21. Quoted by Kluckhohn in DL 23, p. 7.

22. Ibid., p. 6.

23. Ibid.

24. Ibid., p. 7. Cf. also Kasack and Mohrhenn, *Tieck*, vol. 1, p. 228.

25. Cf. the 'Vorerinnerung' to *Ponce de Leon* (K 4, pp. 131–2). The link with the romantic concepts of irony and humour is fairly clear.

26. Cf. Hoffmann's comments on Gozzi and on the *opera buffa* in *Der Dichter und der Komponist* (SB, pp. 84–91).

27. Cf. Kasack and Mohrhenn, *Tieck*, vol. 1, p. 228.

28. Kleist's *Der zerbrochene Krug* is an achievement of at least equal calibre, but some of the qualities which make it so are those which distinguish this author most clearly from the German Romantic Movement.

29. As Schiller shows in his essay *Über den Gebrauch des Chors in der Tragödie*.

30. Cf. above, Chapter 2, note 6 and text.

31. Brentano is here no doubt in part celebrating his friendship with Arnim, out of which the *Wunderhorn* arose, and the first flush of which he was experiencing at the time.

9 HEINRICH VON KLEIST

General Introduction

Kleist belongs chronologically to the romantic generation and his work is not entirely devoid of points of contact with Romanticism. The medieval Swabian setting and doom-laden plot of *Die Familie Schroffenstein*, for example, do call to mind Tieck's early 'Schauertragödie' *Karl von Berneck*.[1] The format of *Das Käthchen von Heilbronn* contains elements not only of the 'Ritterstück' but also of the 'Märchendrama' and we have already seen how Tieck could seize on it as an example of romantic dramatic technique.[2] The passionate nationalism of his later years and above all, perhaps, his distrust of rationalism and the strong emphasis which he places on 'Gefühl', allied to his tragic inability to achieve control in his own life, do place him genuinely closer to Romanticism than to Classicism. But there are important differences, both in the aspects mentioned and in others, which make it impossible to integrate Kleist into our concept of Romanticism.

Not the least significant of the ways in which Kleist stands out as an exception in his generation is the fact that he is a natural dramatist, to a greater extent even than Werner. Metaphysical problems and the subtleties of human psychology interest him deeply, but he feels the need to work them out in terms of a real action and conflict, to characterise with sharpness and colour and to make his figures speak a language which may not be simple, but which is truly the speech of individual people in a 'real situation. There may well be a link between these characteristics and the fact that Kleist's general attitude to reality differs very markedly from the typically romantic one.

Kleist found the concepts of truth and right, as they arise in the context of human relationships in the practical world, essentially problematic. His uniqueness in his own time consists in the fact that he could not exercise the idealist option of finding compensation for the discrepancy between ideal and real in a transcendental sphere of pure truth. He has this at least in common with the 'Aufklärung' that his religious sense seems to have been weak. Nor could he solve his problem by taking the path followed by so many 'moderns', that of accepting that the world lacks coherence, but continuing to act and think as if it did not. The result is confusion, not the fruitful confusion of the intellect which the Romantics often see as the first step to truth,

126

but a potentially corrosive confusion of the heart, the 'Verwirrung des Gefühls' which was accurately observed by Goethe as a strong tendency in Kleist's work.[3]

If we were to seek a predecessor for Kleist, in fact, the only real candidate would be the younger Goethe and that only in the sense that he perceived, as early as *Werther*, the danger of inner disruption in the type of idealist represented by Werther and later, by Tasso, who wants the Golden Age here and now. Indeed, he spent a large part of his thinking and writing life trying — with reasonable success — to develop an antidote to this poison, as he conceived it, and it is small wonder that he was frightened and repelled by what must have seemed to him to be a virulent manifestation of it in the work and personality of Kleist. He spoke once, indeed, of the 'Schauder und Abscheu' which, in spite of the best intentions, he always felt on contact with Kleist.[4]

The 'labyrinth of the breast', to quote another Goethean expression, is Kleist's special province. Without any of the lyrical effects of the Romantics proper, he, in his own way, gives priority to what he calls 'Gefühl' — a concept to which we shall return — and this gives rise to a number of features in his dramatic practice which are, to say the least, unclassical. His plots are not symmetrically or rationally constructed. He shows noticeably less concern than does Schiller for exposition, motivation, variation of pace and the provision of points of rest for the audience.[5] His plays sweep forward at a hectic pace, making almost excessive use of mystery and tension. Characters often behave strangely and with abrupt changes of mood, sometimes talking past rather than to each other, sometimes distrait, sometimes even fainting. The blank verse is frequently broken up into apparently disjointed exclamations and interjections and even in connected passages, the author's inner state of disturbance can at times give rise to striking distortions of the syntax. A true Romantic could well have agreed that the workings of the human heart are mysterious, and eccentric behaviour is by no means uncommon among romantic characters, but just as for him, in most cases at least, the heart would have found a way to resolve the apparent discrepancies, so he would have been incapable of an imagery as strained and a syntax as twisted as are often evident in Kleist, for example in these lines from *Robert Guiskard:*

So steigt der Leiche seines ganzen Volkes
Dies Land ein Grabeshügel aus der See![6]

'Ein jeder Busen ist, der fühlt, ein Rätsel,' says Prothoe in *Penthesilea* (line 1286), a thought which is not, perhaps, in itself unromantic, but which, expressed in this tortuous form, takes on an aura of painful and tragic complexity which makes it unmistakably Kleistian.

In the early years of his intellectual development, Kleist approached life with a strong faith in the capacity of rationally thinking man to understand the world and fashion a 'Lebensplan' which would render him independent of the 'tyrant' Fate.[7] He believed firmly in the real existence of a state of 'virtue' which was the source of true happiness and towards which, through study and self-improvement, he could approach ever more closely 'so wie es sich in meiner Seele nach und nach mehr aufklärt', as he puts it in his *Aufsatz, den sichern Weg des Glücks zu finden* (1799). The determined optimism of such utterances does recall that of the 'Aufklärung' up to a point, but there is a note of earnest intensity in the young Kleist, an implied demand that the world *must* make sense, to which no 'Aufklärer' would have allowed himself to be drawn. They had learnt to settle for much less. Kleist, however, had made himself frighteningly vulnerable and the collapse of his optimism — the first of several such collapses — would have occurred in any case, even if he had not brought it upon himself by his reading of Kant.[8] His reaction was predictably violent. He became convinced that there is an endemic discrepancy between conscious human thought and true reality, between 'Bewußtsein' and 'Wirklichkeit', as Friedrich Koch phrases it,[9] and felt that the basis of all rational and moral certainty had been destroyed. 'Kann Gott von solchen Wesen Verantwortlichkeit fordern?' he demanded of his fiancée Wilhelmine von Zenge.[10] As Gerhard Fricke says in what, despite the intricacy of its language, is probably the best general study of Kleist, our author's longings were certainly metaphysical, but also realist, in the sense that for him, fulfilment had to be not merely conceived, but *lived* in actuality. The idea of a 'Lebensplan', however naïve it might appear, is an expression of the fundamental desire for a practical life which embodies ultimate meaning.[11]

This is, of course, a very special kind of realism (if it is such at all) — Korff, indeed, goes so far as to speak of 'metaphysical realism'[12] — and it is probably better to think in terms of an emotional attitude rather than a philosophy of life, of 'Lebensgefühl' rather than 'Weltanschauung'. Whatever one calls it, it helps us to understand the pattern of Kleist's life; a series of attempts to find integration and fulfilment in the world, all of which eventually broke down, an alternation of euphoric hope and anguished crisis ending, almost inevitably, in suicide, itself perhaps a last, spectacular throw of the dice, for it contained ecstasy as well as despair.

Man's best hope, for Kleist, lies in what Fricke, commenting on *Amphitryon*, calls 'die rettende Macht des Gefühls'.[13] We are not entirely without guidance in the labyrinth. Humans, or at least the more finely organised among them, have an inner capacity for distinguishing truth from falsehood and right from wrong. It is more instinctive and emotional than conscious and rational in its operation and hence Kleist identifies it, in a specialised use of the word, as 'Gefühl'. In its pure state, it is as delicate and accurate as a pair of gold-balances,[14] but it is not, as it might have been for a full-blooded Romantic, a means of emancipating oneself from the finite dimension. It is yoked to the finite world and thus to rational consciousness and when the two are out of phase, as often occurs, the result is a stern and painful conflict and often error and confusion in the feeling itself. In an extreme case, the latter can become perverted into its negative, destructive mirror-image. Fineness of soul is then no protection: indeed, it seems to feed the process with its own strength, as in the case of Penthesilea, who 'sank, weil sie zu stolz und kräftig blühte,' as Prothoe says (line 3040).

As an example of the Kleistian 'Gefühl' and of the way in which it can become confused, we may take the situation of Alkmene in *Amphitryon*. When Jupiter takes advantage of the absence of her husband Amphitryon to assume the latter's shape and visit her, she, convinced that it is her husband to whom she is giving herself, experiences the fulfilment of love at a higher pitch than ever before. When the real Amphitryon denies her, she chides him, secure in the feeling of her own innocence and fidelity, as an 'Unedelmütiger' (line 857), but is later thrown into confusion when she discovers that the diadem which the apparent Amphitryon left with her bears not an 'A' but a 'J'. Her serving-maid, Charis, is appalled:

	Entsetzlich! solltet Ihr getäuscht Euch haben?
Alkmene.	Ich mich getäuscht!
Charis.	Hier in dem Zuge mein ich.
Alkmene.	Ja, in dem Zuge meinst du — so scheint es fast.
Charis.	Und also — ?
Alkmene.	Was und also — ?
Charis.	Beruhigt Euch
	Es wird noch alles sich zum Guten wenden.
Alkmene.	O Charis! Eher will ich irren in mir selbst!
	Eh will ich dieses innerste Gefühl,

> Das ich am Mutterbusen eingesogen,
> Und das mir sagt, daß ich Alkmene bin,
> Für einen Parther oder Perser halten. . .

Charis.   Ihr seid doch sicher, hoff' ich, beste Fürstin?

Alkmene.   Wie meiner reinen Seele! meiner Unschuld!. . .

> . . . Und wenn er's flüchtig nur betrachtet hätte,
> Und jetzt mit allen Feldherrn wiederkehrte,
> Und die Behauptung rasend wiederholte,
> Daß er die Schwelle noch des Hauses nicht betrat!. . .
> Ein Zeugnis *wider* mich ist dieser Stein,
> Was kann ich, ich Verwirrte, ihm entgegnen? (II, 4)

Alkmene's deepest inner feeling assures her of her innocence. It has in fact guided her correctly in causing her to accept Jupiter as her husband and it will do so in the final scene where she chooses the god instead of her real husband, but again, chooses him *as Amphitryon*. The purity of her feeling is demonstrated and the god calls out 'Du Göttliche!', which lends support to the relatively positive interpretation of the ending which Fricke propounds and with which we agree.[15] Even so, it is clear from the extract quoted, in the broken dialogue at the beginning and in Alkmene's speeches, that she cannot take refuge in the stronghold of her feeling. She has to live in the world of material reality, where rational consciousness cannot be denied. The thought of a discrepancy between this latter and her inmost feeling is torture to her. When Jupiter tries to make her believe, not only that a god came to her in the night, but that the 'husband' who is talking to her at this present moment is in fact the god, she finds the thought painful. Throughout this crucial scene (II, 5), in spite of all the Jesuitical twists and turns which Jupiter gives to the argument, she will not allow her love to be detached from her real husband. In reply to Jupiter's final test, she replies that, if she knew that the man now holding her in his arms to be the god, and if the real Amphitryon were standing there as well:

> so traurig würd ich sein, und wünschen,
> Daß er der Gott mir wäre, und daß du
> Amphitryon mir bliebst. . .

And then she adds, 'wie du es bist' (lines 1566–8). At this point, where her integrity and fidelity shine through most brightly, the god is moved (as later in the climactic scene) to pay homage to the human. But while the ending is a triumph for her, there is sadness in it too. She has been exalted, but at the cost of considerable suffering. The privacy of her relationship with her husband has been violated. With this in mind, we can understand the ambiguity of her final exclamation: 'Ach!'

In his plays – and the same is true of his *Novellen* – Kleist often confronts us with the exotic and extraordinary, not because he feels a romantic impulse to stimulate fancy or to create a sense of wonder and of the transcendent, but because he needs such situations as dramatic images, to express the complexity and depth of his experience of the problem of human 'Gefühl'. This is no doubt the reason for the extreme violence which he often introduces into his plots, and it seems also to have affected his use of poetic images. This latter is not as technically advanced as that of Novalis or the later Brentano. It seems in most cases to be metaphorical rather than symbolic in nature: to arise, that is, out of parallelism rather than association, wit rather than fancy.[16] But as in the case of the syntax, the disturbed nature of Kleist's feeling is reflected in it, often suggesting an odd, indeed unpoetic comparison which makes the metaphor or simile more than usually expressive, as when Ottokar says to Jeronimus in *Die Familie Schroffenstein:*

> Das Gefühl
> Des Rechts! O du Falschmünzer der Gefühle!
> Nicht einen wird ihr blanker Schein betrügen;
> Am Klange werden sie es hören, an
> Die Tür zur Warnung deine Worte nageln (I, 1, lines 142–6).

And Kleist's imagery is also striking by the very frequency of its occurrence in his dramatic speech, sometimes with the use of recurring motifs, as for example that of the sun, and of brilliance in general, in *Penthesilea.* The object here is surely not to decorate but to find some way of at least partially articulating feelings of great intensity and complexity.

The Plays

Die Familie Schroffenstein (1803)

'Wenn ihr euch totschlagt, ist es ein Versehen.' This cryptic remark by Ursula (line 2705) embodies several characteristics of this play, the first of Kleist's dramatic projects to be completed. We find there, not only the tendency to sententiousness of expression and involuntary comedy which are typical of the work, but also the extreme pessimism, the view of a world in which all nature, goodness and truth are violated by some malevolent force beyond human control, which bespeaks an origin in Kleist's first great crisis. This is the breakdown of faith which Kleist expresses in his letter to Wilhelmine of 15 August 1801 to which reference has already been made. It was written in Paris, the city which had come to symbolise for him all that was perverted and evil in modern existence and in particular the fall of man from his former state of natural goodness and innocence. With a naïve Rousseauism which sits uneasily beside that almost 'modern' despair, he castigates the sophisticated and scientifically advanced Parisians for their falling-off from nature and contrasts their behaviour with that of two lovers in a park. It may seem to be a far cry from nineteenth-century Paris to medieval Swabia, but this is nevertheless the core-concept of *Die Familie Schroffenstein.*

The majority of Kleist's plots, whether invented or derived, and while they retain the 'real' quality of practical dramatic actions, still cry out to be seen as images of metaphysical issues. That of *Die Familie Schroffenstein* certainly falls into this category. When Rupert of Rossitz, mistakenly imagining that his cousin, Sylvester of Warwand, has caused the murder of his younger son, cries out:

<blockquote>
nichts mehr von Natur.
Ein hold ergötzend Märchen ist's der Kindheit (lines 42 ff)
</blockquote>

we recognise the preoccupations of the Paris letter. The natural bonds of love and trust have been destroyed, or at least badly damaged. The only hope of redemption lies in the pure love of the young scions of the warring families, Ottokar and Agnes, and the former, in fact, sees himself as 'Ein Gehilfe der Natur' (lines 2486 f). This couple, in their essentially idyllic relationship, recall the lovers in the park. When we see the play as an image of the crisis described in the Paris letter, we are better able to reconcile ourselves to the action with its extravagances, heaped improbabilities and contorted metaphors. For even in some of these moments, the intensity and metaphysical profundity of the experience aroused by Kleist's perception of an anarchical confusion in the world are reflected. This is more than just another run-of-the-mill example of the blood-and-thunder 'Schauertragödie' about a fated family in a crumbling castle which was in vogue at that time.

Rupert and Sylvester have drifted into mistrust and (in Rupert's case) hatred of one another largely as a result of an 'Erbvertrag', a

contract (Rousseau again!) by the terms of which, should one branch
of the family die out, the other will inherit its possessions. Sylvester,
who fights against this evil influence, hears that Rupert has declared a
life-and-death feud against him, on the grounds of his supposed
complicity in the murder of Rupert's son. He responds with an
emphatic expression of his bewilderment:

> Einer von uns beiden muß
> Verrückt sein; bist du's nicht, *ich* könnt' es werden,
> Die Unze Mutterwitz, die dich vom Tollhaus
> Errettet, muß, es kann nichts anders, *mich*
> Ins Tollhaus führen. — Sieh, wenn du mir sagtest,
> Die Ströme flössen neben ihren Ufern
> Bergan und sammelten auf Felsenspitzen
> In Seen sich, so wollt' — ich wollt's dir glauben;
> Doch sagst du mir, ich hätt' ein Kind gemordet,
> Des Vetters Kind. . . (lines 625–34)

The assumption of absurd impossibilities for contrastive emphasis in an
argument is, of course, a traditional rhetorical device, but whether or
not Kleist is consciously employing it as such, the effect, in this context
of nature twisted into incomprehensibility, is one of deadly earnest.
Sylvester is being put under severe strain. He desires above all harmony
and clarity and has always resisted the mistrust with which even his own
wife, Gertrud, is infected. Now his conviction of his own innocence is
in conflict with the 'evidence' and with the conviction of others. At the
end of the scene, indeed, when Jeronimus supports the accusation, he
falls in a faint. It seems almost as if he is being forced against his will
into the position which his cousin has already adopted. The murder, at
Rupert's instigation, of Jeronimus, who had gone to Rossitz as his
peace-making emissary, tips the balance in him. His faith, too, snaps
and he expresses his sense of confusion and of fate in a powerful image:

> Es ist ein trüber Tag
> Mit Wind und Regen, viel Bewegung draußen.
> Es zieht ein unsichtbarer Geist gewaltig
> Nach einer Richtung alles fort, den Staub,
> Die Wolken und die Wellen (lines 2019–23).

In the fifth act, Sylvester and Rupert kill their own children, each under
the mistaken impression that he is killing the other's child. Too late,

the misunderstandings which gave rise to the feud are resolved and a kind of despairing reconciliation between the cousins takes place. The last word, however, is had by the madman Johann, who says to Ursula (who was partly responsible for the initial confusion):

> Geh, alte Hexe, geh. Du spielst gut aus der Tasche,
> Ich bin zufrieden mit dem Kunststück. Geh.

That the final image should be one of deception and complexity is appropriate, for the play is deeply and tragically pessimistic. The deadly seriousness of the issue and the strength and intricacy of the psychological disturbance to which it gave rise and which Kleist succeeds in communicating, give a certain power and sincerity even to the more strained images (such as the rivers which flow uphill!) and absurdly hectic scenes.

Robert Guiskard (1803–8)

This was the project (begun in 1801) on which Kleist was working in the early 1800s and on which, encouraged, no doubt, by the appreciative reaction of Wieland to his recitation of extracts from it, he pinned his hopes of achieving fulfilment in literary greatness and fame. His hope was to blend together the best qualities of Shakespeare and of the Greeks. It was an ambition which led to the predictable savage disillusionment and on a second visit to Paris, in 1803, he burned the manuscript. All that we now have is a fragment reconstructed (one presumes, from memory) and published in the journal *Phöbus* in 1808, and which cannot, of course, be relied on to give any detailed knowledge of the mood and attitudes of the original. Wolff[17] speculates, not unpersuasively, that the Guiskard of the *Phöbus*-fragment, who could be seen as having some of the virtues of the leader which are later to be embodied in the ideal figure of the Elector in *Prinz Friedrich von Homburg*, has been ennobled by comparison with what is likely to have been the original conception. However this may be, it seems reasonable to assume that the central and fundamental conflict in both versions is that between an absolute, though human, will and an unpredictable and uncontrollable non-human force.

Guiskard, the Duke of the Normans, is leading the siege of Constantinople. A mysterious and terrible pestilence is ravaging the Norman army and (although he has so far managed to conceal the fact) has at last laid its hand on the leader himself. The published fragment takes us only to the point at which Guiskard, appearing to the people

in an attempt to quell rumours that he is infected, gives a clear sign of
weakness, though not incontrovertible proof of the presence of the
disease itself. It ends with one of a number of powerful descriptions of
the effects of the plague and an appeal that Guiskard should lead his
people home.

The action is presented with a brilliant management of tension and
suspense which is also observable elsewhere in Kleist, above all in *Der
zerbrochene Krug*. He uses an analytical technique reminiscent of that
of Sophocles in *Oedipus Tyrannos*, allowing us to guess at the truth
before it is revealed in carefully calculated stages. The undeniable
grandeur of the theme is realised to an extent sufficient to make us
regret that the project was never completed. There is a truly tragic
terror in the way in which the plague is brought before us and given
the status of a kind of Nemesis. Guiskard, its human antagonist, is
endowed with an equally impressive strength of mind and character.
Abälard describes him in his suffering:

Und als die Kaiserin mit feuchtem Blick,
Ihm einen Becher brachte, und ihn fragte,
Ob er auch trinken woll'? antwortet' er:
'Die Dardanellen, liebes Kind!' und trank. . .
        . . . Doch das hindert nicht,
Daß er nicht stets nach jener Kaiserzinne,
Die dort erglänzt, wie ein gekrümmter Tiger,
Aus seinem offnen Zelt hinüberschaut.
Man sieht ihn still, die Karte in der Hand,
Entschlüss' im Busen wälzen, ungeheure,
Als ob er heut das Leben erst beträte (lines 355–64).

It is good to know that Kleist had so much grandeur in him. The
yearning for sublimity which, as his letters show, was always with him,
was not empty dreaming and one feels that this play, had it been
completed in the same vein, could have become a more satisfactory
realisation of his vision than any of his finished works. At the same
time, his personal tragedy is reflected in its fate, for it is unlikely that
he could ever have achieved a sufficient inner serenity to carry out the
undertaking.

Der zerbrochene Krug (1805–6)

This, Kleist's only true comedy, is the first completed product of the
period during which, having recovered from the breakdown of 1803, he

worked as a civil servant in Königsberg. He seems, at this time, to have acquired a renewed confidence in man's inner resources, though now in those of feeling rather than reason, and to have felt able to dispense with the aid of general, abstract principles in his search for meaning in life. As a project, the play dates back to the period spent in Switzerland in 1802, when he entered into a compact with Zschokke, Ludwig Wieland and Heinrich Gessner, to develop in literary form the theme of a picture, showing simply a woman before a court, holding a broken jug. He makes of it at the same time a successful 'Volksstück', and a subtle examination — this time from the comic perspective — of the problems of truth and trust which we met in *Die Familie Schroffenstein.*

Ruprecht Tümpel, son of a peasant in a village near Utrecht, finds that his betrothed, Eve Rull, is entertaining a male visitor at night. He breaks into the room (dislodging the jug from its ledge in the process), just in time to see the unknown visitor departing by way of the window. Unable to trust Eve ('Was ich mit Händen greife, glaub' ich gern,' he says (line 1176)), he brands her as a slut. She denies any misbehaviour and in the haste of the moment seems to confirm the suspicion formed by her mother, Marthe, that it was Ruprecht who was responsible. It is at this point that the action of the play begins. Marthe is now accusing Ruprecht before the village magistrate. What she does not know, and what Eve fears to divulge, is that the nocturnal visitor was in fact this same magistrate (whose name is Adam!), who has been threatening to send Ruprecht to face death as a soldier in the Indies if she denies him her favours. Chance, as so often happens in Kleist, intervenes, but on this occasion in a benevolent capacity, and brings a visiting Inspector, Walter, to the village on precisely the day of the hearing, and he forces Adam to conduct what the audience gradually divines is his own trial. Walter, as *deus ex machina*, ensures that his desperate attempts to cheat justice and obfuscate the truth are frustrated.

As can be seen from this summary, typically Kleistian themes (the problematic nature of 'truth' and 'justice') are present, but their potentially tragic implications[18] are kept in the background. We are aware that, had the Inspector not been present, Adam might well have escaped undetected and the relationship between Eve and Ruprecht been incurably poisoned. But apart from Eve, who is perhaps a prototype of the great souls to be portrayed in the succeeding plays, the characters here are visualised comically. Ruprecht really is a 'Tümpel' and his manner of addressing the court is exactly the long-winded, roundabout and 'chatty' style in which one rustic 'Gevatter' might talk to another. Adam's cunning and malice are rustic too, and lack the aura of threatening evil which could make us fear or hate him. Issues and events are also seen from the comic perspective. The chaos, or at least anarchy, in the administration of the law which Michael Kohlhaas sees to such destructive effect appear here in a comic light when the maid brings sausage from Adam's registry, wrapped up in a legal document (scene 2). The state of confusion in which Adam begins his day ('Es geht bunt alles über Ecke mir,' line 266), and from which he never recovers, is handled with a consistent feeling for the ridiculous and produces some genuinely comic ideas, as when Adam, seeking an excuse for the fact that he is at present wigless, invents the excuse that the cat — 'das Schwein'! — has produced a litter of kittens (one of which mythical beasts he offers to his clerk, Licht) in that judicial headgear. Misunderstanding too can be comic and is so when — with a nice but unintended symbolism — Brigitte mistakes Adam for the Devil as he flees headlong from Eve's house, 'Schwefeldämpfe von sich lassend' (line 1767).

The arrangement of the action is a technical *tour de force*. It runs remorselessly from the opening to the appointed end, in a close-knit, tense sequence of scenes in which Adam's progressively more frenzied attempts to stave off an exposure which grows progressively more certain, combined with the well exploited irony of the situation, keep our interest high throughout. Concentration is of the essence of Kleist's technique here. It was thus a crowning irony when Goethe, to whom Kleist had sent the play, divided it into three acts and produced it in Weimar (in 1808) in the more formal Classical style. The result was a resounding failure, and so recognition, for which Kleist thirsted and which he needed more than any other writer, was denied him in the place where it would have been most sweet.

Amphitryon (1806)

This work, which grew from the plan of a straightforward adaptation of Molière's comedy of the same name, into a play which — in the main action — constitutes a totally new treatment of the theme, has already been discussed at some length in the first section of this chapter. We will limit ourselves here to a complementary treatment of the portrayal of the three central characters. The comic sub-plot of Amphitryon's servant Sosias and his divine double, Mercury, need not detain us long. It follows very much the lines of Molière's version, and is as entertaining here as it was there. Amphitryon is developed into something more than simply a cuckolded husband. He is not ignoble and his situation causes him a torment which earns our sympathy. He even wins through to a degree of trust which enables him to proclaim the purity of Alkmene's heart and to say that Jupiter *is* Amphitryon 'for her' (line 2290). At the same time, he cannot rival his wife's greatness of spirit. His capacity for faith is too firmly bounded by his 'five senses' (cf. lines 693–704) and there are times when he does give way to baser impulses and speaks with a wildness, even viciousness of expression, which recall the Rupert of *Die Familie Schroffenstein.* There are others when he is more like Ruprecht Tümpel. Some, at least, of his pain is self-inflicted.

Kleist's concept of Jupiter oscillates between immanent and transcendent in a not entirely convincing manner. In an existentialist sense, perhaps, Kleist could be said to have some kind of religious perception,[19] but when he talks of God, or of gods, one receives little impression of a belief in a transcendent spiritual reality such as is to be found even in those Romantics in whom the mystical impulse is relatively weak. He attempts here to make Jupiter into a god in the real sense of the word, principally through the infusion of a rather vague pantheism,[20] but the attempt is at best a partial success. Jupiter is best seen as a secularised equivalent of the divine: that degree of insight and sureness of feeling which is above the confusion which mortal flesh is heir to, but to which it has the capacity to rise, as is demonstrated by the example of Alkmene.

She experiences the greatest suffering and gains the greatest glory. The suffering consists chiefly in the disruption of her sense of her own inner integrity ('meiner Seele Frieden', III, 11: line 2262). Jupiter's divine powers enable him, not only to take on Amphitryon's shape, but to *be* Amphitryon for the loving and trusting wife. As he himself says at the beginning of this scene (line 2171), no one but her husband has 'approached her soul'. Confronted by the two Amphitryons, however, she is misled by logical reason into thinking that the inferior of the two (who is therefore, to her *instinct*, an impostor, though he is in fact the 'real' Amphitryon) must be the one to whom she gave herself the previous night. Her feeling had led her correctly then, as it does now, but the discrepancy between emotional reality and rational appearance can cause confusion in her too. So there is pain even in her glory and triumph. And uplifting as this vision of human greatness of soul undoubtedly is, it must not be forgotten that happy outcome depends on divine intervention. The tragic approach to confusion and clarification of feeling adopted in the case of Penthesilea, whose forerunner Alkmene is in some respects, is exceptional. Korff points out, very reasonably, that the majority of Kleist's plays are not, in fact, tragedies.[21] But the devices by which he avoids a tragic ending, in some cases, make one wonder whether they might not have been more totally satisfying as such.

Penthesilea (1808)

'Es ist wahr', Kleist wrote of this play in a letter composed in late autumn 1807, 'mein innerstes Wesen liegt darin. . . der ganze Schmerz zugleich und Glanz meiner Seele.'[22] He went on to question whether it could succeed on the German stage as it then was, dominated by the moralistic and sentimental taste of the average female playgoer. It was not only the ladies whose taste was too delicate for its uncompromising presentation of the horrors of which the human heart, in a state of extreme disorientation, is capable. Goethe himself, who was well aware of these depths, nevertheless felt that in art, the horrific needed to be moderated and controlled in its expression by the 'Schönheitssinn' of the artist.[23] His attitude to Kleist's play, as expressed in his letter of 1 February 1808, is a decidedly negative one, if put in reasonably conciliatory terms.

Penthesilea concentrates its light single-mindedly on the inner 'Gefühl' and the light here is of a blinding intensity such as we find nowhere else in Kleist's work. Intensity is indeed the key word of the whole. Vocabulary and imagery are dominated by expressions of brilliance, speed and force. The dramatic form, an unbroken sequence of 24 scenes in which there is only one episode – the idyll of scenes 14 and 15 – which can count as a point of (relative) rest, corresponds to, and reinforces, this tendency. The principal characters, Penthesilea and Achilles, spend the majority of their time in restless, often violent, physical activity, moving up and down across a precipitous landscape in a hectic duel which is also a kind of mating-dance, and one in which the male plays a decidedly subordinate role. Without robbing the other characters of personality, Kleist concentrates attention on the central figure to a greater extent in this play than in any other.

The inner action, for which the physical one acts as an appropriate image, concerns the interaction between reason, or 'law', and feeling, a feeling which has been dammed up, unnaturally confined, and is now breaking free as a flood, in which the individual must either learn to swim, or be swept to destruction. Penthesilea is thrown into a state of radical confusion which none of the other characters, not even her bosom friend Prothoe (who does at least grasp that what the High

Priestess calls Penthesilea's 'foolish heart' cannot and should not be subordinated to an abstract principle)[24] can truly understand. She does not simply abandon herself to this confusion, but can achieve a measure of control only after it has driven her to the peak of error (line 2981: 'So war es ein Versehen. . .' etc.) in the killing and mutilation of Achilles.

Penthesilea is Queen of the Amazons, who are, or rather have become, the 'daughters of Mars'. In reaction to their ravishment by barbarian conquerors, a previous generation founded a state in which womanly nature as Kleist sees it — this is anything but a feminist tract! — is in part, at least, denied.[25] Tenderness of feeling towards men as such is not condemned and suppressed, but it is acceptable only in certain circumstances. A mate, when required, may be obtained by vanquishing in battle the man whom the god — who bears a strong resemblance to Chance — chooses to send. Penthesilea phrases it thus:

> Hier dieses Eisen soll, Gefährtinnen,
> Soll mit der sanftesten Umarmung ihn
> (Weil ich mit Eisen ihn umarmen muß)
> An meinen Busen schmerzlos niederziehn.
> Hebt euch, ihr Frühlingsblumen, seinem Fall,
> Daß seiner Glieder keines sich verletze (lines 857–62).

The beginnings of an awareness of the contradictions in her situation are apparent in these lines. Penthesilea has already become aware that the feeling which Achilles has awakened in her is 'confusing' (line 641), that it disrupts the (to her) normal Amazonian state of mind and has spoken of the 'Trotz' and 'Widerspruch' in her soul (line 680). What has happened is that she has fallen in love; to us, the most natural thing in the world, but to the Amazons, a terrifying departure from the norm. To them, Cupid's darts are 'poisonous' (lines 1075–6) and the High Priestess sees this turn of events as 'impossible' and 'horrible' (lines 1080 and 1088). As directed by Mars, Penthesilea has led the Amazons to Troy. But now, instead of submitting herself to the law and accepting the god's decision as revealed in battle, she pursues Achilles like a huntress (the motif is a recurrent one in the play), to the point of losing the prisoners already taken and suffering defeat in single combat at his hands. Seeing her fall, Achilles, who previously intended to treat her as he had Hector, finds his enmity turned to love and, at Prothoe's suggestion, pretends briefly to have been vanquished by her.

This provides the basis for an idyllic picture of harmonious love (scenes 14 and 15), in which Penthesilea can give free expression to the beauty and sensitivity of her heart, but still with such an intensity of feeling that we, knowing that the idyll is founded on deception, can only fear for the future. For her mind is still conditioned by the law within which she has grown up. And not only her mind: her feeling, too, is so conditioned. The law is ingrained into it and so she cannot as yet even gain the relief of rebellion. The force of her emotion turns inwards rather than outwards and — rather as in the case of Sylvester's fainting-fit — gives rise to moments of paralysis of mind and body (e.g. lines 1237 ff), even of 'madness' (1374 ff).

After her disillusionment and unwelcome rescue, Penthesilea is roused from despair by a challenge from Achilles. He intends to submit to her in the combat, thus enabling her to love him on her terms, but she misinterprets the challenge as a denial of love in favour of the law of battle and the mutually distorting interaction of 'Gesetz' and 'Gefühl' produces an extreme perversion of her love into a destructive frenzy, in which she kills him most brutally and then joins her dogs in rending his body. The modest maiden, 'so voll Verstand und Würd' und Grazie' (line 2680), has become a monster. Unnaturalness has taken its course. She returns in a trance-like state, from which she awakens at first to a feeling of bliss. As in the idyll episode, she is aware only that Achilles has been overcome and — as she does there — feels an ecstatic 'ripeness for death'.[26] The knowledge that she has killed him does not in itself precipitate the crisis. This occurs on her discovery of the mutilation and gradual conviction that it was she who caused it, when all she feels is love for him, a love more uninhibited than it ever was before. She realises that it was love, albeit deluded and distorted by the influence of the law, which was pouring itself out in her attack on him:

> So war es ein Versehen. Küsse, Bisse,
> Das reimt sich, und wer recht von Herzen liebt,
> Kann schon das eine für das andre greifen (lines 2981—3).

She finally cuts herself free from the law (line 3012) and goes to join her beloved by turning her own feeling, like a dagger, against herself. It was not weakness, as the High Priestess (not an unsympathetic, but an uncomprehending figure) believed, but her strength of soul which made her capable of becoming untrue to Diana and now that same strength demonstrates itself again. There is, indeed, both 'Schmerz' and 'Glanz' in this ending: the play seems to teach that 'des Lebens höchstes Gut' (line 1287) is attainable only in dream or death, but in this tragic conclusion, the power and the glory of human feeling are also made manifest. That is the meaning of the epitaph pronounced over the dead queen by Prothoe, replying to the High Priestess:

> Sie sank, weil sie zu stolz und kräftig blühte!
> Die abgestorbne Eiche steht im Sturm,
> Doch die gesunde stürzt er schmetternd nieder,
> Weil er in ihre Krone greifen kann.

Das Käthchen von Heilbronn (1808, published 1810)

In the letter to Henriette Hendel-Schütz from which we quoted apropos of *Penthesilea*, Kleist also gives a characterisation of this play. Käthchen is 'die Kehrseite der Penthesilea, ihr andrer Pol, ein Wesen, das eben so mächtig ist durch gänzliche Hingebung, als jene durch Handeln'. That this play does not achieve the aesthetic level of its sister product is due in part, no doubt, to concessions made to the *popular* romantic taste of the time,[27] but in greater measure, probably, to the fact that the heroine, almost totally emptied of consciousness in a way which inevitably suggests the puppet of Kleist's essay *Über das Marionettentheater*, does not provide an adequate *dramatic* image of the Kleistian theme. On the other hand, there is too much of the latter to permit of a success on truly romantic lines. The result is an uneasy mixture of action and 'Stimmung', of hard and soft tones.

The sprawling action, which is overgrown with many romantic tendrils (a sinister secret court, the rescue of a damsel in distress, a burning castle and a trial by combat), is correspondingly hard to summarise. In essence, it is a story of painful misunderstanding and eventual clarification in the relationship between Käthchen (ostensibly the daughter of a smith but in fact the natural daughter of the Emperor) and Graf Wetter vom Strahl. Käthchen has had a dream in which she was visited by vom Strahl at night and firmly believes he will become her husband. She follows him in complete submission to his will, even to the extent of obeying him when he orders her to leave him, though this causes her to fall in the faint which a first consciousness of the discrepancy between feeling and the reality of the ordered rational world often causes in Kleist's finer characters. Unable to return to her old life, she takes to aimless wandering, and chances to overhear a plot against vom Strahl, to whom she gives a timely warning. He, meanwhile, has become captivated by the charms of Kunigunde von Thurneck

which, unbeknown to him, are entirely synthetic. Käthchen exercises
a strong attraction upon him which he cannot understand and when he
learns (as she talks in her sleep in the play's most Kleistian scene
(IV, 2)) that her dream corresponds to one which he had
simultaneously, he falls into a state of extreme confusion:

> Weh mir! Mein Geist, von Wunderlicht geblendet,
> Schwankt an des Wahnsinns grausem Hang umher!
> Denn wie begreif' ich die Verkündigung,
> Die mir noch silbern wiederklingt ins Ohr,
> Daß sie die Tochter meines Kaisers sei?

In a somewhat rushed and unconvincing fifth act, the mystery is
unravelled, poisonous malice is defeated and punished and Käthchen
and vom Strahl are united in a festive and stagey finale.

The lines quoted above take us into that part of the play which is of
greatest significance. Whether it is intended or not, it is the man, in
this case, who carries the greater dramatic interest. Development (a
purification and clarification of feeling) is possible only in his case.
His 'Gefühl', at the deeper level, impels him towards Käthchen, but the
evidence of reason and senses suggests that there is no possibility of
a union between them and favours that with Kunigunde. A confusion
of his love results from this; indeed, the possibility of the perversion of
the natural and lovely into the monstrous and hateful is suggested by
the fact that vom Strahl, not for the first time,[28] threatens Käthchen
with his whip (III, 6). That this is, or would have been, a 'Versehen',
as Penthesilea's rending of Achilles is, is inherently probable and the
argument for this point of view is strengthened by the fact that vom
Strahl seems eventually to wake from a kind of trance and has no idea
of his reasons for taking down the whip. This is very much a situation
of potential tragedy. We have seen from the extract quoted how the
apparent breakdown of rational order leads the Count to the brink of
madness and in Act V, scene 6, when he sees how his feelings have been
led into error in the case of Kunigunde, he talks of suicide.

The solution in this play is not developed out of the human
situation, but is imposed on it by fairy-tale means: the humble maiden
turns out to be a lost princess. A convincing resolution of the problem
through *Märchen* would not have been impossible, but it would have
required a belief in the effective reality of the spiritual dimension
whose source is love, in the romantic sense. Tieck exaggerates the
'romantic' nature of the play's structure, as we saw, and he does the

same in characterising its spirit. He sees it as 'so ganz vom reinsten Hauch der Liebe beseelt und erfrischt. . . dem Wunder des Märchens und doch der höchsten Wahrheit so verschwistert, daß es gewiß als Volksschauspiel immer unter uns leben wird'.[29] This is Kleist seen through the roseate haze of Tieck's own romantic feeling and is more illuminating as a guide to what the latter aimed, at least, to achieve in his own dramatic versions of medieval legends. Kleist, on the other hand, while he means the transcendental dimension of his play to be taken seriously — as in the case of *Amphitryon* — portrays it without full involvement or poetic power. It is characteristic that he does not actually show vom Strahl's conversion to faith in it. Even after the revelations of the dream scene, in Act V, scene 1, he still speaks of 'ein Märchen, *aberwitzig, sinnverwirrt'* (my emphasis). We have to imagine the conversion as taking place between the eighth and eleventh scenes of this act, so that in the fine twelfth scene, love can be truly set free. This scene is the true culmination of the *Kleistian* action and one feels a little dissatisfied that the actual conclusion should allow that to be swathed in a relatively superficial 'romantic' drapery.

Die Hermannsschlacht (1808)

This, Kleist's only genuine 'Zeitstück', was intended as a rallying-call to the Germans at a time of national degradation. Whether it would have been effective as such is hard to determine; circumstances, in fact, prevented even its publication until 1821. Certainly, it is propaganda of a xenophobic nature and its workmanship, as well as its spiritual quality, is inferior. At the same time, it should not be dismissed out of hand as nothing more than that.

The plot is familiar enough: Hermann manages to overcome the egotism of the Germanic tribal leaders and unite them to victory over the Romans. The latter of course, represent the French. Kleist adds a sub-plot of his own invention in which Hermann's wife, Thusnelda, takes revenge on a Roman legate, Ventidius, with whom she has been engaged in a mild flirtation, by luring him into an enclosure where he is torn to pieces by a starving bear.[30] Previously an advocate of humane standards, she has been turned into an avenging fury by the discovery that Ventidius intends that her hair shall grace the head of the Empress Livia.

That this is not mere gratuitous sadism is shown by the fact that Thusnelda's German companions, like the Amazons who look with horror and disgust at Penthesilea in her hour of aberration, react with the same natural repulsion. That Thusnelda herself should fall in a faint when her revenge has been consummated is an indication that this is an act which is totally against her nature and has imposed an enormous strain on her. The true cause lies in the perversion of feeling arising out of the situation in which she is placed. Hermann too knows that humanitarian values *should* be paramount and it is precisely this knowledge that makes him curse a noble act on the part of an individual Roman. In the situation in which one nation is oppressed by another, hatred is his office and revenge his virtue (line 1725) and anything which undermines the integrity of his feeling is unwelcome: 'Ich *will* die höhnische Dämonenbrut nicht lieben!' (line 1723)

These examples of 'Verwirrung der Gefühle' demonstrate that this is a play by Kleist. But no one would pretend that it deserves to be ranked with the major works. It was produced in a hurry and shows the effects of that in its sketchy motivation, aesthetically unjustified anachronisms, faulty versification and often merely odd, rather than expressive, imagery. It may be that the circumstances of composition can be blamed, in part at least, for the play's most serious, moral flaw, its failure to show clearly that the horrors and bloodthirsty language are meant symbolically; as an expression, that is, of the unnaturalness of the situation in which the Germans find themselves and of the depth and strength of the feeling which it calls forth and which drives them to seek freedom. Single-minded concentration on the struggle against the one common enemy is essential and when Egbert demands the punishment of those Germans who had collaborated with the Romans, Hermann replies, significantly: 'Verwirre das Gefühl mir nicht!' (line 2285) But however impressive absolute feeling and devotion to a cause may be, there is no way in which they can justify inhumanity. It may well be that Kleist would have agreed with this view, and would have argued that he intended only to demonstrate, and to inculcate *intensity* of feeling, but even accepting that, one would have to reply that he does not succeed, in the text, in giving that impression.

Prinz Friedrich von Homburg (completed 1811)

Tieck's opinion, namely that this is Kleist's 'reifstes und vollendtstes Werk',[31] is shared by the majority of critics and it is a judgement which it is hard to dispute. Its handling of dramatic verse, construction and exposition and its portrayal and motivation of a wide range of characters show a new mastery and there is a captivating brilliance about its presentation of the triumph of 'Gefühl' at a level 'above tragedy', as Koch writes, [32] a level where 'feeling' and 'law' can be reconciled without recourse to fairy-tale methods or idealist abstractions. It is only with reluctance that the present writer can bring himself to confess that the solution offered by Kleist does not convince and that the play is easier to admire than it is to love.

It is not the famous 'fear-of-death' scene which creates the difficulty. This, rather, is one of the dramatic high points of the play, as, indeed, it is its axis. The Prince, an officer under the Elector of Brandenburg, is brave and noble, but obsessed with the dream of glory. He is in general very much a dreamer and we first see him in a somnambulistic state, making himself a laurel wreath. The Elector plays a trick on him by having his niece, Natalie, make as if to present to him the wreath, around which the Elector's chain has been wrapped. This draws forth an expression of his love for Natalie. He tries to snatch the wreath, but grasps only her glove, as the Elector's party retires in some disorder. Next day, during the briefing of officers before the battle of Fehrbellin, the Prince's attention is devoted more to the ladies than to military duties, especially when he notices that Natalie has lost a glove. What he had thought dream becomes reality for him and he feels that an irresistible tide is sweeping him on to fortune. During the battle, he is even more obsessed with thoughts (which are really dreams) of glory and attacks before the order is given, thus helping to win a victory but also infringing the fundamental Prussian law of discipline. But his 'Gefühl' does not accept this as a real crime. Even after he has been condemned to death by a court-martial, he confidently expects to be pardoned. His friend, Hohenzollern, convinces him that the Elector may wish to be rid of him because his relationship with Natalie stands in the way of a marriage of political convenience. He goes to plead for help from the Electress and, on the way, sees his own freshly dug grave. This is the moment of full awakening to reality and it produces a collapse as spectacular, in its way, as that of Penthesilea. In Act III, scene 5, he renounces his beloved — in her presence — and pleads for nothing but bare life:

Ich will auf meine Güter gehn am Rhein,
Da will ich bauen, will ich niederreißen,
Bis mir der Schweiß herabtrieft.

Natalie, her love (and esteem!) for him unabated, pleads for him to the Elector, who is completely taken aback ('verwirrt', as the stage direction puts it) at the news of Homburg's collapse. For him, a solely rational acceptance of law is not sufficient: it must be assented to by feeling as well. His own heart tells him that the sentence is just, but he senses and reveres in the Prince a sure feeling which, it now appears, does not accord with his. Hence the confusion. He writes to Homburg, telling him that if he is willing to state that an injustice has been done him, he is free. The Prince, having grovelled before, now stands fully upright (Act IV, scene 4) and submits himself freely to the law, though he is now convinced that the sentence will be carried out. He is determined to 'glorify' the law by a free death. This in turn puts the Elector in a position to pardon him, in fact, it makes it a necessity, for harmony between feeling and law has now been achieved, and to execute the Prince would renew dissonance. In a final scene which betrays a taste for the operatic, the Prince, expecting death and immortality, is confronted by a repetition of the 'dream' of Act I, scene 1, but this time in all seriousness as reality. He has become almost a living symbol of Prussia and the work ends with a kind of ritual chant by the whole cast: 'In Staub mit allen Feinden Brandenburgs!'

Korff is surely right to connect this play with the movement for 'renewal' in Prussia after her shattering defeat by Napoleon and with the efforts of such as Fichte (in the *Reden an die deutsche Nation*) and Arndt to arouse a national spirit.[33] The political ideas of Adam Müller, his friend, in which 'Ausgleich der Gegensätze'[34] played an important part, will have helped to create in Kleist's mind the image of a harmonious relationship between the individual and the state. At the same time, the play has clear links with the more personal preoccupations of its author: the awakening of 'feeling' at the deeper level as a response to and a guide through the ultimate realities of life, its susceptibility to confusion and its ability to rise again after a fall.

Kleist never lost the taste for the sublime. Almost all his plays show it in some form or other and if *Die Familie Schroffenstein* is exceptionally pessimistic in its conclusion, it does contain, in Sylvester's words to Jeronimus on recovering from his faint, a striking statement of the Kleistian vision of heroism:

Nicht jeden Schlag ertragen soll der Mensch
Und welchen Gott faßt, denk ich, der darf sinken,
– Auch seufzen. Denn der Gleichmut ist die Tugend
Nur der Athleten. Wir, wir Menschen fallen
Ja nicht für Geld, auch nicht zur Schau. – Doch sollen
Wir stets des Anschauns würdig aufstehn.

Our present play shows just such a glorious rise after a fall and in this case, the brilliance of the glory is not dimmed (as in *Penthesilea*) by a consciousness of discrepancy between the truth of feeling and that of objective, rationally observed reality. And yet one is constrained to wonder whether we are not being presented with what is a paper solution only. Homburg has been caught up by a vision of sublime heroism, of a 'glorious' victory over pride and rebelliousness (Act V, scene 7). His death will help to lay the foundation for the victorious war and harmonious peace to be enjoyed by Brandenburg: the individual's problem, perhaps, solved in and through the state. He feels, in his speech in Act V, scene 10, the 'divinity' of a man in a state of harmonious bliss, rather than the heroic greatness of the suffering hero as we see it in *Penthesilea* (scene 14). His 'ripeness for death' recalls the state of the heroine, not at the tragic climax, but in the idyll scenes of the play:

> Es weht, wie Nahn der Götter um mich her,
> Ich möchte gleich in ihren Chor mich mischen,
> Zum Tode war ich nie so reif als jetzt (lines 1680–2).

It is impossible to blot out the knowledge of Kleist's suicide, which was to be forthcoming in only a few months and of the contrasting moods expressed in letters of that period, though we know, of course, that the letters cannot in themselves be said to *prove* that he had such and such an intention in the play. But they can suggest a fruitful approach to the text. There is depression, of course. His hopes of finding a vocation in the rebuilding of Prussia seemed on the point of collapse.[35] But there is also ecstatic euphoria[36] at the thought of the glorious sublimity of the 'Freitod', which the personality of Henriette Vogel, the incurably ill woman with whom he had entered into a suicide pact, no doubt fanned into a flame. Death (as opposed to the mixture of glory and tragic necessity in *Penthesilea*) now becomes the last great gesture in which the soul expresses and fulfils itself. The thought of death as the culmination of self-fulfilment is one which Kleist has expressed in a letter to Ulrike (1 May 1802), written from his rustic retreat in Switzerland, in adding: 'Denn das Leben hat doch immer nichts Erhabneres, als nur dieses, daß man es erhaben wegwerfen kann!' Writing now to Marie (9 November 1811), 'mitten im Triumfgesang [sic!], den meine Seele in diesem Augenblick des Todes anstimmt', he uses the formula we have seen employed by Penthesilea and the Prince in their moments of ecstatic anticipation:

> Nur so viel wisse, daß meine Seele, durch die Berührung mit der

ihrigen [i.e. Henriette's] zum Tode ganz reif geworden ist; daß ich die ganze Herrlichkeit des menschlichen Gemüts an dem ihrigen ermessen habe, und daß ich sterbe, weil mir auf Erden nichts mehr zu lernen und zu erwerben bleibt.

What the Elector has offered the Prince is the chance to make just such a sublime gesture. In its longing for glory and triumph (cf. Act V, scene 7), the Prince's serene, indeed joyful, embracing of death is linked, not with the healthier, if more painful, experience of reality, but with the more dangerous, if brilliant, ecstatic visions of glory to which Kleist is prone. The play attempts to build a bridge between these and reality, but one is more inclined to echo Kottwitz's remark in the final scene: 'Ein Traum, was sonst?' It could be that this reflects at least a subconscious awareness that this ending is a kind of self-indulgence: Kleist at last finding the glory that real life had denied him. This feeling, in combination with the overt Prussianism, in which even a faint echo of the xenophobia of *Die Hermannsschlacht* can be heard, explains why, for one reader at least, the technical mastery of this play is not enough to give it equal status with the painful and personal honesty of *Penthesilea*.

Notes

1. Cf. H. A. Korff, *Geist der Goethezeit*, 2nd edn (4 vols., Leipzig, 1954), vol. III, p. 459. The tradition of medievalising 'Schauerromantik' had been inherited from the pre-romantic period and existed in a dramatic form (with Goethe's *Götz von Berlichingen* as a distinguished ancestor) and an epic one (popular novels such as those of Veit Weber or Benedicte Naubert).
2. Cf. above, p. 110.
3. In a diary entry of 1807, apropos of *Amphitryon*. Quoted in Kleist, *Werke*, E. Schmidt, G. Minde-Pouet and R. Steig (eds.) (Leipzig–Vienna, n.d.), vol. 1, p. 199.
4. Quoted by H. Kasack and A. Mohrhenn, *Ludwig Tieck* (Berlin, 1943), vol. 1, p. 381.
5. A partial exception is *Prinz Friedrich von Homburg*, but even this play has its technically 'Kleistian' features.
6. Lines 12–13. Had Kleist wished to do so, he could no doubt have fitted the normal order into his metrical form.
7. Cf. his letter to his sister Ulrike (May 1799).
8. For the 'Kantkrise', cf. H. M. Wolff, *Heinrich von Kleist. Die Geschichte seines Schaffens* (Berne, 1954), pp. 115 ff.
9. Cf. F. Koch, *Heinrich von Kleist. Bewußtsein und Wirklichkeit* (Stuttgart, 1958), Part I.
10. Letter of 15 August 1801.
11. Cf. G. Fricke, *Gefühl und Schicksal bei Heinrich von Kleist* (Berlin, 1929), *passim*. For the 'Lebensplan', cf. particularly p. 8.

12. *Geist der Goethezeit*, vol. IV, pp. 47–52.

13. *Gefühl und Schicksal*, p. 76.

14. Cf. *Amphitryon*, lines 1395–6.

15. For the opposite view, cf. Koch, *Bewußtsein*, pp. 123 ff and especially W. Silz, *Heinrich von Kleist. Studies in his Works and Literary Character* (Philadelphia, 1961), pp. 50 ff.

16. This impression is confirmed when one looks at Kleist's (not very distinguished) lyric poetry. He can speak, for example, of 'ploughing the ground of Fate with the ploughshare of hard work' (*Für Wilhelmine von Zenge*, stanza 1).

17. *Heinrich von Kleist*, pp. 139 ff.

18. P. Witkop sees the action as a 'parody of the struggle of the tragic hero', a judgement endorsed by Koch (p. 86).

19. Cf. Fricke, *Gefühl und Schicksal.*

20. Cf. particularly Act II, scene 5, lines 1415 ff, and Act V, lines 2296–3000.

21. *Geist der Goethezeit*, vol. IV, pp. 53–4.

22. Kleist, *Werke*, vol. 5, G. Minde-Pouet (ed.) (Liepzig–Vienna, n.d.), p. 358. The editor suggests Henriette Hendel-Schütz as the addressee.

23. Cf. Goethe's essay *Über Laokoon.*

24. Cf. lines 1280–1.

25. Achilles calls the Amazon law 'unweiblich. . . unnatürlich' (line 1903) and there can be little doubt that he is speaking for Kleist here.

26. Cf. line 1682. This – to say the least – dangerous tendency to states of ecstatic exaltation, which will be discussed in greater detail in the section on *Prinz Friedrich von Homburg*, is perhaps more in place here than anywhere else in Kleist's work.

27. No doubt Kleist responded genuinely to the romantic charm of the material and to romantic thinking about the unconscious mind (he would have learned something of 'magnetism' from his Dresden acquaintance, G. H. Schubert). But he did also have an eye to the saleability of the product: cf. his emphasis of the 'romantic' nature of the work in his letter to the publisher Cotta of 7 July 1808.

28. Käthchen tells of a previous occurrence of the same threat in Act I, scene 2.

29. *Käthchen von Heilbronn*, in Kasack and Mohrhenn, *Tieck*, vol. 1, p. 387.

30. Whether this is a prophetic vision, in symbolic form, of the crucial role eventually played in Napoleon's downfall by Russia, the present writer is unable to say!

31. Cf. Kasack and Mohrhenn, *Tieck*, vol. 1, p. 398.

32. *Bewußtsein*, p. 193.

33. *Geist der Goethezeit*, vol. IV, pp. 287 ff.

34. Ibid., pp. 295–6, and Wolff, *Heinrich von Kleist*, pp. 226 ff.

35. Cf. his letter to Marie von Kleist, 10 November 1811.

36. Cf. the letter to Marie (12 November 1811) in which he states that 'ein Strudel von nie empfundener Seligkeit' has taken possession of him.

10 EPIC WRITING (GENERAL): (A) THE NOVEL

We have already commented on the deliberately undisciplined nature of the romantic approach to genre and on the tendency to romanticise the traditional forms which, in the case of drama, was hardly an unqualified success. We anticipated that the epic forms would prove more congenial to the romantic spirit. Fancy and love should be less inhibited by considerations of practicality and probability and the spirit of *Märchen*, the canon of all poetry according to Novalis,[1] should inform these genres more easily, and not only in the specific short form which bears the name. Friedrich Schlegel, indeed, expects that in all the epic forms, which he sees as 'esoteric' by nature, the structure should be 'nach Art eines Märchens'.[2]

The romantic novel represents an interruption — and in Germany a particularly radical one — in the progress of the form from its traditional associations of the 'adventurous' and improbable[3] towards probability and realism. Wieland, though less boldly than Fielding, moves in *Agathon* (1767) from the wondrous to the 'natural', that is, to the character of ordinary, rather than exotic, life and the subsequent trend of the German novel, though it showed the effects of the romantic tendency and of idealism as they appeared in the later eighteenth century, was in the same general direction. The Romantics saw the genre as one of fancy, love and poetry. A true novel, says Novalis, must be 'durch und durch Poesie' (KS III, 558); it should be 'the highest fulfilment of romantic poetry and philosophy', and 'approximate representation of the infinite'.[4] It is an all-embracing form. True, Friedrich Schlegel distinguishes different emphases (he speaks of philosophical, psychological and sentimental novels), but the ideal is the 'absolute novel', one which comprehends all these and blends 'absolute individuality' with 'absolute universality'.[5] The novel can combine a wide variety of forms and styles; it is encyclopedic as the mind of a romantic person is encyclopedic and its unity is the unity of such an individual *Gemüt*: 'Mancher der vortrefflichsten Romane ist ein Kompendium, eine Enzyklopädie des ganzen geistigen Lebens eines genialischen Individuums.'[6] The romantic novel, then, does not impose a form on the *Gemüt* and its faculties; rather, it is the form assumed by these in their organic self-expression.

It was not as unnatural as it may seem to a reader schooled in the realistic tradition of the nineteenth-century novel that the Romantics, with Schlegel in the vanguard, should have singled out the novel as an essentially un-realistic form. For their conception of it, they went back to the more 'romantic' ages and climes; to earlier Italian, and above all to Spanish, literature. Schlegel gives his most characteristic definition in the context of a discussion of Cervantes. He talks of a texture made up of all kinds of interwoven stylistic threads, liberally ornamented with verse of a wide variety of types, large in extent and containing 'die bunteste Verwicklung, Fülle und Mannigfaltigkeit'. No requirement for unity of tone limits the author, who can alternate between the serious and the playful and 'abandon himself completely to his fantastic caprice and to the outpourings of his own moods and the playful impulses of humour'.[7]

As always, it was the general spirit rather than the precise form of older literature which the Romantics tried to revive and in this case, it was in fact a modern work, Goethe's *Wilhelm Meisters Lehrjahre*, which provided the decisive stimulus to the development of the German romantic novel. As is well known, Goethe's work represents the high point of the form usually called the 'Bildungsroman', in which the threads of event ('Begebenheit'), discursive treatment of ideas ('Meinungen') and sentiment, which run haphazardly through the typical earlier eighteenth-century novel, are drawn together and placed in an integrated relationship through the theme of the moral and spiritual development of a central character. It is the formal achievement of the work, its combination of variety and unity, rather than its 'Classical' ideal of 'Bildung', which the Romantics find fruitful. Friedrich Schlegel comments enthusiastically on that aspect in his *Charakteristik von den Meisterischen Lehrjahren von Goethe.* In addition, in spite of the relatively realistic and rationalistic tendencies of the book, Goethe's awareness of the other factors in life and in particular of the importance of emotion and imagination is strong enough – certainly by comparison with any other novel of the preceding decade – to give ample satisfaction to the romantic hunger for poetry. While Novalis was quite justified in eventually deciding that it does not pay to poetry the full tribute which romantic taste demands, Schlegel can also make a persuasive case, with the aid, perhaps, of a little wishful thinking, for his view of this book as one in which spirit triumphs over, if it does not entirely transfigure, matter. A progressive escalation towards spirituality is a feature of its structure and the sense of mystery aroused by Goethe's presentation of Wilhelm's various encounters and of the interventions in his life of the emissaries of the 'Turmgesellschaft', a feature which recalls the popular 'Bundesroman', the novel of mystery based on the machinations of a secret society, is something which we shall find also in Jean Paul and Hoffmann.[8]

In his commentary on *Wilhelm Meister*, Schlegel exaggerates the mysteriousness, the lack of clear coherence of the plot, which he sees as being balanced by an 'inner' coherence, which arises out of the pervasive presence of an indwelling 'genius'. Whether or not this is accurate as a description of Goethe's work, it certainly represents the dominant romantic conception of novel structure. A loosely constructed plot (as W. Müller-Seidel says in commenting on Hoffmann's *Die Elixiere des Teufels*), which is only a 'foreground'[9] that is constantly being broken, or robbed of its solidity to reveal the real content behind it, becomes the standard romantic practice. A certain lack of discipline becomes a virtue. This is fitting for a mentality which emphasises the freedom of the spirit and sees all things as parts of an all-embracing unity. But if the real, romantic unity and coherence is to emerge, formal indiscipline needs to be accompanied by a compensating inner mental and moral discipline which forms the basis of the true content, the spiritual substance out of which that unity and coherence are to arise. Brentano shows his awareness of this when he admonishes his friend Achim von Arnim who constantly runs the risk of letting his fancy run away with him, 'Arnim, lieber Arnim, wenn du nur ein wenig strenger arbeiten wolltest und nicht so aneinander binden...'[10] It is possible to see links between the myriad characters and episodes in Arnim's novels and stories, but it is also true that the reader sometimes has to do what is strictly the author's work; to locate the message and apply it. Arnim, at least, creates the substance. In the case of Tieck, Friedrich Schlegel even doubts whether this is present: 'Tieck hat gar keinen Sinn für Kunst sondern nur [für] Poesie-Kunst; für Genialität, Fantasmus und Sentimentalität...' He has the romantic externals, but this is not enough: 'Es fehlt ihm an Stoff, an Realismus [sic!], an Philosophie.'[11] Whether this is quite a fair judgement on Tieck, we shall see in due course. It certainly shows us that the romantic relaxation of outer discipline is not meant as an excuse for relaxation of artistic and mental effort.

A not dissimilar observation can be made in the matter of the treatment of character. The real 'character' of a romantic novel resides in the unifying spirit dispersed through the whole. The figures who appear on the stage have largely the function of reflecting that spirit, as bodies reflect light. Even the central hero or heroine usually lacks a distinct personality and is outwardly passive. Inwardly, on the other hand, these figures show a great deal of activity; they have the rich and sensitive *Gemüt* which one associates with the artistic temperament and, indeed, the *Künstlerroman* is very much a romantic form. These characters are often contemplatives of the type portrayed by Novalis in Chapter 6 of *Heinrich von Ofterdingen*. They resemble Goethe's Tasso in some respects, but lack the dramatic dimension with which that character is endowed. Even when they are described as active, they do not engage the reader's interest through emotional power, but rather function in such a way as to stimulate a poetic state of mind. They are not empty shells, but they are presences, rather than individual people.

At its least successful, the German romantic novel melts into a kind of haze, without contours or real impact. At its best, it has a quality of musicality, by which we mean here not only its liberal use of song, or of melodious language – though these are aspects of the phenomenon – but the presence of substance and structure in spite of the absence of solidity and architectonic form. The fact that, as Professor Pascal notes, *Heinrich von Ofterdingen* has a relatively 'insubstantial' character[12] does not necessarily invalidate it as a novel in general, but only in relation to a specific type of novel. There is another approach, which has been called by one critic 'non-epic',[13] but for which we have chosen the term 'musical', rather as Friedrich Schlegel talks of a musical structure in one of his basic models, *Don Quijote*.[14] The unity of a work of this kind depends less on plot than on the recurrence of symbols and motifs and on the organisation of the figures, not as a dramatic grouping, but through their relation to a common centre, like variations on a theme. Novalis speaks with some justice of the 'Variationsreihen' of characters in *Wilhelm Meister*[15] and he himself takes this tendency much further in *Heinrich von Ofterdingen*. His figures are barely identified, but are thematically interrelated in a close orchestration. This musicality of structure, complemented by other, often lyrical, techniques, is calculated to activate the fancy or in Schlegel's terminology, 'wit', the starting-point of music proper,[16] and love, the spiritual energy which lies at its heart. The romantic alienation-effect[17] in which the grip of logic on the *Gemüt* is decisively loosened is gradually achieved and the novel approaches the free-floating state of the *Märchen*. As Novalis says, 'alle Romane, wo wahre Liebe vorkommt, sind Märchen – magische Begebenheiten.'[18]

The romantic novel, then, works best with a loose epic framework: but at least a rudimentary epic framework there still must be. A collection of descriptions, reflections and anecdotes, all of which happen to be concerned with the nature of art and its role in life, does not constitute a novel, not even a romantic one. Such is the case with the *Herzensergießungen eines kunstliebenden Klosterbruders* (1796) of *W. H. Wackenroder*. All the pieces are linked by the fact that they emanate from the pen of the art-loving monk, but not only is the latter not involved in any action whatsoever, but he also lacks all spiritual presence. He is a neutral, psychologically inactive agent and so cannot lend coherence to the various pieces in the collection, whose orientation remains predominantly theoretical. Within this truly non-epic framework, however, Wackenroder has created one figure who is in embryo such a characteristically romantic novel-hero that he deserves to be briefly discussed here. That figure is the artist-hero, the musician Joseph Berglinger,[19] a self-portrait in origin, but one which has been raised to a general and symbolic level, which makes it capable of articulating the romantic problem of the dualism of the spiritual ideal and the material reality. The form chosen, the narration of the alternating ecstasy and anguish of the artist, presages the *Künstlerroman*, for which Wackenroder's friend Tieck, was soon to lay the foundation with *Franz Sternbalds Wanderungen*.

Friedrich Schlegel could appreciate and analyse the creative imagination, but he did not possess it within himself. He is at best a minor and occasional poet and in his *Lucinde* (1799), we have a conception, rather than a realisation, of an interesting novel. It is in the ideas rather than the poetic quality that the interest lies. The theme is the nature of love, in its full romantic harmony of sense and spirit; the final synthesis, as Esther Hudgins shows, of the dialectical interaction between the 'male' and 'female' principles, in which marriage need not necessarily play any part. In many marriages, indeed, such a synthesis does not take place. The hero, Julius, finds his perfect complement in Lucinde; the active principle finds the passive, 'Witz' finds 'Phantasie' and system 'chaos'. In the process of portraying this development, Schlegel says much that is interesting and the loose and unsystematic form, in which Julius asserts his 'right to a charming confusion',[20] is certainly no hindrance to a romantic effect. But Schlegel cannot give his ideas poetic substance. Even the dream-allegory ('Allegorie von der Frechheit'), in which he tries to evoke the harmony of 'Phantasie' and 'Witz', remains intellectual and conceptual in nature and the synthetic

quality of Schlegel's attempted lyrical mysticism emerges clearly in a
passage like the following:

> Wer kann messen und wer vergleichen was eines wie das andere
> unendlichen Wert hat, wenn beides verbunden ist in der wirklichen
> Bestimmung, die bestimmt ist, alle Lücken zu ergänzen und Mittlerin
> zu sein zwischen dem männlichen und weiblichen Einzelnen und der
> unendlichen Menschheit?[21]

The underlying experience may be a genuine one, but Schlegel can find
neither the words nor the images to articulate it in a poetic form. One
has only to place this language alongside that of Novalis to realise its
essential hollowness.

Novalis left both of his essays in narrative prose, *Die Lehrlinge zu
Sais* and *Heinrich von Ofterdingen* (1802), unfinished, but in different
stages of incompleteness. Whereas the latter has already acquired a
momentum and a fairly clear structural pattern, the former, consisting
of two only loosely connected fragments, is more a sketch for a novel
than the torso of an uncompleted work. It seems quite likely that the
Lehrlinge, on which work was begun first, and which is the product of
the scientific and philosophical studies of the Freiberg period – when
Novalis studied under the 'Naturphilosoph' A. G. Werner – was
dropped in favour of the Ofterdingen-theme when Novalis became
aware of the much greater philosophical and aesthetic potential of the
latter.

The gist, indeed, of the *Lehrlinge* seems to have been assimilated
into the later work. The main preoccupation is nature and man's
relation to and capacity for understanding it. It is a mystery written in
a hieroglyphic language and the seeker's best chance of insight lies in
cultivating a poetic and childlike *Gemüt*. Man, in his present fallen
state, can achieve at best fleeting glimpses of the mystery behind the
veil of Isis, but there are hints of a restoration to come, both in the
references to a (perhaps Messianic) blue-eyed child who has departed
and to whom, on his return, the present Teacher will yield his place
and in the motif of the unveiling of the statue of Isis, prefigured in the
Märchen of Hyacinth and Rosenblütchen and spelt out in the well-
known distich in the paralipomena:

> Einem gelang es – er hob den Schleier der Göttin zu Sais –
> Aber was sah er? Er sah – Wunder des Wunders – sich selbst.

As it stands, *Die Lehrlinge zu Sais* (apart from the charming 'Hyacinth' episode) represents thought trembling on the brink of poetry. Certainly, the approach is imaginative — very much a poeticised science in so far as the term 'science' is applicable at all! — the language sensitive and evocative rather than abstract and descriptive, and some passages more or less lyrical in their analysis of states of mind. But the work lacks movement. The working out of the potential romantic epic concept (that of a quest) has not been truly begun. Such a development would have been possible and might well have led to a pattern of escalation of understanding such as is present in the *Hymnen an die Nacht* and also forms the structural basis of *Heinrich von Ofterdingen.*

Hiebel rightly calls this work the 'novel of poetry'. If the quest for the Blue Flower (symbolising the goal of romantic longing in general), which begins in the first chapter and was intended to end in the (uncompleted) second part of the novel, gives an outward narrative framework, the inner revelation is that of poetry and its inner action is a process of progressive poeticisation, both in the hero's personal development and in the world about him, in which he was to have played, eventually, a Messianic role. The first chapter of Part One serves as a prologue and presents two contrasted dreams: Heinrich's revelatory dream of the Blue Flower, an image which becomes immediately implanted in his mind and impels him forward on the poetic path, and that experienced long ago by his father, which was also a call to the poetic life but remained ineffective as a result of his (the father's) inability to liberate himself from the mentality of the material, 'gegenwärtige Welt'. This lays the foundation for the constant theme of a dual reality (prosaic and poetic, 'Welt' and 'Traum'), such as we saw earlier in the *Hymnen an die Nacht.*[22] Although Novalis concentrates attention primarily on the poetic, positive dimension, surrounding his hero with favourable influences and eschewing the uncanny altogether, the existence of the other possibility is not forgotten and it appears from time to time as a foil, for example in the figure of the 'Schreiber' in Klingsohr's *Märchen* (Chapter 9) or in the reference in stanza 4 of the miner's second song (Chapter 5) to those who seek gold for gain and 'ahnden nicht, daβ sie gefangen'.

Heinrich lives in a poetic era (the Middle Ages) and has himself an 'Anlage zum Dichter', as is made clear in Chapter 2. Chapters 2–5 take the hero through a series of encounters which further the development of this potential in a steadily escalating inward progression from legends and fairy-tale stories of poets (documents of the poetic primal age), through the worlds of the Crusades and of the Orient (Chapter 4) to the inner spiritual truth of nature and history (the miner and hermit of Chapter 5, whose underground lives emphasise symbolically the fact that while at the superficial level, Heinrich is making a journey from Eisenach to Augsburg, the real journey is a spiritual one into his inner Self). At this point, Novalis judges the moment to be right for the beginning of the initiatory process proper. The change is marked by the arrival in Augsburg at one level and a detailed analysis (at the beginning of Chapter 6) of the poetic *Gemüt* at the other, after which the process itself begins.

As the hero's eventual mission is to be one of restoration, it is appropriate that the powers which preside over his initiation should be those which (as has been shown in the 'Atlantismärchen' of Chapter 3) ruled in the Golden Age, namely poetry and love, embodied here in the figure of Klingsohr and his daughter Mathilde (Chapters 6–8). The restoration of the Golden Age is prefigured by a *Märchen* told by Klingsohr, which constitutes the ninth and final chapter of Part One and contains the whole work in microcosm as, indeed, in a more fragmentary form, do many other episodes. This, however, is but the end of the stage of 'Expectation' (the sub-title of Part One). Heinrich still has much progress to make.

The love relationship with Mathilde has set free his independent spiritual consciousness, symbolised by the sidereal being Astralis, who sings at the beginning of Part Two (sub-titled 'The Fulfilment' and devoid of chapter divisions) of the need for the experience of death and parting if true spiritual freedom is to be achieved. Mathilde has been drowned and Heinrich, now a pilgrim, is roused from despair by an experience of her continued living presence. He is led by her emissary, Cyane, to Sylvester, his final teacher in the completed text, who introduces him to the concept of the fundamental, universal spiritual principle called 'Gewissen', which takes individual shapes in individual people and confers 'mastery', as the culmination of human 'Bildung'. The decisive breakthrough to a new dimension has still not yet occurred, however, at this, the final point of the completed text. The *Report* given by Tieck of plans for a continuation, together with material left behind by Novalis himself, makes it seem likely that this was to occur during a visit to a strange 'monastery', the end effect of which would have been a complete understanding of death and the decisive liberation of the spirit from the material world ('Erdgeist, deine Zeit ist um,' runs the last line of the poem already written for this section). After this, Heinrich was to have ranged freely and widely in time and space and eventually to have effected a second breakthrough, into a world beyond the bounds of nature as at present constituted, one like that of Klingsohr's *Märchen*. Here, he would have been finally united with Mathilde (simultaneously finding the Blue Flower) and would have fulfilled the prophecy of the 'Atlantismärchen' of Chapter 3, becoming the poet-king and founding a new Golden Age.

In a manner entirely typical of Novalis, then, this work is planned, and partially executed, as one in which spirit not only illuminates the material world, but one in which it 'becomes world', a veritable 'apotheosis of poetry', as Friedrich Schlegel put it.[23] One. is struck, not only by the universality of the grand design, but also by the (entirely romantic) organisational capacity which informs it. It is the only romantic novel which scores a convincing success in realising the 'encyclopedic' ideal so boldly set up in theory by Friedrich Schlegel.

It is Novalis's success in rendering the fact that the world is both infinitely multifarious and at the same time united by a single universal spiritual force which makes this such a *radically* romantic novel and so consistently and continuously poetic in the romantic sense. This certainly means that it demands a great deal of the reader in terms of dedicated concentration, but it also offers much, no less, in fact, than a romantic Gospel. Poetry, though not itself the ultimate truth, is the means by which that truth can be made manifest. Love can inspire poetry ('Du wirst mich zu den höchsten Anschauungen begeistern,' says Heinrich to Mathilde (KS I, 289)), but love is 'dumb' without poetry, which is the spirit's means of self-expression, 'die eigentümliche Handlungsweise des menschlichen Geistes', in the words of Klingsohr (KS I, 287).[24] It is the key factor which creates in what, to the casual observer, might appear a loosely constructed novel with an exiguous plot, a dense and highly integrated texture. It ruled in conjunction with love, in the pre-historical Golden Age; it will do so again in the post-historical one of the future, when the tyranny of time has been abolished. It is the common factor which binds together the various strands of Heinrich's experience. War, which he encounters through the Crusaders, has the tendency to become 'Dichtung' and the participants, 'unwillkürlich von Poesie durchdrungene Weltkräfte' (p. 285). The Orient (known through the 'Morgenländerin') is 'das Land der Poesie' and can, by virtue of its roots in the remote past, become 'die zauberische Dichtung und Fabel unserer Sinne' (p. 237). The Miner, who represents the understanding of nature, has the poet's 'Erhebung über die Welt' (KS I, 241; cf. ibid., p. 267) and the sum of his wisdom is expressed in poetic form. The hermit (in whom mysticism and the sense of history are combined) shows that the true historian is also a poet (p. 259).[25] Love itself can be defined as 'die höchste Naturpoesie' (p. 287) when it is experienced as a human relationship. The unity provided by this common orientation is underpinned by the constant recurrence of figures (e.g. the Teacher-figure), motifs (such as the colour blue, the Golden Age, the apprentice who marries the master's daughter[26]) and by the sense of *déja vu*, a feeling of familiarity in an entirely new experience.

As we saw, the very first chapter establishes the coexistence of two levels of reality: the practical, 'realistic' one on which Heinrich's parents live — his mother, for example, diagnoses his pensive inwardness of spirit as a sign of sickness or depression — and the inner, romantic one which Heinrich enters at the outset and never for a moment leaves. In the second chapter, where the plot proper begins, we are given first a sensitive evocation of the spirit of the Middle Ages, followed by the departure for Augsburg, which is also the beginning of a spiritual journey and is rendered in terms of the hero's state of mind: 'Er sah sich an der Schwelle der Ferne. . . Er war im Begriff, sich in ihre blaue Flut zu tauchen' (p. 205). As the novel progresses, we do not lose the sense of time and place altogether, but these seem of little account and we are so successfully weaned away from the objective, 'realistic' perspective on events, that this seems not to matter; indeed, as in a *Märchen*, the unusual begins to seem natural. We have already seen, in Chapter 5,[27] an example of the process of romantic alienation on which this effect is based. There, as very often, indeed, imagery is the principal vehicle for it. But we should not forget the contribution made by the narrative style in general which, while it is formally straight-forward, is consistently melodious and luminous and avoids all harsh or prosaic effects. It is always a style which favours reflective inwardness or at the very least, preserves the state of detachment of the spirit from close involvement with the details of material reality.

The final effect of the book is indeed 'märchenhaft' in Novalis's sense. It produces an impression, if not of life on another planet, at least of life on another plane, and is a successful communication of its author's experience and view of life. To be completely successful in its own terms, it needs, perhaps, to convince the reader of the actuality and validity of the higher spiritual dimension of which it aims to be a revelation, and it is hard to avoid being swept along by its strong, smooth current, once the initial resistance to its deliberately strange atmosphere and technique has been overcome. But even those who remain immune to its spiritual message will value it as a profound and exhaustive portrayal of the romantic *Gemüt*.

Clemens Brentano, in his novel *Godwi oder das steinerne Bild der Mutter* (1800–02), takes the freedom inherent in the romantic concept of the novel to the point of amorphousness. He presents us with a wide range of intricately interrelated characters, and a liberal expenditure of lyricism, wit and fancy, canvassing ideas and probing into the human consciousness in an interesting manner. Yet it seems to be all subject and no object, all thinking and no specific thought. The book lacks a focal point and all its agitated movement cannot compensate for the absence of a sense of direction. The common need of all the characters, including the 'author', Maria, for salvation from their chronic instability and disorientation, a salvation they seek in love, is not in itself enough to produce an integrated structure, and the organisational power of a Novalis is lacking here.

For Brentano does not succeed in conveying to us an idea of what love, in his view, is, or should be. It is not only a question of the emancipation of the individual heart from conventional social morality (though that is clearly a preoccupation of the author's). Violetta, for example, begs Godwi to save her from the life of licence towards which her 'emancipated' mother is driving her. Asceticism, or 'Classical' renunciation, represent no solution to her problem, but neither does the system of 'Zügellosigkeit' to which her mother, the Countess, subscribes (cf. K 2, 440). Eventually, she is united with Godwi, 'not by a priest, nor by life, but by love alone' (p. 444), but we have no very clear idea of what that love is.

A harmonious balance of the sensual and spiritual may be the essence of this ideal. This may be what Molly has in mind when she says of Godwi: 'Er kann nur durch Liebe, die heftigste, ruhigste Liebe, . . . ruhig und unendlich viel werden' (K 2, 87). But it is discord and restlessness that predominate here. Violetta, torn between two extremes, recalls the similarly contradictory figure of Perdita in the fragment of what might have become a good romantic picaresque novel. *Der schiffbrüchige Galeerensklave vom Toten Meer* (1811).[28] As we saw in Chapter 6, Brentano was still struggling much later in life with the problem of reconciling sacred and profane love and here, in spite of the rather bland indication that Godwi does find peace, we are tempted to use of him — and indeed of the book as a whole — Molly's comment: 'Er ist ein Spiegel der trübbarsten und beweglichsten Flut, und nichts als ein Spiegel' (K 2, 87).

Like several other Romantics, Brentano delved into the romantic ages of the past, and not only in the *Wunderhorn*. He indulged in the retelling of old stories (e.g. Jörg Wickram's *Der Goldfaden*) and was

largely successful in re-creating the naïve simplicity and piety of the
Middle Ages in the long, unfinished *Chronika eines fahrenden Schülers*
(1802–6; second version 1818). This is a genuinely romantic re-
creation, with the psychological subtleties and sadness intermingled
with sweetness which bespeak the nostalgia of the modern for a lost
innocence, as they do also Brentano's own feeling that he has been
orphaned. But there is none of the hothouse atmosphere which
sometimes makes itself felt in *Godwi*, and although the loose chronicle
form has been adopted, the sense of disoriented flux which we have in
that novel is absent. Brentano has been able to find a point of reference
outside his own individual preoccupations and the work has a firm
thematic centre. There are even moments of an almost Eichendorffian
serenity, as in the opening paragraph:

> In dem Jahr, da man zählte nach Christi, unsers lieben Herrn,
> Geburt, 1358, im lieblichen Monat Mai hörte ich, Johannes, die
> Schwalbe früh an meinem Kammerfenster singen, als ich erwachte,
> und ward innig durch den frommen Gesang des Vögeleins erbaut
> (K 2, 518).

It is pleasant to be able to leave Brentano, temporarily at least, in a
relaxed and harmonious mood, one which recalls the *Wunderhorn* and
the sunnier *Märchen*. It is not, perhaps, his most authentic voice, but
it is still genuinely his and should not be altogether disregarded.

Achim von Arnim undoubtedly did his best work in the epic genres,
but was better served by the shorter forms, which imposed at least an
elementary discipline of limitation on him. For that reason, our more
detailed general characterisation of him as a writer is to be found in
Chapter 12. His novels, however, cannot be passed over in silence.
They are: *Armut, Reichtum, Schuld und Buße der Gräfin Dolores*
(1810) and *Die Kronenwächter* (vol. 1, 1817; vol. 2 – in a fragmentary
and unrevised form – published posthumously by Bettina in 1854). In
each, we find the breathless, un-lyrical narrative style, the deep concern
with moral issues, the tendency to the comic grotesque and the peculiar
interpenetration of the material and psychological, leading to a kind
of romantic surrealism, which we shall meet also in the shorter stories.
Since we do not wish to discuss these works in a vacuum and since in
any case it is through the detail, rather than a general description, that
Arnim is most fairly represented, we feel justified in quoting a single
example here.

Our chosen episode – by no means the oddest or most animated in
Arnim's novels – is that in the first volume of *Die Kronenwächter* in
which Berthold, who has recovered his health after a transfusion of
blood from Anton and who wishes to acquire knightly accomplish-
ments, goes to practise riding on the wooden 'Trojan Horse' left behind
in the Waiblingen 'Rathaus' after a theatrical performance:

'Nun gebt die Sporen, dann geht's fort,' rief Fingerling, 'Aber haltet
die Zügel fest, daß es nicht durchgeht, nicht zu fest und nicht zu
wenig.' Auch das tat Berthold, bemerkte aber plötzlich solche
Bewegung in dem Rosse, daß er die Zügel immer stärker anzuhalten
für nötig fand, was aber alles nicht half, denn unaufhaltsam stürzte
der stolze, von der Sonne ausgetrocknete Holzbau zusammen,
Berthold an die Erde, und aus dem hohlen Bauche sprang Anton
schlaftrunken, sich die Augen reibend, hervor. Fingerling half
erschrocken seinem lieben Berthold auf, fragte ihn sorglich, ob er
sich Schaden getan, dieser hörte aber nicht auf ihn, sah Anton
verwundert an und sprach: 'Ist's mir doch wie ein bedeutsamer
Traum, daß du aus meiner verunglückten Ritterfahrt so froh
hervorgehst; begegnest du mir vielleicht noch oft?'[29]

This is indeed more than just an oddly comic incident. Berthold and
Anton are strangely linked and the latter is indeed to 'emerge' as the
main hero in succession to Berthold. The abortive 'Ritterfahrt' is a
symbolic reference to Berthold's situation as at one and the same time
a 'Bürger' (in fact, the Mayor of Waiblingen) and a descendant of the
Hohenstaufens and through this, to the unsatisfactory social and
political state of the German nation, not only under Maximilian, but in
the early nineteenth century.

Our main concern here, though, is with the way in which this
anecdote, itself of no great significance in the main plot, is narrated:
with a mass of solid detail whose solidity is emphasised, and yet at the
same time, although the dreamy atmosphere of the romantic *Märchen*
is lacking, an alienating strangeness which makes it impossible to speak
of realism (unless there be such a thing as 'romantic realism'!) and
which justifies the author's explicit invocation of the dream-motif.
Arnim's peculiar characteristic is that he distorts the perspective from
which the reality is observed and stimulates the inner activity of the
Gemüt without removing our sense of the *materiality* of the world
described. The most striking single feature of the passage quoted is the
expression '[daß du] aus meiner. . . Ritterfahrt *hervorgehst*' (my

emphasis), which echoes the earlier, purely descriptive 'sprang. . .
hervor' and combines a clear abstract force with the concrete image of
the boy emerging from the wreckage of the stage-horse, rubbing the
sleep from his eyes.

Gräfin Dolores has a modern, and *Die Kronenwächter* a medieval,
setting; both, in fact, are very much concerned with the political,
social and moral state of contemporary Germany. It was the question
of spiritual values in general, rather than 'external' political forms,
which exercised Arnim. He would not have denied that change was
inevitable, but in the change that was going on around him, he saw
mainly decay, a drift into an unstable and indeterminate state in which
all firm character and morality could be lost. This trend is very much in
his mind in his novels, as in his stories,[30] and not only in the portrayal
of the chief characters. The figure of the 'ugly Baron', a total egoist
and unprincipled joker who flits through the pages of *Gräfin Dolores*,
serves to bring home to the hero, Graf Karl, the dangerous nature of
such detachment and to keep his reforming zeal within bounds:

> Mit Schrecken dachte er, daß eine Revolution gerade notwendig
> solche Menschen an ihrer Spitze tragen müsse, und mancher
> jugendliche Umwälzungsplan, den er mit dem gärenden Most der
> Zeit getränkt hatte, verschwand vor seinen Augen in dem einen
> bedeutenden Augenblicke; nur der Ruchlose fängt eine neue Welt an
> in sich, das Gute war ewig; das Bestehende soll gut gedeutet
> werden. . . Es wurde ihm so wohl, indem er rasch fortschreitend
> dieser ruhig fortschreitenden Bildung des geliebten Vaterlands
> gedachte (SRE 1, 67–8).

This passage illustrates not only Arnim's reformist-conservative political
position, but also the way in which the details and episodes can be
integrated into the whole. The incident out of which it arises is of no
importance in the plot, but it can be, and is related by the author to the
fundamental theme which underlies Karl's thinking and striving: that
of the search for creative, constructive, non-egotistic self-fulfilment.
The novel ends, indeed, on the idea of 'true and loyal service' to the
German nation.

The main plot is constituted by the story of the marriage of Karl
and Dolores, her infidelity and moral regeneration through penitence
and penance, and her eventual death, brought about by the mistaken
idea that Karl is about to leave her for another. Dolores is a child of
her time, not evil, but morally indeterminate. She slides into infidelity

almost without realising it and her moral character develops only afterwards, in awareness of guilt and humble acceptance of a life of service. The novel is certainly a counterblast to Goethe's *Die Wahlverwandtschaften* in its defence of the sanctity of marriage, which many felt that Goethe had called into question. It is not Dolores who is the centre of interest, however, but Karl, who succeeds in overcoming his passions and achieving firmness of purpose amidst the shifting sands of instability all around him.

The Karl–Dolores plot is in fact a framework only, and anything but a restrictive one. Arnim feels free, in typical romantic fashion, to use the novel form as a receptacle for a large number of poems and playlets, and even a mini-novel, *Hollins Liebeleben*, a study of undisciplined sensibility which recalls Goethe's *Werther*.[31] All this material could conceivably have been unified in a thematically organised romantic structure and some degree of integration is indeed observable. The *Hollin*-story, for example, and that of Frank, the rootless erstwhile preacher, are fairly clearly examples of the sickness of the age which the novel is attempting to diagnose and treat. The figure of the poet Waller, on the other hand, to which considerable attention is devoted, is not thoroughly integrated into the main texture. That this would not have been impossible is shown, for example, by the comment (on p. 193) in which Arnim exposes his lack of true character, his unwilling-ness to give liberally of his time and effort to create worthy art. In general, however, the figure too often serves as an excuse for a poem or an episode of comic oddity and the reader finds himself hard put to it to hold together all the various impressions he is offered. Arnim might perhaps have replied to such a criticism with a reference to the principle of 'ewige Berührung in allem', which is in fact invoked to justify one somewhat questionable inclusion (p. 425), but even a romantic novelist cannot expect his readers to do for themselves the work of identifying these relationships. This is a work of interest and merit, but Arnim's remorseless accumulation of material produces in the end a somewhat disorderly abundance which bewilders, rather than delights the fancy.

This last point applies with even greater force to *Die Kronenwächter*. It is true that we do not possess a finally revised form of the complete work, but it would have taken an organising genius far beyond Arnim's to produce even a romantic order (i.e. a 'musical' unity within apparent confusion) out of this genuine chaos. Arnim's original concept, as Bettina tells us (SRE 1, 1055), was a four-volume historical tapestry encompassing the 'Geschichte, Sitten und Gebräuche von ganz

Deutschland'. What we are given is not the great German historical
novel which one senses in potential in this concept, but an enormous
and disorganised archive, into which all the results of Arnim's
researches into late fifteenth- and early sixteenth-century Swabia,
every figure, factual or legendary, and every character and story he can
imagine, are crammed. The result is like a huge carnival procession; full
of colour and movement and showing great inventiveness and power in
individual details but hardly a finished work of art. If Scott, in the
preface (of 1831) to *Quentin Durward*, expresses some uncertainty as
to whether, faced by an 'abundance of material', he has succeeded in
bringing his story 'into a pleasing, compact and sufficiently intelligible
form', what, one wonders, would his reaction to *Die Kronenwächter*
have been?

Arnim was not, of course, aiming to produce an historical novel of
the type so successfully established by Scott. The latter had learned to
let romance take precedence over history, not only in the sense of a
willingness to depart from factual accuracy but also in the more
important matter of the kind of interest which he brings to the past
and which he communicates to his readers. He wishes to tell 'a good
story', and to build it around characters, events and milieux which are
heroic and 'interesting' (exotic), in the first place because they belong
to the past. The 'Walter Scott Model', if we may so call it, is represented
in the German novel of our period only by relatively minor figures like
Zschokke (hardly a Romantic!), Fouqué and Wilhelm Hauff, whose
Lichtenstein (1826), the best German work in this line, turns to
sixteenth-century Swabia for its superficially romantic, 'interesting'
qualities: 'auch wir hatten eine Vorzeit, die, reich an bürgerlichen
Kämpfen, uns nicht weniger interessant dünkt als die Vorzeit des
Schotten.'[32] As might be expected, Hauff's book is quite a fresh and
colourful tale of action — though not on a par with Scott or Dumas —
but lacks the deeper spiritual and psychological dimensions
characteristic of the major German Romantics. Arnim's approach to
history is more like that of Novalis;[33] he is interested in characters and
events, less for their own individual sake than for the way in which they
reflect the workings of the eternal spirit in what, in the long and
important Introduction to *Die Kronenwächter*, he calls 'die Schule der
Erde' (SRE 1, 518).

The basic plan of the work is centred on parallel situations of crisis
and confusion on both the individual and the national planes. The
principal characters stumble desperately in the attempt to find a firm
footing and direction in an unreliable and often sordid reality. The

national theme is no less than the whole past, present and future of Germany, which are inextricably entangled. The past is represented by the Hohenstaufens, both an ideal of glory and unity (symbolised by the crown and the fairy-tale 'Kronenburg') and (as a surviving factor in the present state of the Empire), an alien and potentially disruptive force. The present is that of the Emperor Maximilian and his attempts to control and reform the Empire, in which task he often comes into conflict with the Guardians of the Crown, a secretive and rather sinister body whose agents intervene, in both positive and negative ways, in the lives of various representatives of the later generation of the Hohenstaufen line, through whom they hope to achieve some mysterious, and probably not very praiseworthy, end. Their odd and somewhat squalid residence of Hohenstock seems designed to be a concrete symbol of their actual nature, a clear parallel and contrast to the 'Kronenburg', the symbol of the ideal. As to the future, we have the feeling that all the striving, confusion and suffering which we are witnessing represent the birth-pangs of something new, but it is not at all certain what this will be. On the national as on the individual level, there is effort, even good will, but also an alarming degree of suscepti- bility to error and sin. The forces of chaos seem stronger than those of constructive order. But we know that Arnim did believe in the eventual victory of the spirit over the forces of evil. He does seem to have envisaged an eventual redemption in *Die Kronenwächter* and we shall find later clear evidence of his faith in the saving power of the spirit, above all in the story *Der tolle Invalide.* . .

Eichendorff produced in his *Ahnung und Gegenwart* (written in 1811– 12, but not published until 1815) a 'Zeitroman' which is at least as thoroughgoing in its Romanticism, and certainly more successful as a romantic novel, than *Gräfin Dolores.* He had a good opinion of Arnim's book, which he expressed through his hero, Graf Friedrich, in Chapter 12 of *Ahnung und Gegenwart*, but was also critical of its formal capriciousness and delight in oddity. His own taste is conditioned, as in the lyric poetry, by an indwelling sense of beauty and proportion which – in the romantic context at any rate – one might almost call Mozartian; indeed, it is suggested that he was influenced by Mozartian opera, in particular *Figaro*, during the period of study in Vienna when the novel was composed.[34]
   From the brilliant initial evocation of youth, as Friedrich stands among his fellow students on the ship 'in stiller beschaulicher Freude',

to the more muted, but still romantically serene, ending (which, like the beginning, takes place at sunrise, always a positive motif in Eichendorff), the author's mastery of tone and of poetic language rarely deserts him. As in the case of Novalis, we see here that the romantic novel form offers particular opportunities to the lyrical genius and Eichendorff takes full advantage of these, not only in the songs, of uniformly high quality, which are strewn through the book, but also in his descriptions, above all those of landscapes. We have already seen something of his ability to evoke spiritual reality and to stimulate and articulate the inner life of the *Gemüt*.[35] This capacity is consistently in evidence and its effect is not merely decorative. It forms just as important a part of the novel's substance as those discussions in which ideas are directly formulated, by keeping our minds attuned to the spiritual reality to which we must hold in the interplay of 'Ahnung' and 'Gegenwart' which is central to human life. A landscape can indeed become a vehicle in a more direct sense for the author's moral and spiritual message, as for example the Rhine valley in Chapter 15, or the mountain landscape to which Friedrich refers the 'unbändig' Romana when he is admonishing her for her unwillingness to submit to God's authority and live 'in weiser Ordnung und Frömmigkeit' (BG 2, 223).

It is for this ideal of spiritual stability which Friedrich stands and which he achieves, and which is also Eichendorff's hope for his own nation. Germany, as he saw it, was going through a period of crisis, a 'gewitterschwüle Zeit der Erwartung, Sehnsucht und Schmerzen' as he called it in a letter to Fouqué of 1 October 1814. Both of the principal male characters, Friedrich and Leontin, feel the need to work constructively, but the current social and political situation offers no really satisfactory sphere of activity for either. Leontin, indeed, has relapsed into a subjective, 'poetic' existence which may preserve the spirit from infection by the sickness of the age, but carries with it the danger of isolation, and the egotistic 'Verwilderung' which is the lot of Romana and Friedrich's brother Rudolf. The saving grace, in Leontin's case, is his love for Julie. Friedrich involves himself in a wider variety of experience and successfully avoids the two main dangers, represented by the two women in his life: Romana, to whom reference has already been made and who falls victim to her self-assertive and self-destructive hypersensibility, and Rosa, who is sucked into the slough of philistine materialism. His range of experience includes, in addition to love, friendship, politics, war and poetry, the last of which comes closest to providing him with a fulfilling mission in life. But he cannot accept as sufficient in itself a poetry divorced from morality and practical living, a purely abstract and aesthetic activity, such as is represented by the literary society into which he strays in Chapter 12, and by the unattached, 'professional' poet Faber. 'Ich möchte nicht dichten,' he says to the Prince, 'wenn es nur Spaß wäre, denn wo dürfen wir jetzt noch redlich und wahrhaft sein, wenn es nicht im Gedicht ist?' (BG 2, 195). The poet should be the paladin of the spirit, but not in egotistic 'independence'. His true freedom, and his guarantee of truth, lies in making himself the servant of God and the brother of the martyrs.[36] The poet, like everyone else, must build his life on a foundation of religion, the only source of stability in the Babylonian confusion of 'Poesie, Andacht, Deutschheit, Tugend und Vaterländerei' which Friedrich sees around him. All this is expressed in the final summation of Chapter 24. In the light of that, Friedrich's final decision to enter a monastery should be seen not as a confession of despair, but as a sign of faith and of determination to prepare for the constructive work which the future will make possible and demand.

Eichendorff's second novel, *Dichter und ihre Gesellen* (1834) is, like its predecessor, a highly poetic work and, like the earlier novel, has a typically romantic structure, centred on the travels of the principal character, Baron Fortunat. It too is concerned with the quest for the true path in life and for clarification of the role of poetry therein. It shows, however, a certain slackening of the spiritual discipline and control that such a structure demands and a less positive confidence in the capacity of poetry to cope with the pitfalls which life contains. Eichendorff's sense of the dangers of introversion seems to be sharper; poetry itself contains a 'Lockung' (BG 2, 572), a devilish temptation to indulge in deception (p. 649). One poet, Otto, ends in collapse and even the one who most successfully maintains control, Viktor, is a more ascetically inclined figure than his counterpart, Friedrich, in *Ahnung und Gegenwart*. It is not the fact that Viktor becomes a priest that makes the difference, but his vision of himself as a kind of Savonarola, descending 'auf den alten, schwülen, staubigen Markt von Europa' (p. 727) to throw down the idols which the people now worship. This is not exactly a denial of poetry. Fortunat feels that Viktor's path is in essence the same as his, but his formulation of his own poetic path is somewhat lacking in confidence: 'ich habe nun kein anderes Metier dafür, als meine Dichtkunst' (p. 727). Viktor closes the work with a religious reflection and a warning: 'Du schöne Welt, nimm dich in acht!' and we may be forgiven for thinking that this is the voice of the older Eichendorff, the voice, not of a renegade, but of a veteran of Romanticism who sees it as belonging more to the past than to the future and cannot now write about it without a certain elegiac sadness. On the other hand, there is no sign, as there is with the later Tieck, for example, of an accommodation with the 'realistic' spirit of the post-romantic epoch.

Notes

1. Cf. above, p. 42.

2. Cf. the essay 'Literatur' in *Europa*, reprint, E. Behler (ed.) (Darmstadt, 1963), p. 55.

3. Adelung, the foremost lexicographer of the 'Aufklärung', defines 'Roman' as 'im weitesten Verstande eine jede erdichtete, wunderbare Geschichte. . . im engsten Verstande. . . eine wunderbare, oder mit Verwirrungen durchwebte Liebesgeschichte'.

4. Cf. G. Schulz, 'Poetik des Romans bei Novalis', in R. Grimm (ed.), *Deutsche Romantheorien* (Frankfurt–Bonn, 1968), pp. 81 and 87.

5. H. Schanze, 'Friedrich Schlegels Theorie des Romans' in Grimm, *Romantheorien*, pp. 66–8.

6. Ibid., p. 64.

7. Cf. his discussion of Spanish literature in the Vienna lectures of 1812, printed with introduction by E. Behler in *Hochland*, Jg. 52, 5, p. 456.

8. Further to this type of novel, cf. Marianne Thalmann, *Der Trivialroman des achtzehnten Jahrhunderts und der romantische Roman*, reprint (Nendeln, 1978).

9. In his edition of *Die Elixiere des Teufels/Lebens-Ansichten des Katers Murr* (Darmstadt, 1970), p. 672.

10. Quoted by R. Steig, *Achim von Arnim und die ihm nahe standen*, reprint (3 vols., Berne, 1970), vol. 1, p. 266.

11. *Literary Notebooks*, no. 65. Cf. also F. Mennemeier, *Friedrich Schlegels Poesiebegriff* (Munich, 1971), pp. 282 ff and 290–1. 'Realismus' in Schlegel could well correspond to what we have called 'substance'.

12. R. Pascal, *The German Novel* (Manchester, 1956), p. 31.

13. Cf. Esther Hudgins, *Nicht-epische Strukturen des romantischen Romans* (The Hague–Paris, 1975).

14. Mennemeier, *Schlegels Poesiebegriff*, p. 91.

15. Schulz, 'Poetik des Romans bei Novalis', p. 91.

16. Schanze, 'Schlegels Theorie des Romans', p. 75.

17. Regarded as very important by Novalis (KS III, p. 685).

18. Quoted by Schulz, 'Poetik des Romans bei Novalis', p. 81.

19. *Das merkwürdige musikalische Leben des Tonkünstlers Joseph Berglinger* in Wackenroder, *Herzensergießungen*, ed. Gillies (Oxford, 1948), pp. 88–107.

20. *Lucinde* (Frankfurt, 1964), p. 8.

21. Ibid., p. 80.

22. Cf. above, pp. 67–8.

23. Letter to Schleiermacher, 5 May 1800.

24. Cf. also the double invocation of love and poetry in the dedicatory sonnets.

25. The same view is evident in *Die Christenheit oder Europa.*

26. The pattern of the 'Atlantismärchen', repeated in the life of the miner and of Heinrich himself.

27. Cf. above, pp. 67 and 75.

28. Two chapters are extant, printed in K 2. For a thorough discussion, see the edition by W. Rehm (Berlin, 1949).

29. A. von Arnim, *Sämtliche Romane und Erzählungen* (cited as SRE), W. Migge (ed.) (Munich, 1962), vol. 1, p. 616.

30. A brilliant study of the 'modern disease' is *Mistris Lee* (see Ch. 12 below).

31. It had already been published in epistolary form in 1802.

32. W. Hauff, *Lichtenstein*, 'Einleitung', p. 49.

33. Cf. above, p. 67. Further to this topic, see M. Nußberger and W. Kohlschmidt, 'Historischer Roman' in W. Mohr (ed.), *Reallexikon der deutschen Literaturgeschichte*, 2nd edn (Berlin, 1958).

34. Cf. P. Stöcklein, *Eichendorff* (Hamburg, 1963), p. 112.

35. Cf. Chapter 7 above, pp. 97–100. Further to Eichendorff's descriptive technique, see the excellent essay by R. Alewyn, 'Eine Landschaft Eichendorffs' in P. Stöcklein (ed.), *Eichendorff Heute* (Darmstadt, 1966), pp. 20 ff.

36. Cf. Friedrich's words to Faber in Ch. 3 (BG 2, pp. 31–2).

11 THE NOVEL (EXCURSUS: JEAN PAUL)

The positioning of this section has caused no little heart-searching. Jean Paul Friedrich Richter (to give him, for the one occasion, his full name) presents, in our context, a problem to which there is no perfect solution. He was born in 1763 and, after some not very successful forays into the field of satire, published his first major epic work, *Die unsichtbare Loge*, in 1793; some three years, that is, in advance of Tieck's *William Lovell*. He is a novelist of major importance and by no means without affinities to Romanticism, and must have had some influence on the Romantics proper. It could be argued that this chapter should have preceded the general discussion of the romantic novel. Our decision to adopt the present order is based on the consideration that the fundamental duty of a historical study of this kind is to relate the literary works treated to the central concept around which the whole is organised. To introduce, before the general characterisation of the romantic novel had been carried out, an author whose relation to Romanticism is problematic would be to run the risk of confusing beyond redemption an already complex issue. Since one of the primary questions which we must seek to answer is that of the extent to which Jean Paul's work can be designated as 'romantic', it seemed better, on balance, to give him here the status of an 'Extrablättchen', to use one of his own ironic expressions for the digressions and appendices of which he was so fond. As in the case of Jean Paul himself, this procedure implies no lack of respect for the material which we shall be treating in this chapter. The period with which we shall be principally concerned is that stretching from 1792 to 1805, which embraces all the major novels, from *Die unsichtbare Loge* to the *Flegeljahre*. The later work, and in particular the substantial fragment *Der Komet* (1812–22) cannot, and will not, be entirely ignored, but it is the earlier writing which is the more characteristic, influential and, on the whole, aesthetically important.

Jean Paul's novels, with their fanciful titles and chapter headings, frequent digressions, supplements and pseudo-prefaces (under equally unusual headings) and complicated intrigues, full of mysterious and tangled relationships and other features reminiscent of the popular novels of the time,[1] make, at first glance, an almost hyper-romantic impression. Formally, *Ahnung und Gegenwart* and even Part One of

Heinrich von Ofterdingen seem almost sober by comparison. But though one could certainly find parallels in, for example, Hoffmann's *Kater Murr* or in the elaborately capricious fancies of the half novel, half satirical fantasy, the *Nachtwachen des Bonaventura* (1805), and while the disrespect for formal discipline which this denotes is indeed a feature which Jean Paul has in common with Romanticism in general, it is questionable whether the motivation behind this approach is a purely romantic one. It might be better to call it 'Gothic', in the sense in which Will Vesper uses the term, to convey Jean Paul's all-inclusiveness in the service of a peculiar blend of the earthly and the infinite.[2] For on reflection, we feel that the very mechanical intricacy of its form gives Jean Paul's work a quality of intellectualism and solidity which sets it apart from the typical romantic novel, whose plot (in so far as it has one at all), generates an inconsequential and unforced atmosphere. Both are fantastic, but the fancy is used differently. The Romantic has a tendency towards the *Märchen*; Jean Paul's novels (which suffer, if anything, from a surfeit of 'plot'), make an impression of calculation, of fantasy dependent on a device.

A parallel tendency is apparent in Jean Paul's style. He writes well at times, but always in an elaborate and deliberately cultivated manner which makes the author a tangible presence in his own work to a greater extent even than is the case with the most 'ironic' of the Romantics. This very tangibility, however, leads, for good or ill, to an effect which differs from the free play of fancy in romantic irony. After a time, it begins to seem contrived, as that of Sterne is often contrived.[3] Jean Paul's style is compounded in more or less equal parts of three elements, sentiment, fancy and a third which can be called 'wit', but not in the free and creative sense in which a Romantic like Friedrich Schlegel would use the term. Jean Paul's wit is more reminiscent of that of the eighteenth century and above all, the 'Aufklärung', which consisted in essence in the capacity of the intellect to see 'similarities', to link disparate things by virtue of a quality which, in the abstract, they might be said to have in common. This is a world away from the associative links made by romantic fancy, which arise out of and arouse a sense of the spiritual unity, the 'symptomatic' nature, to quote Novalis, of all things.[4] The Jean Paulian wit, which is of course more a producer of metaphors than of symbols, does not remove our sense of the disparate nature of the things compared, but rather leaves an impression of the ingenuity of the author in finding a point of comparison.

If that impression of ingenuity is so strong as to appear to us

unusual, even perhaps 'unnatural' (i.e. a special effort is required to
conceive and to understand the parallel), we tend to speak of a
'baroque' wit. It is no accident that Jean Paul's wit has sometimes been
so described.[5] He is not, of course, in any meaningful sense a 'baroque'
writer, but the similarity is not entirely fortuitous. The imagination is
not as free from intellectual interference in his imagery as it might be,
and is in a Novalis or even an Arnim. Here too, we sometimes sense an
intricate clockwork driving the machine. Hermann Meyer affords us a
glimpse into the workshop in his essay on *Flegeljahre*. Jean Paul was
an inveterate excerptor and had a huge collection, the source of many
of his striking allusions and metaphorical comparisons, which he had
indexed for easy reference, using 'about two hundred' abstract concepts
for classification. One is reminded of the lists of possible metaphorical
applications and combinations in baroque works on poetics,[6] or the
specialised poetic lexica, such as M. Bergmann's *Deutsches Aerarium
Poeticum oder Poetische Schatzkammer* (Jena, 1662) in which the
poet whose invention was flagging could find metaphors for all
occasions. Meyer does not see a baroque connection here, nor would
we wish to drive the comparison too far, but to neglect this side too
much in favour of the element of pure play[7] would also be wrong.

Chapter 22 of the second 'Bändchen' of *Flegeljahre* will help us to
make our point. It opens with the hero, Walt, preparing himself for his
first appearance in Hasslau society. He intends to be seen as 'ein in
einem Dorfe gebrochener Juwel, der sich auf der Edelsteinmühle der
Stadt schon sehr ausgeschliffen'.[8] There is nothing unduly obtrusive
about the intellectuality of this image, though it does not contain a
great deal of food for the imagination. In the description of the
furniture in Neupeter's drawing-room, the basic technique is still
metaphorical, but one has the feeling that the metaphors have arisen
naturally as the fancy, in truly humorous mood, ranged freely over the
objects described. This is a humour very closely allied to that of the
Romantics, though it does not appear in a purely romantic form:

> Er glänzte sehr, der Saal, die vergoldeten Schlösser waren aus den
> Papier-Wickeln herausgelassen, dem Lüstre der Staub- und Bußsack
> ausgezogen, die Seiden-Stühle hatten höflich vor jedem Steiß die
> Kappen abgenommen (M 2, 737).

Between these two passages, however, there occurs one of Jean Paul's
'baroque' moments. Walt puts on his best coat, the gold-coloured
material of which presents an irresistible opportunity for the display of

ingenious wit. A nankeen garment turns into metal-work; the gentle
poetic dreamer becomes a brass-founder: 'Walt goß sich bei Zeiten
seinen Sonntags-Beschlag, den Nanking, als sein eigener Gelbgießer
über' (p. 736). Such is the mixture which Jean Paul offers: a unique
blend of, or rather, oscillation between poetry and contrivance.

The former outweighs the latter, as the idealist impulse is stronger
than the 'realistic' one, though in this latter respect too, there is an
oscillation between the two poles and in the end product, Jean Paul's
presentation of spiritual reality is weighed down somewhat by a non-
romantic ballast. We shall be dealing with the question of his 'realism'
in detail later, but one aspect of his response to the material world
deserves to be singled out here, because it too casts light on the nature
of his imagination and taste. He was immensely interested in the more
curious facts and phenomena of the material world around him and
decorates and animates his narratives with many examples, which he
presents both as a stimulus to the imagination and as an interesting
entertainment for the scientifically and mechanically minded. Thus in
Hesperus (M 1, 552 f), he shows us a chair which, by virtue of an
ingenious mechanism, can become, literally, a musical one. The idea of
an 'Isolier-Schemel', a device for allowing a subject to feel electricity
without physical ill-effects, prompts, in *Flegeljahre* (M 2, 841), a
comparison with first love, which is said to act in much the same way.
In each case, the author creates an effective image, which lifts the
reader clear of mundane rationalism, but also directs his attention to
solid objects and mechanical processes and the ingenious intellect of
their inventors.

There is undoubtedly a realistic side to Jean Paul, at least relatively,
in his historical context. Wolfgang Harich, who wishes to see him as a
'revolutionary democrat',[9] speaks of his 'Dringen auf Lebenswahrheit
und Realismus', his 'Gegenwartsbesessenheit'.[10] Harich's approach, an
attempt to correct the distortion arising out of the 'bourgeois'
interpretation of his hero, is itself too one-sided. But it is certainly true
that Jean Paul, in contrast to the Romantics, tended to the left in
politics and showed a special awareness of the material realities of life.
His generally democratic cast of mind and deep dislike of courts and
aristocrats are not hard to trace in his books, nor is his understanding of
the life of the poor, which is much more than just a sentimental
sympathy or the response of a sophisticated poet to naïve simplicity.
Jean Paul knew of the harsh realities of their existence, which he calls,
in a typical metaphor, a 'harte Pritsche in der Wachtstube des Lebens'
(in *Flegeljahre*, M 2, 858). Public life and public issues are sometimes

reflected in his work. But it is in the private sphere that his main
interest lies. He is the child, and to a great extent the chronicler and
analyst of the era of subjectivistic sensibility which began with the
breakthrough to prominence of the romantic tendency in the eighteenth
century. The influence on him of the pre-romantic generation,
especially of Klopstock (the sentimentalism of whose *Messias* is recalled
by many of Jean Paul's love scenes), Lavater, Fritz Jacobi, Karl
Philipp Moritz[11] and above all, his greatest idol, Herder,[12] is stronger
than on the Romantics proper. His thinking is not, surely, realist in the
proper sense of the word, but he shies away from the radical idealism
of some romantic thinkers, above all Fichte. The latter's doctrine of the
Self is criticised on a number of occasions, especially in the *Clavis
Fichtiana* which forms part of the 'Comic Appendix' to *Titan*.

Nevertheless, Jean Paul cannot simply be grouped with the older
generation. He undoubtedly feels within himself the more intense
inwardness which characterises the romantic outlook and despite his
relative respect for everyday reality, which he describes with more
loving care than is to be found in Tieck, or even Hoffmann, the inner
world of the *Gemüt* has priority. In what is generally agreed to be the
most nearly 'realistic' of his novels, *Siebenkäs* (1796–7), the main
thrust is still idealist. The detail of the hero's life as a poor lawyer in a
provincial backwater is carefully described and undeniably carries
weight in its own right, but its main function is still to act as a foil to
the superior spirituality of Siebenkäs himself. Even the portrayal of
everyday life in Jean Paul's so-called 'idylls' is problematic, viewed
from the point of view of realism of technique. In the 'Reichsmarkt-
flecken' Kuhschnappel,[13] the setting for *Siebenkäs*, the author provides
a contrasting background of 'dumpfe, im dicken Erdenblute
schwimmende Menschenherzen' (M 2, 236) against which the free,
heroic soul of the hero shines all the more brightly. Similarly, while
Siebenkäs's wife, Lenette, is portrayed with some understanding, her
main function as a busy and fussy housewife and housekeeper is to
throw into relief the suffering of a poetic mind cramped and caged by
marriage to a being whose head can accommodate no thoughts other
than those of 'Spitzen, Hauben, Hemden und Kochtöpfen und
Bratpfannen' (M 2, 290). The plot turns on his emancipation from this
prison of banal domesticity and in order to achieve it, Jean Paul does
not scruple to allow Siebenkäs to welsh on his obligations by means of
the characteristically Jean Paulian device of a 'Scheintod', which sets
him free to begin a new existence. Indeed, when he wishes to unite his
hero with an intellectually and spiritually more suitable mate, Jean

Paul, after a gesture of sympathy in Lenette's direction, disposes of her through the convenient method of having her die in childbed.

Siebenkäs's ability to rise above the narrowness of his environment is evidence of the fact that he belongs to the line of 'hohe Menschen', as Jean Paul calls them, which begins with Gustav in *Die unsichtbare Loge* and culminates in the twin heroes of *Flegeljahre*, Vult and Walt. In the late period, in which Jean Paul's idealism is muted and his humour has acquired a sharper, more destructive edge reminiscent of the satirical tone of his literary beginnings, no comparable figure appears, not even in *Der Komet*. But in the idealist middle period, Jean Paul is able to present with conviction a type of man (and woman) who could be described as his equivalent of the romantic poet-hero, though only one of the series, Walt, is a poet in practice and even then — characteristically — in an idiosyncratic prose form which one hesitates to call lyrical. This type of person has the capacity to see beyond the material to a higher reality, a 'zweite Welt' (*Hesperus*: M 1, 603 ff). This insight guarantees true freedom, even in poverty, and renders its possessor immune against infection by the mean materialism of the common realist, if not always against scepticism and even spiritual and mental disorientation, which Jean Paul shows to be a danger in the case of those 'lofty men' who take the more radical, more pronouncedly romantic road to freedom followed by Roquairol and Schoppe (in *Titan*), or Leibgeber (in *Siebenkäs*). It is often associated by commentators with the appreciation of the meaning of death, such as came to Jean Paul in the experience which he recorded in his diary for 15 November 1790,[14] and which opens the mind to the experience of eternity, at the same time showing the relative nature of earthly life and time. Paradoxically or not, this liberated him from the sceptical and satirical rut in which he had previously been confined and rendered him capable of seeing human life with that mixture of humour and compassionate sentiment which is typical of the major novels.

The 'lofty man' may be embroiled in material reality and unable to render himself quite as independent of it as could, say, Novalis, but he does have a number of defences and escape routes which, like the evening star,[15] provide balm for the wounds which the workaday world inflicts on the sensitive soul. At the humblest level, the bed is such a refuge, an 'anchorage safe against storms' into which Siebenkäs can climb when he is 'wundgedrückt vom Tage' (M 2, 216). For the suffering and steadfast Liane, the martyr-heroine of *Titan*, it is the 'sanctuary of the day' where she can release the 'Tränen, die ein schwerer Tag gekeltert hat' (M 3, 416). Here, we have the neo-

Klopstockian Jean Paul, who is capable of burdening the novels with a streak of sticky sentimentality (in particular in the love scenes), which we would rather not notice, but which cannot be left entirely out of account in a balanced picture. It could, of course, be argued that such passages and episodes, like similar ones in Hoffmann, are written with purely commercial considerations in mind. That they were a major factor in the wide popularity which Jean Paul's novels achieved cannot be doubted and Jean Paul was not in a position to be indifferent to the question of financial return. But this is an argument to be used with caution. It implies that a craftsman is willing to flaw his own work and also that he is capable of thinking himself into a sub-literary frame of mind sufficiently thoroughly to produce a 'fake' that can carry conviction, a rare combination, one would think, in a major writer.

Certainty is unattainable in the absence of firm documentary evidence as to Jean Paul's intention in specific cases. But it is by no means inconceivable that, when dealing with sentimental situations, he became genuinely sentimental himself. It is true that he seems to feel that the spirituality of the young lovers, Walt and Wina, in *Flegeljahre* is a little over-refined, but he surely takes their love seriously and it is hard to believe that he would have been prepared deliberately to make them look ridiculous. And yet, in the scene in which Wina discovers that Walt is a poet, he drifts, in his attempt to suggest their delicate affinity, into what is most assuredly *Kitsch*: 'Aber einander verborgen hinter den froher nachquellenden Tränen, glichen sie zwei Tönen, die unsichtbar zu *einem* Wohllaut zittern;[16] sie waren zwei gesenkte Maienblümchen, einander durch fremdes Frühlingswehen mehr nachbewegt als angenähert' (M 2, 1042). Like that of another great humorous novelist, Dickens, Jean Paul's taste is not always secure when he has to present a serious, poetic love.

Among other defences against domination by the material world, the Jean Paulian hero has at his disposal music and nature and, above all, he possesses the capacity for freedom in his own mind. By the power of the imagination and of the related faculties of memory — the 'Gedächtniskunst' through which Walt rekindles the mentality of childhood (M 2, 1018) — and of hope[17] and consistent spirituality of vision, whether serious or humorous, he can demonstrate and maintain his freedom. Siebenkäs is probably the one among this group of characters who is most desperately embroiled with the everyday world and he makes a correspondingly liberal use of humour: 'er verhing sein schönes Herz mit der grotesken komischen Larve. . . und machte das kurze Spiel seines Lebens zu einem Mokierspiel und komischen

Heldengedicht' (M 2, 292). As we shall see, the humorist is not the only type of lofty man portrayed by Jean Paul, nor does he (in theory at least) represent the highest form of that genus, though he is perhaps the most successful and characteristic of the author's creations. It is doubtful whether Jean Paul wished to convey with the word 'grotesque' all the associations which modern critics have discovered in it. Certainly, it is going too far to place him, as Philip Thomson does, 'firmly in the tradition of satanic and black humour'.[18] Eccentric his humour and his humorists certainly are, but by comparison with the master of the eccentric and grotesque, Hoffmann, in whom we really do sense the awakening of irrational and dark forces, he indulges this tendency with a caution born of quite strong residual rationalistic inhibitions.

Nevertheless, Jean Paul's willingness to enter into this territory, going further along the path taken by Moritz's Tobias Hartknopf, is a clear indication of at least an affinity to the romantic mentality. And that impression is strengthened by the constant tendency of his narratives to turn 'inwards', into the exposition and analysis of states of mind, in which an impressively wide and sensitive vocabulary is displayed. The 'external' world and the sensibility of the 'higher' characters or of the author who can represent them in their absence seem often to form a continuum. Perceptions of the outer world are transposed easily and quickly into feelings and the sensitively and sentimentally analytical author is at hand to articulate the latter. Sometimes he delegates the task to a character, a prime example being Liane in *Titan*, the extreme case of unadulterated sensibility in Jean Paul's work. In a letter to her friend Elisa, she writes of her feelings as a convalescent in the early morning:

> In einer unendlichen Seligkeit schweb' ich wie verklärt. . . schwach, aber leicht und frei, ich hatte die drückende Hülle — so war es mir — unter die Erde gelegt und nur das pochende Herz behalten, und im entzückten Busen flossen warme Tränenquellen gleichsam über und bedeckten sie hell (M 3, 209).

Liane, it is true, is deliberately created as an example of extreme spirituality. She is one of the characters whose 'Einkräftigkeit', to quote Jean Paul himself,[19] put in perspective the central theme of this book, the quest for and achievement of a balanced mentality, in the context of the confusion of mental and emotional states that this generation is heir to. It comes as no surprise that Liane is too incorporeally hyper-spiritual to stand a chance of surviving to the novel's end. But it would be wrong to assume that her portrayal is carried out as a negative criticism of the idealistic tendency. She may represent a beauty which, in its pure form, is too good for this earth, but she is still very much a positive heroine, designed to be admired and mourned. This novel, we must remind ourselves, is slightly atypical in that its tenor and tendency are unusually close, for Jean Paul, to the spirit of 'Classical' Weimar. But while one does sometimes receive the impression of older and wiser experience surveying from its vantage-point the strivings and mistakes of idealistic youth, there can be no real doubt that even here, sympathy lies more with the warmth of the latter than with the cool restraint of the former, as represented by the scheming, cold egotist Gaspard, who could well have been conceived as a somewhat caricatured portrait of Goethe.[20] If Jean Paul had had to choose between him and his antipode, the passionate and destructive egotist Roquairol, he would doubtless have chosen the latter. Classical restraint does not represent a natural attitude for Jean Paul, as Walter Höllerer points out in his comments on the (more characteristically Jean Paulian) comic companion-piece to *Titan, Des Luftschiffers Giannozzo Seebuch.*[21] The idealising light in which hope and memory see the world may, as Jean Paul puts it in an authorial intervention in *Titan* apropos of the exaltation of Albano's love for Liane, be a 'feines Gift' (M 3, 221), but it is one which he prefers to the philistine sleep of safety. Albano himself may be Jean Paul's Wilhelm Meister, but he is a much more passionate and idealistically enthusiastic one than his prototype.

On the other hand, Jean Paul is not insincere in the gesture of respect which he makes to the 'Classical' ideal of balanced 'Humanität' which he makes in *Titan.* He cannot trust subjective idealism to quite the extent that the pure Romantic can. He is not as confident in the ability of the free Self to provide its own, organic and non-rationalistic control (the romantic 'Besonnenheit') which will preserve it from the dangers of which they, as well as he, are aware. Nor, on the positive side, does he seem to be able to envisage such a satisfaction of longing, as sweet a release and consummation, as the Romantics, at their best, can evoke. His portrayal of perfect love, for example, always seems forced. Peace and harmony he can conceive, but not those which pass all understanding. Transcendence is a state which he wishes to achieve, just as he yearns for assurance of the immortality of the soul.[22] Here, the inadequacy or, if preferred, the essentially eighteenth-century, rationalistically inhibited nature of Jean Paul's religious feeling is a crucial factor. He posits a God, who can be experienced (as can Werther's) in nature or in moments of some ill-defined kind of ecstasy. The guru Emanuel in *Hesperus*, for example, feels Him as a kind of abstract spiritual essence. Jean Paul's, however, is at best a pseudo-mysticism. His God is an abstraction only and his 'second world' a theologically empty concept. It stands, in fact, for 'God in man' (*Hesperus*, M 1, 605).[23] On the other side of the coin, Jean Paul lacks a convincing perception of evil. With the possible exception of the 'leather man', 'Kain' in the late novel *Der Komet*, one can think of no figure in which a sense of the hostile and uncontrollable force which can enter a man's life and destroy him — and against which the only defence is divine grace — is conveyed. The uncanny in Jean Paul, when it occurs, is the product of trick-effects, such as those of the 'Uncle' in *Titan*, and reminds one of nothing more than of the mysteries of Schiller's *Geisterseher* and the popular 'Bundesroman' of the type represented by Karl Grosse's *Der Genius* (1791–4).[24]

Jean Paul, then, wishes to fly but is unable or unwilling to break the umbilical cord which links him to earth and acts effectively as a tether on his imagination. We have seen how rationalistic and realistic factors, while hardly predominant in him, nevertheless have their inhibiting effect. The element of ingenious calculation which is part of that is evident also in his treatment of nature. We are not thinking primarily here of the great descriptive set-pieces, the colourful sunsets and sunrises shot through with intimations of the infinite, though even here, it is fair to say that one does hear the wheels of rhetoric turning rather too distinctly.[25] It is in Jean Paul's fondness for man-made natural effects, in parks and gardens, that this tendency makes itself most strikingly felt and above all in the long descriptions of Lilar, the park in *Titan*. This is undoubtedly a place designed to delight and stimulate the *Gemüt*, a fantasy-park like the one in Bayreuth which Siebenkäs visits (M 2, 364 ff), only more so, since in this imaginary context, the author is free to indulge his inventive fancy, making use of a good knowledge of eighteenth-century garden technology. Jean Paul sets important parts of the action in Lilar, and exploits its romantic potential, but at the same time displays a keen interest in the mechanics by which the effects are obtained, so that his descriptions sometimes read like baroque conceits realised in terms of plants, trees and fountains, with added sound-effects (e.g. the 'Flötental'). The episode in which Roquairol sets in motion the hydraulic devices which produce what Jean Paul calls 'nach Himmel gekehrter Regen' (M 3, 385) is a *tour de force* in this mode.

Nor are even the best of Jean Paul's famous dream-sequences, for all their boldness of imagery and rhythmically effective prose, as satisfying for at least one reader as they are reported to have been for Carlyle,[26] as food for the imagination. They could be described as Jean Paul's equivalent of the romantic *Märchen*; constructions whose purpose is to lift the work in which they appear on to the metaphysical plane, but without entirely losing contact with earth. The present writer cannot agree that Jean Paul is consistently successful in creating a situation in which, as J. W. Smeed puts it in commenting on Albano's dream (*Titan*, M 3, 552 ff), 'idea is almost completely dissolved in image and dream-sequence', and an effective 'magic fable' devised to render the abstract theme in terms congenial to the *Gemüt*.[27] The 'dreams' contain many happy ideas and images, but they are also over-long and overblown and in their accumulation of 'Einfälle' they sometimes impose on the imagination the strain which one feels in reading Klopstock's portrayals of imagined ethereal realms in *Der Messias*.

In the last analysis, Jean Paul cannot share the Romantics' faith in the possibility of complete spiritual freedom. His analysis of the dualism of real and ideal agrees with theirs in many respects, but he can see only the prospects of consolation for the man locked in the 'prison' of earthly reality (*Siebenkäs*; M 2, 385), or at best of an escape, such as Siebenkäs himself achieves. We know, and Jean Paul himself surely knows, that this is no real solution to the problem. His sympathies lie strongly with the idealist who can preserve the purity of his faith, like Walt in *Flegeljahre*, in whom the emotional faculties clearly predominate. Yet he is shown to need at least *something* of the (relatively) realistic view of life of his brother Vult. The latter is a potentially tragic victim of undisciplined self-assertion and nihilistic scepticism, but Walt is too naïve; as Jean Paul himself puts it: 'In der Tat braucht der Mensch bei den besten Flügeln für den Äther doch auch ein Paar Stiefel für das Pflaster' (M 2, 869). If a happy end is to be envisaged at all, some measure of education is necessary for the idealist-hero and Berend's reconstruction of the planned ending of *Flegeljahre* (M 2, 1173) suggests a clear process of maturation through experience which, like *Titan* and perhaps also *Die unsichtbare Loge*, has points in common with the 'Bildung' of *Wilhelm Meisters Lehrjahre*.

Nor is the duality overcome by absorption into the little world of obscure, backwater reality. This is the way of the 'Kauz', the hero of Jean Paul's 'idylls' *Schulmeisterlein Wuz* (1793) and *Quintus Fixlein*

(1796), to which might be added the later, perhaps somewhat more satirically inclined *Leben Fibels* (1812). This type of character is able, consciously or unconsciously, to carry out a kind of miniaturisation of the world of the spirit and find his satisfaction within a controllable enclave where the discrepancy between ideal and real no longer has its usual numbing effect, because the former has been tailored to fit the latter. The life of such a character is, as the full title and the opening line of *Wuz* establish, 'sanft und meerstille' and above all, 'vergnügt' (contented, with a suggestion of complacency). Wuz is poor, but he is proof against the feeling of spiritual privation. This is not by virtue of the heroic independence of spirit which we saw in the case of Siebenkäs. Wuz represents the imagination at work at a lower level: when he finds he has not the money to buy new books, he writes them for himself on the basis of the information he can put together from catalogues and reviews. He is happily unaware of the limitations of the spiritual universe which he inhabits, which enables Jean Paul to depict him with a certain affectionate envy of his happy lot, but without compromising his own ideals. His presentation is, in fact, a blend of envy and humorously tolerant criticism. He makes certain that we are not caught up in Wuz's self-satisfaction by introducing himself, as the detached and analytical narrator, and as the chronicler, musing at the bedside of the dying man on the eternal dimension of existence, ignorance of which is a precondition of the little schoolmaster's bliss.

The 'Kauz' is treated in greater detail in *Quintus Fixlein*. Without falling into a destructively satirical tone, Jean Paul still exposes the village priest's pedantry and over-cautious, limited spirit. Fixlein, the happy swain awaiting his wedding-day, remains, thanks to his inner regulator, his 'Mäßigkeit', in complete control: 'in diesen heißen Strudeln der Lust. . . bewegtest [du] deinen Fischschwanz [i.e. 'reason'] und schriebest dir eine rechtläufige Bahn durch die Wogen vor' (M 4, 145).

This is not, however, a direct 'romantic' attack on philistinism. There are points in common between 'Kauz' and 'Philister', it is true, but the former has achieved his bliss with the aid of the imagination and as Max Kommerell says, it is, if limited, still 'ein durchaus geistiger Zustand'.[28] It is not wise to despise these 'Blattminierer', who crawl on a leaf and imagine it a continent (M 4, 132). Jean Paul can see the poetry of small-town reality and has discovered here a vein which the post-romantic 'Biedermeier' writers were to mine with assiduity and success.

For Jean Paul, the surest path to happiness seems to be a kind of oscillation between the heroic and the idyllic, as he formulates it in the 'Billett an meine Freunde' prefaced to *Quintus Fixlein* (M 4, 10–13). The dualism at the heart of his view of life remains unresolved and the resulting manner is one characterised by shimmering light and constant movement: the mixture (*not* blending!) of high and low, serious and comic, romantic and unromantic of the middle-period work. In the books written after 1805, Jean Paul did not change his spots entirely. His feeling for the comic and fantastic did not desert him, nor did his appreciation of greatness and goodness. But the sentiment and sunnier humour give way to a view of life tinged with the satirical bitterness of the disappointed idealist. Those idealists he now portrays (above all Nikolaus in *Der Komet*) are Don Quijotes in whom the ridiculous tends to outweigh the sympathetic; the 'little men', like the 'heroes' of *Doktor Katzenbergers Badereise* and *Des Feldpredigers Schmelzle Reise nach Flätz* (both 1809) are pilloried in a way which entirely supports Smeed's description of the mood of the late work as one of 'disillusionment'.[29] There had, of course, been moments of doubt and darkness before (e.g. the 'Rede des toten Christus' in *Siebenkäs*) but there had always been ample compensation for such visions of negativity. There is none such for the demonic figure of the 'leather man' in *Der Komet*.

Notes

1. Both the 'Bundesroman' and the 'humoristic' novel. For the latter at the popular level, see L. L. Albertsen, *Die Eintagsliteratur in der Goethezeit* (Frankfurt–Berne, 1975), pp. 194 ff.

2. In the Introduction to *Jean Pauls Träume* (Munich, 1906). Cf. p. 5: 'Es gibt in unserer Literatur nichts "Deutscheres", ich meine nichts Gotischeres als Jean Paul. . .' etc.

3. For the influence of Sterne on Jean Paul, see P. Michelsen, *Lawrence Sterne und der deutsche Roman des achtzehnten Jahrhunderts* (Göttingen, 1962), pp. 311–94.

4. Cf. above, p. 68.

5. See U. Schweikert, *Jean Paul* (Stuttgart, 1970), pp. 76–7 and the works by W. Zucker and R. Benz mentioned there (p. 77).

6. E.g. the list of 'Verblümte Reden und kunstzierliche Ausbildungen' in Part III of G. P. Harsdörffer's *Poetischer Trichter* (Nuremburg, 1663).

7. Cf. H. Meyer, 'Flegeljahre' in B. von Wiese (ed.), *Der deutsche Roman* (Düsseldorf, 1965), vol. 1, p. 229.

8. Jean Paul, *Werke*, N. Miller (ed.), 3rd edn (Munich, 1971), vol. 2, p. 736. Cited as M.

9. W. Harich, *Jean Pauls Revolutionsdichtung* (E. Berlin, 1974), pp. 92 ff.

10. Ibid., p. 536.

11. Cf. R. Unger, 'Zur seelengeschichtlichen Genesis der Romantik' in *Zur*

Dichtungs- und Geistesgeschichte der Goethezeit (Berlin, 1944). Unger speaks also of Novalis, but the connection with Jean Paul is closer. Moritz was an enthusiastic advocate of *Die unsichtbare Loge* and is said to have been the model for Emanuel in *Hesperus* (cf. Schweikert, *Jean Paul*, p. 29).

12. Dian in *Titan* and 'Plato' in *Flegeljahre* seem to have been intended as homage to Herder.

13. This milieu also provides an opportunity for some social and political satire, but that too is secondary.

14. Quoted by most writers on Jean Paul, e.g. Schweikert, p. 26.

15. Cf. *Hesperus*, M 1, p. 582 and the reference to peace as the 'Hesperus des müden Herzens', ibid., p. 587.

16. The use of the comparative form 'froher' and of the verb 'zittern' contains a strong suggestion of Klopstock!

17. I.e. escape from the present into the past or future. Cf. the discourse on the 'natural magic of the imagination' appended to *Quintus Fixlein* (M 4, p. 195): 'Gedächtnis ist nur eine eingeschränktere Phantasie' and the reference in *Der Komet* (M 6, p. 601) to past and future as 'die beiden reichen Indien der Phantasie'.

18. P. Thomson, *The Grotesque* (London, 1972), p. 16.

19. Letter to Jacobi, 8 September 1803.

20. Cf. W. Harich, *Jean Paul* (Leipzig, 1925), p. 579.

21. M 3, pp. 1139 ff. Giannozzo, the daring aeronaut whose mind and wit, in the 'Ich-Besteck' of the body (p. 983), range as freely as his balloon, crashes, but crashes gloriously. Albano, in *Titan*, has, as Höllerer says (ibid., p. 1150), to pay for his classically harmonious 'happy end' by a severe reduction in the scope and colour of his life.

22. He even went to the length of attempting to prove it in a book (*Selina*, 1823–5), a thing for which no true Romantic would have felt the need. Cf. also *Das Kampaner Tal*, particularly the ending, where balloons are used to raise poetic souls from an earthly to an infinite vision: a 'romantic' flight by mechanical means!

23. Cf. also Albano's reference in *Titan* to 'the god in me and over me' (M 3, p. 772), and Spener's exposition of man's relationship with God (ibid., p. 827).

24. This influenced Hoffmann and also made an impact in England, in a translation under the title *Horrid Mysteries*. In addition to *Titan*, it is possible that *Die unsichtbare Loge* was influenced by the 'Bundesroman'.

25. *Titan* is particularly rich in such purple passages. The Ischia-episode (Jobelperioden 28–9) contains perhaps the finest examples.

26. Carlyle, apparently, was carried away by their 'vastness' of imagination; cf. J. W. Smeed, *Jean Paul's Dreams* (London, 1966), p. 3.

27. Cf. Smeed, *Jean Paul's Dreams*, p. 27.

28. M. Kommerell, *Jean Paul*, 4th edn (Frankfurt, 1966), p. 284.

29. Cf. Jean Paul, *Des Feldpredigers Schmelzle Reise nach Flätz*, J. W. Smeed (ed.) (London, 1966), p. 14.

12 EPIC WRITING (GENERAL): (B) SHORT FORMS

The *Novelle* and *Märchen* are both forms in which the Romantics produced work of distinction. Both had begun to establish themselves in Germany during the eighteenth century but only exceptionally, in the isolated case of Goethe, can they be said to have achieved the status of true literary respectability. As with the case of the novel, though less decisively, it was Goethe who, in his *Unterhaltungen deutscher Ausgewanderten* (1795), provided a stimulus. The stories and *Das Märchen* in this work represented an advance on the approach of Musäus, Wieland and others in their aesthetic ennoblement of the narrative technique and deepening of the content. He cannot, however, be said to have performed the historical role of emancipating the short narrative genres entirely from their sub-literary status. After the *Unterhaltungen*, he left the *Märchen* proper alone and tended to use the short story in a subordinate role in novels. His late masterpiece, the *Novelle* (so entitled) of 1828, is an exercise in the typical late Goethean symbolist style, without forbears or progeny and comes, in any case, well after the Romantics had fully developed both forms.

A long time previous to this, Tieck, as ever the innovator, had begun a development which led to a veritable blossoming. *Der blonde Eckbert* (1796), *Der getreue Eckart und der Tannenhäuser* (1799) and other works established a romantic tradition in which, from the start, it was by no means easy to distinguish between *Novelle* and *Märchen*. Indeed, criticism has at times found it necessary to employ the term 'Märchennovelle'[1] to do justice to the constant interplay and interaction between the two forms in our period. The new factor was the refusal of the Romantics to draw a clear dividing-line between the two distinct worlds to which the eighteenth century assigned the two different forms. Even Goethe, in *Das Märchen*, kept the wondrous firmly encapsulated in a sphere of consciously artificial aesthetic play. It is perhaps possible to see some influence from this work on Novalis's handling of the *Märchen*-form in *Heinrich von Ofterdingen* (especially in Klingsohr's tale), but even here, there is a difference of basic attitude. Whereas for Goethe, the form is probably the most important aspect of the exercise, Novalis is writing a deeply serious romantic allegory, not so much play as pure dream, which is at the same time the higher reality. The Romantics as a group knew that such total spiritual freedom demands an ability to live in a highly rarefied atmosphere which few possess, and they indulged themselves in this but seldom. What is much more common with them is an interpenetration of the two realities of which they were conscious, something along the lines laid down by Hoffmann in his description, in a letter to his publisher Kunz (19 August 1813), of his approach in *Der goldene Topf*: 'Ein Märchen. . . feenhaft und wunderbar aber keck ins gewöhnliche alltägliche Leben tretend und seine Gestalten ergreifend.' In the pure *Märchen*, as Eberhard Lämmert puts it, the wondrous is presented as a 'poetic fact': no one wonders at it.[2]

This effect, which is more the product of narrative style than of any other factor, is not necessarily 'romantic' in the sense in which we use the term in this book. That would require the creation of an impression of the truly magical, of the 'bizarre', in the special sense given to the word by Friedrich Schlegel in his distinction between *Novelle* and *Märchen*:

> Wie die Novelle in jedem Punkt ihres Seins und ihres Werdens neu und frappant sein muß, so sollte das poetische Märchen und vorzüglich die Romanze unendlich bizarr sein; denn sie will nicht bloß die Fantasie interessieren, sondern auch den Geist bezaubern und das Gemüt reizen.[3]

The bizarre, Schlegel continues, consists in 'gewisse[n] willkürlichen und seltsamen Verknüpfungen und Verwechslungen des Denkens, Dichtens und Handelns'. It estranges the mind more radically from everyday 'normality' than does the 'baroque' element in Schlegel's 'architectonic wit' which, according to *Athenäum* fragment no. 383, is the source of the 'schöne Seltsamkeit' of the *Novelle*.

In essence, then, *Novelle* and *Märchen* would seem to differ from one another in romantic theory and practice in the degree of estrangement which is produced in the reader's mind. The former is distinguished, formally, by the fact that it remains anchored in material reality and introduces the supernatural dimension only by suggestion, as in the episode of the visit to the executioner in Brentano's story of *Kasperl und Annerl* when the movement of the sword in its cupboard certainly brings to our minds the idea of a hostile force threatening the little girl, but the surrounding narrative prevents the suggestion from maturing into a certainty. The unusual nature of the central event — the *Novelle* is a development of the anecdote rather than of the fable or moral tale — can of itself produce estrangement, or this can arise

out of what Tieck calls 'a striking and odd turning-point', some central
factor which diverts the story from its originally 'normal' path, yet
without overtly flouting the laws of natural possibility ('und doch
natürlich').[4] The *Märchen* extends the concept of nature to include the
supernatural.

This is not in itself, however, enough to make the *Märchen* intrinsically romantic. The *Kinder- und Hausmärchen* (1812–14) of the Grimm
brothers do not, on the whole, develop through their style and narrative
technique the potential Romanticism of their material. The Grimms
adopted a primarily antiquarian approach to their stories, seeing the
folk-tale as an expression, through an individual speaker, of a
'community experience' ('Gemeinschaftserlebnis').[5] They aimed,
Jakob especially, at authenticity rather than poetry of form, and
disapproved strongly of Brentano's tendency in his *Märchen* to
elaborate, to revel in the sophisticated romantic consciousness of the
freedom of the spirit. Arnim's defence of Brentano is revealing:

> es ist nämlich keineswegs wie Eure Sammlung etwas, das im
> Kinderkreise gelebt ohne weitere Verdauung zu den Kindern
> übergehen kann, sondern ein Buch, das in den Ältern die Art der
> Erfindsamkeit anregt, die jede Mutter, die recht gebildeten
> ausgenommen, im Notfall zeigt, ihren Kindern einen Umstand,
> dessen Reiz sich ihnen entdeckt hat, in einer längern Erzählung zu
> einer dauernden Unterhaltung zu machen.[6]

Brentano himself replied more succinctly by describing the style and
method of the Grimms as 'boring'.[7] Novalis's anti-realistic definition
of the genre, or rather, of its spirit, we have already met.[8] It is, in fact,
the spirit rather than the form which is at issue: whatever the ostensible
link with the nursery, the romantic *Märchen* is meant for adult,
sophisticated, modern man and it is meant to convey to him a spiritual
and psychological message. This message is in essence concerned with
the nature of reality and it is capable of being conveyed in other
genres as well (hence Novalis's dictum: 'Alles Poetische muß märchenhaft sein'[9]), but the *Märchen* as genre offers special opportunities. In
the remainder of this chapter, we shall see how these opportunities,
and those afforded by the *Novelle*, are exploited by the principal
romantic practitioners of the two genres, and we will be examining the
stories of Kleist who, once again, will be found to stand in a special
relationship to the Romantic Movement.

Fouqué

Friedrich, Baron de la Motte Fouqué has been spoken of earlier in this book in somewhat disparaging terms. We do not intend now to retract any of these criticisms, even in attempting to do justice to his real literary merits, for the very fact that he does have such merits increases the danger than his relatively superficial Romanticism could act as a barrier to the appreciation of the genuine article. That said, however, it behoves us to recognise that most of his work is genuinely romantic in *intent*, and that he does not always fail to hit the mark. His poems, plays and novels may safely be left to their well-earned oblivion, but some of his shorter narrative works are still worthy of attention. The *Geschichte vom Galgenmännlein* (1810) earned Hoffmann's approval and *Undine* (1811) and *Sintram und seine Gefährten* (1814) are rightly singled out by Josef Nadler for a place in his collection of the best *Romantische Novellen*.[10] Each contains, and to some extent at least, exploits a genuine romantic potential for which parallels can be found in more important authors. *Undine*, the main source for which seems to have been Paracelsus's account of the elemental spirits and which tells the story of a marriage between a human and a water-sprite, deals with the interpenetration of the human and supernatural planes in a way which recalls the theme, if not quite the narrative power, of Tieck's *Die Elfen.* In *Sintram*, a story inspired, apparently, by Dürer's engraving *Ritter, Tod und Teufel*, the hero has to battle against diabolical forces let loose on him by the pagan cruelty of his father. The conflict of good and evil principles within him is not unreminiscent of stories by Hoffmann, for example *Das Fräulein von Scuderi.* These works of Fouqué's are not pure *Märchen*, but the emphatic introduction of the supernatural (much more emphatic than in the case of the story by Hoffmann which was cited) makes one inclined to see them as 'Märchennovellen'.[11] In both, he makes a genuine attempt to penetrate beyond the merely exotic and decorative aspects of the material, and to achieve the psychological depth which distinguishes much of Tieck's work in this field. His success at this level is at best partial. In fact, his true merits lie elsewhere and in fairness to him, we should discuss these other aspects before attempting a final assessment of him on the more profoundly romantic criteria.

All medievalism is by definition backward-looking to some extent, but not all is as much so as Fouqué's. As we tried to show in Chapter 2,[12] the more serious purpose of the major Romantics who turned to the Middle Ages was — above and beyond considerations of 'period

charm' – to influence the present, and to look to the future, through
the revivifying stimulus of the spirit of the past. To be effective in this
role, of course, it had to be distilled in a form capable of being blended
with a sophisticated modern sensibility. Too much of the solid material
detail of medieval life, and too much of its vocabulary, would hamper
the author in this attempt, and it is no accident that Novalis, for
example, gives us very little medieval 'local colour' in *Heinrich von
Ofterdingen.* It may be that Fouqué seriously hoped, as he hints, for
example, in the dedicatory poem of *Sigurd, der Schlangentöter* (1808),
that he could contribute to a revival of the heroic 'old German' virtues
at a time when the need for German national feeling was felt to be
acute, but if so, it must be said that his work is much less effective in
this respect than the ballads of Uhland. One misses in him the deeper
motivation which, as Friedrich Schlegel says, should inspire the quest
for 'romantische Ferne', namely the desire 'die prosaische Wirklichkeit
durch Witz und Abenteuer. . . zu einer Gattung der Poesie zu
erheben'.[13] Fouqué lays too much emphasis on the external medieval
forms and makes too liberal a use of archaic vocabulary; his imagination
is stirred by the old Germanic world, but it is not sufficiently informed
with the modern romantic fancy, or 'wit', to be capable of transcending
'Wirklichkeit' as Schlegel demands. His chivalric world is in fact one of
'Waffenhallen und Minnelauben', to quote the original title of the novel
Der Zauberring (1813). His 'altkräft'ge Pracht'[14] is a world away from
the Tieckian 'mondbeglänzte Zaubernacht'.

Adventure, colour and physical animation his work does possess in
plenty. Wild weather and scenery, ancient castles, colourful medieval
clothing and armour, these and things like these excite him and he
can communicate his excitement, though not in a very subtle form. In
Chapter 2 of *Der Zauberring*, for example, Gabriele and Archimbald –
the names are not untypical! – appear almost like figures in a fashion-
parade:

> Es gab einen hübschen Anblick, wie nun die Frau und der Ritter
> sich lustwandelnd neben einander auf dem Rasen ergingen; der Dame
> Gewand von himmelblauem Sammet, mit großen Bogen von goldner
> Stickerei am Saum; des Ritters Harnisch in tiefer Schwärze glänzend,
> und mannigfache Sinnbilder von leuchtendem Silber darauf
> eingelegt.[15]

There is no romantic mystery here: the function of the emblems on
the armour is simply to introduce another colour. There is nothing

here of the transparency, the predominance of mood over matter, of a description by Eichendorff. Even so, this is not mere 'Kitsch'. Fouqué does convey a response to colour, brilliance and richness ('in tiefer Schwärze glänzend', for example, is a telling phrase) which is romantic in a sense. There are many such pretty pictures in Fouqué's stories and it would be churlish to deny them all charm, though a constant diet of such fare would soon begin to cloy.

There is also a good deal of action, much of it violent, and all described in a rousing style. This is not confined to jousts and battles. Dramatic scenes, usually in correspondingly dramatic settings and climatic conditions, can be found in *Undine* (e.g. the storm-sequence in Chapters 2–3 and the rescue of Bertalda in Chapter 14) and in *Sintram* (e.g. the opening scene in Chapter 1 or the bear hunt in Chapter 17). The narration in these scenes is fired with a considerable energy, and there is also often a genuine attempt to suggest more than physical forces at work, thus switching the main thrust of the story from the material to the mental plane. The opening chapter of *Sintram*, in which the Nordic knights, carousing on a stormy night, are interrupted by the terrified boy fleeing from a bad dream, is calculated to arouse fear and a sense of the uncanny. But as he tends to do all too often, Fouqué lays the colour on too obviously and too thick. 'Wunderlich' and 'wunderbar', 'Entsetzen' and 'entsetzlich' occur so frequently that one notices the intention and feels a revulsion against the intended effect. Fouqué lacks a sufficient awareness of the creative sensitivity of the *Gemüt*.

That he is genuinely concerned to link the external level of Romanticism with the inner, psychological one, at least in the stories under discussion, is evident from those moments at which he specifically draws attention to the inner processes in his heroes. In *Undine*, the motif of isolation, of alienation from 'normality', is established with some skill in the opening description of the fisherman's habitat and used to underpin the description of the gradual process by which the mind of Huldbrand, the knight who has strayed into this environment, is detached from the plane of everyday reality:

> Ihm war zumute, als gäbe es keine Welt mehr jenseits dieser umgebenden Fluten. . .[Huldbrand] war in tiefe und seltsame Gebilde seines Innern verloren. Die Gegend jenseits des Waldwassers zog sich seit des Priesters letzten Worten immer ferner und dunkler von ihm ab; die blühende Insel, auf welcher er lebte, grünte und lachte immer frischer *in sein Gemüt hinein* (Nadler, pp. 236 and 239: my emphasis).

A similar moment in *Sintram* is that in which the devilish tempter Kleinmeister calls out to the hero, during the ride through the Valley of Terrors: 'Ergib dich lieber mir. Im Augenblick – denn schnell sind *deine Gedanken*, schnell ist meine Macht – im Augenblick stehst du in der Normandie' (Nadler, p. 310: my emphasis).

But such moments are moments only and do not act cumulatively to produce a genuine romanticisation of the material. And even in them, Fouqué betrays the shallowness, or perhaps one should say relative coarseness, of his psychological perception. The critical moment in Chapter 17 of *Sintram*, when the lying words are spoken which send Folko to what is intended to be his death, provides an excellent opportunity for the blurring of the dividing-line between outer and inner reality. But the opportunity is not utilised. Certainly, we are made aware of Sintram's inner conflict, but by identifying the speaker as someone other than, and outside, Sintram himself, Fouqué misses his chance to project the principle of evil, which Kleinmeister represents, into the hero's mind. Not a clear identification, but a romantic confusion, an impersonal 'es', perhaps, is required here. The confusion in fact exists in Folko's mind, but Fouqué will have none in the mind of the reader: 'Folko meinte, Sintram habe gesprochen, und glitt pfeilschnell hinab, während dieser sich umsah. Kleinmeisters verhaßte Gestalt fiel ihm ins Auge' (p. 293).

If we were forced to choose between the categories of *Märchen* and *Novelle* on formal grounds in this case, we would be inclined to plump for the former. The supernatural is portrayed as an objective reality, largely independent of the minds of the protagonists; the story proceeds in a direct, evenly flowing line from beginning to appointed end and is not organised around a 'Wendepunkt', or other narrative centre. At the same time, the virtues of these works are more those of the *Novelle*: they come closer to being 'frappant' than 'bizarr' in the terms of Friedrich Schlegel's definition. The fairy-tale material needs to be lifted clear of everyday reality in tone as well as in logic, whereas in Fouqué, it still has something of the stiffness of a waxwork. In the following passage from *Undine*, he tries to achieve a sense of the uncanny in describing a head appearing on the surface of the Danube:

Kaum aber daß sie [Undine] die Augen geschlossen hatte, so wähnte jedermann im Schiffe nach der Seite, wo er grade hinsah, ein ganz abscheuliches Menschenhaupt zu erblicken, das sich aus den Wellen emporhob, nicht wie das eines Schwimmenden, sondern ganz senkrecht, wie auf den Wasserspiegel gerade eingepfählt (p. 257).

The fact that the author takes us by the hand and explains in what way his apparition is uncanny, thus placing a fatal obstacle in the way of the direct appeal to the *Gemüt*, is a clear indication of the fact that his emancipation from rational restraints is less than total.

Very little of Fouqué's writing still appeals and even in his own day, when he enjoyed a period of great popularity with the broad mass of the reading public, there were those among the Romantics who could not take him quite seriously. Eichendorff, basing himself on the fact that Fouqué remained satisfied with the surface reality of the medieval world, called him the Don Quijote of Romanticism. It is hardly fair, though, to lay at his door all the sins of what Nadler calls the Dresden 'Afterromantik', with its 'rationalistische Nüchternheit, sentimentale Rührseligkeit und phantastische Romantik'.[16] Fouqué at his best did *feel* his vision of chivalry and his imagination was truly stirred by romance. But it is certainly true that he either could not or would not see the need to translate it into modern terms and his heroes, for all their occasional charm, remain for the most part 'Gäste aus der alten, großen Welt'.[17]

Arnim

In a previous chapter,[18] we had a foretaste of the special blend of the realistic and the fantastic which is the characteristic tone of Ludwig Achim von Arnim. His stories — with only one clear exception in *Der tolle Invalide* — do not have the close-knit narrative organisation which one associates with the *Novelle*, and he himself, like his most recent editor, is wary of the term, using it only in the general subtitle of *Der Wintergarten*, in which case the memory of Boccaccio's collection may have been an influence, and in a few individual cases,[19] in which there seems to be no special reason for its use. His fondness for working — as far as plot is concerned — within the bounds of material reality precludes the *Märchen* proper (the Goethe-parody, *Wunder über Wunder*, is much more satire than *Märchen*, in spite of its sub-title). And yet, within his own sphere, he often produces an analogous effect. He narrates directly, as does the teller of fairy-tales, in an economical, almost objective style, but makes, if anything, an anti-realistic effect by virtue of his consistent choice of curious, comic and grotesque material and his presentation, which often comes down to a hectic and — to the logical mind — inconsequential accumulation of details and events. He conveys a strong awareness that the layer of 'reality' on which he moves is a thin and brittle covering over spiritual depths. Görres puts it well when he talks of Arnim's 'Schlittschuhtritt, der bisweilen so tief einschneidet, daβ das Grundwasser durchbricht und den Leuten in die Augen spritzt'.[20] Fantasy, laced with humour, and a serious, moralistically inclined spirituality are the foremost constituent features of Arnim's literary personality.

He is as aware as some others of a spiritual world which exists in and around the material one. In *Die Majoratsherren* (1820), he even refers to the 'higher' or 'inner' world (SRE 3, 39 and 63) to which one has access through the *Gemüt*, but apart from this story, which shows farily clear influence from Tieck (cf. *Liebeszauber*) and Hoffmann and also seems to have been affected by contact with the thought of romantic scientists like Steffens and Schubert,[21] he is not strongly inclined to introduce it directly. Those romantic techniques which can most directly liberate the *Gemüt* from logical control do not feature very prominently in Arnim's writing. The suggestion, for example, through the supernatural or irrational and uncontrollable forces which can work within the psyche is (with the exception, again, of *Die Majoratsherren*) not a favoured method in his case. He prefers on the whole to work without specific invocation of the supernatural and when he does employ it, it is more the moral than the mental dimension of the inner life which seems to be his chief concern. In the two stories which make particular use of magic, *Isabella von Ägypten* and *Melück Maria Blainville* (both 1812), this factor is not a decisive one. In the first, indeed, it exists only at the level of the comic grotesque, a malevolent force, certainly, but one which can make no *internal* impression on the heroine, and to which she is triumphantly superior. And while it gives Melück *physical* power over Saintree's heart,[22] it has no power over his 'higher' love[23] for Mathilde and this higher principle eventually triumphs over magic in Melück herself.

While he takes a more oblique path to it, or at any rate a different one from that taken by most Romantics, which involves the elimination, or serious weakening, of the sense of material reality, Arnim is as aware as they of the irrational and subconscious factors in the psyche and ascribes to them as important a role. However superficially matter-of-fact the narrative technique, Arnim's rapid-fire sequence of intrinsically odd events and situations creates an atmosphere conducive to awareness of a psychological and spiritual layer of significance under the crust of 'reality' and there is no lack of direct references to show that Arnim is strongly interested in the motivation and mental and emotional processes of his characters. The compression which the shorter narrative

form brings with it naturally enhances this effect. Thus, *Mistris Lee*,
the most original and important story of *Der Wintergarten* (1809),[24]
studies a problem also broached in *Gräfin Dolores*, namely the
indeterminate and unstable character of modern man, but does so
with greater concentration, and conveys a stronger sense of the odd
and brittle nature of the character's psychology. It is on the surface a
rather banal story: a woman who has drifted into a disastrous marriage
and lives estranged from her husband meets again the two brothers,
Laudon and Lockhart Gordon, the companions of her youth, and the
memory of an early love, tinged with the influence of Richardson's
novels, is revived. After some hesitation, she runs away with the
brothers, but after one night spent at an inn, denounces them to their
pursuers and is reunited with her husband, with whom she lives
henceforth in contented 'Gewöhnlichkeit' (SRE 2, 273).

The tale is in fact an effective evocation of a character which is
neither good, nor evil, but 'gestaltlos' (p. 253). Mistress Lee is not
capable of clear vision or resolute purpose. The elopement, the idea of
which seems simply to 'arise', without a definite decision (p. 262),
becomes frightening to her when she is faced with the reality, but she
cannot take resolute steps to prevent it. Her denunciation of the
brothers is the result of her sudden realisation that she loves, not
Laudon, with whom she spent the night (out of fear of sleeping alone),
but his bolder brother. As usual, she acts on impulse which is 'des
Teufels Gewalt auf Erden' (p. 271), and against which she has no real
defence, unless grace is vouchsafed her: and in the only moment in
which she applies to the source of grace, she is disturbed (p. 268).
Arnim shows her consistently in a state of agitation and confusion,
speaking and acting in an inconsequential manner which puzzles those
around her, as when she speaks to her maid as if it were to her own
soul, which had stepped outside her body (p. 268), makes a reference,
out of the blue, to a portrait of herself (p. 267) when the subject is
elopement, or attempts to demonstrate her presence of mind as the
three drive away in the coach:

> Mistris Lee wußte wenig von sich; bald fiel es ihr ein, sie müßte sich
> stärker zeigen und fragte: 'Hab ich nicht meine Gegenwart des
> Geistes gezeigt?' Dann fragte sie wieder, ganz als wäre nichts
> vorgefallen: Ob wohl Feuer im Wohnzimmer angemacht wäre?
> (p. 269)

Arnim achieves the romantic alienation, then, the shift from the

level of 'normality' in feeling and thought, without stripping the
reality he describes of its solid, everyday qualities to the extent which
can be observed in the majority of Romantics. This, paradoxical as it
might seem at first sight, often increases the sense of oddity which his
narrative style and technique of presentation produces. It is a hard-
edged oddity, lacking in the dreaminess and musicality which makes it
easy for us, reading Eichendorff for example, to detach ourselves from
logical patterns of thought. In Arnim, even moments of the formally
fantastic, such as dreams, can have a quality of pronounced materiality,
as for example in the narrator's dream in *Die Ehenschmiede*,[25] whose
purpose is to show how strongly his mind is preoccupied with Aura.
The indigestion born of an injudicious late meal becomes involved in a
grotesquely comic interaction with romantic imagination – the quality
which Aura herself embodies – and he feels that instead of kissing her,
he has 'swallowed her':

> nun scherzte, tanzte, sang die Schöne in meinem Magen, endlich
> nahm sie sogar Reitstunde, vielleicht weil ich die Herzogin zu
> Pferde am vorhergehenden Tage gesehen hatte. Ich fühlte, wie ihr
> Fuß gegen die Wände der Bahn schlug, ich fühlte jeden Tritt des
> beschlagenen Pferdes. . . (SRE 3, 549)

Another effective instance of the interweaving of the material and
psychological is the episode at St Benno's pool in *Owen Tudor* (1821)
in which the Queen detaches herself from the sense of responsibility
and fidelity to her late husband and turns inwardly to her real love,
Owen (being as yet unaware of his presence). His prowess as an
underwater swimmer enables him first to remove the king's ring from
her hand, then, with the ring in his mouth, to blend his face with her
reflection in the pool. Imagining that this is the miraculous apparition
of the saint, she exclaims: 'Heiliger Owen, Heiliger Benno, dein Bild
küßt mein Bild im Wasser, darum bewahre den Ring, als ob ich dir
vermählt wäre' (SRE 3, 92).

   This 'strange but real' effect is a central principle in Arnim's choice
and treatment of narrative events. His penchant for the odd is
apparent to all who read him: the wooden leg which catches fire at the
beginning of *Der tolle Invalide*, the consort of musical cooks in *Der
Pfalzgraf, ein Goldwäscher*, or the discovery of a text on the subject
of marriage in the stomach of a dead cow in *Martin Martir* (SRE 3,
709) are representative examples of the multitude of such details
which often seem to swarm around the central characters and plots, in

themselves eccentric enough. They serve also to illustrate the fact that, serious as Arnim's mentality and preoccupations undoubtedly are, he has a strong and very individual sense of humour. This fantastic humour is both romantic in its psychologically liberating effect, and peculiarly Arnim-esque in that it does not encourage or, often, even permit of relaxation. The ideas come and go, literally, so thick and fast, that while one appreciates that calculated indiscipline is a constitutive principle of Arnim's art, one also sometimes feel that he has over-estimated his readers' capacity to maintain balance and control under constant bombardment.

Among the most successful of Arnim's predominantly humorous stories are *Fürst Ganzgott und Sänger Halbgott* (1818), a lighthearted comic variation on the romantic theme of the 'Doppelgänger' and — on a more ambitious scale — *Die Ehenschmiede.* The former encloses a little political parable on the regeneration of an ossified German aristocracy within an amusing and fanciful story which shows a relative lightness of tone at times recalling the *Märchen* of Brentano. The troop of 'prophetic' tame mice, which follows Halbgott's fortune-telling mother about the house and is eternally getting in the way, is a pretty touch and plays a useful role in helping to motivate Halbgott's original flight from the theatre, though in this episode (SRE 3, 16 f), one feels that only a little more embroidery would have been needed to push an enjoyable and fruitful confusion to the point at which it imposed a genuine strain on the reader's imagination. The episode as it stands, though, is a good example of the controlled comic grotesque. *Die Ehenschmiede* is surely Arnim's masterpiece in that manner.

Eccentricity is the order of the day in this story. The narrator, an itinerant entomologist, becomes involved with a group of characters living in or near a castle on the Scottish coast. At the centre of the whole group stands Aura, the embodiment of caprice, 'das wahre Wasserstoffgas' (SRE 3, 538). This will-o'-the-wisp attracts a number of suitors but cannot be domesticated and leads the whole company a merry dance before she finally takes her leave, though not until she has left the men well provided for in a series of weddings at Gretna Green, the smithy of the title. It is as well that she does not remain. She represents a necessary factor in the happiness of the society she has left behind, but can only fulfil her function if she is left free, if no attempt is made to integrate her: 'So flüchtig ist sie eben herrlich,' as the Captain remarks, 'wenn wir sie festhielten, störte sie mit fatalen Späßen unser freudiges Mittagsmahl' (p. 585).

Gaiety must be tempered, in the human spirit, with firm seriousness of character. Arnim is always critical of characters who lack such spiritual firmness or, rather, the ability to recognise and accept the grace through which it is offered to man. Thus *Isabella von Ägypten* (1812) at the same time celebrates the spiritual purity of the heroine and condemns Karl (Charles V of Spain) for his inability to rise to its challenge. Similarly, *Der Pfalzgraf, ein Goldwäscher*[26] depicts a life of gay (though good-natured) frivolity which is redeemed when the Count Palatine is made aware, as a gift of grace, of the nullity of the hedonistic life and of the 'Ernst der Welt' (SRE 3, 650), in the simple and arduous gold-seeker's life into which he entered, ironically, in order to rid himself of the fat which stands in the way of a marriage with the Emperor's sister. And so in *Die Ehenschmiede*, Karl von Starkader, the former adherent of the Kantian Categorical Imperative, comes to see that God is not a mere invented abstraction and kneels in gratitude 'für die Gnade, die mir nach so vielem Umherirren, nach so falscher trostloser Wahl zu Teil geworden' (SRE 3, 584). Sara, the wife he has rescued from hunger and degradation, links him with the serious reality of life;[27] with Aura, his life would have been dissipated in an unproductive void.

But this is not meant as an invalidation of fancy and gaiety. As Arnim says in *Der Pfalzgraf, ein Goldwäscher*, humour is also a 'gift of heaven' and a path to truth (p. 650) and the story ends in a great outburst of comic good humour. Provided that the moral base is secure, there is no necessary opposition between these qualities and true, productive spiritual seriousness. Aura, after all, brings the couples together. It is she — symbolically — who adorns Sara for the wedding and who, as if by a fairy-tale wonder,[28] provides the Indian birds' nests which are the crowning glory of the Captain's turtle soup, of which the assembled company all partake, in festive mood but not without a certain ritual solemnity (p. 585, 'mit Andacht') in the concluding paragraph. The whole story, in fact, celebrates the triumph of the humorous and fantastic spirit over that of rationalistic, false solemnity. Aura rises above all attempts to tie her down and the best-laid plans of the other characters usually go awry. A further intrusion of the spirit of fancy (or at least of that area of reality which borders on the fanciful) is provided by a shipwreck, which decants on to the Scottish coast a whole menagerie of exotic animals, which play an important part in the episode of the 'exploding Captain', one of Arnim's *tours de force* in the comic grotesque.

The Captain is acting as second in a duel in the castle grounds. He intends later to arrange a firework display as a birthday surprise for the Duchess and has stuffed his pockets full of fireworks (though at first these are assumed to be sausages). The duel having come to nothing, the mood switches into merriment at the antics of some turtles on the shore, and as abruptly into terror, when a Bengal Tiger appears. The Duchess, who has been given as a present a small model of the 'fire-dragon', a device invented by the ingenious mechanic Rennwagen for hurling fiery darts at French invaders, directs this useful weapon at the tiger, but hits the Captain instead:

> Der Tiger machte ein krauses Gesicht und drückte den Kopf ein, der Hauptmann dagegen fing Feuer, sein Herz knallte, noch lauter seine Rocktaschen, sein Rock platzte überall, seinen Hosentaschen entstiegen Schwärmer, seinem Bauche Leuchtkugeln, Frösche hüpften aus seinen Westentaschen. . .[er] sprang in die brausende Flut und duckte bis zum Kinn unter, aber das Feuer war darum noch nicht erloschen. . . es puffte und platzte und warf das Wasser in die Höhe, er schien ein Vulkan im Meeresgrunde, wohl gar eine untergegangene oder auftauchende Insel (p. 568).

Arnim has not really tried to conceal what is in fact happening, but he describes it in such a way as to mingle the material and the fantastic. The fact that in many cases, the fireworks seem to come out of the Captain (e.g. 'seinem Bauche [entstiegen] Leuchtkugeln') and the introduction of the motif of bursting, do indeed conjure up the image of a man who has, as the Duchess fears, eaten 'a strange dish of gunpowder, which has ignited in his stomach'. Reality remains solidly material, but becomes simultaneously fantastic, a genuinely grotesque effect which has something of the phenomenon of 'estrangement' which Wolfgang Kayser sees as typical of this mode, or of the disruption of the feeling of rational control and of the cause-and-effect nexus which T. Cramer mentions as its main characteristic.[29] One thinks, inevitably, of that mixture of the material and the phantasmagorical which can be observed in surrealist painters, and modern writers like Breton or Bulgakov.[30]

But the temptation to interpret Arnim as in any sense a 'modern' should be resisted. His is not a meaningless universe, however much the common run of everyday existence may seem to be divorced from spiritual truth. There is, for Arnim, a transcendental spiritual dimension to which man has access, largely, as we have seen, through grace and which can be present and active in earthly affairs. History is a very valuable source of understanding of that truth for Arnim, as for other

Romantics[31] and the bulk of his stories, as well as *Die Kronenwächter*, are set in past epochs, about which he was at some pains to inform himself, and in which he seems to have felt the power of the spirit to have been more active and accessible, even if men were not necessarily more virtuous in consequence. This awareness is particularly strong and single-minded in *Der tolle Invalide auf dem Fort Ratonneau* (1818), and this undoubtedly is the cause of the untypically close-knit, *Novelle*-like structure of the story, to which reference was made at the beginning of this section. The thematic centre is the battle between the good and evil principles, working in and through humans. This battle is always implicitly present in Arnim, but here, it appears in a much more explicit form and, in a way characteristic of the *Novelle*, crystallises around tangible motifs, such as that of war itself (Francœur against Marseilles) and of the Devil (whose flag the mentally disturbed soldier actually flies). The concluding verse-motto sums up succinctly:

> *Gnade* löst den Fluch der *Sünde*
> *Liebe* treibt den *Teufel* aus

The emphases here, which neatly point up the opposition between hostile forces, are Arnim's own.

The French sergeant, Francœur, is wounded in the head and made a prisoner during the Seven Years' War. A German girl, Rosalie, falls in love with him and cleaves to him, in defiance of her mother's curse, which consigns her to the Devil. She suffers considerable mental distress until after her marriage to Francœur, after which she gains relief, but he begins to act wildly and conceives an antipathy towards churches and clergy. The couple return to France and Rosalie's mind is completely set at rest after the birth of her child. Her husband's malady does not abate, however, and she confides in the Commandant of Marseilles, who assigns him to the island fort of Ratonneau, to keep his behaviour out of the public eye. An unguarded remark by a friend reveals to Francœur that Rosalie has 'betrayed' him and he expels her and their child from the fort and declares war on Marseilles in the name of the Devil. It seems that only a violent solution is possible, but Rosalie, whose initial flight from the fort was made in a kind of daze ('bewußtlos': SRE 2, 746), and with the child's safety in mind, now resolves the crisis by walking alone into the path of the guns with which her husband is bombarding the city and offering herself as a sacrifice. The climactic passage (too long to be quoted in full) has something of the tone of a biblical casting-out of a devil:[32] a confrontation between a calm, loving principle and a wild, destructive one. Arnim's narrative style is naturally more dramatic and elaborate, but the basic pattern of a simple and sublime confrontation is the same. Rosalie kneels in silence and trust; Francœur, as the battle of 'two natures' rages within him, tears at his clothes, then his hair and strikes his brow. Then, in a passage which could be said to contain faint, but daring, echoes of the crucifixion-accounts,[33] the crisis arrives:

> Da öffnete sich die Wunde am Kopfe in dem wilden Erschüttern durch Schläge, die er an seine Stirn führte, Tränen und Blut löschten den brennenden Zundstrick, ein Wirbelwind warf das Pulver von den Zundlöchern der Kanonen und die Teufelsflagge vom Turm. . .
> (p. 753)

Love, strengthened by grace, triumphs and Francœur is cured. As is usual in his stories, Arnim avoids introducing the supernatural outright — a possible psychological explanation for Francœur's madness is presented in the shape of a splinter of bone lodged in the head-wound — but the stylistic level at which he narrates, especially in the final scenes, and the unusual nature of the situation and some of the detail[34] raise the tone above that of mundane realism. Furthermore, to explain as mere coincidence the fact that Rosalie's mother dies on the very same day, released from the burning remorse which plagued her from the time of the imposition of the curse and from which she begged Rosalie, in a dream-vision, to redeem her, is to stretch that concept rather too wide for comfort. It seems rather to strengthen the impression of a real curse, as the description of the climactic scene strengthens the impression of a genuine demonic possession, or at least of the influence of a dark spiritual force which only a corresponding holy one can combat. It reminds us that when called upon to surrender in the name of the King, Francœur had replied: 'In mir ist der König aller Könige dieser Welt, in mir ist der Teufel. . .' (p. 747).[35] The final effect is a demonstration of the power of the spirit, a romantic rather than a Schillerian sublimity: grace, that is, given in response to faith.

Brentano

Brentano's work in this field comprises a substantial collection of *Märchen* (composed 1805–12)[36] and the stories *Die Schachtel mit der*

Friedenspuppe (1815), *Die mehreren Wehmüller und ungarischen
Nationalgesichter* (1815–17) and *Die drei Nüsse* and *Geschichte von
dem braven Kasperl und dem schönen Annerl* (both 1817). In addition,
there should be mentioned the fragments *Die Rose* (1800) and *Der
Sänger* (1801). These latter two works belong more to the sphere of
Godwi than to any other. Although *Die Rose* is sub-titled 'ein Märchen',
it is unlike Brentano's *Märchen* proper and bears rather the marks of a
Tieckian re-telling of an old romance, with clear signs of the tendency
to subjective introversion characteristic of the early Brentano. *Der
Sänger*, more overtly autobiographical, deals with the poet's loss of the
sense of integration with the world around him (contingent on the
death of the mother) and his quest for its restoration in love, and shows
that tendency more clearly still. Its slow, meandering course, frequent
pauses for reflection and 'inwardly' oriented lyricism and nature
description all point towards a novel of the type of *Godwi*.

We have seen how Brentano's concept of the *Märchen* differed from
that of the Grimm brothers.[37] He did not despise the 'Volksgeist';
indeed, he felt that the naïve spirit which had flourished in earlier times
was in many ways superior to the sophisticated, disunited modern one.
But his aim was not to preserve monuments for posterity, but to speak
directly to his own generation (and to some extent, to himself, though
he is less entangled in subjectivism in the short than in the long
narrative form). This meant more freedom for the modern writer,
particularly in matters of form and phrasing: a trend already evident in
some of the *Wunderhorn* poems. Brentano found the narrative style
and technique adopted by the Grimms aesthetically inadequate and
much preferred the Low German *Märchen* of P. O. Runge, *Von den
Machandelboom* and *Von den Fischer un syne Fru* (1806).[38] He
himself certainly does not adopt the relatively self-effacing manner of
the Grimms and achieves a quality which is at once childlike in its free
acceptance of and delight in the wondrous, and sophisticated and
personal in its wit, its truly romantic ironic humour, and freely
indulged lyricism. The romantic spirit has, as it were, created its own
nursery, in which the restraints imposed elsewhere on fancy and on the
sense of beauty no longer apply.

The *Märchen* fall into two groups, the 'Rheinmärchen' and the
'Italian', so called because they are based on the collection by
Giambattista Basile, though thoroughly Germanised in spirit and setting.
The 'Rheinmärchen' form a unit, being rather loosely linked together
by the framework-story of the miller Radlauf and his bride Ameley,
who is given to him by his friend and protector, the Rhine. The river,

the 'alte[r] treue[r] Rhein' (K 3, 9), with its associations of Germanic spirit and legend, is the symbolic and thematic centre of the whole and the dualism of faithfulness and faithlessness is a recurrent central motif in both the framework and the inset stories. One is reminded of Brentano's stated aim, in the *Wunderhorn*, of restoring 'die frische Morgenluft altdeutschen Wandels'.[39] But the predominant mood is more one of gaiety and free fancy (the Rhine also leads 'a free life, dancing, along by the vines, through the solemn night' (p. 9)). There are many scenes of gay and chaotic, even crazy, humour, as for example those in which the soldiers of Trier, out of pure exuberant valour, stand on their heads and present arms with their feet (K 3, 41), and the State Cat of Mainz chases the State Rat of Trier (pp. 161 ff). And there are others of magical colour and musicality, as when the goldfish sees the river lit up by moonlight and hears the beautiful song 'Himmel oben, Himmel unten' (pp. 84–5).

Among the 'Italian' tales, that of *Gockel, Hinkel und Gackeleia* must be singled out, for the fact that Brentano returned to it in the 1830s and developed it into a profound, if typically convoluted, expression of his whole experience of and insight into life.[40] This he achieves, not by destroying the light-hearted charm of the original, but by grafting on other elements. He has added an important autobiographical *Dedication*, evoking with considerable imaginative and emotional power the world of his childhood, in which a (still innocent) fancy played such an important part. And he has developed from hints present in the basic story a second, *adult* fairy-tale stratum which, while it retains the prettiness and capricious playfulness of Brentano's typical style, has a serious, even mystical tone. The theme of the basic *Märchen* is the discovery, loss and recovery of the magic ring of Solomon, which has been handed down from generation to generation of the cockerels belonging to Gockel's family. The potential of the ring as a symbol of harmony is clear. The idea of its long history enables Brentano to introduce the figure of the 'Ahnfrau' (modelled, probably, on the love of his later years, Emilie Linder) and himself, in the guise of a lost, confused and frightened child, seeking integration and stability like the gleaner seeking grains of corn. The main hope seems to lie in the perception of a mysterious, indeed mystical link between the earthly and heavenly, indescribable, but capable of being invoked through the 'Stern und Blume' formula of the 'Ahnfrau', which we have already met[41] in our discussion of the poem 'Eingang', which in fact brings the second version finally to an end. These words, of which the 'Ahnfrau', to whom they are a kind of charm, herself says: 'Ich verstand sie durch und durch und konnte sie doch nicht erklären. Ich verstand ihr Wesen und hatte keine Worte für sie als sie selbst' (K 3, 857), represent very well the nature and style of this part of the *Gockelmärchen*. The naïve fairy-tale is lifted to the level of complex symbolism, but without suffering undue intellectualisation in the process. Serious spiritual and psychological depths are suggested, and the style of the prose and above all the verse[42] is as concentrated and allusive as any in the late Brentano, but the ideal of childlike wholeness which Brentano perceives, albeit with the simultaneous consciousness that he cannot be in constant and serene possession of it, is not swamped by all the complexity.

The stories have in common complexity of plot (in which the unravelling of a mystery is the central thread) and a practical, somewhat spare, narrative style. All have their romantic aspects. The *Wehmüller* story exploits from the comic angle the chaotic situation of a travelling portraitist who is hampered in his efforts to reach his destination by an epidemic, while a rival is impersonating him and reaping his harvest. The story of the main character, and the tales told by the people whom he meets, reflect in their wild and irrational nature the terrain in which the story is set and while it all ends harmlessly enough, there is certainly no comfort here for the philistine. The other three stories all have definite suggestions of the demonic. They are centred on dark deeds, on guilt and retribution. The power of evil is strong; even honourable men and women are not immune against it and sin must and will be punished, however cunningly devised, even well-meaning, may be the attempts of humans to prevent it. Nemesis, in the guise of chance, can and does intervene to ensure this, as at the end of the *Kasperl und Annerl* story, when the noise of gunnery practice going on nearby foils the attempt of the Prince to pardon Annerl.

Those who are tempted, by this last example, to posit a Hardy-esque pessimism in Brentano should remember the words of the character who speaks for him, the grandmother: 'Gerechtigkeit ist besser als Pardon' (K 2, 798). God is the judge: His justice and providence can and should be trusted. There is a positive counterpart to the dark fate of those who fall victim to the temptations of this world. Amelie, in *Die drei Nüsse*, who had seemed fated to remain caught up in sin and shame, is led by providence to the very place where she can be relieved of that burden. In *Die Schachtel mit der Friedenspuppe*, the chance which brings to the Baron's house the two miscreants responsible for the crime with which the box is connected brings also the innocent victims and the solution of the mystery is also the source of clarification and restoration for them. And the coming together of the narrator and the grandmother in *Kasperl und Annerl* is providential in a number of ways. True, Annerl and the seducer Grossinger, have to die, but the latter's sister and the Duke are saved from committing a sinful act and the two main characters receive their honourable grave and a reasonable hope of salvation on the final, and more important, Day of Judgement.

The status of the *Geschichte vom braven Kasperl und dem schönen Annerl* as one of the greatest of romantic *Novellen* depends very largely on the author's ability, while remaining his sophisticated and uncertain self, to create, in the grandmother, a portrait of simple and secure faith which deserves the overworked adjective, 'archetypal'. Her calm, and unshakable consistency in holding to eternal verities and brushing aside other considerations (for which her favourite saying, 'Gib Gott allein die Ehre,' can stand as symbolic), achieved by masterly narrative technique and stylistic control, make her stand out with a completely romantic sublimity like a rock in a swirling sea of doubts and confusions. She is also the structural centre of the work: it is she alone who sees events *sub specie aeternitatis*, she who links the framework with the inset story and the present with the past and the future, and through whom all the various occurrences and motifs can be related together.

The old woman has come to the 'Residenzstadt' to plead for an honourable burial for her grandson Kasperl, who has shot himself in despair on learning that his father is a thief and that his 'honour' is therefore besmirched, and for his beloved Annerl, who has been seduced by a nobleman (whose name she will not reveal), has killed her child and is to be executed next day. The narrator finds her preparing to spend the night in the doorway of a nobleman in whose service she was as a young girl and she enlists his aid in petitioning the Duke, in the process telling him the story of the unhappy lovers. We thus have an outer framework, in which she is an actor, and an inner one in which she functions as narrator, and the subtlety of the story's structure is enhanced by Brentano's manipulation of the time factor. Past, present and future overlap and interact. We have the past in the inner story of Kasperl and Annerl and a more remote past introduced in the inner framework through the grandmother's references to her own youth. The present, of course, is the action of the outer framework, in which she and the primary narrator are involved and the future consists not only of the impending judgement to be carried out the next day, but in the grandmother's preoccupation with the Day of Judgement, the reason for the request which has brought her to the town. In his creation of a sense of complexity together with unity, of a multiplicity of figures and motifs which are both disparate and yet quite naturally related together, Brentano has achieved an effect which is both highly romantic and, on the aesthetic level, matched only by his best lyrics.

Chamisso

Like his lyric poetry, Chamisso's story *Peter Schlemihls wundersame Geschichte* (1814) stands close to the periphery of the Romantic Movement. Critical opinion is divided on the question of its historical attribution, as it is also on the question of genre (*Märchen* or *Novelle*?). One's first instinct is to decide for Romanticism: the story is indeed 'wundersam', dealing as it does with the fortunes of a character who exchanges his shadow for the magic bag of Fortunatus, lives to regret the exchange bitterly, but refuses to buy back the shadow at the cost of his soul (or is saved from doing so by a convenient fainting-fit), finally finding some consolation in a pair of seven-league boots, which enable him to roam the earth, studying it as a scientist. Another magical motif, that of the bird's nest which renders its bearer invisible, is added for good measure. It can, however, and has been argued that the strange and wondrous elements in the subject-matter have not been exploited in a positively romantic way. Benno von Wiese emphasises that it is everyday life in the material world rather than the inner life of the *Gemüt* which is Chamisso's main preoccupation, and sees the shadow as a symbol of 'bürgerliche Solidität und menschliche Zusammengehörigkeit'[43] (rather than some more purely spiritual good), and its absence as not a romantic 'liberation', but a real deprivation for Chamisso. The conciliatory ending von Wiese sees as confirmation of his view, since it is not a quasi-mystical experience of nature, but rational, scientific understanding of it which becomes Schlemihl's principal occupation and pleasure.

There is much force in this argument and we can agree immediately that this is no true *Märchen*. It contains wonders, but not the strong sense of wonder which that designation would imply. There are uncanny moments, but the sense of horror communicated lacks the depth which, in the great romantic masters, arises out of a sense of *inner* disorientation. As in the case of Fouqué, we feel that the author does not wish to introduce into our minds that radical confusion, those 'seltsame Verknüpfungen und Verwechslungen des Denkens' of which Schlegel spoke[44] and which are there even in Arnim. But — again as with

Fouqué – we would rather, on balance, speak of a muted, or inhibited, Romanticism in this case than of a positive impulse towards the relative realism and 'quietism'[45] of Biedermeier.

What, then, has Chamisso communicated? The symbolic force of the shadow is strong, but hard to define. The effect of its loss is clear; it makes Schlemihl an outsider in society. But should we cease, at this point, to think at the symbolic level and simply relate this to Chamisso's view of man in general, and himself, as an *émigré* Frenchman, in particular, in his social context? Should we, in other words, begin to think realistically, or is there not a deeper level of spiritual and psychological significance, even if one admits that Chamisso does not bring it out as effectively as he might? Solitude (e.g. that of the hermit) is certainly not a negative state for the Romantics, but isolation is a different matter. There is a qualitative difference between the 'Waldeinsamkeit' portrayed by Tieck in *Der blonde Eckbert*, in which Bertha is in fact able to transcend her individual self and find a healthy relationship with the universal spiritual dimension, and the solipsistic 'Einsamkeit' in which Eckbert has locked himself and which sends him mad.[46] Schlemihl's isolation is, of course, to some extent social, but there is also a sense of a different and more fearsome loneliness in it, something resembling that feeling of being totally cut off from a lost or inaccessible paradise which occasionally makes even Eichendorff's Taugenichts 'zum Sterben bange' (BG 2, 355). There is a flash of this feeling at the beginning of Chapter 6 of *Peter Schlemihls wundersame Geschichte*, in the scene on the desolate heath, and a stronger indication in Chapter 2, in which Schlemihl, sleeping on a bed of gold pieces, dreams of his friend – and 'double' – 'Chamisso': 'Ich betrachtete dich lange und jedes Ding in deiner Stube, und dann dich wieder, du rührtest dich aber nicht, du holtest auch nicht Atem, du warst tot' (*Werke* 1, 420). The deliberate strangeness of this episode makes one think that the author's intention is to open a window into the inner psychological world, in which the sense of a transcendental one also plays a part.

There is certainly no lack of suggestions of the demonic about the devil-figure which pursues the hero and the 'soul' at the cost of which Schlemihl could redeem his shadow is surely a little more than his 'better self', as von Wiese formulates it.[47] Its surrender, which would bring about the restoration of the shadow, would place him on a level with Thomas John, the rich, complacent man whom the sinister stranger already has, literally, in his pocket. Even the noble impulses of love could not justify the selling of the soul, and Schlemihl recognises that the faint which prevented him from doing so was the intervention of a 'weise Fügung'. It was an act of grace, indeed, as becomes clear in the next chapter (the eighth), in which a specifically religious dimension appears. Schlemihl charges the tempter in God's name to show him where John is, whereupon the devil reluctantly draws the rich man from his pocket, 'pale and disfigured', and repeating the words of Bidermann's Cenodoxus: 'Justo judicio Dei judicatus sum. . . Justo judicio Dei condemnatus sum.'[48] Schlemihl then abjures all commerce with the devil in words recalling Christ's rebuke of Satan in the Wilderness: 'So beschwör ich dich im Namen Gottes, Entsetzlicher! hebe dich von dannen. . .' (*Werke* 1, 452)

There are certainly 'Biedermeier' writers whose psychological depth and poetic sensitivity are superior to those of Chamisso. But none of them would have treated this subject in quite this way. His nearest, if still not exact, equivalent among the narrative artists of his age is his friend Fouqué and it may well be no accident that there is a 'Galgen-männlein' among the magical treasures offered to Schlemihl and that in the dream-vision of 'Chamisso', the 'healthy' alter ego of the narrator, the two books representing literary, as against scientific, activity are 'a volume of Goethe' (whose influence, through *Faust*, is evident) and Fouqué's *Der Zauberring*. Our present story has, in fact, much in common with *Sintram*, though it should be added that it represents a considerably higher achievement as a piece of narrative literature. Whatever literary trend is seen as predominating in it, it remains a good story, well told.

Eichendorff

The question of a possible relationship with 'Biedermeier' arises also in the case of Eichendorff's stories and while we are not inclined to answer it in the affirmative, the question itself is a fruitful one, because it concentrates our attention on certain aspects of the work to be discussed which might be obscured by exclusive concentration on a narrow range of 'traditional' romantic themes. The 'Biedermeier' writer has a sophisticated awareness of the dangers which man faces, and of his limitations, and ultimate inability to make himself independent of reality. While this movement often looks back with some nostalgia to the heady days of the Age of Idealism, and still adheres, to a large extent, to the values of the 'Goethezeit', it feels consistently the need to achieve a compromise between poetry and

everyday reality. The writer of this generation may be a reluctant
realist, but he is on balance a realist nevertheless.

Even if the reality in which Eichendorff's stories are anchored is one
in which drab and mundane considerations, when they do intrude,
seem to offer no serious threat to the freedom of the poetic existence,
it is felt as a real world, as Benno von Wiese points out.[49] Exoticism is
rare and, when it occurs, as in *Eine Meerfahrt* (1835–6?), is clearly less
congenial to Eichendorff's characteristic tone than the familiar German
and Italian settings. It is true also, as we have indeed seen before, that
Eichendorff instinctively distrusts the eccentric and immoderate and
that the majority of his outsiders and rebels end in unhappiness. The
warning issued at the end of *Das Schloß Dürande* (1837) against
arousing the 'wild beast' in one's own breast might seem to reflect the
sentiments of 'Biedermeier', as might the fact that the nomadic life of
the Taugenichts eventually ends in domesticity. Even Werner
Bergengruen, who sees Eichendorff unequivocally as a Romantic,
speaks of a touch of 'kleinbürgerliche [r] Biedermeierei' in this
ending.[50]

But acceptance of the fact that *absolute* freedom for the self is not
viable and horror at the thought of complete isolation and self-loss are
not to be equated with the concession of authority to the material
world and its practical ethos. We remember that the romantic ideal
included a social dimension of 'Geselligkeit', but one which at the
same time did not surrender the principle of the superiority of the
poetic to the practical. Eichendorff still believes in the possibility of
such a true spiritual freedom without isolation, the kind of freedom
which Grillparzer seems, in *Der arme Spielmann* (1849), to be
declaring an impossible pipe-dream. The 'Biedermeier' writer is not
exactly hostile to idealism, but realism has invaded his outlook to a
significant extent, an observation which could also be made in the case
of Jean Paul, the true precursor of 'Biedermeier' in our period.

Freedom, for Eichendorff as for the other Romantics, is a gift of
grace, won through the faith of the pure in heart who can ward off
modern egotism and nihilism and go courageously out into a world
full of hazards and 'fight their way through', to adopt Diego's phrase
in *Eine Meerfahrt*. The stories all centre on the distinction between
true and false freedom and celebrate the former, the possibility of
which is never in doubt, even if not all the endings are entirely happy
ones. In *Das Schloß Dürande*, for example, the central character,
Renald, fails to achieve it. In consequence, he does not recognise true
love and positive freedom in the unconventional behaviour of his sister

Gabriele, who has run away to be with her aristocratic lover. He makes
common cause with the French revolutionaries in a quest for 'justice',
kills the supposed seducer and — in error — Gabriele herself and ends
in despair and obliteration. It is against this false, rebellious, self-
liberation and its passions that the final sentence, addressed by the
narrator to the reader with the image of the ruined castle in mind,
warns: 'Du aber hüte dich, das wilde Tier zu wecken in der Brust, daß
es nicht plötzlich ausbricht und dich selbst zerreißt' (BG 2, 849). The
triumphant, or at least serene, ending accorded to Gabriele, symbolised
in the fire which destroys the castle, rising 'wie eine Opferflamme,
schlank, mild und prächtig' (p. 849), sets off by contrast the negative
nature of Renald's fate. And to confirm that it is not fear of, or a
sceptical disbelief in, freedom which dictates the final integration of
the 'Taugenichts' into a social context, but rather the symbolic and
festive celebration of the triumph of the pure in heart, we can set
beside that ending that of *Die Glücksritter* (1841), in which Klarinett,
escaping from a philistine fate worse than death, remains in the forest
with Denkeli, 'selig verschollen'.

Die Entführung (1839) is another story in which the tragic aspect of
the theme looms large, though not, perhaps, to the extent of
invalidating the happy ending. Graf Gaston stands between two women,
in a not uncommon situation in Eichendorff: between the shy, fresh
blossom Leontine and the colourful hothouse flower Diana, between
the Germanic and the Italianate beauty, the Virgin- and the Venus-
figure.[51] He eventually chooses Leontine, in part at least because
Diana, who really holds the centre of the stage, fails to rise to the
challenge of the elopement by achieving true freedom of spirit. She
attempts to maintain the wilful, 'wild' freedom in which, not unlike
Romana in *Ahnung und Gegenwart*, she has lived and is unable or
unwilling to make the leap to the childlike trust and self-abnegation
which are adumbrated in the 'Kaiserkron' und Päonien' song.[52]
Ironically, perhaps, her failure becomes more firmly imprinted in the
reader's mind than Leontine's implied, but not clearly delineated,
success.

The other major stories have unclondedly happy endings. The
dualism between positive and negative freedom is clearly present in
both *Das Marmorbild* (1819) and *Die Glücksritter*. In the former, it is
worked out rather too obviously and emphatically to be entirely
satisfactory and the character of Florio, the 'man in the middle', is so
insipid that one wonders whether he deserves to be saved, as he in fact
is. The atmosphere of *Die Glücksritter* is much fresher. We are given a

convincing portrayal of positive spiritual freedom in the figure of the travelling musician Siglhupfer ('Klarinett'), whose gay and trusting openness to life make us confident that he will be given grace to avoid the pitfalls which life, aided by his own *naïveté*, places in his path. The negative foil is provided by the band of marauders led by Schreckenberger, a character with more than a little of the baroque 'miles gloriosus' about him,[53] but whose criminality is real enough. He and his associates represent destructive indiscipline. They are soldiers of fortune, as indeed is Siglhupfer, but theirs is the disorderly and fickle Fortuna whose attributes are the wheel and the rolling sphere. Siglhupfer's 'Glück' is like that of the 'Taugenichts' and it is significant that, after he has escaped from the false good fortune of the comfortable landowner's life, he is able to 'own' the forest which would have been legally his possession, in a more spiritually meaningful sense: 'es war alles, alles wieder sein' (BG 2, 933).

This is a variant of the formula, as Paulsen rightly calls it,[54] which occurs in a number of Eichendorff's narrative works, and in its best-known form at the end of *Aus dem Leben eines Taugenichts* (1826): 'und es war alles, alles gut!' This is indeed a phrase which implies a feeling of relief in the speaker at the thought of difficulties and dangers overcome, but Paulsen is on more dangerous ground when he attempts to use that fact to cast doubt on the spiritual depth of Eichendorff's characteristic serenity, which appears in its purest form in this work. To experience the complacent 'schmunzelnde Zustimmung' of which Paulsen speaks[55] is surely to fall into the trap against which we warned in our discussion of the lyric poetry.[56] Eichendorff is no escapist, 'painting the clouds with sunshine' and refusing to face the fact that all is not always well in the best-organised of worlds. We are meant to take the vision of poetry which the story presents seriously, but not literally, as if Eichendorff believed in the existence of a kind of romantic 'Schlaraffenland'. He has made the artificial, quasi-'märchenhaft' nature of the world which his hero mainly inhabits quite clear to all who read with due care and attention. Providing that we maintain a proper spiritual and intellectual discipline, our awareness of what *romantic* reality is, we can afford ourselves the luxury of enjoying what Bergengruen has called 'one of the most enrapturing stories in the [German] language'[57] without feeling that we are giving way to an unworthy nostalgia for a 'heile Welt' which would in fact mean a regression to the nursery.

The 'Taugenichts' is sent out by his disgruntled father, a miller, to earn his own keep in the world. Being a completely naïve creature, in both the positive and the negative sense, he often blunders and falls, but his sure faith, expressed in a song which deliberately recalls a well known hymn,[58] preserves him from sin and ensures that he finally falls on his feet. He falls in love with a girl whom he takes for a Countess (but who in fact is the niece of the castle porter) and after many misunderstandings, in which he is employed as an unwitting pawn in an aristocratic love-intrigue, is rewarded with the hand of his beloved and a 'weißes Schlößchen', where he is now writing this retrospective account of his career.

The distinction between the narrator and the younger 'Taugenichts' of the story proper needs to be kept in mind, for while the former takes his 'hero' seriously and has retained his faith in the reality of poetry — which is expressed in this work in a more sustainedly lyrical form than anywhere else in Eichendorff — he also looks at his younger self with a detached humour which prevents complete identification with him. The intense beauty of the early morning scene in the garden when the 'Taugenichts' observes his lady at a window is entirely valid in itself, but the narrator guards against its abuse as a kind of escapist drug by introducing a tinge of irony. The 'Taugenichts' is overcome by a sneezing-fit brought on by a 'fatale Fliege' (BG 2, 354). Whether Eichendorff intends it or not, we cannot help but be reminded of the delicious combination of the poetic and the comic in Mozart's Cherubino.

This reminiscence of an opera which we know Eichendorff greatly appreciated and which contains, in its plot at the very least, a strong 'Rococo' element, is not fortuitous. Eichendorff, who had spent his youth in an aristocratic environment and had spent a happy and formative period as a student in Vienna, had a better understanding of the Rococo culture (which of course still survived in aristocratic circles) than any other Romantic. He was aware both of its capacity for poetic gracefulness — which he renders, for example, in the brilliant description of a minuet in *Die Entführung* (BG 2, 862–3) — and of its old-fashioned and artificial nature. He is as scathing as any in his judgement of Wieland[59] and in the poem 'Prinz Rokoko' (in *Der Adel und die Revolution*) expresses quite clearly his view that whatever its former charm, it now looks stiff and out of place:

Daphne will nicht weiter schweifen
Und Damöt erschrocken schmält,
Können beide nicht begreifen,
Was sich da der Wald erzählt (BG 2, 1044).

He has used this ambivalent feeling to infuse a necessary ambivalence into the *Taugenichts*. Reminiscences of the Rococo are frequent in the language of the story and the plot itself is a self-consciously complicated intrigue which makes one think of the Rococo *opera buffa*. Eichendorff underlines this, indeed, by direct comment. Leonhard tells the hero that he has been playing a part in a love-intrigue ('Roman', in the eighteenth-century usage: cf. p. 431) and the priest who appears towards the end of Chapter 9, possibly as an authorial intrusion, sees 'Konfusion, nichts als Konfusion!' (p. 424), a fact which causes him no little amusement, at the hero's expense. This is not a satirical laughter, however, directed against the illusions of a comic 'Schwärmer', but the serene play of a romantic humour, rooted in the sure and certain knowledge of the higher spiritual reality, of which the whole work is a revelation and for which the 'Taugenichts', even at his most naïve, acts at least as a catalyst.

Kleist

Kleist's *Novellen*, composed during the period 1805–10, were published in their final form in two volumes under the title *Erzählungen* (1810 and 1811).[60] They show, not surprisingly, very much the same attitudes and preoccupations as have been noted in connection with the plays. There is the same interplay of 'Schmerz' and 'Glanz', of attachment to reality and awareness of the metaphysical. Human nature is still capable of sublimity (portrayed with particular force in *Die Marquise von O*), still capable of having its feeling perverted by mistrust (e.g. *Die Verlobung in St. Domingo*). Greatness of soul is still no guarantee of immunity against error: as in the case of Penthesilea, it is precisely Michael Kohlhaas's depth of soul which drives him to crime: 'Das Rechtgefühl. . . machte ihn zum Räuber und Mörder.'[61]

This last quotation points to an important difference (though one of degree) between the dramas and the *Novellen*, one which probably has to do with the nature of the genre and Kleist's handling of it. The tendency of the *Novelle* is towards concentration: whether or not there is a central symbol or 'Wendepunkt', some identifiable *point* of concentration, all the things that are done and said tend to relate together, not necessarily as parts of the story, but through a common central orientation. In Kleist, this is often provided by a thematic preoccupation; justice in *Michael Kohlhaas*, for example, the inner potential of 'Gefühl' in *Die Marquise von O*, the force of evil in *Der*

Findling, the mysterious and apparently capricious ways of God in *Das Erdbeben in Chili* and *Der Zweikampf*, mistrust and misunderstanding in *Die Verlobung in St. Domingo*. The sense of paradox which is expressed so forcefully in the words quoted from *Michael Kohlhaas* and which is an aspect of Kleist's essentially pessimistic conception of the perverted present state, the 'gebrechliche Einrichtung'[62] of the world, is present also in the plays, but its expression there is less overt and less sharp. The villainy of a Kunigunde (*Käthchen von Heilbronn*) cannot compare with that of Nicolo in *Der Findling*; the violence of the plays impinges much less vividly and painfully on our minds than that of the *Novellen*. Even Penthesilea's treatment of Achilles does not give the shock of horror of the moment in *Das Erdbeben in Chili* in which Pedrillo seizes Fernando's child by the legs, swings it round in the air and smashes its brains out against the sharp edge of — bitter paradox again! — a church-pillar.

Kleist's narrative style does much to enhance this intensification of his themes. It is hard-edged and direct, dominated by action and speech, the lean language of the anecdote, of which Kleist was in fact a master, most notably in *Das Bettelweib von Locarno*.[63] It makes little concession to the reader's need for rest and relaxation of tension. Paragraphs of 1,500 to 2,000 words are not uncommon and sentences are extremely long, swelled by the author's liking for the accumulation and encapsulation of subordinate clauses.[64] One almost feels that Kleist's ideal would be the single-sentence *Novelle*! This style is certainly neither romantic nor realistic. Here is a relatively moderate example from *Der Zweikampf*:

> Littegarde stand, bleich wie Kreide, vom Boden auf; sie bat, indem sie seinen Mißhandlungen schweigend auswich, ihr wenigstens zur Anordnung der erforderten Abreise die nötige Zeit zu lassen; doch Rudolph antwortete weiter nichts, als, vor Wut schäumend: 'Hinaus, aus dem Schloß!' dergestalt, daß, da er auf seine eigne Frau, die ihm, mit der Bitte um Schonung und Menschlichkeit, in den Weg trat, nicht hörte und sie, durch einen Stoß mit dem Griff des Schwerts, der ihr das Blut fließen machte, rasend auf die Seite warf, die unglückliche Littegarde, mehr tot als lebendig, das Zimmer verließ; . . . (*Sämtliche Werke*, ed. Laaths, p. 799)

The sentence is still not at an end, but the recent translators of the story, quite properly aware that there are limits beyond which English syntax cannot 'reasonably be pushed',[65] call a halt at this point, and

smooth out the syntactical convolutions of the sentence a little.
'Dergestalt, daß, da . . .', for example, becomes simply 'and since'.[66]
This style, which most would surely agree is incapable of reproduction
in another language, succeeds in being simultaneously laconic and
labyrinthine and is a, possibly the, crucial factor in the creation of the
inimitable tenor of Kleist's stories.

This could perhaps be defined as combining toughness, an almost
brutally[67] hectic pace, and a dense and intricate texture. In spite of the
apparent haphazard 'hypotactic'[68] confusion in which the clauses
tumble down the page, like an avalanche, everything is working towards
the desired end. The opening of *Das Erdbeben in Chili* tells us first that
Jeronimo is about to hang himself. Then, in a huge parenthetical
exposition, we learn that he has got with child Josephe, whom her
father had sent to a nunnery to prevent just such an eventuality, but
who had gone into labour on the cathedral steps during a religious
procession and who is now to pay the penalty for fornication, if by a
form of execution which a bigoted and cruelly sensation-hungry public
opinion regards as too lenient. Jeronimo has prayed in desperation to
the Virgin Mary for deliverance, but the day of execution has dawned,
and all seems lost. Then, at the last minute, an earthquake shakes
Santiago, killing many people, but rescuing the lovers from death.
Almost everything here points towards the thematic centre, while at
the same time the narrative hurries forward at a breathless pace. While
Jeronimo and Josephe cannot, in the strict sense, be described as
completely pure and innocent, they command our sympathy and their
love is no crime. It becomes one only in the human environment in
which they are placed, where natural relationships are perverted by
lovelessness and wrath: Josephe's brother is 'hämisch', her father
'entrüstet', civil and (with the worthy exception of the Abbess)
ecclesiastical opinion is harshly condemnatory − the vocabulary is
dominated at this point by words like 'scharf', 'Erbitterung' and
'Entrüstung' and the climax comes when Kleist describes, with a
scathing irony, the eagerness of pious society to see the outcast suffer:

> Man vermietete in den Straßen, durch welche der Hinrichtungszug
> gehen sollte, die Fenster, man trug die Dächer der Häuser ab, und
> die *frommen* Töchter der Stadt luden ihre Freundinnen ein, um
> dem Schauspiele, das der *göttlichen Rache* gegeben wurde, an ihrer
> *schwesterlichen* Seite beizuwohnen.[69]

We are face to face, again, with the perverted, 'gebrechlich' state of the world, in which only by the most monstrous of paradoxes, a gigantic upheaval (which is described in vivid, almost apocalyptic terms), can love be restored. This is the 'Rettung' for which Jeronimo has prayed and for which he thanks God once he has escaped from the city. Yet it has cost the lives, as Kleist has already laconically observed in the opening sentence, of 'many thousands of people'. Kleist does not here add the epithet 'innocent' which one is tempted, as if by a conditioned reflex, to insert, but he does later specifically draw attention to the death of the charitable Abbess, which occurs 'auf eine schmähliche Art', whereas Josephe is saved 'als ob alle Engel des Himmels sie umschirmten' (p. 720). The story proceeds, in the same concentrated and closely integrated style, to show the lovers, with their child, enjoying marital and familial love and finding acceptance in the harmonious society of the survivors, in a paradisal natural setting,[70] where the meanness and divisions of modern society have fallen away. The grim paradox of the opening, however, spans the story like an arch, for no sooner do the happy and serene survivors return to the town to thank God for their deliverance, than hate and bigotry reassert themselves, and Jeronimo and Josephe are brutally clubbed to death just outside the church. In a final, very Kleistian twist, their child is saved by an error of Pedrillo, the ringleader of the lynch-mob, who seizes instead the son of the man who has befriended them. Chaos, it seems, has reasserted itself and the Being which rules this planet seems to be indulging an almost sadistically ironic sense of humour. But the twist itself has a twist, for the bereaved father, Fernando, adopts the orphaned love-child Philipp, who serves as a reminder of an episode which was not only tragic, but also glorious. It brought him, after all, to the peak of selfless heroism. He is, in fact, the true hero of the story ('dieser göttliche Held', p. 729) and that moment, like the child itself, is in a way a gift of God. Hence the ambivalence of the final sentence: 'und wenn Don Fernando Philippen mit Juan verglich und wie er beide erworben hatte, so war es ihm fast, als müßt er sich freuen.'

We have done little more than scratch the surface even of *Das Erdbeben in Chili*, but this chapter is already very long, and we have no room for another. If space permitted, the temptation to develop this analysis further and to give detailed treatment to *Die Marquise von O* and *Die Verlobung in St. Domingo*, each a *Novelle* of the highest quality, would be well nigh irresistible. As things stand, we have room for only a brief account even of *Michael Kohlhaas*, the longest by far of the stories. It does contain some inconsistencies and the introduction of the sub-plot of the gypsy-woman Elisabeth, while it does chime in with the basic theme of justice,[71] imposes a certain strain on the structure. But it is still Kleist's greatest narrative work, by virtue of the tragic depth and grandeur with which it realises its theme. It is based on an old chronicle which tells the story of one Hans Kohlhaas. The change of name is probably explained by the following passage:

> Fünf Tage nach Zersprengung dieser beiden Haufen stand er vor Leipzig und steckte die Stadt an drei Seiten in Brand. – Er nannte sich in dem Mandat, das er bei dieser Gelegenheit ausstreute, 'einen Statthalter Michaels, des Erzengels, der gekommen sei, an allen, die in dieser Streitsache des Junkers Partei ergreifen würden, mit Feuer und Schwert, die Arglist, in welcher die ganze Welt versunken sei, zu bestrafen' (p. 625).

At first sight, it seems that we are dealing with a madman; indeed, Kleist does speak shortly after this of 'a kind of madness'. What has the Archangel Michael to do with Kohlhaas, the leader of a band of outlaws? How, indeed, could a man who, as we are told in the introductory paragraph, is the epitome of uprightness and kindliness, come to such a pass? Kohlhaas is not mad; he is the victim of an upheaval in the moral and emotional sphere as shattering as was the Chilean earthquake in the physical, one which arises out of the collision between his deep emotional commitment to Right and the 'gebrechliche Einrichtung der Welt'.

The transformation of an upright citizen into a murderous outlaw is brought about by a chain of events which expose, with a measured, almost majestic tragic inexorability, the corrupt nature of human justice. Kohlhaas, a horse-dealer from Brandenburg, is cheated by the Saxon nobleman Wenzel von Tronka, who appropriates two of his finest horses and misuses them. Kohlhaas's attempts to obtain proper restitution through regular legal channels are frustrated by human error and malice, the last straw being the death of his wife from a blow received when attempting to present a petition on his behalf. This event opens a gulf behind him and forces him to go forward: his deep sense of outrage and equally deep love for his wife (most movingly indicated in his wordless grief during the burial-episode) merge together to constitute an insuperable barrier to a conventional reconciliation or accommodation. He gathers a band of followers, storms and destroys von Tronka's castle in a scene of terrifying violence and then pursues him and carries on a campaign of terror against any town in which he knows or imagines him to be. His obsessive craving, however, is for satisfaction for his sense of justice; he appeals to Luther (to whom he goes in disguise in one of the most powerfully dramatic scenes of a highly dramatic story), whose intervention with the Saxon authorities produces an amnesty and a formal examination of his case against von Tronka. The latter has relations in high places and they manage to trick and pressurise Kohlhaas into a compromising position and have the amnesty set aside. He is saved by the Elector of Brandenburg, who demands his return to his native land to stand trial there. After highly complex legal procedures, he is condemned to suffer for his crimes as an outlaw, but before he dies, has the satisfaction of revenge against the Elector of Saxony through the withholding from him of the prophecy given by the gypsy-woman, and of victory in the case against Tronka and the return of the horses in their original healthy condition. He dies content; his sons are ennobled and will enjoy a prosperous future.

For all their cultivation of the extreme and unusual and their anything but classical form and style, Kleist's *Novellen* are not positively romantic in effect, any more than are his plays. His message is that of the breakdown of rationalism and of man's need to find out of resources of his own which have nothing to do with romantic fancy and love, a means of coping with a world which does not of itself make sense. He lacks the Romantic's ability to grasp within the *Gemüt* a transcendental reality — his inability to create a satisfying supernatural effect is one sign of this[72] — and offers only the hope that man can, descending into the depths of pain, become, as does the Marquise von O, 'mit sich selbst bekannt' (p. 700) and find a strength which will enable him to conquer fate. His portrayal of his characters and of the world in which they live is formally realistic, even if he also normally allows a metaphysical dimension to become apparent, as for example in the brilliantly written episode in *Michael Kohlhaas* in which the knacker brings the horses 'um derenthalben der Staat wankte' (p. 640) to Dresden. The whole scene is concerned with degradation and cannot but be seen in relation to the fate of Kohlhaas himself, but the actual details are sober, clear and solid, sometimes drastically so, rather than dissolved in mood or atmosphere, as might have been the case in a romantic description. Korff's 'metaphysical realism' is perhaps as good a description as any. Certainly, romantic or not, Kleist's four best stories belong among the greatest in the language.

Notes

1. As used for example, by H. Himmel in his *Geschichte der deutschen Novelle* (Berne-Munich, 1963), p. 90, to describe Tieck's *Der Runenberg.*
2. E. Lämmert, *Bauformen des Erzählens*, 3rd edn (Stuttgart, 1968), p. 181.
3. *Athenäum*-fragment no. 429.
4. H. Kasack and A. Mohrhenn, *Ludwig Tieck* (Berlin, 1943), vol. 2, p. 299.
5. Cf. L. Denecke, *Jakob Grimm und sein Bruder Wilhelm* (Stuttgart, 1971), pp. 73 and ff.
6. Quoted in R. Steig, *Clemens Brentano und die Brüder Grimm*, reprint (Berne, 1969), pp. 187–8.
7. Cf. Denecke, *Grimm*, p. 83.
8. Cf. above, p. 42.
9. DL 3, p. 230.
10. Nadler, *Romantische Novellen* (Bonn, Wahlband der Buchgemeine, n.d.: originally J. Habbel, Regensburg). References will be to this edition.
11. Nadler (*Romantische Novellen*, p. xxiv) holds that they are 'very close' to this type, but we do not want to split hairs quite so finely.
12. Cf. above, pp. 23–4.
13. *Vom Roman* in DL 12, p. 91. On Fouqué's contribution to the nationalistic revivalism of the German Romantic Movement, see H. A. Korff, *Geist der Goethezeit*, 2nd edn (4 vols., Leipzig, 1954), vol. IV, pp. 259 ff.
14. Cf. DNL 146, p. 7.
15. Ibid., p. 204.
16. Cf. *Romantische Novellen*, p. xxvi. There is a good account of this aspect of the decadence of Romanticism in this work, pp. xxv–xxvi.
17. Cf. DNL 146, p. 8. Heine is quite justified in finding Fouqué's 'ewige Rittertümelei' out of date (*Die Romantische Schule*, p. 133), but not necessarily in rejecting *Undine* on the ground that it does not present 'wirkliche Gestalten des Lebens'.
18. Cf. above, pp. 162–7.
19. E.g. *Angelika, die Genueserin, Die Verkleidungen des französischen Hofmeisters* and *Die Ehenschmiede.*
20. Quoted by W. Migge in SRE 2, p. 885.
21. SRE 3, pp. 758–9.
22. Arnim even permits himself a (typical) slightly grotesque joke at the idea of a 'herzfressende Zauberin' (SRE 2, p. 572). Frenel establishes an ascendancy over the enchantress by purely mundane methods.
23. Cf. SRE 2, p. 567. This suggests the dualism of sacred and profane love of Gryphius's *Cardenio und Celinde* which was the basis, of course, for Arnim's *Halle und Jerusalem.*
24. This collection is largely a re-working of material from older German literature, in a spirit similar to that of the *Wunderhorn*, but with less success.
25. The date of composition of this story (published posthumously) is uncertain. The material makes one think of an early date (the visit to Britain was made in 1803), the technique of a late one, perhaps in the 1820s.
26. First published in 1841. Migge (SRE 3, p. 809) suggests that Arnim may have begun work on the story shortly after the completion of *Isabella von Ägypten*, in 1812.
27. It is also in degradation and need that Martin Martir receives the decisive revelation and shakes off the illusions which have veiled true reality from his sight (cf. SRE 3, p. 722).
28. Cf. p. 584: 'Wunder geschehen noch heut. . .' etc.
29. Cf. T. Cramer, *Das Groteske bei E. T. A. Hoffmann* (Munich, 1966), pp. 15 and 21–7.

30. Arnim's direct influence on the French Surrealists is documented by Migge (SRE 3, p. 846). I know of no such influence on Bulgakov, but the romantic grotesque in general certainly did help to form his narrative technique, through Hoffmann and Gogol.

31. Cf. the Introduction to *Die Kronenwächter*. Even Ranke declares: 'In aller Geschichte wohnt, lebet, ist Gott zu erkennen' (letter of 1820, in DL 13, p. 207).

32. E.g. Luke 4, 33 ff.

33. One thinks of the flow of water and blood (John 19, 34) and the upheavals in the natural world reported, for example, by Matthew (27, 51). Certainly, it is not easy to see Arnim's account as realistically 'natural'.

34. E.g. the firework-display discharged from cannon.

35. Cf. John 12, 31 and 2 Cor. 4, 4.

36. Cf. Kemp's account of the composition and publication in K 3, pp. 1066 ff.

37. Cf. above, p. 188.

38. Cf. K 3, pp. 1066–7. The tales by Runge mentioned here are in DL 14, pp. 13–24.

39. Cf. above, p. 87.

40. Published in 1838. Both versions, with the illustrations designed by Brentano for the 1838 version, are in K 3.

41. Cf. above, pp. 82–3.

42. In addition to *Eingang*, we should mention 'Wenn der lahme Weber träumt', a poem which renders the lack of, and longing for, integration in a succession of powerful images centred on the theme of a destroyed illusion.

43. Cf. the essay on *Schlemihl* in B. von Wiese, *Die deutsche Novelle von Goethe bis Kafka* (Düsseldorf, 1956), p. 110.

44. Cf. above, p. 187.

45. Von Wiese, *Novelle*, p. 102.

46. Cf. above, pp. 29 and 34. On Tieck, see further Ch. 13 below.

47. Von Wiese, *Novelle*, p. 111.

48. The exclamations occur, in a slightly different form, in scenes 4 and 6 of Act V of *Cenodoxus*, the powerful play by the seventeenth-century German Jesuit dramatist Jakob Bidermann, the central figure of which, a great scholar, is blinded by pride and becomes the Devil's property.

49. Von Wiese, *Novelle*, pp. 88 ff.

50. 'Nachwort' to Eichendorff, *Erzählungen* (Zurich, Manesse Bibliothek der Weltliteratur, n.d.), p. 659.

51. In *Das Marmorbild*, the only story in which the supernatural is invoked, Venus herself appears in this role.

52. Cf. above, pp. 101–2.

53. The story is set in Germany, just after the Thirty Years' War. Whether Gryphius's *Horribilicribrifax* suggested the Schreckenberger figure is not clear, but not beyond the bounds of possibility!

54. Paulsen, *Taugenichts*, pp. 49 and ff.

55. Ibid., p. 53.

56. Cf. above, p. 95.

57. Eichendorff, *Erzählungen*, p. 658.

58. Namely 'Wer nur den lieben Gott läßt walten', by Georg Neumark (1621–81).

59. Cf. *Geschichte der poetischen Literatur Deutschlands*, pp. 182 ff.

60. For the dating of the Novellen, cf. H. M. Wolff, *Heinrich von Kleist* (Berne, 1954).

61. H. von Kleist, *Sämtliche Werke*, E. Laaths (ed.) (Munich, Knaur, n.d. [1954?]), p. 597.

62. Cf. *Die Marquise von O* (ibid., p. 716); *Michael Kohlhaas* (p. 603).

63. *Die heilige Cäcilie*, especially in the shorter first version, has more the quality of an anecdote than that of a *Novelle*. There are also a number of well told anecdotes among Kleist's contribution to the *Berliner Abendblätter*.

64. Cf. Emil Staiger's comments on Kleist's style in 'Heinrich von Kleist: Das Bettelweib von Locarno' in J. Schillemeit (ed.), *Deutsche Erzählungen von Wieland bis Kafka* (Frankfurt, 1966), pp. 90 ff.

65. Kleist, *The Marquise of O and Other Stories*, David Luke and Nigel Reeves (trans.) (Harmondsworth, 1978), p. 49.

66. Ibid., p. 296.

67. In the case of *Das Erdbeben in Chili*, definitely so.

68. Cf. Staiger, 'Bettelweib', p. 90.

69. *Sämtliche Werke*, pp. 717–18 (my emphases). One recalls the gratuitous cruelty with which Littegarde is cast out (by her brother!) and the picture of the innocent lovers in a perverted environment in *Die Familie Schroffenstein*. P. Witkop, *Heinrich von Kleist* (Leipzig, 1923), pp. 180–2, makes a plausible case for linking the two works.

70. The Garden of Eden motif is specifically evoked (p. 721).

71. The gypsy-woman, associated, but not clearly identified with, Kohlhaas's dead wife, gives him a paper containing a prophecy which the Elector of Saxony is desperate to know. As the Elector has broken faith with him, Kohlhaas rejoices in the opportunity which possession of the paper affords him to obtain satisfaction ('Genugtuung').

72. Though it should be recorded that Hoffmann, who in general thought highly of Kleist, praises his achievement, in *Das Bettelweib von Locarno*, of an effect of '[das] Grauenhafte, . . . mehr in Gedanken, als in der Erscheinung' (SB, p. 928).

13 LUDWIG TIECK

The work which we shall be discussing in this chapter is that written in the period up to and including the collection of narrative and dramatic writing, *Phantasus* (1812–16). This did not by any means mark the end of Tieck's significant career as a writer, nor would anyone claim that the work he produced in his later period lacks all trace of Romanticism. There is more than a touch of it, for example, in the charming late *Novelle, Des Lebens Uberfluß* (1839), in which the poetic and imaginative spirit of the lovers, who, to keep warm, have chopped up and burnt the staircase which links them with the rest of the world, is clearly seen as superior to the materialism of their landlord. The older Tieck cannot make common cause with the 'Young Germans', whom he attacks, for example, in the self-styled 'Märchennovelle' *Das alte Buch*.[1] But if he is not a realist, or at least not always so, it is true that he is now in what G. W. Field calls a 'post-romantic phase',[2] and what is probably the greatest achievement of his later years, the novel *Vittoria Accorombona* (1840), is hardly a romantic work.[3] The romantic elements in the writing of this period show what R. Stamm, in commenting on the treatment of the wondrous in *Die Vogelscheuche*, calls a muted quality ('Dämpfung'),[4] the feeling of attraction without complete conviction which makes one think of Heine, in *Atta Troll*, singing what he himself describes as 'das letzte freie Waldlied der Romantik' (Kaput 27).

In the earlier period, there can be little doubt that Tieck's approach was a romantic one. But as we have already had occasion to point out,[5] his Romanticism not infrequently seems less than full-blooded. His psychological constitution seems to contain some inhibiting factor which prevents him from attaining a sufficient practical (as opposed to theoretical) independence of logical rationality and realism. He is a little afraid both of the journey into the inmost recesses of the Self and of that into the infinite: 'der unendliche Geist', in Ermatinger's formulation,[6] 'erscheint bei ihm verendlicht, verstofflicht, versinnlicht.' His attitudes often drew harsh judgements from his romantic contemporaries, as for example from the great apostle of mysticism and romantic love, Baader, who, consciously or unconsciously echoing Böhme, writes that Tieck slinks, like the cat in Lady Macbeth's adage, 'around the one thing that is needful, nibbles, but never risks burning a paw'.[7] Even in his narrative works, where he develops and analyses romantic themes much more thoroughly than elsewhere, we still sense an unwillingness to go quite as far in his investigations of the world of the *Gemüt* as he might profitably have done. No doubt these inhibitions made him more susceptible than many to the change in the literary climate of the 1830s, when he was even able to condemn Hoffmann as 'fratzenhaft',[8] but at the same time, the suggestion that he was simply a romantic Laodicean is surely unfair.

The penchant for the horrific which Tieck shows in such lurid juvenilia as the novel *Abdallah*, or the final chapter which he wrote for F. E. Rambach's popular thriller, *Die eiserne Maske*,[9] is not just the product of derivative and commercially motivated sensationalism. No doubt that played its part. But amid the predictable, operatically orchestrated terrors, one hears also a note of genuine existential fear: the fear of the void, of chaos, perhaps of madness, the spectre which haunted more than one Romantic:

> [Ryno] empfand itzt das fürchterliche Gefühl, einsam dazustehen, eine Beute der Qualen seiner Seele; um ihn her kein Ton, der das Grausen versteckte, keine Gestalt, die die fürchterlichen Bilder des Todes verscheuchte. Diese feierlich gräßliche Stille konnte Ryno nicht dulden (*Werke* 1, 13).

This is not a mood which has been artifically induced for literary purposes and can be 'switched off' as soon as it has served those purposes. Such was no doubt the case with a Cramer, Spieß or Grosse.[10] The young Tieck, on the other hand, writes to some extent from experience. It is known that he was subject to fits of black, destructive melancholy in his cultivation of the inner life and that the inner balance which is the Romantic's only real safeguard in such excursions was precarious in him. His friend Wackenroder urges him, in a reply to a letter (12 June 1792) in which he had described a vision of 'schwarze Nacht und grause Totenstille' and a feeling of approaching madness, to desist from such 'verderbliche[n] Ausschweifungen in den Genüssen des Geistes'.[11] Tieck had to establish control over this tendency, and it may well be that what seems an unduly gingerly attitude on his part to the irrational, the occasional apparently perverse refusal to follow a brilliant beginning into the deeper layers of the mind, in fact represents the working of an unconscious inner defence-mechanism.

The Novels

Both of Tieck's major romantic novels, *Die Geschichte des Herrn William Lovell* (1795–6) and *Franz Sternbalds Wanderungen* (1798),[12] are studies in depth of the romantic temperament and its problems. In *William Lovell*, Tieck considers the danger of mental and moral disorientation which emancipation of the Self brings with it; in *Franz Sternbald*, he examines the artistic life as a possible solution to the problem of establishing a viable relationship between the emancipated individual and his environment. In both, we seem at times to catch echoes of Goethe, and in particular of *Werther* and *Faust*, though almost always, the tune is transposed into a romantic key. We are reminded of Faust's 'im Genuß verschmacht' ich nach Begierde'[13] when Lovell writes (Book IV, letter 36) of his inability to find lasting satisfaction with Rosaline. Both heroes find themselves relentlessly driven forward by an inner urge, but whereas in Faust, we sense a fundamentally healthy moral and mental constitution which can and will enable him to save his soul, Lovell makes a more febrile, passive and radically introverted impression:

> Welcher böse Geist ist es, der uns so durch alle Freuden anwinkt? Er lockt uns von einem Tage zum andern hinüber, wir folgen betäubt, ohne zu wissen, wohin wir treten, und sinken so in einer verächtlichen Trunkenheit in unser Grab.

Lovell's external antagonist is a mere man, but his is a romantic *Gemüt*; an ocean, that is, on which, without grace to guide it, the conscious will drifts helplessly.

In a similar way, the description of Franz's experience of nature in Part Two, Book Two, Chapter 5 of *Franz Sternbalds Wanderungen* recalls that described by Werther in the letter dated 10 May in Book One. Among the features which the two descriptions have in common are characteristic motifs such as 'Herrlichkeit', 'vergehen', and of course that of the embrace. But while both show the romantic tendency in their use of the nature-experience to activate the life of the *Gemüt*, the pre-romantic *Werther* retains more of a balance between the inner and outer worlds. The latter retains its solidity, whereas in Tieck, it threatens to melt, like a romantic landscape, into movement, musicality and the play of colour and light. Passive 'Stimmung' rather than energetic emotion is favoured:

Franz streckte die Arme aus, als wenn er etwas Unsichtbares an sein
ungeduldiges Herz drükken wollte, als möchte er nun erfassen und
festhalten, wonach ihn die Sehnsucht so lange gedrängt; die Wolken
zogen unten am Horizont durch den blauen Himmel, die Wider-
scheine und die Schatten streckten sich auf den Wiesen aus und
wechselten mit ihren Farben, fremde Wundertöne gingen den Berg
hinab, und Franz fühlte sich wie festgezaubert. . . (p. 249)

In both *William Lovell* and *Franz Sternbald*, the central narrative
thread is provided by a journey undertaken by the hero as part of his
general education for life and in both, the outer quest is symbolic of
an inner one, that for stability, for a viable relationship between the
free Self and the objective 'Welt'. In each case, the treatment of the
theme is romantic, certainly by comparison with Goethe's *Werther,
Faust* or *Wilhelm Meisters Lehrjahre*, the last of which clearly influenced
the form of *Sternbald*. As opposed to other Romantics, however, Tieck
seems to have no clear vision of a solution to the problem which he sets
his characters. To that extent, the author seems to stand somewhat to
one side at times, rather as Goethe does in *Werther*, though with a less
positive motivation. The pre-romantic path is closed to Tieck, but the
echoes of Goethe which we hear much more clearly in him than in
other Romantics suggest a certain hankering after the pre-romantic
position, a reluctance to risk full romantic commitment.

William Lovell is a thoroughly pessimistic work. It is a story of
mental and moral decline, in which structural elements of the
'Bundesroman'[14] are grafted on to the basic journey-pattern. Lovell
and his German friend Balder, both characters of a deep but highly
unstable sensitivity — descendants of Werther, but romantically
'gesteigert' — become victims of the malicious master-schemer 'Andrea',
whose real name is Waterloo (!) and who has long been an irreconcilable
enemy of Lovell's family. He is able to work on them because their
'Hang zum Wunderbaren' (p. 467) is not kept under control by the
inner balance essential to the Romantic, and he produces in them,
as opposed to the (healthy) romantic spiritual independence of the
'real' material world, a complete alienation from it. Balder ends in
madness, Lovell in moral bankruptcy, the extreme of isolated egotism.
The external world is a chaos to him; truth resides only in the 'Self'
(pp. 353 ff). He seeks salvation in sensuality (Book IV), but this brings
only a sense of nihilistic disassociation (p. 451 f). 'Andrea' now
intervenes and by manipulating Lovell's sense of the Wondrous, brings
him eventually to a conviction of the meaninglessness of the real world:

'alle Gegenstände umher erscheinen mir nur als leere Formen, als wesenlose Dinge' (p. 534). Only he himself matters; the others, to whom he causes suffering, are of no account (p. 537). He is moving towards the total 'irony' (absolute subjectivity) which Fritz Brüggemann sees as the central theme of the novel.[15] He almost reaches the point of inner death, but Tieck is unwilling to condemn him completely and in his last letter, he still feels some spark of spiritual activity within him, and asserts that he 'is still capable of love'. But Tieck is not willing to save him either, and he falls to the avenging bullet of Karl Wilmont, whose sister he has earlier seduced.

Tieck can diagnose the sickness, but has no clear idea of a cure. He can see the dangers of what the eighteenth-century observer would call a 'hypochondriac' disposition and an 'over-heated' imagination, as can Eichendorff and Hoffmann, but he seems less convinced than they that the romantic 'inner' path *can* be walked with safety and that it is indeed the true path to glory. The positive counterparts offered to Lovell seem a little pallid. The simple piety of his servant Willy falls considerably short of the depth of naïve spirituality observable in corresponding figures in other romantic works. The more sophisticated characters, Mortimer and Wilmont, learn from life, and particularly from the fate of Lovell, the dangers of excessive preoccupation with the Self and the need for a positive, active attitude, a 'frohe Gemütsstimmung', as Wilmont calls it (pp. 509–10). In theory, Mortimer grasps the principle of the healthy spiritual core ('Urverfassung') which preserves him among the temptations and pressures of life. What is missing is a clear impression of this principle working in practice. We have to take Mortimer's word for its activity and Wilmont even suffers a fall from grace at the end. It is as if Tieck himself suffers from the periodic self-doubt which plagues his other main romantic hero, Franz Sternbald.

Franz Sternbalds Wanderungen remained a fragment, though it was a long time before Tieck entirely abandoned the idea of completing it. It seems to have been consistently conceived as ending happily, with Franz finding his predestined beloved and his own firm place in life. Everyone, in fact, was to have been content.[16] The narrative structure has two principal strands: Franz's journey, as a young artist, in search of mastery of his craft, and the twin mysteries surrounding his parentage and his relationship with a girl (Marie), glimpsed fleetingly in early youth, whose image accompanies him on his travels as his ideal of love, and whom he finds, eventually, in Rome.

The mystery plays only a subordinate part in the completed text

and the theme of painting, while it bulks quite large in terms of the space
devoted to it, grips the imagination of the author and reader less firmly
than that of the hero's search for his true self and his true relation to
the world around him. Unlike Lovell, Franz, who is a favourite pupil of
Dürer (with Raphael, Wackenroder's great aesthetic hero[17]), has found
in art a framework for the cultivation of the life of the spirit and since
he genuinely and humbly seeks the true and the good, the influence,
which affect his course are broadly favourable. Through the spiritual
revelation of nature, and through many experiences and encounters —
above all that with Florestan — the world shows him more of its poetic
than of its darker side and when temptation does threaten, he is
prevented from falling deeply into sin.

Even so, his salvation is anything but a foregone conclusion. He has
a significant measure of the morbid introversion which eventually
destroys William Lovell. In his important early letter to Sebastian, the
friend he has left behind, he describes himself as still 'ein weichherziges
Kind' (*Franz Sternbald*, ed. Anger, p. 77) and conjures up an archetypal
image of healthy spirituality in his picture of '[der] vielgrüne Wald'
(pp. 80 ff), only to cancel it out with a vision of decay (p. 83). The
novel sets out, no doubt with *Wilhelm Meisters Lehrjahre* in mind, to
show how this dangerous tendency is overcome. Franz will continue to
strive towards the light, albeit in the more passive manner of the
romantic hero: 'Ich will daher immer suchen und erwarten,' he writes
(p. 79). The true spirit of Romanticism is generously poured out on
him in poetic encounters and acquaintanceships, and in the experiences
of nature, art and love. But it is hard to discern any progressive
development towards clarity and stability. We know that this is a
possibility, we are even told at one point, when Franz is strangely and
unexpectedly united with Marie (Part Two, Book Two, Chapter 6), that
the breakthrough has been achieved. And yet we cannot tell *how* it has
happened: there is no bridge which leads from the insecure, confused
hero who is still able, but four chapters before the end, to look into
his inner life and see nothing but 'ein rauschendes, tosendes Rätsel'
(p. 358), to the picture of serene romantic harmony with which Tieck
leaves us:

> Lautenklang mein ganzes Leben,
> Herz verklärt in schönster Schöne,
> Wundervollem Glanz und Weben
> > Hingegeben (p. 401).

The melodiousness of these lines cannot conceal their lack of substance. Nor does the fragment of a Third Part reprinted by Alewyn[18] solve the mystery; here, Franz and Marie are portrayed in the enjoyment of serene bliss, but quite unable to explain how it has come about: 'Ist es nicht, hub [Franz] an, als wenn eine gütige Gottheit meinen Lebenslauf wie ein anmutiges goldenes Kindermärchen vor mir hin, gewebt hätte?'[19]

But if Tieck is unable to realise the positive romantic message in narrative terms here, if Franz, with his occasional heavy solemnity, can become tiresome, and if the discussions of painting have their undeniable *longueurs*, it is also true that, if one *listens* to the work as a whole, without concerning oneself too closely with the hero and the plot in which he is involved, one can hear, as did Friedrich Schlegel, 'eine süße Musik von und für die Fantasie',[20] the music of the free romantic spirit. The sense of the Wondrous, of a 'magic' dimension in the world, which in *William Lovell* is infected by the hero's sterile egoism and becomes a trap for him, here fulfils its proper liberating function, opening the mind to a higher truth. It is part of Franz's experience of love and appears more clearly in other aspects of his experience, notably art, nature and (in the general sense) 'Poesie'.

Franz's vocation as an artist in the narrower sense — his outlook and development as a painter — is taken seriously. This is the part of the book in which Wackenroder's influence is strongest and it certainly seems in its turn to have had some influence on painters, such as Runge, the 'Nazarene' school and perhaps even the Pre-Raphaelites.[21] More important is the quasi-religious philosophy of art which emerges in discussions and statements of faith and which has a more general applicability. The artist is seen as above all the servant of the spirit. His function is to achieve the Divine and to reveal it, as is laid down in the crucial discussion in Antwerp (pp. 173–9). The true artist is a vehicle of divine revelation (p. 253) and his productions are 'geheimnisvolle Wunderwerke' (p. 282). It may seem that Franz's later development in Italy, his new appreciation of Correggio and of the life of the senses (Part Two, Book Two, Chapters 3–4) set up an unresolved dichotomy between 'German Spiritualism' and 'Italian Sensualism',[22] but Tieck does not wish to imply an unbridgeable gap between spirit and sense. It is only the one-sided, 'leichtsinnig' sensualism in the Italian world that Franz rejects and it is an Italian, Michelangelo, who reawakens in him the sense of the spiritual nature and function of art. After all, 'medieval' Nuremberg and Renaissance Italy exist happily side by side in Wackenroder's *Herzensergießungen*. It has to be admitted, though, that in this field, Tieck can do little more than hint at harmony.

Poetry, rather than painting, is his *métier* and it is in that part of
the novel where 'Poesie', in both the narrow and the broad sense, is
dominant that he is most successful in conveying the positive romantic
message. It is no accident that in this part, Franz is together with the
novel's most poetic character, Florestan, whose unquenchable cheer-
fulness of spirit and responsiveness to the poetry of life act as a welcome
corrective to the melancholic tendency which is present in Franz. It is
present in the author too, who is occasionally moved to express
reservations about the 'frivolity' ('Leichtsinn') of his most attractive
character. He even does so (through Franz) in connection with
Florestan's inspired speech on the wondrous dimension in life in Part
Two, Book One, Chapter Three. But Franz confesses that he feels
himself carried away by Florestan's words and there can be little doubt
that they express a genuine romantic experience on the part of the
author, even though he might not be as ready to endorse the
emancipation of the mind from the 'ordinary run of life' as is the
reader himself:

> 'Fühlst du nicht oft,' sprach Rudolf weiter, 'einen wunderbaren Zug
> deines Herzens dem Wunderbaren und Seltsamen entgegen? Man
> kann sich der Traumbilder dann nicht erwehren, man erwartet eine
> höchst sonderbare Fortsetzung unsers gewöhnlichen Lebenslaufs. . .
> dann ist es, als wollte der Waldstrom seine Melodie deutlicher
> aussprechen, als würde den\Bäumen die Zunge gelöst, damit ihr
> Rauschen in verständlichern Gesang dahinrinne. Nun fängt die Liebe
> an, auf fernen Tönen heranzuschreiten. . . Ein Zirkel von Wohllaut
> hält uns mit magischen Kräften eingeschlossen, und eine neue,
> verklärte Existenz schimmert wie rätselhaftes Mondlicht in unser
> wirkliches Leben hinein' (p. 221).

It is in the Florestan section too that nature functions most
consistently as a channel for the revelation of a higher spiritual reality.
The sunsets, sunrises, landscapes and forest scenes almost always
contain an intimation of a higher presence, sometimes explicitly, as in
the passage in Part Two which we cited earlier, and in which there is
even mention of a Schelling-esque 'Weltgeist' (p. 249), sometimes
indirectly, through a certain spiritual quickening which communicates
itself to both characters and readers, an effect of which Eichendorff,
who must have learnt much from Tieck, was a master. Eichendorff, in
fact, was to outdo Tieck in the art of poetic 'Stimmung', as was
Hoffmann in matters of mystery and of the plumbing of the

subconscious. Romanticism remains only partially fulfilled in Tieck's novels. But his importance as a Founding Father is enormous and it would be churlish to deny him, over and above that merit, a significant romantic achievement in his own right.

The Stories

The important stories of our period are *Der blonde Eckbert* (1796), *Der getreue Eckart und der Tannenhäuser* (1799), *Der Runenberg* (1802) and *Liebeszauber, Die Elfen* and *Der Pokal* (all 1811), of which the first three are the best, and the most pronouncedly romantic in tone and substance. All involve the presence of the supernatural in an active role[23] and to that extent, can legitimately be described as *Märchen*, as they are by Marianne Thalmann in the *Werke* (vol. 2). And yet one misses the sense of radical estrangement, the clear liberation of spirit from logic, which one expects from the *Märchen* in its pure form. Tieck prefers to work in the border-area and to oscillate, in fact, between the supernatural and psychological. He is the creator of the 'Märchen-Novelle', a form to be perfected by Hoffmann, in which the inner processes of the *Gemüt* tend to be the dominant interest. It is a form which can produce great mystery and above all, tension, as the mind struggles to come to terms with the incomprehensible and to fight off the threat of disorientation.

It was undoubtedly Romanticism which raised the 'tale of mystery and imagination', to use Poe's term, to the status of true literature and the role played by the Germans in this process was a very important one. In terms of ideas, the outstanding feature of this form is its insight into the relative and indeterminate nature of merely human 'truth' and 'reality'. We should end with a feeling of the mysteriousness of the universe which man inhabits, rather than of mystery 'solved' in the full sense of the word. A phrase from *Der blonde Eckbert*, 'er konnte sich nicht aus dem Rätsel herausfinden' (*Werke* 2, p. 25), sums up the general tendency very well.

All the stories, like *Lovell* and *Sternbald*, are inward-looking. They investigate the world of introversion, in which the imagination is cultivated, and show it as a garden full of delights but also of deadly dangers. Tieck shows his characters trying to find 'die rechte Bahn', as it is called in *Der blonde Eckbert* (p. 17), but like Bertha in that story, they often find it hard to do so. We know that Tieck does not regard it as impossible. Bertha, in *Der blonde Eckbert*, does enjoy harmony in

her life with the old woman, the steadfast virtue of Eckart is set against
the mental and moral fragility of Tannhäuser and in *Der Pokal*, Tieck
even shows a muted optimism. Franziska maintains her inner stability
throughout and even Ferdinand, who has stumbled and fallen into
outsider-hood, is given a second chance, one which he is able to grasp.
The goblet no longer exercises its magic influence upon him and he is
released from the state of stultifying isolation which his inability to
exercise self-control on a previous occasion, and distinguish between
the phantom produced by the goblet and true reality, brought upon
him.

The pessimistic ending is, however, the more characteristic in
Tieck's case – in itself, perhaps, a sign of the reservations which he had,
as a Romantic, about the romantic way. He seems to have been able to
achieve a happy end only at the cost of a muted Romanticism; when
he surrenders himself to it more fully, as in his best stories, the result
is gloom and doom. Eckbert has an insight similar to that of Ferdinand,
but it comes too late, or rather, only in time to add a crowning, bitter
irony to his last moments. The physical isolation in which he has lived
with Bertha, and which was described without sinister overtones in the
opening paragraph, is now recalled, as he dies both physically and
mentally, in the phrase: 'in welcher entsetzlichen Einsamkeit hab' ich
denn mein Leben hingebracht!' (p. 26). Eckbert has been living in an
incestuous relationship with his half-sister Bertha, a fact of which he
has always had a vague premonition. It is now confirmed for him by
the witch-figure who provides the fairy-tale dimension of the story.
Bertha has lived with her in her cottage in a remote and strange area in
the hills, and has absconded, stealing her magic bird. But unlike Jack
with his beanstalk, she cannot destroy the bridge between the worlds of
Märchen and reality, and the witch comes to exact retribution in the
guise of Eckbert's 'friends' Walther and Hugo. By allowing egotistic
thoughts of self to predominate in her, Bertha has turned the magic
dimension from a beneficent into a malevolent one.

Eckbert, through choosing to marry Bertha, has entered a prison. It
is the same kind of prison as that in which William Lovell lives: the real
incest is a mental and spiritual one. The motif of 'entering' is present
(often in a very obvious physical form) in all the stories. Tannhäuser
begins the journey which leads eventually to the 'Venusberg' when he
enters the garden (p. 51), Christian wanders into the territory of the
'Runenberg', Marie into that of the elves. Ferdinand crosses the
borderline when he follows the recluse Albert into a mysterious back
room and succumbs to the sorcery of the goblet. In *Liebeszauber*, Emil

crosses the threshold with the decision to go to the ball, which, it seems, releases in him the 'Wahnsinn' (p. 97) which makes him susceptible to the charm.

These characters have crossed from one reality — or mode of perceiving reality — into another which, from the point of view of our everyday logic, can be called a 'dream'-reality. When the awakening comes, when the two dimensions seem to intersect in the mind, as in the final episode of *Der blonde Eckbert*, the effect can be shattering. The most spectacular instance is probably the fit of murderous frenzy which overcomes Emil at the end of *Liebeszauber*. The danger of a breakdown of control is always there. Tieck consistently blurs the distinction between the two realities[24] and indulges in frequent crossing and re-crossing of the borderline between the two. The awareness of discrepancy between them can occur as one travels in either direction, and often manifests itself in the form of a sense that one or other of them is a 'dream'. Thus Christian feels at various times, in *Der Runenberg*, that his visit to the magic mountain on the one hand, and his settled, ordinary and domesticated life in the village on the plain on the other, are dreams (pp. 68—9 and 77 respectively). This is an oscillation between two states of mind, a fact which is brought home to us with particular force in *Der Runenberg*, when the figure on the tablet, which symbolises his entry into the inner, irrational world, actually enters into his 'inmost being' (p. 68). It can be contained, but this demands a firm control, which is often symbolised by the fairy-tale motif of the keeping of a trust (Bertha) or a secret (Eckbert, Marie). When that control lapses, the intersection of realities can occur in a destructive way and real madness can ensue, as with Eckbert, Christian, Tannhäuser and Emil.

A good example is the crucial episode, in *Der getreue Eckart*, in the story of Tannhäuser. Having lost Emma and (as he thinks) killed his successful rival, he has succumbed to the temptations of the 'Venusberg', but divine grace has given him a chance of redemption. He is on a pilgrimage to Rome when he meets his friend Friedrich and, at the latter's insistence, tells him his story. Friedrich, who was in fact the rival, and who is happily married to Emma, attempts to disabuse him of the illusion, the 'strange madness' (p. 57), which hides the true reality from him. But Tannhäuser takes the latter for an illusion ('Blendwerk'), and after failing to obtain absolution in Rome, returns to cancel out the reality which so disrupted his equilibrium and made his salvation — at least on the mental plane — impossible:

Einige Monden waren verflossen, als der Tannenhäuser bleich und
abgezehrt, in zerrissenen Wallfahrtskleidern und barfuß in Friedrichs
Gemach trat, indem dieser schlief. Er küßte ihn auf den Mund . . .
Hierauf entfernte er sich eilig. Friedrich ermunterte sich, der
unglückliche Pilger war schon verschwunden. Er ging nach dem
Zimmer seiner Gattin, und die Weiber stürzten ihm mit Geheul
entgegen: der Tannenhäuser war hier früh am Tage hereingedrungen
und hatte die Worte gesagt: 'Diese soll mich nicht in meinem Laufe
stören!' Man fand Emma ermordet (pp. 57–8).

Friedrich too is lost. Tannhäuser's kiss draws him inexorably into the
mountain. Nor can he be called an innocent victim, for it was he, after
all, who showed the fatal curiosity which precipitated the catastrophe
which has now overtaken him.

The interest in and fear of unusual and potentially pathological
states of mind which predominates in these stories is a clear indication
that their main thrust is psychological. Tieck seems to be warning us
against playing with fire. The 'Wahnsinn' which he describes would
seem to have two possible stages: a primary one of isolation, in which
the 'inner' reality supersedes the outer and in which one is subject to
hallucination, as is Tannhäuser, and as was Tieck himself.[25] The second
stage is the complete and often terrible disorientation which we saw in
Tannhäuser's case and which can also be observed, if not always in such
a spectacular form, in those of Emil, Eckbert and Christian. This
psychologising tendency points in the direction of the *Novelle*, in that
it locates the principal action and interest in the human sphere. But the
supernatural dimension is not mere decoration, nor is its function
exhausted by the capacity, which it obviously does have, for under-
pinning and perhaps symbolising the irrational dimensions of human
consciousness. The old woman in *Der blonde Eckbert* could be seen as
symbolising the irrational areas of the *Gemüt*, which revenge themselves
on those who misuse them, and therefore act indirectly as a cause for
Eckbert's neurotic suspiciousness. But that she should actually *appear*
as Walther and Hugo is plain magic. The bird which lays eggs containing
jewels belongs to the same sphere, as do the 'Venusberg'-description in
Eckart, the account of the realm of the elves in *Die Elfen* and the
hocus-pocus of Albert in *Der Pokal*.

In the case of the dragon in *Liebeszauber*, which Emil sees as he
watches the ritual murder involved in the love-charm, everything
depends on the way in which the apparition is described:

die Alte zuckte murmelnd das Messer und durchschnitt den weißen
Hals der Kleinen. Da wand sich *hinter ihnen* etwas hervor, *das beide
nicht zu sehen schienen, sonst hätten sie sich wohl ebenso inniglich
wie Emil entsetzt.* Ein scheußlicher Drachenhals wälzte sich schuppig
länger und länger aus der Dunkelheit. . .[etc.] (p. 100: my emphasis)

Is the author's intervention meant to convey that this is an hallucination? It would be possible to argue to that effect, but our impression is
that the intended effect is the opposite one. Tieck need not have stated
specifically that the dragon was behind the group involved in the
murder. He makes it less likely, in fact, that they could have seen it and
then adds that they would have been horrified had they done so. The
suggestion seems, on balance, not to be that it was not there, but that
it was. The same point is made in a different way in *Der Runenberg*.
We have already drawn attention to the way in which Tieck links the
tablet with Christian's inner psychological processes by making the
figure enter into him. But the supernatural moment is not entirely
absorbed into the psychological one, even though the latter is the more
important. The tablet, and the whole experience in the mountain, could
possibly be explained as hallucinatory, except for one thing:
Christian's father sees the tablet as well and senses something of its
frightening mystery (p. 78).

Whereas Hoffmann's 'magic' worlds tend to be private ones, in that
some figure or object from the everyday environment provides a crucial
point d'appui and therefore eases the transition from supernatural to
psychological, Tieck's stories oscillate between the worlds of the *Gemüt*
as such and the familiar 'Volksmärchen', in which witches, for example,
can be frightening in the manner of the traditional stereotype, but will
not appear as door-knockers, as does the 'Äpfelweib' in Hoffmann's
Der goldene Topf. The description of the 'Waldweib' in *Der Runenberg*
reflects this oscillation. At first, Christian takes her for the stranger who
left money with him earlier (which, in another shape, of course, she
was!), but then the relativity of reality makes itself felt: 'die Umrisse,
welche er wahrzunehmen gewöhnt, zerbrachen in sich selber.' The
influence of the mind on the eye of the beholder is clearly indicated.
But the description which follows is very much the conventional witch-
figure of the 'Kindermärchen': ugly, old, possessed of a 'fearsome'
voice, and so on. Indeed, she herself says: 'Jedes Kind weiß von mir zu
erzählen' (p. 78). The subtler kind of mystery in which we have a
feeling of an *inner* breakdown of rationality is tempered by a less
disturbing variety in which a human and a magical world are juxtaposed,

but not merged. Tieck's unwillingness to draw all the logical conclusions from a romantic insight asserts itself once more. He seems himself to have been plagued by a secret fear of madness. A spell cast by a wicked witch is in a way less frightening than one cast by one's own mind and Tieck's desire to keep the wondrous at least partially external to the mind could well be prompted by the instinct for self-preservation.

Notes

1. 1835. Cf. *Werke*, M. Thalmann (ed.) (Munich, 1963), vol. 4, p. 1045.

2. *The Nineteenth Century* (London, 1980), p. 94.

3. For this novel, cf. the study by W. F. Taraba in B. von Wiese (ed.), *Der deutsche Roman* (Düsseldorf, 1965), vol. 1, pp. 329–52. On *Des Lebens Uberfluß*, cf. B. von Wiese, *Die deutsche Novelle von Goethe bis Kafka* (Düsseldorf, 1956), pp. 117–33.

4. R. Stamm, *Ludwig Tiecks späte Novellen* (Stuttgart–Berlin–Cologne–Mainz, 1973), p. 137.

5. Cf. above, p. 48.

6. *Deutsche Dichter*, vol. 2, p. 135.

7. Letter to von Stransky, 1 June 1840; quoted in DL 1, p. 130. Böhme had compared the 'Schul-Zäncker', who distrusts the direct, irrational approach in religion, to the cat circling round the hot porridge (cf. *Sämtliche Werke*, W.-E. Peuckert (ed.) (Stuttgart, 1957), vol. 5, p. 31).

8. Cf. Stamm, *Novellen*, p. 134.

9. The chapter is printed by Marianne Thalmann under the title 'Ryno' in vol. 1 of Tieck's *Werke.* References, wherever possible, are to this edition. Rambach wrote prolifically in a style suited to the cruder popular taste. 'Wenn ich einmal stecken bleibe', he is reported to have said, 'knirsche ich mit den Zähnen und es geht frisch weiter' (cf. R. Köpke, *Ludwig Tieck*, reprint (Darmstadt, 1970), p. 118).

10. C. G. Cramer (1758–1817), C. H. Spieß (1755–99) and K. Grosse (1761–1800), all exponents of the popular horror novel, for which see M. Thalmann, *Die Romantik des Trivialen* (Munich, 1970).

11. Quoted by H. Lippuner in *Wackenroder, Tieck und die bildende Kunst* (Zurich, 1965), pp. 13–14.

12. Thalmann (*Werke*, vol. 1) prints the 1843 text. We shall be quoting in this instance from the reprint of the 1798 version, A. Anger (ed.) (Stuttgart, 1966).

13. *Faust* I, line 3250. The 'Wald und Höhle' scene, where this line occurs, first appeared in the 'Fragment'-version of 1790. A direct influence is made very probable by the corresponding phrase in Lovell's letter: 'und auch im höchsten Genusse lauert gewiß schon eine neue Begierde.' At the same time, the use of the verb 'lauert' is evidence of Tieck's more passive and pessimistic attitude.

14. Cf. above, pp. 153, 181.

15. Cf. F. Brüggemann, *Die Ironie als entwicklungsgeschichtliches Moment* (Jena, 1909).

16. 'Alle sind glücklich,' concludes the report on the plan in Tieck's 'Nachrede' to the 1843 version (*Werke*, vol. 1, p. 986).

17. Cf. the *Herzensergießungen*, pp. 43–51. Wackenroder's influence on *Sternbald* must have been considerable. His friendship with Tieck is clearly mirrored in that of Franz and Sebastian and one of Tieck's contributions to the

Herzensergießungen is a letter from a German artist in Rome to his friend Sebastian in Nuremberg (pp. 69–74) which contains, as Gillies remarks, the 'basic plan' of the novel.

18. *Jahrbuch des freien deutschen Hochstifts*, 1962. Reproduced by Anger in *Sternbald*, pp. 495–501.

19. *Sternbald*, p. 495.

20. Letter to Caroline Schlegel, 29 October 1798, quoted by Anger in *Sternbald*, p. 508.

21. Cf. Anger, 'Nachwort' to *Sternbald*, p. 547 and note 24 to Ch. 5 above.

22. Cf. Eichendorff's development of the German-Italian dualism.

23. In the case of *Liebeszauber*, this involves accepting that the evil spirit which Emil sees in the spell scene is an objective reality, a point to be dealt with later.

24. Eckbert, for example, kills Walther in a kind of trance ('ohne zu wissen, was er tat': p. 23). We are left in doubt as to how much objective reality we are to ascribe to this occurrence.

25. Cf. Margaret E. Atkinson, 'Introduction' to *Der blonde Eckbert*, edited together with Brentano's *Kasperl und Annerl* (Oxford, 1958), p. xxiv.

14 E. T. A. HOFFMANN

General Introduction

Hoffmann's career as a writer spans the period from *Ritter Gluck* (1809) to *Meister Johannes Wacht, Des Vetters Eckfenster* and *Meister Floh* (1822). It is fitting that the *Novelle* and *Märchen* should both begin and crown his career, for though he did write two important novels, *Die Elixiere des Teufels* (1815–16) and the unfinished *Lebens-Ansichten des Katers Murr* (1819–21), it was in the former genres that he showed the greatest mastery of narrative prose and technique. In the novels, good as they are in their strong passages, his limitations as a writer are also more fully exposed. Their somewhat 'gothic' attitude to plot and tendency to cliché, of expression and situation, reveal a genuine (if not necessarily a deep) affinity to the popular novel of the time. *All* the passages which recall Grosse and his ilk cannot have been written tongue-in-cheek.[1] And the more sustained attempts to realise the romantic ideal of poetry, while sincere, show the more clearly that he lacks the poetic depth of Novalis, who may well have been his chief model in this regard. His talent lies primarily in the field of the uncanny, the grotesque and the ironically humorous, and he displays this talent, with increasing strength and versatility, throughout the period under discussion.

Hoffmann's love of the grotesque and his ironic, even 'caustic' tone have led some critics to query the depth of his Romanticism. Gabrielle Wittkop-Menardeau follows this trend in her monograph (Hamburg, 1966), in which our author is described as romantic 'only in a qualified sense' and linked, somewhat fancifully, with Heine, Börne and even Grabbe (pp. 113–14). It is true, as we shall see, that he is not entirely convincing as a 'serious' Romantic, and that he has a sharp satirical eye for the pseudo-romantic cults of 'genius' and refined sensibility as revealed, for example, in his portraits, of the 'artistic' lady (Cäcilia's mother) in *Nachricht von den neuesten Schicksalen des Hundes Berganza* (1814), the educated ape Milo (*Fantasiestücke* IX, 4) and 'die jeanpaulisierende Clementine' in *Das steinerne Herz* (1817: FN 598),[2] and in a more tragic key, of the overstrained poet Nathanael in *Der Sandmann* (1816). It is true too that this tendency, which grows stronger as Hoffmann grows older, goes together with an awareness of the inadequacy of undisciplined imagination and of the fact that however apparently unpoetic the world of everyday reality, man has to live in it. With the possible exception of Anselmus in *Der goldene Topf* (1814), Hoffmann's dreamers have to come back to earth: Peregrinus Tyss, for example, in *Meister Floh*, finds love and rest, not with a princess, but with the simple bookbinder's daughter Röschen Lämmerhirt, who provides him with the 'ruhiges häusliches Glück' which Clara, in *Der Sandmann*, enjoys as a well earned reward after the travails she has suffered in her love for the unbalanced Nathanael.

But none of this is inconsistent with a fundamentally romantic outlook. We have seen romantic satire of would-be romantic philistinism before, for example in Eichendorff,[3] and the domestic bliss which Peregrinus and others like him enjoy does not mean captivity in or resignation to the prosaic 'Alltag'. Peregrinus is not only a 'Bürger', but a king, the possessor of the talisman which raises him to the heights of human existence, a 'miracle' wrought by love (SW 810–14). This brings us directly to the serious romantic basis which underlies all Hoffmann's best work, the ironic and grotesque in 'Callot's manner'[4] just as much as the visions of harmony and goodness in works like *Meister Martin der Küfner und seine Gesellen* (1819) and *Das Fräulein von Scuderi* (1820). Certainly, Hoffmann was not a deeply religious man and he tended to distrust mysticism,[5] but he did possess a strong sense of a transcendent spiritual reality, manifested in moral qualities (Mademoiselle de Scudéry or the 'Großonkel' in *Das Majorat* (1817: FN 499–500)), in the arts (especially music) and in the phenomenon of love. His experience of pure beauty, which reached its peak in his unfulfilled love for his pupil Julia Marc, who was still for him, in 1820, an indwelling ideal of 'alle[r] Herzensgüte, alle[r] Himmelsanmut wahrhaft weiblichen Sinns',[6] is transposed into a vision of angelic, redeeming purity which recurs with striking, indeed monotonous regularity in his works. Julia was to him what Sophie had been to Novalis. It is worth pausing, at this point, to consider briefly Hoffmann's relation to that, at first sight perhaps rather unlikely, predecessor.

We are told by Wittkop-Menardeau (p. 53) that Hoffmann read Novalis assiduously during his early years in Berlin and even without that knowledge, it would be hard for anyone who had read *Der goldene Topf* to believe that he had not. It is somewhat disconcerting to find, in the index to the *Briefwechsel*, only one reference to Novalis and even that turns out to be rather offhand. Writing to Kunz (25 November 1816), he comments disparagingly on the *Lotosblätter* of Novalis's not very successful disciple, O. von Loeben, and continues with the remark that 'ein gewisser Novalis' has produced 'ähnliche, nicht ganz unebene Fragmente'. This is hardly the language of an acolyte and it is certainly true that Hoffmann does not share Novalis's profound poetic ethereality. But that he can appreciate it as something real and valid is shown by the characterisation which he gives of him in the *Berganza*-story. He is praised for his 'kindliches Gemüt', illuminated by 'die reinsten Strahlen der Poesie', and his constant quest for 'das Höchste, das Heiligste', and defended against charges of bombastic obscurity (cf. FN 136). The glory is dimmed, perhaps, for us by the fact that Hoffmann couples Novalis with his friend Fouqué, but that certainly was not his intention. Novalis is presented as the *pure* poet. Pure spirit, it may be agreed, is not Hoffmann's natural element, but as an ideal, it is an essential component of his romantic balance. It *exists* in a realm outside our present reality, but it forms the basis of the faith which keeps us whole (and truly sane) within that reality. The 'other' realm impinges on men through various 'forces'. These can be destructive as well as beneficial, but it is the latter with which we are concerned here and, as we have said, art and love are the principal channels through which these become manifest, and in discussing both of them, Hoffmann makes reference to a 'realm' of the spirit. Music is 'die geheimnisvolle Sprache eines fernen Geisterreichs';[7] it is, as 'Donna Anna' puts it in *Don Juan* (1813), 'das wunderbare, romantische Reich. . . wo die himmlischen Zauber der Töne wohnen' (FN 71). We recall Novalis's 'Reich der Liebe' in the *Hymnen an die Nacht* and we are not surprised to find a (relatively secularised) version of this concept in Hoffmann, for example in the treatment of the Medardus-Aurelie relationship in *Die Elixiere des Teufels* (the phrase itself, for example, occurs on EM 288). The close relationship between music and love as revelations of the absolute is evident in the figure of Kreisler in *Kater Murr*. In love, man can transcend his earthly self, as indeed does Peregrinus; very much the same is said of the 'hero' of Mozart's opera in the much earlier *Don Juan*: 'Es gibt hier auf Erden wohl nichts, was den Menschen in seiner innigsten Natur so hinaufsteigert, als die Liebe' (FN 75). This conception can, when the guardian angel of humour nods, give rise to aesthetically undistinguished but sincere passages of rhetorical pathos or exaltation, such as those in which, sublimating his rage against Julia Marc's husband, Groepel, Hoffmann shows the sensual beast attempting to violate the virginally angelic beauty,[8] or this attempt to render Peregrinus's feelings in *Meister Floh*:

Dem Peregrinus kam Röschen in diesem Augenblick vor, wie ein höheres Wesen, jedes ihrer Worte wie Trost des Himmels. Ein unbeschreiblich Gefühl der reinsten Wonne durchströmte sein Innres[9], wie milder, süßer Frühlingshauch. Er war nicht mehr der Sünder, der vermeßne Frevler, für den er sich gehalten, er glaubte mit Entzücken zu erkennen, daß er wert sei der Liebe, der holdesten, engelreinsten Jungfrau (SW 804).

There is an echo of Novalis here, but the poetic conviction is missing, as it is in another usage reminiscent of Novalis which we find in *Märchen* like *Der goldene Topf, Nußknacker und Mausekönig* (1819), *Meister Floh* and *Prinzessin Brambilla*, namely the construction within the plot of a mythical world of abstract spirit, with which the action in the material world is mysteriously linked. The difference lies in the fact that in Hoffmann, the transition between 'Dream' and 'World' and vice versa is much less smooth and easy.

The ironic outlook of the 'humorist', the basis of which is a deep feeling of the *gulf* between the ideal and material reality and which represents the idealist coming to terms with, rather than resigning himself to, that fact and the ubiquitous duality of life which arises from it, is much more truly characteristic of Hoffmann than the triumph of the myth, as presented in *Der goldene Topf*. For all its very real literary virtues, this story has always seemed to me a little too solemn in its overall tone, and its resolution of the duality of life in '[das] Leben in der Poesie, der sich der heilige Einklang aller Wesen als tiefstes Geheimnis der Natur offenbaret' (FN 255), while doubtless sincerely meant, leaves too many questions unanswered and lacks the *poetic* conviction which Novalis might have given it. Hoffmann is certainly more capable than, say, Jean Paul of writing romantically evocative poetic prose (as, for example, in Anselmus's first vision of Serpentina, FN 182–3), but he is not the complete idealist poet, and he is at his best when he recognises this. That does not mean any denial of the ideal, but rather a greater scepticism as to the possibility of realising it.

Such an attempt could more easily have a tragic outcome, as in *Der Sandmann* or *Doge und Dogaresse*, which we shall consider later. Even in the deliberately idyllic *Meister Martin der Küfner und seine Gesellen*, there is the suggestion that Friedrich's ability to combine devotion to Rosa with devotion to his artistic ideal is exceptional. The painter Reinhold, his co-hero, finds that he cannot marry 'das Himmelskind, wie ich es im Herzen trage' (SB 462) and comments that Friedrich's art is 'more capable of accommodating domesticity' than is his (p. 471).

It is the recognition and humorous acceptance of the duality of ideal and real which saves Reinhold, as it is the lesson learned by Traugott in *Der Artushof* (1817). This is the story of a clerk who is awakened to his artistic vocation by love for Felizitas, the daughter of the mad artist Berklinger. His search for her in the real, Italian Sorrento rather than the house of that name near Danzig where she actually resides is symbolic of the fact that such beauty can only be possessed as an artistic ideal and after an initial reaction of sharp, near-tragic pain, he comes happily to this realisation. Only the positive, romantic 'Sehnsucht' remains. The *true* Felizitas exists on canvas and has nothing to do with '[die] klägliche Existenz des Alltags' (SB 169), at which level she is in fact degraded to the status of 'Kriminalrätin Mathesius'. The story has a very romantic moral, for artists and non-artists alike, namely the doctrine of humour which, as Lothar remarks in the discussion immediately following its conclusion, arises out of the recognition of irony, and is the basis of 'Serapiontic' serenity.

This doctrine developed progressively in Hoffmann's mind and culminates in *Prinzessin Brambilla*, which we shall examine later in this chapter. But it was always present in potential at least, and underlies the choice of Callot's manner as a stylistic model. In the opening piece of the *Fantasiestücke*, Hoffmann has already moved close to an enunciation of his concept of the fantastic and grotesque, which is based on an insight into a deeper poetic truth which the rationalistic philistine and the ponderous, unimaginative critic cannot see:

> Die Ironie, welche, indem sie das Menschliche mit dem Tier in Konflikt setzt, den Menschen mit seinem ärmlichen Tun und Treiben verhöhnt, wohnt nur in einem tiefen Geiste, und so enthüllen Callots aus Tier und Mensch geschaffene groteske Gestalten dem ernsten tiefer eindringenden Beschauer alle die geheimen Andeutungen, die unter dem Schleier der Skurrilität verborgen liegen (FN 12–13).

In its truly Hoffmanesque form this grotesque humour is free from bitterness, as it is in *Signor Formica* (1819) which, if it is perhaps somewhat undisciplined, remains probably his most completely *funny* story and is also characteristic in its use of the Italian impromptu comedy as a channel for the expression of the 'humoristic' mentality. Mere eccentricity, which can have a 'splenetic' element, is not enough. Such is the case with the eponymous 'hero' of *Rat Krespel* (1816), whose oddness of behaviour is less an expression of imaginative and spiritual freedom than a necessary compensation, a 'Blitzableiter' (SB 43) for the inner tensions of a man living mentally, as his daughter is physically, on a knife-edge, as a result of the unresolved discrepancy between the artistic constitution and the harshness of reality. He lacks the childlike purity of spirit which characterises the hermit 'Serapion' and which enables Salvator Rosa, in *Signor Formica*, to see life positively, even though the world refuses him recognition as an artist.

Insight into the duality of life, in combination with purity of soul, constitutes the best defence against the dangers to which the non-philistine soul is regularly exposed, the 'finstere Mächte' which threaten even Anselmus and Peregrinus. Romantic spirituality brings with it, for Hoffmann, a delicate mental constitution and the majority of his stories constitute a battle fought out on that ground, or at least presuppose such a battle. Hoffmann's concentration on human psychology (a field in which he was a well informed layman) does not mean a desertion of the romantic belief in the objective existence of a separate spiritual dimension in the physical and moral universe. In the discussion on 'magnetism' in the *Serapionsbrüder* (SB 261 ff), the (relative) sceptic, Lothar, does not deny that this phenomenon belongs to the area in which the human dimension is touched by another which is 'geisterhaft' (p. 263) and alien. He stipulates only that such processes must occur 'naturally', that is without deliberate human manipulation, '[das] unheimliche Spiel mit einer fremden Gewalt' (p. 265). It is, however, the possibility of a damaging psychological effect which chiefly concerns Hoffmann, the fear that such arrogant and ignorant dabbling 'mein eignes Leben rettungslos verstören könnte' (SB 265).[10] Mental, or, in the broader sense, spiritual self-loss is Hoffmann's greatest fear and it is this fear which lends force and depth to his treatment of the uncanny and supernatural.

The feeling of the uncanny with which Hoffmann invests his study of the psychology of the gambler, *Spielerglück* (1818–19) is not mere decoration. We do have a vivid sense of an alien fate which drives the gambler in spite of all good intentions and resolutions, of a 'hostile power' stretching out its 'Krallenfäuste' (SB 717) towards the hero, Baron Siegfried. Hoffmann sees the threat in this case as essentially a moral one: loss of 'Reinheit der Gesinnung' (SB 720) and slavery to Mammon (p. 721), which was for Hoffmann a spiritual sickness unto death. The attack can come mysteriously and unpredictably. In Siegfried's case, the motive is the relatively understandable one that he wishes to prove that he is not mean. In that of Theodor in *Das öde Haus* (1817), an apparently chance glimpse of a hand at a window, wearing a brilliant gem and holding a crystal glass bottle, is enough to start the process in a mind already attuned to mystery and a mirror pressed on him by an odd and importunate pedlar strengthens the hold of the 'alien power' over him.

Theodor becomes more and more entangled in a psychological problem which is one of Hoffmann's central preoccupations, the 'double' nature of reality[11] and the corresponding danger of a split in the individual personality and complete mental alienation. He feels himself to be 'auf dem Wege zum Tollhause' (FN 474), to the fate which threatens Kreisler and has already overtaken the central figure of Hoffmann's first story, *Ritter Gluck*. But as he finds when he visits the doctor, man is not helpless in this situation. A clear awareness of the duality of existence and a pure will can overcome the attacking force. We shall be able to follow this process, in both positive and negative examples, later in this chapter.

That Hoffmann, without entirely 'breaking free' from Romanticism, took at least an important step towards realism is a suggestion made by, among others, Klaus Günzel in his essay 'Zu Hoffmanns Entwicklung als Schriftsteller'.[12] Günzel makes considerable play with Hoffmann's undeniable recognition of the importance of material reality and points particularly to development in the field of the *Märchen*, from Anselmus, who is transported to Atlantis, to Peregrinus, who 'finds his happiness in this earthly life'.[13] But this is no vindication of what is called in *Der Artushof* 'die klägliche Existenz des irdischen Augenblicks' (SB, 169), just as the realisation that one cannot live constantly in fantasy does not constitute an invalidation of the truth of the latter. Not dissimilarly, the use of the grotesque has been seen as a move in the direction of realism.[14] But it can just as easily be seen as an *anti*-realistic effect, the 'Hineinschreiten des Abenteuerlichen in das gewöhnliche Leben' which Hoffmann values so highly in the *opera buffa (Der Dichter und der Komponist,* SB 90). The fantastic, arising partly out of the oddnesses of some characters, partly out of 'the bizarre play of chance', steps with a rather aggressive boldness[15] into everyday life and 'turns it upside down'. Hoffmann shows the intersection of the absolute and the earthly *in* reality, but nowhere implies that the truth is *of* reality. The development in his approach to the *Märchen* in late works like *Klein Zaches genannt Zinnober* (1819) and *Meister Floh* does mean that the fantastic aspect cannot retain as much unadulterated, abstract wondrousness as in earlier work, and that satire, though hardly a newcomer on the scene, does play a somewhat larger role. There is political and social satire, in particular in the two works mentioned,

directed against the repressive and sterile approach of government to
the governed in the Metternich era, particularly after the Carlsbad
Decrees of 1819. *Klein Zaches*, indeed, has been described as in essence
an attack on the restored *ancien régime*,[16] and it is easy to see in it
echoes of Metternich's dislike of independent thinkers and enthusiastic
sects, examples of the 'presumption' which he saw as the chief sickness
of the age.[17]

But Metternich's mentality, like the enlightened despotism which
was the sum of his political wisdom, was much more in tune with
'Aufklärung' than with Romanticism, and the political satire, while real
enough in itself, is secondary. The central attack is surely directed
against complacent, unimaginative, indeed essentially obscurantist
rationalism, which threatens to stamp out poetry and fantasy and
which needs to be combated, not so much by satire, as by humour.
Hoffmann was entirely justified, in his preface to *Prinzessin Brambilla*,
in calling the earlier work 'die lose, lockre Ausführung einer
scherzhaften Idee' (SW 211). The tone in this case *is* the message, and
madness is his method: 'ein superwahnsinniges Buch', he called it in a
letter to Friedrich Kralowsky (5 December 1819). It is a blow against
philistinism, against the spiritual, rather than the political *ancien
régime*.

The Novels

Die Elixiere des Teufels

A summary of the plot of this novel, which constitutes the memoirs of
the monk Medardus, looking back over what is, to put it mildly, a
chequered career, including flight from the monastery (after drinking
from a bottle reputedly given by the Devil to St Antony), fraudulent
assumption of a second identity, love and lust, murder in thought and
deed, madness, repentance and eventual expiation of a family curse and
return to the monastic life, might give the impression that this is just
another melodramatic extravaganza in the tradition of Matthew
('Monk') Lewis. Lewis's novel did indeed influence Hoffmann[18] and
there are occasions when this influence shows in subject-matter and
style ('Mit eiskaltem Schauer durchbebte mich der Gedanke': EM 198).
Underneath this gaudy mask, however, it is a penetrating study of the
mental and moral problems of the romantic personality in general and
of that of Hoffmann in particular. Its subject is the battle between the
principles, or forces of light and darkness, played out in the mind and
heart of the hero and to a lesser extent of his beloved, Aurelie, who are

predestined to love and then lose one another as fleshly desire gives way to 'something higher'.[19]

Hoffmann himself defines the issue neatly enough in a letter to Kunz (24 March 1814);

> Es ist darin auf nichts geringeres abgesehen, als in dem krausen, wunderbaren Leben eines Mannes, über den schon bei seiner Geburt die himmlischen und dämonischen Mächte walteten, jene geheimnisvollen Verknüpfungen des menschlichen Geistes mit all' den höheren Prinzipien, die in der ganzen Natur verborgen und nur dann und wann hervorblitzen, welchen Blitz wir dann Zufall nennen, recht klar und deutlich zu zeigen.

Medardus is called to bring about, through the achievement of inner purity, the expiation of a curse of violent lecherousness which has come down from a previous generation of his family and which he has to combat within himself. The Devil (or the 'evil principle') is concerned to prevent this and so he often seems to be driven hither and thither by forces over which he has no control, and which well up inside him as apparently irresistible impulses. At the point where marriage to Aurelie seems assured, when his 'Doppeltgänger' is being taken away to suffer for the crimes *he* has committed, Medardus is swept away:

> Da wurden die Geister der Hölle in mir wach, und bäumten sich auf mit der Gewalt die ihnen verliehen über den frevelnden verruchten Sünder. – Ich erfaßte Aurelien mit grimmiger Wut, daß sie zusammenzuckte: 'Ha ha ha . . . Wahnsinniges, töriges Weib . . . *ich* . . . *ich* . . . dein Buhle, dein Bräutigam, bin der Medardus . . . ich bin König . . . ich trinke dein Blut!' (EM 206)

The narrator goes on to describe how he seized his knife (the 'Mordmesser' which has come down to him, like the curse, from his father) and stabbed Aurelie, before making his escape. It later transpires that this murder was a hallucination, like the double who appears through the stone floor of the prison and gives Medardus the knife (EM 171 f). He is both mentally and morally under attack, often unable to distinguish with certainty between reality and illusion.[20]

If Medardus is unable to distinguish true from false and right from wrong, can there be any question of sin, or, indeed, redemption? It is a question which Medardus himself puts to the Pope (EM 248). But the retrospective narrator has a spiritual freedom which enables him to view his former self with the balanced detachment of a 'higher principle' (EM 288) and he constantly provides the moral perspective, the consciousness of sin, which the Medardus of the story proper, who is in the clutches of a Satanic power to whose influence he is exposed by his own inherent sin of egotistic pride, often lacks. Medardus *is* responsible and the Pope, in his reply to his question, mentions the indwelling principle of insight and control ('Bewußtsein', p. 248) which should give him the victory over the mad desire to possess, indeed to violate the pure ideal (this novel is written very much under the sign of the Julia-experience). In potential, at least, here is a saving power and one which will be more to the fore in Medardus's successor, Kreisler. Had it been more definitely operative here, it would have introduced a therapeutic and very welcome element of irony, perhaps even humour, into our intensely passionate and heavily serious hero. As it is, the principle of humour, allied to a somewhat exaggerated oddity, is contained in this book in a separate character, the barber with a second, comic identity, Schönfeld-Belcampo. Belcampo loves Medardus for his 'sublime[n] Tollheit' (EM 252) and warns him against his would-be assassins. But the Hoffmann of the *Elixiere* is not yet in the serenely balanced frame of mind of the *Serapionsbrüder* (which appeared between 1819 and 1821, alongside *Kater Murr*). Neither inner consciousness, nor good advice, nor even severe penance can free Medardus from Satan's power. That liberation comes only in a hazy, quasi-mystical experience at the moment of Aurelie's death. It is a mysticism which sits rather uneasily with Hoffmann's deeper talents and insights, his psychological perceptiveness, his humour and his *artistic* idealism. It seems to owe more to Zacharias Werner than to Novalis and it can hardly be denied that the novel would have been better without it.

Lebens-Ansichten des Katers Murr

Only two of the planned three volumes of this novel were completed, a fact which causes us some difficulty in interpreting it, since Hoffmann, true to his usual practice of constructing his plot along the lines of the popular mystery-novel, has left unclear many details which would no doubt have been explained in the completed version. We do not know, for example, whether the hero of the main story, Kreisler, was to become the mad musician of the *Kreisleriana* (already published in the *Fantasiestücke*). The duality of life is the work's thematic centre; whether the outcome was to have been tragedy or comedy is by no means certain. The psychological climate is, to be sure, less tropically

sultry than was the case in the *Elixiere*. The element of criminal
sensuality has been moved from the centre to the relatively peripheral
figure of Prince Hektor, who is the husband-elect of Princess Hedwiga,
but secretly lusts after her friend Julia, the pure 'angel of light'
(EM 411) and embodiment of the spirit of music. The latter, while she
feels her inner harmony to be under some degree of threat,[21] is not
caught up in a family history of sin as is Aurelie. Her love for Kreisler is
an essentially platonic reply to his 'Liebe des Künstlers' — i.e. the man
of enlightened romantic 'Gemüt' — who finds revealed in love the secret
of ideal beauty and truth which had hitherto slumbered in his breast
and whose love is a 'pure heavenly fire' which 'nur leuchtet und wärmt,
ohne mit verderblichen Flammen zu vernichten' (EM 431).

This is Kreisler's own description and it is no doubt sincere. He is, as
distinct from Medardus, a true artist, for whom beauty (in his case,
music above all) is a revelation of the higher spiritual reality and who,
like Traugott in *Der Artushof* and Salvator Rosa in *Signor Formica*, has
learned the lesson of irony and humour — in theory, at least. Hoffmann
treats this crucial aspect of his character with a studied ambivalence and
there seems to be no way of knowing whether he was in fact planning
an equally ambivalent, 'open' conclusion: a picture of a balance
achieved under constant pressure and needing continually to be fought
for. It is true that Kreisler's old mentor and friend, the eccentric organ-
builder, 'magician' and philosopher Abraham, denies the charge that
Kreisler is embittered and inwardly 'zerrissen'. The 'spirit of true love'
reigns within him, and his humour is that which arises 'aus der tiefern
Anschauung des menschlichen Seins', and is 'die schönste Gabe der
Natur . . . die sie aus der reinsten Quelle ihres Wesens schöpft' (EM
499). Kreisler disturbs the courtly society in which he lives for the
greater part of the novel, because, as Abraham sees it, he is spiritually
above its self-interested, meanly conspiratorial ethos.[22] Rätin Benzon,
to whom he is replying here, is one of those who have sold their
spiritual birthright for a mess of worldly pottage.

But there are also echoes of Krespel in Kreisler. His humour is by no
means always free of corrosive 'spleen', it is, as the Princess says, a
'schneidender Humor (EM 427) and even Julia, who recognises that the
soul out of which it arises is good and true, also sees that it has a
destructive and hurtful side. She herself feels her inner harmony
disturbed by his caprices and changes of mood: 'Dieser Todessprung
von einem Extrem zum andern zerschneidet mir die Brust' (EM 415).
Kreisler himself is pursued by the fear that the balance between longing
for the ideal and ironic detachment which enables him to exist in an

essentially alien reality, this balance which is the basis of his humour, may break down in madness. The thought of his double and *alter ego*, the mad painter Ettlinger, plagues him in his less secure moments, and while it seems to depart from him during the period which he spends as a fugitive in the monastery, there is no guarantee that it will not return. The serenity and pure devotion to art of that period cannot and does not last and at the end of the second volume, Abraham calls him back into the battlefield. Julia is to be married to the imbecile Prince Ignatius, a sacrifice to the ambitions of her mother, Rätin Benzon. The forces of darkness are at work, and what the outcome will be remains uncertain.

We are talking here of Kreisler, and it is time to recognise that important as he is — and Hoffmann's friend Hitzig was probably justified in calling him a self-portrait — his story is not the whole novel. He may be the potentially tragic humorist, but Hoffmann the author, while he is treating in him a central problem of his own life, has not totally identified himself with him. The fragmentary biography of Kreisler, after all, has come down to us only 'in zufälligen Makulaturblättern', left interleaved among the memoirs of a cat, and printed by mistake.

The fiction of an incompetent publisher or printer gives Hoffmann the opportunity to enfold what he himself calls his 'very serious' book within an 'irreverent joke'[23] and thus to provide, in the format and in the constant contrast of tone and subject-matter between the two biographies which appear in alternating fragments, a comic counterpoint which the main Kreisler-action could not contain. Murr, pompous, proud, learned, and above all totally devoid of humour, of the ability to appreciate the relation in which the idea stands to reality, is a philistine, certainly, but also (in an external sense) a *romantic* one. He seizes on the forms of the cults of genius, sentiment, individualism, high-flying 'poetry' and the like, and being incapable of informing them with the true romantic spirit, reduces them unconsciously to comic absurdity. It may well be that Hoffmann overdoes somewhat the element of parody and satire (especially of the 'Burschenschaften') and that the balance of the book would have been improved if Murr had not been allowed to continue his lucubrations at such length, but the device still plays a very important part in the total economy of the novel, in that it serves to reinforce the distinction between Hoffmann and Kreisler, and allows the truly detached humour of the former to blow like a refreshing breeze in what might otherwise have become a rather stuffy atmosphere.

The *Novellen* **and** *Märchen*

Four pieces have been chosen to represent Hoffmann's work in this field, namely *Der Sandmann, Doge und Dogaresse, Das Fräulein von Scuderi and Prinzessin Brambilla* (1820). The first of these belongs to the collection *Nachtstücke* (1816–17), which seems to us to show a decided advance on the (already high) standard of narrative art displayed in the *Fantasiestücke*. Among the other stories in the *Nachtstücke* which, for lack of space, we cannot discuss, *Das öde Haus* (an instructive companion-piece to *Der Sandmann*), *Das Majorat*, which can fruitfully be compared with *Das Fräulein von Scuderi*, and the thematically and stylistically almost Kleistian *Das Gelübde*, deserve to be singled out. Hoffmann's mastery of his craft continued to grow and *Die Serapionsbrüder* (1819–21) contains a high proportion of work of the first rank, including our second and third examples. *Prinzessin Brambilla* belongs to the very last phase, that of *Klein Zaches* and *Meister Floh*. No selection, of course, can do justice to such a rich and large *oeuvre*; on the other hand, even such a low figure as four imposes from the outset a severe restriction on the degree of detail into which we can enter in each discussion.

Der Sandmann is Hoffmann's most penetrating study of mental imbalance. It is not devoid of humour: significantly, immediately after the description of Nathanael's removal, 'in gräßlicher Raserei tobend', to the asylum, we are given an amusing account of the way in which Spalanzani had tricked sophisticated and self-important society by introducing his automaton, 'Olimpia' into its 'vernünftige[n] Teezirkeln' (FN 360). There is humour, too (or at least the clarity and serenity of mind which is its normal accompaniment), in the figure of Clara and the narrator, in his tone and his management of the plot,[24] adds a very necessary element of balance and objectivity to a story which is very much one of the mind, and in which it is often hard to distinguish between fact and fancy. It is, however, as he himself says, a story which is 'gar nicht spaßhaft'.

Nathanael, a student and poet, is pursued by obsessions which took root in him in childhood. His father had been given to alchemistic experiments, which he carried out with a lawyer, one Coppelius, a man of odd appearance and manner who appears in Nathanael's account as devilishly grotesque, who disliked children and had a frightening effect on them. His mother would send the children off to bed when Coppelius was due to visit his father, using the phrase 'der Sandmann kommt,' though only as an expression for sleepiness in the eyes. The unease

which she felt at these visits communicated itself to the child and he
enquired further of his sister's nurse, who turned the sandman into a
terrifying bogeyman whose aim was to steal children's eyes. Coppelius's
chastisement of him when he was discovered spying on the secret
activities in his father's sanctum, coupled with his father's death in an
explosion during an experiment, have finally fixed in his subconscious
mind ideas which owe much to folk-beliefs about the evil eye, pacts
with the devil and the like, and which come to the surface in moments
of mental stress and make him susceptible to hostile forces which, as he
himself puts it in the opening paragraph, could totally disrupt his 'life',
that is, his mental balance.[25]

All these memories have been reactivated by a meeting with Coppola,
an Italian salesman of optical instruments, who seems to be Coppelius,
or his double (as he often does in such points, Hoffmann leaves this
issue in a mysterious half-light), and this has prompted the letter to
Lothar, the brother of Nathanael's beloved Clara, with which the story
begins. He is threatened by a melancholic gloom, a conviction that a
dark and inescapable 'fate' is about to overtake him and neither Clara's
letter to him, in which, like the doctor in *Das öde Haus*, she speaks of
the individual's mental and moral capacity to overcome the 'dark
power' within and out of the resources of his own *Gemüt*, nor even her
'angelic' presence and personal serenity, can dispel that gloom
permanently. A battle within the mind and soul ('Kampf im Innern') as
Clara calls it (EN 340) is in progress and it is a battle for possession of
that territory ('sie [die dunkle Macht] muß . . . unser Selbst werden':
FN 340). This is in fact part of the universal struggle between dark and
light to which humanity is subject – a fact of which the motifs of the
devilish (Coppelius) and the heavenly (Clara: cf. especially FN 361)
serve to remind us – and only the spiritually dead, who lack all sense of
the 'eternal' dimension,[26] and thus of the romantic, can remain totally
untouched by it. There is a poison in Romanticism, as all the great
Romantics recognised, but it can be controlled by the spiritually and
morally healthy.[27] Nathanael's spiritual health, however, is fragile. He
mistakes Clara for a philistine, a 'lebloses, verdammtes Automat'
(FN 348) and is only brought back into balance again when he and
Lothar are on the point of fighting a duel.

His victory over the 'finstere Macht' (FN 349) is only temporary.
Returning to university, he relaxes his inner vigilance (symbolised by
the purchase of a spy-glass from Coppola) and indulges that side of his
nature which takes the in itself legitimate desire for the wondrous to
the point of the 'mystische Schwärmerei' which repelled and bored

Clara (FN 346–7). This makes him susceptible to the deception practised on society by Spalanzani with his 'daughter' Olimpia, who is in fact an automaton. Whereas society in general is deceived only into thinking Olimpia a real person, Nathanael, his poetic perceptiveness perverted by his inner sickness (in contrast, for example, to Balthasar in *Klein Zaches*), compounds deception with self-deception and makes her into his ideal of love, an ideal which he wishes to possess in marriage. The eventual disillusionment, in a grotesquely comic scene in which he sees Spalanzani and Coppola engaged in a (literal) tug-of-war over Olimpia, brings, not a cure, but an outbreak of complete madness.

Once again, friendly influences, above all that of Clara, Nathanael's 'angel', restore him and all seems set fair for a happy ending. But as the lovers stand on a high tower admiring the view, he takes out Coppola's spy-glass to look at a 'grey bush' that seems to be approaching, the madness seizes him again, and he attempts to throw Clara down. She escapes, but Nathanael leaps to his death when he sees the lawyer Coppelius in the crowd beneath. Clara later finds in marriage the happiness 'das ihr der im Innern zerrissene Nathanael niemals hätte gewähren können' (FN 363). He can never be won back securely to reality where the healthy Romantic, however highly developed his appreciation of the ideal and the transcendent dimension, must and can live.

The narrative technique of the story is masterly, particularly in its handling of motifs (above all, that of the 'eye') and in its intermingling of objective and subjective realities so as to produce, in the alert reader, a sense of mystery, but not of hopeless confusion, and to direct the attention firmly towards the psychological dimension. This also serves to provide an alternation between scenes of extreme tension, such as that in which Coppola piles eyeglasses ('Sköne Oke': i.e. 'Augen') on Nathanael's table (FN 351) and others in which the reader, secure in his knowledge of the true reality, can derive an ironic enjoyment from Nathanael's self-delusion. We are meant to sympathise with Nathanael, who appeals as a kind of romantic Werther, but not to identify with him, and there is more than a touch of the self-parody which we saw in Murr in the episode in which the poet, holding the automaton's hand, speaks to her in high-flown language 'which no-one understood, neither he, nor Olimpia'. She replies with her stereotyped 'Ach – Ach – Ach!', which inspires him to call her 'du tiefes Gemüt, in dem sich mein ganzes Sein spiegelt' and to add, as Hoffmann says, 'more in the same vein' (FN 355). It is painful also, of course, to see a man of real poetic potential speaking to a lifeless puppet like Heinrich von Ofterdingen to his Mathilde, for we know that Hoffmann did believe in an ideal of poetic love.[28] But we are clear in this case that Olimpia is no Mathilde and Nathanael no Heinrich, and the comic impression is the stronger. It plays, in fact, an important part in the story, for though it does not prevent us from feeling sad at Nathanael's fate, it makes sure that we stand in no danger of sharing it.

Doge und Dogaresse is not one of Hoffmann's most often discussed *Novellen* and it may be that its inclusion here is an act of self-indulgence on the part of the present author. Certainly, it could be faulted for its rather cumbrous structure, which arises out of the attempt to combine a personal with a political plot, an affair of the heart with affairs of state. Its account of Antonio's childhood meeting with Annunziata – reminiscent, perhaps, of Franz's with Marie in Tieck's *Franz Sternbald* – is not entirely convincing, and the attempt to make Margaretha fulfil the dual function of vehicle for the grotesque and mysterious and of Antonio's former nurse and present protective genius could be said to be over-ambitious. In addition, it has to be admitted that some of the most characteristically Hoffmannesque features, above all his humour and his concentration on the inner, psychological reality, are largely absent. This latter point, however, does not necessarily make the story a lesser work than the others, but merely a different one and there are some compensatory features which would be lacking, perhaps, had it been more 'typical'. We would single out in particular episodes of exciting action like the rescue of the Doge from the storm-tossed bucentaur (SB 363: 'Gleich zerstäubtem Gefieder sah man Gondeln und Barken hier und dort auf dem Meere treiben'), the presentation of the bouquet at the *mardi gras* festival (pp. 386–7) and Antonio's flight on the night of the failed conspiracy (p. 397). To the colour and movement of such scenes should be added the successful evocation of the city of Venice and its life. As Hoffmann himself commented (SB 400), the story is 'individuell lokal', the result of careful use of sources.

But it is not primarily for these reasons that we find this story significant and attractive. It is of interest to us for its genuine tragic sense (paralleled elsewhere in Hoffmann only by *Das Majorat* – and even there, the tragedy is less central) and for its boldness in confronting the theme of human love, an issue which Hoffmann usually treats in a relatively inhibited way, either in an artificially idyllic relationship, or sublimated in a quasi-mystical haze. Perhaps the most crucial statement in the whole *Novelle* is Annunziata's cry: 'ja es gibt noch einen Himmel auf Erden!' (SB 398). That the sea, the Doge's bride, should revenge him on the widow who is 'unfaithful' to his memory and on her lover does not necessarily cancel out this assertion, as we shall see.

Annunziata, young, beautiful and innocent, obediently marries the Doge who is, as he himself says, 'ein achtzigjähriger Greis', at the behest of her politically ambitious great-uncle Bodoeri. One day, she is seen with the Doge by Antonio, who falls into the faint which not infrequently seems to stand, in Hoffmann, for an interpenetration of the conscious and unconscious levels of the mind. In this case, as with Reutlinger in *Das steinerne Herz* (FN 604), a repressed memory from the past has risen in a shatteringly vivid form. Antonio, who at the beginning of the story was eking out a precarious living as a porter at the Fontego, the house of the German merchants, from which condition 'die ewige Macht', in the guise of Fate or Fortune, has saved him by singling him out to save the Doge (SB 363), has been possessed by a mysterious longing for a 'lost Eden' (p. 373) which is connected with an event in his childhood. This, it now transpires, was an incident in which the young Annunziata, not unlike the angel which guards the sleeping children in the fairy-tale *Snow-White and Rose-Red*,[29] saved him as he slept from deadly danger (cf. SB 383–4). The mystery of his childhood and origin is not yet completely explained, but he now knows that the old woman whose grotesqueness of manner and appearance (the result of torture by the Inquisition) have till now prevented him from accepting her as such, is his former nurse Margaretha. He knows too that the meaning of his life is love and that he can find fulfilment only in Annunziata.

She too has felt a sympathetic faintness (p. 382), but awakens in her turn to full consciousness of the situation only when, sailing with her husband in a gondola rowed by the disguised Antonio, she hears the snatch of song ('Ah senz amare . . .' etc.) which is carved into the frame of the picture of a Doge and Dogaressa of which the whole story purports to be an explanation. In this (for Hoffmann) exceptionally successful and moving poetic scene, while the Doge chatters complacently on about the grandeur of Venice and of his position, Annunziata is brought by the sensuous gliding of the gondola, and the music and the words of the song, which tell her that her high position is no compensation for a loveless marriage, to a realisation of her situation (cf. pp. 392–3). Fate seems to offer the lovers a way out of their *impasse* when an attempted *coup* against the Venetian constitution (in which Antonio becomes involved through the fact that his real father, a German merchant, was unjustly executed by the *Signoria*), goes awry and the Doge himself is executed. In an assertion of the supreme validity of their love, Antonio and Annunziata flee from the 'blutige Mordstätte' in a small boat, but are overtaken by a storm, and drowned. Certainly, they can be seen as sinners, though Hoffmann hardly emphasises the point. He sees their love as doomed, but he also sees it as glorious and he manages an ending which, if it is perhaps not entirely free from the effects of the streak of melodrama which is an inalienable constituent of his taste, nevertheless has a genuine tragic grandeur:

> Der Sturm erhob sich und jagte die düstern, zusammengeballten Wolken mit zornigem Toben vor sich her. Hoch auf und nieder flog die Barke. 'O hilf, O Herr des Himmels!' schrie die Alte. Antonio, des Ruders nicht mehr mächtig, umschlang die holde Annunziata, die, von seinen glühenden Küssen erweckt, ihn mit der Inbrunst der seligsten Liebe an ihren Busen drückte. 'O mein Antonio!' – 'O meine Annunziata!' So riefen sie des Sturms nicht achtend, der immer entsetzlicher tobte und brauste. Da streckte das Meer, die eifersüchtige Witwe des enthaupteten Falieri, die schäumenden Wellen die Riesenarme empor, erfaßte die Liebenden und riß sie samt der Alten hinab in den bodenlosen Abgrund! (SB 399)

It is as if Hoffmann has at last decided to face the full power of love.

In *Das Fräulein von Scuderi*, love has again become a minor element. There is a pair of young lovers, Olivier and Madelon, and their role in the plot is not unimportant, since they represent the innocence which is in danger of being swallowed up by the morass of sin and crime which threatens, indeed, to engulf the whole of seventeenth-century Paris, in which the story is set. A series of poisonings, followed by nocturnal (and often deadly) attacks by what is taken to be a gang of jewel-thieves is terrorising the city and even the efforts of the secret court, the *chambre ardente*, represented by the ruthless and rather sinister La Regnie and Desgrais,[30] seem powerless to remove this threat to the civil order. Mademoiselle de Scudéry becomes involved in this situation through her connection with Olivier Brusson, the son of a former protégée, who is accused of having murdered his master, the goldsmith Cardillac. The evidence against him is strong and it is the love for, and faith in him of Cardillac's daughter, the pure and innocent 'angel'-figure Madelon, which convinces the older woman more than anything else. She spares no effort, including a traumatic visit to the 'Gemächer der frevelnden Verruchtheit' (SB 680) of the *Conciergerie* which almost undermines her faith, and eventually succeeds in saving Olivier.

The man responsible for Cardillac's death is in fact Cardillac himself.

He was mortally wounded, in self-defence, by an intended victim and carried home by Olivier, who had followed him in the hope of preventing a murder. For as Olivier discovered, there was no gang: Cardillac had been responsible for the murders and robberies which had so baffled the *chambre ardente*, driven by an irresistible urge which told him that only he had the right to possess the fruits of his own craftsmanship or, perhaps it would be better to say, artistry. This he attributed to a frightening experience which his mother had when she was carrying him, and in which the demonic attraction of brilliantly flashing diamonds played a crucial part. There is no doubt that Hoffmann does accept that an external agency is partly responsible for Cardillac's crimes. He lives, otherwise, a life of faultless rectitude which is not, as Olivier first imagines (he calls him 'heuchlerischer Bösewicht', p. 691) mere hypocrisy, as his genuine veneration for Mademoiselle de Scudéry confirms. The motif of the sharp, flashing light, or glance, is one which Hoffmann often uses to indicate the entry of an alien and hostile principle (Cardillac speaks of a 'böser Stern': pp. 691–2) into the *Gemüt*.[31] And he has no wish to benefit materially from his crimes, nor to hand on the stolen jewels, which his moral sense tells him bear a curse of blood, to his daughter. He is another variant of the common Hoffmannesque figure of the sensitive and artistic spirit with the capacity to apprehend the realm of the wondrous, but not the ability to channel and control its spiritual and psychological effects. His apprehension of reality and truth are flawed, hence the Jekyll-and-Hyde dual personality. The duality of life becomes a destructive split, another not uncommon phenomenon in our author.[32]

But it is not the study of Cardillac's psychology, nor the mystery and tension of the narrative, well sustained as this is, which is this story's main claim to distinction. These features act, in fact, as foils to the central action, the heroic battle of good against evil, of 'Tugend' (the key expression of the story) against 'Frevel', in which a 73-year-old lady, an artistic nature like Cardillac – she is still working on her novel *Clélie* – is the chief protagonist. Her real antagonist is not Cardillac, nor the police investigator Desgrais, though in each of them we feel the approach of her real enemy. This is the moral poison which has infected almost the whole of Paris. The saving of Olivier, important as that is, is less so, one feels, than the deeper, moral and psychological action which, like a lever, it sets in motion: the saving of Mademoiselle de Scudéry from the pit of despair. She does not feel herself to be in serious physical danger, not even when she cries out: 'Welcher Geist der Hölle hat mich in die entsetzliche Geschichte verwickelt, die mir das

Leben kosten wird!' (SB 681). But she is 'auf den Tod angepackt von der höllischen Macht auf Erden, an deren Dasein sie nicht geglaubt' (SB 680).

The 'life' to which she refers in the first of the two passages just quoted is the inner balance and serenity to which we have already seen Nathanael refer with the same expression, 'Leben'.[33] It is that which forms the basis of the 'Tugend' for which she is universally revered, and which has kept her free from the unhealthily brooding, melancholic mood which bedevils the central figure of *Der Sandmann*. It is expressed, with the clarity and even humour which characterise her mentality, in the couplet which has so impressed both the King and Cardillac: 'Un amant qui craint les voleurs, N'est point digne d'amour'. Now, in the climactic section of the story, that stretching from the visit to the *Conciergerie* to the beginning of the interview with Olivier, she becomes aware, for the first time at such an advanced age, of the reality and power of Evil which till now had been, for her, something external and essentially hypothetical. The poison which has infected even the agents of justice[34] has entered her own bloodstream. As is usual with Hoffmann, the real battle is a mental and spiritual one. The temptation for the heroine is to withdraw from the whole affair, to wash her hands of Olivier and Madelon and if this happens, the reader, who remains convinced of their innocence, knows that they will be lost. The crisis comes when Desgrais asks her to see Olivier, who will otherwise be put to the torture and she agrees in God's name to accept the cup which, it seems, may not pass from her:

> Die Scuderi sah tief sinnend vor sich nieder. Es war ihr, als müsse sie der höheren Macht gehorchen, die den Aufschluß irgend eines entsetzlichen Geheimnisses von ihr verlange, als könne sie nicht mehr den wunderbaren Verschlingungen entziehen, in die sie willenlos geraten. Plötzlich entschlossen sprach sie mit Würde: 'Gott wird mir Fassung und Standhaftigkeit geben; führt den Brusson her, ich will ihn sprechen' (SB 682).

There is still much tension to be endured in this *Novelle*, which is also, incidentally, a fine early example of the genre of the detective or 'mystery' story which Poe and others were later to develop, but the real crisis is now over, and we feel confident, even at this stage, that all will end happily.

We turn finally to what is, by common consent, Hoffmann's finest *Märchen*, *Prinzessin Brambilla*, which achieves what is conceived, but

not executed with complete success, in *Der goldene Topf*: a romantic
myth which is at the same time a completely satisfying story, in which
reality and ideality, seriousness and humour, find as nearly harmonious
a balance as we have a right to expect from Hoffmann. The solution
offered in *Der goldene Topf*, to which this tale is in many ways a
counterpart, with Anselmus safely ensconced in a too obviously
mythical Atlantis and the author, acutely aware of the inadequacies of
reality, offered the somewhat pale consolation of a 'life in poetry', does
not convince because Hoffmann is not Novalis, however much he might
at that moment like to be. In *Brambilla*, he has given up any such
ambition. In contrast to the earlier Atlantis myth, he presents myth
with an irony which does not rob it of its serious meaning, but refines
out of it the heavy, conceptual would-be mysticism which ballasts the
earlier story. Fancy, in this story, is ironically self-aware: Celionati even
gives voice to his awareness that *Prinzessin Brambilla* is a 'Caprice' and
that he and the others are characters appearing in it (SW 310). And in
him, the prime mover of the plot and representative of the author,
irony and the wondrous (he is 'selbst ein Abenteuer': p. 258) exist in a
harmonious balance, whereas in the corresponding figure in *Der goldene
Topf*, Lindhorst, they are in an uneasy juxtaposition: the spirit-prince
yoked to an observer of the world whose humour often has an
uncomfortable sharp cutting edge.

    Any attempt at an orderly résumé of the plot of *Prinzessin Brambilla*
would be almost an act of vandalism. Its structure is more romantic,
perhaps, in its deliberate cultivation of confusion,[35] than any other
work by this author, *Kater Murr* included. The spirit of caprice, of the
Roman carnival amidst which it is set and of the *commedia dell'arte*
from which the principal 'masks' are chosen and which triumphs over
tragedy in the story, give the tone to the narrative technique. It is also a
Märchen in its cultivation of the wondrous in general and in the
'mythical' action of the land of Urdar, the pollution of its magical
spring and the pilgrimage to Italy, the 'Land, des blauer Sonnenhimmel
der Erde Lust in reicher Blüt entzündet' (SW 288) in search of
restoration and the release from enchantment of the Princess Mystilis,
all of which takes place under the aegis of the magician Ruffiamonte.
The echoes of Novalis, once again, are there for all to hear. But as it is
Ruffiamento's friend, Prince Postoja (acting for the most part in his
'other' personality as the *ciarlatano Celionati*), who is endowed with
more than ordinary wisdom but still human, who usually holds the
centre of the stage, so the wondrous, without losing its essential
character, tends to be transferred to the human, psychological

dimension. Rather as, in the *opera buffa*, the wondrous steps into everyday life and the 'Spuk' is rooted in reality (SB 90–1), so here, we have 'das bunte Maskenspiel eines tollen märchenhaften Spaßes' (SW 315).

The lifting of the fairy-tale spell becomes in essence a background to the dis-enchantment of the two lovers, the sempstress Giacinta and the tragic actor Giglio, on the latter of whom the light mostly falls. As we see them at the beginning, they are not unpleasant people, but infected by the vanity and materialism of this world. Giacinta, by trying on a mysterious dress, and Giglio, through a number of experiences culminating in the purchase of magical spectacles from Celionati, become involved in a fantastic action in which they pursue a prince and a princess respectively and in which they appear in *commedia dell'arte* costumes based, in fact, on engravings by Callot, Giacinta fades rather into the background, but we follow Giglio step by step as he vacillates between his serious, everyday self and a comic second self which eventually gains possession of him. Ordinary mortals like the tragic poet Chiari think him mad and he himself speaks to Celionati, who is directing his progress almost like a puppet-master, in terms reminiscent of Nathanael: ' "Ihr seid", erwiderte Giglio, "Ihr seid ein fürchterlicher graulicher Mensch! – Was dringt ihr ein in mein Leben? was wollt Ihr Euch meines Seins bemächtigen?" ' Celionati's reply gives us the correct humorous perspective:

'Das', rief Celionati laut lachend, 'das verlohnte sich der Mühe, die hochwichtige Person des Herrn Exschauspielers Giglio Fava dermaßen einzugehen! – Doch, mein Sohn Giglio, du bedarfst in der Tat eines Vormundes, der dich auf den rechten Weg leitet, welcher zum Ziele führt' (SW 242).

The 'goal' is the same as that indicated in the 'Urdar' myth as the secret of harmony and happiness, namely self-realisation, insight into the duality of life and mastery of it through irony and humour. King Ophioch and Queen Liris, in the inner *Märchen*, look into the spring, see 'ihr eignes Ich in verkehrter Abspiegelung', become aware of a glorious new world previously invisible to them, and respond with a laughter which is '[der Ausdruck] . . . der Freude über den Sieg innerer geistiger Kraft' (SW 256). In the restoration scene, Princess Brambilla and Prince Cornelio, who are the chief actors in the *Roman* fairy-tale action in which Giglio and Giacinta have become involved, look into the spring, 'recognize themselves for the first time', and laugh in the same way (p. 321). At the conclusion of the whole story, we find Giglio and Giacinta as actors of the *commedia dell'arte*, happy in their love and in their worldly lot and morally, at least, a prince and princess in their ability to join the 'wings' of fancy to the 'body' of humour. Only this combination, as Pistoja tells them in his wryly self-deprecating allegorical explanation of both the psychological and the fairy-tale action, is capable of giving true freedom, of exorcising the demon 'der Zobelmützen und schwarze Schlafröcke trägt' (p. 324). *Prinzessin Brambilla* is indeed an allegory of humour, and a thoroughly romantic one. It leaves the spirit where all romantic presentations of its condition essentially leave it, whatever the details of the individual formulation: involved and entangled in a reality which is far from ideal, but possessed of the capacity, at least, to achieve an inner freedom and balance which will preserve the ideal in it and itself in an often hostile environment. That, in essence, is the message which all romantic literature, satirical or idyllic, grave or gay, aims to leave with its readers.

Notes

1. The genuine enthusiasm which the young Hoffmann felt for Grosse's *Der Genius* is expressed in his letter to Hippel of 19 February 1795 (*Briefwechsel*, F. Schnapp (ed.) (Munich, 1968), vol. 1, pp. 53 f). The reservations which the flood of popular novels of mystery called forth in the romantic mind are mirrored in A. W. Schlegel's ironic comment: 'Von den Femegerichten, den geheimnisvollen Bündnissen und den Geistern ist vollends keine Rettung mehr' (quoted in A. Ward, *Book Production, Fiction and the German Reading Public* (Oxford, 1974), p. 154).

2. Hoffmann's works are quoted from the edition in 5 volumes by W. Kron, W. Segebrecht and F. Schnapp, with 'Nachworte' by W. Müller-Seidel (Darmstadt, 1970–1): *Die Elixiere des Teufels. Lebens-Ansichten des Katers Murr* (cited as EM), *Fantasie- und Nachtstücke* (FN), *Die Serapions-Brüder* (SB), *Späte Werke* (SW), *Schriften zur Musik. Nachlese* (SMN).

3. Cf. above, p. 96.

4. Cf. *Fantasiestücke in Callots Manier* and the late work, *Prinzessin Brambilla*, which is based on a number of engravings by Jacques Callot, a French engraver with a particular talent for the grotesque and a fondness for the *commedia dell'arte*, both of which Hoffmann shared (see A. Blunt, *Art and Architecture in France 1500–1700* (London, 1953), pp. 126 ff.

5. Cf. his portrait of Zacharias Werner, SB pp. 850 ff.

6. Quoted by Müller-Seidel, FN p. 757.

7. Cf. *Der Dichter und der Komponist*, SB p. 83.

8. E.g. the pursuit of 'die holde, fromme Julia' (EM p. 572) by Prince Hektor, of whose 'giftige Verderbtheit' (p. 475) we are made well aware, or the bedroom scene in *Berganza*: 'Wie er nun so schamlos mit der nie zu befriedigenden Begier des entnervten Lüstlings die geheimsten Reize des keuschen Mädchens enthüllte' (FN p. 123).

9. Compare – and contrast! – Goethe, *Iphigenie auf Tauris*, IV, 3: 'Denn wie die Flut, mit schnellen Strömen wachsend, Die Felsen überspült . . . so bedeckte

ganz Ein Freudenstrom mein Innerstes', and Novalis: 'Unendlich und geheimnisvoll Durchströmt uns süßer Schauer' (HN 6). Hoffmann's is a genuine attempt at poetry, but he can here manage no more than cliché.

10. Further to Hoffmann's interest in Mesmer and all that followed in his wake, cf. the story *Der Magnetiseur*. Hoffmann seems to have been inclined to side with the 'spiritualist' school of Barbarin, which rejected physical agencies as far as possible, and stressed the role of faith and will (cf. FN p. 787).

11. Cf. Lothar Köhn, *Vieldeutige Welt. Studien zur Struktur der Erzählungen E. T. A. Hoffmanns und zur Entwicklung seines Werkes* (Tübingen, 1966), especially pp. 5 ff, 59 f, and 134 ff. The list of figures in which this 'double' consciousness finds expression would be a long one; as examples, we might cite Medardus, Berganza (half-dog, half-human), Coppola-Coppelius and Salvator Rosa-Signor Formica.

12. (1972) Reprinted in H. Prang (ed.), *E. T. A. Hoffmann* (Darmstadt, 1976: 'Wege der Forschung', CDLXXXVI).

13. Ibid., p. 378.

14. E.g. by W. F. Mainland, Introduction to Hoffmann, *Der goldene Topf*, W. F. Mainland (ed.) (Oxford, 1947), p. viii.

15. 'Keck': Hoffmann uses the word to characterise Callot.

16. J. Walter, 'E. T. A. Hoffmanns "Klein Zaches gennant Zinnober." Versuch einer sozialgeschichtlichen Interpretation' in Prang, *E. T. A. Hoffmann*, pp. 398–423.

17. Cf. his 'Confession of Faith' in the famous memorandum to the Russian Emperor Alexander, dated 2 December 1820.

18. Aurelie, the pure 'Julia Marc' figure in the book, has read Lewis's *Ambrosio, or The Monk* (1795), to which she refers (EM pp. 198–9). Cf. EM p. 697, note.

19. Cf. EM p. 288: 'Es gibt Höheres als irdische Lust . . .' etc. Aurelie has to be murdered by Medardus's mad double as she is taking her vows, before the hero can experience this final spiritual liberation. One cannot but be reminded of Zacharias Werner (e.g. *Wanda*, cf. above, Ch. 8) whom Hoffmann had, of course, known from youth.

20. For the deliberate ambivalence of the treatment of reality in this work, see further Köhn, *Vieldeutige Welt*, pp. 44–90.

21. EM p. 636: ' "Barmherziger Himmel," rief Julia mit emporgerichteten [!] Blick, "schütze mich nur vor mir selber!" ' How far Hoffman intended to develop this hint of an enemy within is a matter of speculation.

22. That this setting (the small court beloved also of Jean Paul) gives rise to biting and often amusing political and social satire hardly needs to be stressed. But here, as elsewhere in Hoffmann, such satire has a secondary, rather than a primary function.

23. Cf. his remark to Friedrich Speyer (letter of 1 May 1820): 'Ein wirklicher Kater . . . gab mir Anlaß zu dem skurilen Scherz, der das eigentlich sehr ernste Buch durchflicht.'

24. Cf., for example, his ironic discussion with the reader of possible ways of beginning his narrative, culminating in the decision 'not to begin at all' (FN 343–4).

25. Cf. the expression used ('mein . . . Leben rettungslos verstören') to render Hoffmann's antipathy to the forcible invasion of the subject's will in some forms of Mesmerism (SB p. 279).

26. Hoffmann often speaks, for example, of an 'ewige Macht', which can be both positive and negative in its working.

27. Cf. *Das öde Haus* (FN. p. 478): 'nur geistige Krankheit – die Sünde macht uns untertan dem dämonischen Prinzip.'

28. That Hoffmann appreciated Novalis's portrait of the inspired poet in that novel, even if he did not follow the same lines in his own presentation of Ofterdingen, is evident from the comment made by Theodor in the discussion following *Der Kampf der Sänger* (SB p. 316).

29. Cf. the *Kinder und Hausmärchen* of the Grimm Brothers, F. von der Leyen (ed.) (Jena, 1927), vol. 2, p. 315: 'da sahen sie ein schönes Kind in einem weißen glänzenden Kleidchen . . .' etc.

30. Hoffmann, although a legal official and not particularly favourably disposed to the 'demagogues' against whom the Prussian government was taking repressive measures, intensely disliked the illiberal police state which seemed to be developing under Metternich's influence. He himself was under investigation at the time of his death.

31. E.g. the effect of the diamond ring and crystal bottle on Theodor in *Das öde Haus*.

32. Cf. above, p. 243.

33. Cf. above, pp. 242, 250.

34. Cf. the exchange: ' "Und Madelon," rief die Scuderi, ". . . die treue unschuldige Taube." – "Ei," sprach La Regnie mit einem giftigen Lächeln, "ei, wer steht mir dafür, daß sie nicht mit im Komplott ist" ' (SB p. 678).

35. Cf. above, pp. 17–18.

BIBLIOGRAPHICAL APPENDIX

We do not intend to compete with the specialist bibliographies, to which the scholar in search of exhaustive information will no doubt turn. The purpose of these lists is, first, to facilitate identification of works cited in the text and, secondly, to provide the student with *starting-points* for further study. He will find further bibliographical information in many of the works listed. In addition, there are very useful bibliographies in the volume by Stahl and Yuill listed below (Section A), together with short biographies of the main authors of the period. The Introductions to the various volumes of DL, *Reihe Romantik* are usually stimulating and informative. The articles in W. Kohlschmidt and W. Mohr (eds.), *Reallexikon der deutschen Literaturgeschichte*, 2nd edn (Berlin, from 1955) and W. Stammler (ed.), *Deutsche Philologie im Aufriß*, 2nd edn (Berlin, 1957–62) are usually worth consulting and the volumes on romantic authors and topics in the series 'Sammlung Metzler' (Stuttgart, J. B. Metzler) and 'Rowohlts Monographien' (Rowohlt, Hamburg) can also be recommended.

A. General Studies

(i) History

Gooch, G. P. *Germany and the French Revolution* (London, 1920).
Pinson, K. S. *Modern Germany. Its History and Civilization*, 2nd edn (New York-London, 1966).
Ramm, A. *Germany 1789–1919. A Political History* (London, 1967).
Thomson, D. *Europe since Napoleon*, 2nd edn (Harmondsworth, 1966).

(ii) History of Literature and Thought

Barzun, J. *Classic, Romantic and Modern* (London, 1962).
Canat, R. *La littérature française. Par les textes* (Paris, n.d.).
Ermatinger, E. *Deutsche Dichter, 1700–1900* (Bonn, 1949), vol. 2.
Field, G. W. *The Nineteenth Century* (London, 1975).
Gundolf, F. *Romantiker* (2 vols., Berlin–Wilmersdorf, 1930).
Huch, R. *Die Romantik* (Leipzig, 1924).
Kluckhohn, P. *Das Ideengut der deutschen Romantik*, 5th edn (Tübingen, 1966).

Kohn, H. *The Mind of Germany* (London, 1965).
Korff, H. A. *Geist der Goethezeit*, 2nd edn (4 vols., Leipzig, 1954).
Lukács, G. 'Die Zerstörung der Vernunft' in *Werke* (Neuwied, 1962), vol. 9.
Lucas, F. L. *The Decline and Fall of the Romantic Ideal* (Cambridge, 1936).
Mittenzwei, J. *et al.* (eds.) *Romantik* (E. Berlin, 1967).
Prawer, S. S. (ed.) *The Romantic Period in Germany* (London, 1970).
Reed, T. J. *The Classical Centre. Goethe and Weimar, 1775–1832* (London, 1980).
Sengle, F. *Biedermeierzeit* (2 vols., Stuttgart, 1971).
Stahl, E. L., and Yuill, W. E. *German Literature in the Eighteenth and Nineteenth Centuries* (London, 1970).
Taylor, R. *The Romantic Tradition in Germany* (London, 1970).
van Tieghem, P. *Le Préromantisme* (3 vols., Paris, 1924).
Unger, R. 'Zur seelengeschichtlichen Genesis der Romantik' in *Zur Dichtungs- und Geistesgeschichte der Goethezeit* (Berlin, 1924).
Wellek, R. 'The Concept of "Romanticism" in Literary Theory', *Comparative Literature*, vol. 1.

B. Topics

(i) Art and Architecture

Brion, M. *The Art of the Romantic Era* (London, 1966).
Flege, G. *Caspar David Friedrich* (Hamburg, 1977).
Hilton, T. *The Pre-Raphaelites* (London, 1976).
Pevsner, N. *An Outline of European Architecture* (Harmondsworth, 1961).

(ii) Drama

Ulshofer, R. *Die Theorie des Dramas in der deutschen Romantik* (Berlin, 1935).
Wendriner, K. *Das romantische Drama* (Berlin, 1909).

(iii) The Grotesque

Kayser, W. *Das Groteske in Malerei und Dichtung* (Hamburg, 1960).
Thomson, P. *The Grotesque* (London, 1972).
(See also T. Cramer, under 'Hoffmann').

(iv) Irony

Brüggemann, F. *Die Ironie als entwicklungsgeschichtliches Moment* (Jena, 1909).

Strohschneider-Kohrs, I. *Die romantische Ironie in Theorie und Gestaltung*, 2nd edn (Tübingen, 1977).

(v) Love (theme and concept of)

Kluckhohn, P. *Die Auffassung der Liebe im achtzehnten Jahrhundert und in der Romantik*, 3rd edn (Tübingen, 1966).

(vi) Lyric

Ermatinger, E. *Die deutsche Lyrik seit Herder* (3 vols., Leipzig–Berlin, 1925).
Prawer, S. S. *German Lyric Poetry* (London, 1952).
von Wiese, B. (ed.) *Die deutsche Lyrik. Form und Geschichte* (Düsseldorf, 1957).

(vii) Märchen

Lüthi, M. *Märchen*, 2nd edn (Stuttgart, 1964).

(viii) Music

Grove, G. *Beethoven and his Nine Symphonies*, reprint (New York, 1962).
(See also monographs on Beethoven (F. Zobeley), Schubert (M. Schneider) and Schumann (A. Boucourechlier) in 'Rowohlts Monographien', and articles on romantic composers in R. Hill (ed.), *The Concerto* (Harmondsworth, 1952); A. Jacobs (ed.), *Choral Music* (Harmondsworth, 1963); and R. Simpson (ed.), *The Symphony. I: Haydn to Dvořák* (Harmondsworth, 1966).

(ix) Narrative Forms (general)

Lämmert, E. *Bauformen des Erzählens*, 3rd edn (Stuttgart, 1968).

(x) The Novel

Forster, E. M. *Aspects of the Novel* (Harmondsworth, 1962).
Grimm, R. (ed.) *Deutsche Romantheorien* (Frankfurt–Bonn, 1968).
Hudgins, E. *Nicht-epische Strukturen des romantischen Romans* (The Hague–Paris, 1975).
Pascal, R. *The German Novel* (Manchester, 1956).
von Wiese, B. (ed.) *Der deutsche Roman*, I (Düsseldorf, 1965).

(xi) The Novelle

Arx, B. *Novellistisches Dasein* (Zurich, 1953).
Himmel, H. *Geschichte der deutschen Novelle* (Berne–Munich, 1963).

von Wiese, B. *Die deutsche Novelle von Goethe bis Kafka* (Düsseldorf, 1956).

(xii) Political Thought

Droz, J. *Le romantisme allemand et l'état* (Paris, 1966).
Hartau, F. *Metternich* (Hamburg, 1977).
Reiss, H. S. *Politisches Denken in der deutschen Romantik* (Berne, 1966).

(xiii) Popular Literature

Albertsen, L. L. (ed.) *Die Eintagsliteratur in der Goethezeit. Proben aus den Werken von Julius von Voss* (Berne–Frankfurt, 1975).
Thalmann, M. *Der Trivialroman des 18. Jahrhunderts und der romantische Roman*, reprint (Nendeln, 1978).
—— *Die Romantik des Trivialen* (Munich, 1970).
Ward, A. *Book Production, Fiction and the German Reading Public* (Oxford, 1974).

(xiv) Religion

Kantzenbach, F. W. *Schleiermacher* (Hamburg, 1967).
Lütgert, W. *Die Religion des deutschen Idealismus und ihr Ende* (4 vols., Gütersloh, 1923–30).

(xv) 'Romantic' (word and concept)

Immerwahr, R. 'The Word "Romantic" and its History' in Prawer, *Romantic Period*.
Prang, H. (ed.) *Begriffsbestimmung der Romantik* (Darmstadt, 1968).
Ullmann, R., and Gotthard, H. *Geschichte des Begriffes "Romantisch" in Deutschland* (Berlin, 1927).

C. Authors

Arnim, L. A. von and Bettina von

Rudolph, G. *Studien zur dichterischen Welt Achim von Arnims* (Berlin, 1958).
Steig, R. *Achim von Arnim und die ihm nahe standen*, reprint (3 vols., Berne, 1970).
Vordtriede, W. *Achim von Arnim und Bettina in ihren Briefen* (Frankfurt, 1961).
—— 'Die Kronenwächter' in J. Schillemeit (ed.), *Deutsche Romane von Grimmelshausen bis Musil* (Frankfurt, 1977).

266   *Bibliographical Appendix*

Brentano, C.

Enzensberger, H. M. *Brentanos Poetik* (Munich, 1961).
Frühwald, W. *Das Spätwerk Clemens Brentanos* (Tübingen, 1977).
Hoffmann, W. *Clemens Brentano. Leben und Werk* (Berne-Munich, 1966).
Killy, W. ' "Gemütserregungskunst": Clemens Brentano' in *Wandlungen des lyrischen Bildes* (Göttingen, 1956).
Migge, W. *Clemens Brentano. Leitmotive seiner Existenz* (Pfüllingen, 1968).
Prawer, S. S. 'Brentano: *Der Spinnerin Lied*' in *German Lyric Poetry*.
Steig, R. *Clemens Brentano und die Brüder Grimm*, reprint (Berne, 1969). (Cf. also Steig, *Achim von Arnim*, vol. 1).
Stopp, E. ' "O Stern und Blume": Its Poetic, and Emblematic Context', *Modern Language Review*, vol. lxvii (1972).

Chamisso, A. von

Mann, T. 'Chamisso' in *Essays of Three Decades* (New York, 1947).
von Wiese, B. 'Peter Schlemihls wundersame Gesichte' in *Die deutsche Novelle von Goethe bis Kafka*.

Eichendorff, J. von

Alewyn, R. 'Eine Landschaft Eichendorffs' in Stöcklein, *Eichendorff Heute*.
Hillach, O. *Eichendorff-Kommentar* (2 vols., Munich, 1971).
Kunz, J. *Eichendorff. Höhepunkt und Krise der Spätromantik* (Oberursal, 1951).
Paulsen, W. *Eichendorff und sein Taugenichts* (Berne–Munich, 1976).
Seidlin, O. *Versuche über Eichendorff* (Göttingen, 1965).
Stöcklein, P. *Eichendorff* (Hamburg, 1963).
—— (ed.) *Eichendorff Heute* (Darmstadt, 1966).

Fouqué, F. Baron de la Motte

Schmidt, A. *Fouqué und einige seiner Zeitgenossen* (Karlsruhe, 1958).

Grimm, J., and Grimm, W.

Denecke, H. *Jakob Grimm und sein Bruder Wilhelm* (Stuttgart, 1971).
(Cf. also Steig, *Clemens Brentano* and *Achim von Arnim*, vol. 3.)

Hauff, W., Kerner, J., Schwab, G.

Stortz, G. *Schwäbische Romantik* (Stuttgart, 1967).

Hoffmann, E. T. A.

Cramer, T. *Das Groteske bei E. T. A. Hoffmann* (Munich, 1966).
Günzel, K. 'Zu Hoffmanns Entwicklung als Schriftsteller' in Prang, *Hoffmann*.
Köhn, L. *Vieldeutige Welt. Studien zur Struktur der Erzählungen E. T. A. Hoffmanns und zur Entwicklung seines Werkes* (Tübingen, 1966).
Mainland, W. F. Introduction to Hoffmann, *Der goldene Topf* (Oxford, 1947).
Prang, H. (ed.) *E. T. A. Hoffmann* (Darmstadt, 1976).
Walter, J. 'E. T. A. Hoffmanns Märchen "Klein Zaches genannt Zinnober" ' in Prang, *Hoffmann*.
Wittkop-Menardeau, G. *E. T. A. Hoffmann* (Hamburg, 1966).

Hebel, J. P.

Kully, R. M. *Johann Peter Hebel* (Stuttgart, 1969).

Jean Paul (Richter)

Harich, W. *Jean Paul* (Leipzig, 1928).
—— *Jean Pauls Revolutionsdichtung* (E. Berlin, 1974).
Kommerell, M. *Jean Paul*, 5th edn (Frankfurt, 1966).
Meyer, H. 'Flegeljahre' in von Wiese, *Der deutsche Roman,* I.
Michelsen, P. *Lawrence Sterne und der deutsche Roman des 18. Jahrhunderts* (Göttingen, 1962).
Schweikert, U. *Jean Paul* (Stuttgart, 1970).
Smeed, J. W. *Jean Paul's Dreams* (London, 1966).
—— Introduction to Jean Paul, *Des Feldpredigers Schmelzle Reise nach Flätz* (Oxford, 1966).

Kerner, J.

See *Hauff.*

Kleist, H. von

Fricke, G. *Gefühl und Schicksal bei Heinrich von Kleist* (Berlin, 1929).
Koch, F. *Heinrich von Kleist. Bewußtsein und Wirklichkeit* (Stuttgart, 1958).
Reeves, N. B. R., and Luke, D. Introduction to Kleist, *The Marquise of O. and Other Stories* (Harmondsworth, 1978).
Silz, W. *Heinrich von Kleist. Studies in his Works and Literary Character* (Philadelphia, 1961).
Staiger, E. 'Heinrich von Kleist: "Das Bettelweib von Locarno" ' in J.

Schillemeit (ed.), *Deutsche Erzählungen von Wieland bis Kafka* (Frankfurt, 1966).

Witkop, P. *Heinrich von Kleist* (Leipzig, 1923).

Wolff, H. M. *Heinrich von Kleist. Die Geschichte seines Schaffens* (Berne, 1954).

Müller, W.

Cottrell, A. P. *Wilhelm Müller's Lyrical Song-Cycles* (Chapel Hill, 1970).

Just, K. G. 'Wilhelm Müller und seine Liederzyklen' in *Übergänge* (Berne–Munich, 1966).

Novalis

Dick, M. *Die Entwicklung des Gedankens der Poesie in den Fragmenten des Novalis* (Bonn, 1967).

Hederer, E. *Novalis* (Vienna, 1949).

Heftrich, E. *Novalis. Vom Logos der Poesie* (Frankfurt, 1969).

Hegener, J. *Die Poetisierung der Wissenschaften bei Novalis* (Bonn, 1975).

Hiebel, F. *Novalis*, 2nd edn (Berne–Munich, 1972).

Ritter, H. *Der unbekannte Novalis* (Göttingen, 1967).

—— *Novalis' Hymnen an die Nacht,* 2nd edn (Heidelberg, 1974).

Schanze, H. *Romantik und Aufklärung. Untersuchungen zu Friedrich Schlegel und Novalis* (Nuremberg, 1966).

Schulz, G. 'Die Poetik des Romans bei Novalis' in Grimm, *Deutsche Romantheorien.*

Schlegel, F.

Behler, E. *Friedrich Schlegel* (Hamburg, 1966).

Mennemeier, F. *Friedrich Schlegels Poesiebegriff. Dargestellt anhand der literaturkritischen Schriften* (Munich, 1971).

Schanze, H. 'Friedrich Schlegels Theorie des Romans' in Grimm, *Deutsche Romantheorien.*

(See also Schanze, under 'Novalis'.)

Tieck, L.

Atkinson, M. Introduction to Tieck and Brentano, *Der blonde Eckbert* and *Geschichte vom braven Kasperl und von dem schönen Annerl* (Oxford, 1958).

Köpke, R. *Ludwig Tieck*, reprint (Darmstadt, 1970).

Staiger, E. 'Ludwig Tieck und der Ursprung der deutschen Romantik' in *Stilwandel* (Zurich, 1963).

Stamm, R. *Ludwig Tiecks späte Novellen* (Stuttgart-Cologne-Berlin-
Mainz, 1953).
Taraba, W. F. 'Vittoria Accorombona' in von Wiese, *Der deutsche Roman.*
von Wiese, B. 'Des Lebens Überfluß' in *Die deutsche Novelle von Goethe
bis Kafka.*
Zeydel, E. H. *Ludwig Tieck, The German Romanticist*, reprint
(Hildesheim, 1971).
(See also Lippuner, under 'Wackenroder'.)

Uhland, L.

Froeschle, H. *Ludwig Uhland und die Romantik* (Cologne-Vienna,
1965).
Thomke, H. *Zeitbewußtsein und Geschichtsauffassung im Werke Uhlands*
(Berne, 1962).

Wackenroder, W. H.

Hertrich, J. *Joseph Berglinger. Eine Studie zu Wackenroders Musiker-
Dichtung* (Berlin, 1969).
Lippuner, H. *Wackenroder, Tieck und die bildende Kunst* (Zurich, 1965).

INDEX

Note: To save space, frequent use has been made of short titles; lyric poems have not been listed, and other works only in the case of major authors.

popular literature 172, 184n1, 193,
223, 235n10, 237, 246, 259n1;
see also Bundesroman,
Räuberroman
Pre-Raphaelites 228
pre-romanticism 12, 14, 15, 37,
176, 224
Protestantism 97
Pückler-Muskau, Hermann von 18
Pushkin, Aleksandr S. 11

Raumer, Karl von 40n72
Rambach, Friedrich Eberhard 223,
235n9
Ranke, Leopold von 220n31
Raphael 227
Räuberroman 22, 38n18
religion 19–20, 21, 27, 31, 32,
40, 69–70, 76–8, 82, 85–6,
87–8, 97, 103, 104, 110, 112,
115, 126, 138, 169, 180–1, 198,
200
Renaissance 228
Reynolds, J. H. 16
Reynolds, Sir Joshua 12
Rhine, theme of 24, 93, 168,
202–3
Richardson, Samuel 195
Richter, J. P. F. *see* Jean Paul
Richter, Ludwig 97–8, 106n7
Ritter, Johann Wilhelm 33
Rococo 212–13
Rousseau, Jean-Jacques 26, 132,
133
Rückert, Friedrich 59
Runge, Philip Otto 18, 28, 32, 202,
228

Sanscrit 34
satire 24, 32, 119, 121, 177, 184,
185n13, 193, 213, 238, 243, 248
Savigny, Karl Friedrich von 24, 35,
83, 93n8
Schauerromantik see horror
Schelling, Friedrich von 19, 20, 43,
108, 110, 229
Schenkendorf, Max von 62n20
Schiller, Friedrich 11–17 *passim*,
22, 38, 41, 59, 74, 114–15,
125n29, 127, 181, 201
Schlegel, August Wilhelm 23, 31,
36, 40n81, 41, 42, 50, 68
Schlegel, Friedrich 15, 17, 20–6
passim, 30–4 *passim*, 42, 43, 50,

74, 109, 110, 119, 151–4 *passim*,
155–6, 159, 173, 187, 190, 192,
206, 228
Schleiermacher, Friedrich 19–20,
21, 32, 34, 35, 64
Schopenhauer, Arthur 15
Schubert, Franz 16, 58
Schubert, Gotthilf Heinrich von 28,
38, 39n52, 149n27, 194
Schuckmann, Caspar F. 25
Schumann, Robert 11, 62
Schwab, Gustav 44n8
Schwind, Moritz von 106n7
science 20–1, 26, 28, 33, 67,
156–7
Scott, Sir Walter 53, 54, 166
secret societies *see Bundesroman*
Sehnsucht (longing for release or
consummation) 19, 36–7, 68,
69–70, 71, 91–2, 99, 220n42,
241
Self ('Ich') 12, 13, 15, 19, 20,
27–8, 71–6 *passim*, 86, 102,
158, 176, 222
Shakespeare, William 41, 43, 51,
108–12 *passim*, 119, 120, 134
Simrock, Karl 24
society, relation to 18, 24–5,
34–5, 66, 206–8, 210
Solger, Karl W. F. 22, 33, 43
somnambulism 28, 146
Sophocles 135
Speyer, Friedrich 260n23
Spieβ, Christian Heinrich 223
Spinoza, Baruch 20, 30, 31
Steffens, Henrik 33, 40n72, 54, 194
Stein Karl, Reichsfreiherr von 23,
94n20
Sterne, Lawrence 173
Stifter, Adalbert 50
Stimmung 28, 47, 48, 50, 52, 55,
56, 76, 81, 86, 88, 96, 97, 191,
224
Stolberg, brothers Friedrich and
Christian von 13
Sturm und Drang 14, 21, 31, 121
subconscious 28, 48, 55–6,
99–100, 101–2, 194–5
supernatural 187, 189, 192, 194,
201, 230, 242–3; *see also* magic
surrealism 32, 84–5, 162, 199
symbolism 28, 33, 43, 66, 68, 76,
82, 84, 86, 91, 92, 131, 154,
167, 173, 204